Regina
The FIRST 100 YEARS

REGINA'S CORNERSTONES

The History of Regina told through its Buildings and Monuments

Regina
The FIRST 100 YEARS

REGINA'S CORNERSTONES
The History of Regina told through its Buildings and Monuments

WILLIAM ARGAN

WITH

PAM COWAN AND GORDON W. STASESON

REGINA – THE FIRST 100 YEARS

by William Argan with Pam Cowan and Gordon W. Staseson

First Printing – October 2002

Copyright© 2002 by
The Leader-Post Carrier Foundation Inc.

Published by The Leader-Post Carrier Foundation Inc.
c/o The Leader-Post Ltd.
1964 Park Street
P.O. Box 2020
Regina, Saskatchewan
Canada S4P 3G4

"The Cultural Industries Development Council gratefully acknowledges the Government of Saskatchewan, through the Cultural Industries Development Fund, for its financial support."

Canadian Cataloguing in Publication Data

Argan, William P.

Regina, the first 100 years : the history of Regina told through its buildings and monuments/William Argan ; with Pam Cowan and Gordon W. Staseson. – Rev. ed.

Previous eds. have titles: Cornerstones and Cornerstones 2.
Includes index.
ISBN 1-894022-77-7

1. Historic buildings – Saskatchewan – Regina. 2. Historic buildings – Saskatchewan – Regina – Pictorial works. 3. Regina (Sask.) – Buildings, structures, etc. 4. Regina (Sask.) – Buildings, structures, etc. – Pictorial works. 5. Regina (Sask.) – History. I. Cowan, Pam. II. Staseson, Gordon W. III. Leader-Post Carrier Foundation Inc. IV. Argan, William P. Cornerstones. V. Argan, William P. Cornerstones 2. VI. Title

FC3546.7.A74 2002   971.24'45   C2002-911227-3
F1074.5.R3A74 2002

Cover Design by
Brian Danchuk, Brian Danchuk Design

Project Coordinator
Dan Marce, Publishing Solutions, A Division of PW Group

Formatting and Index by
Iona Glabus, Centax Books

Printed and Produced in Canada by
Centax Books, A Division of PW Group
Publishing Director and Editor – Margo Embury
1150 Eighth Avenue, Regina, Saskatchewan, Canada S4R 1C9
(306) 525-2304 Fax (306) 757-2439
E-mail: centax@printwest.com   www.centaxbooks.com

TABLE OF CONTENTS

WILLIAM P. ARGAN – ARTIST AND HISTORIAN

*D*uring his school days at Wetmore and Balfour Tech schools, in a seven year period, William Argan set a record for the number of awards won in school exhibits at the Provincial Exhibition and YMCA Boys and Girls Fair. He won over 50 awards, including provincial and national awards.

In 1939, at age 18, he designed and prepared settings for the Wascana Winter Club ice show and painted royal visit plaques and coats of arms for the RCMP Barracks, the Union Station (interior and exterior) and the new Federal Building on Victoria Avenue and Scarth Street.

Argan also had a twenty-year music career beginning in the early 1930s. He played mandolin, violin, clarinet, sax and drums. On Saturday mornings he appeared on CHWC, at the Kitchener Hotel, and on Saturday afternoons on CJRM Talent shows. During the war he played the side drums in a bugle band in Calgary and the clarinet in the Massed Band at Rivers and Winnipeg.

During the war Argan served in the RCAF Navigation Visiting Flight, developing visual training aids for navigators.

In Winnipeg, following the war, Argan designed billboards and posters, winning three international awards. He returned to Regina where he spent 29 years at CKCK-TV. His two television characters "Audy and Vidy" won a national award during television week in 1958. Argan has generously contributed his time and talents to the community in many ways. A Regina street, Argan Drive, was named after him and in 1967 he received the Centennial Medal from the Canadian Government.

A talented graphic artist and amateur historian, Argan researched, wrote and illustrated the book, *Columbianism in Saskatchewan, 1907-1982*. Other books to his credit are *Heartland Tradition*, a curling history of Saskatchewan which was published in 1990, two books entitled *Wetmore School Daze*, *The Spirit of Patriotism* and *Cornerstones 1 and 2 – An Artist's History of the City of Regina*.

As a hobby, Argan began drawing older Regina buildings in the early 1970s. He says retirement is the greatest joy in his life because it gives him the opportunity to document the many wonderful scenes and buildings in Regina. He describes his interest in researching and drawing Regina buildings as obsessive because he spends hours searching for details about a structure's history. "If I don't get it now, I'll pursue it later, even if it takes me five or ten years," Argan says with pride.

The Saskatchewan Wheat Pool Building took the meticulous artist nearly fifty hours to complete, but Argan doesn't begrudge the time because he gets tremendous satisfaction from bringing the past alive for others to appreciate.

On February 19, 1996, the City of Regina Municipal Heritage Award for Education, was presented to Argan for the book titled *Cornerstones – An Artist's History of the City of Regina*, for an outstanding contribution to the conservation of Regina's built heritage. A second City of Regina Municipal award in Education was presented to him for outstanding contribution to the conservation of Regina's built heritage on February 21, 2000.

The Mayor's Community Volunteer Award for the Arts was presented to Argan in 1997 and the Mayor's Most Distinguished Volunteer Award was presented to him in 2001. Saskatchewan Culture Inc., on October 12, 2001, presented him with the Volunteer Award for Culture. Argan's work in the world of curling, Briers and the Knights of Columbus is manifold.

Bill Argan and his wife, Helen, live six blocks from his childhood home on Wallace Street. They have a daughter and two sons. Carole lives in Regina, Darrel in Martensville and Glen resides in Edmonton.

GORDON W. STASESON – CO-WRITER

ord Staseson was born in Regina May 9, 1926. He has been involved in many diverse activities ever since. He performed on the stage of the old Rex Theatre when he was five and was a cast member in the Regina Rotary Club Musical "Racy Days" in 1932. On July 1, 1935 he sold "extras" on the street for the Regina Daily Star during the Regina Riot. He managed his own hockey team in the old Parks Hockey League when he was eleven. Staseson later played hockey for the Regina Junior Abbotts, the Boston Olympics in the Eastern US Hockey League and for the Regina Caps in the old Western Hockey League. He coached minor league hockey in Regina for ten years.

Staseson produced major ice shows for the Wascana Winter Club and was chairman of the Regina Horse Show during its greatest years. He was chairman of Saskatchewan Derby Sweepstakes, the second largest lottery in Canada. He was the chairman of the Canadian Figure Skating Championships in 1984 and the commissioner of the Saskatchewan Pavilion at Expo86 in Vancouver.

Staseson was president of the Saskatchewan Roughriders from 1979 to 1982 and chairman of the CFL Board of Governors in 1983. He was instrumental in the creation of the Plaza of Honor in 1985 and was its first producer. He is a past president and honorary life member of the Regina Construction Association, a founding member of the Regina Housebuilders Association and was their president in 1969.

President of the Regina Exhibition in 1974, Staseson was also chairman for the building of the Agridome in 1977, the Canada Centre in 1984 and the Queensbury Centre in 1987. He was president of Regina Buffalo Days in 1967 and founded Pile of Bones Sunday, held each year in Wascana Park.

Staseson is a life member of the Queen City Kinsmen Club and was president in 1958. He was governor of District 3 in 1964 and national co-ordinator in 1965. He is a 32nd Degree Mason and a Shriner.

He owned his own decorating company from 1951 to 1963 and became managing director of Sherwood Land Development Co. in 1959. He and his partners developed Albert Park, University Park, University Park East and Gardiner Heights subdivisions in Regina. He was also in charge of land development for Harvard Developments in Normanview West and Westhill Park. He developed subdivisions in Alberta in Brooks, Strathmore and Black Diamond.

Staseson was the founding chairman of the Regina Economic Development Authority, a position he held for six years. He later became chairman, president and CEO of the Saskatchewan Gaming Authority, operators of Casino Regina. He was the chairman of the Regina Airport Transitional Committee that led to the transfer of the Regina Airport to the Regina Airport Authority. He served a three-year term on the board of directors of the Vancouver Port authority. He was a member of the City of Regina Planning Commission for 17 years.

An active promoter of Regina, he has received many honors. He was recognized by the B'Nai B'rith Regina Lodge as the sports personality for 1984 and was winner of the Larry Schneider Communications Leadership Award in 1985.

Staseson received an honorary doctor of laws degree from the University of Regina in 1989, the Regina North Rotary Club Humanitarian Award in 1990 and, in the same year, was voted Fairman of the Year by the Canadian Association of Exhibitions. He received the Saskatchewan Roughriders' Al Foster "Unsung Heroes Award" in 1991 and was inducted into the Saskatchewan Roughrider Plaza of Honor in 1993.

Staseson's broad knowledge of the history of Regina was invaluable in the preparation of this book. He is no longer active in the business community and spends his time working with young golfers at the Wascana Country Club.

PAMELA COWAN – CO-WRITER

P amela Cowan has resided in Regina since 1977 and is the mother of two daughters, Trina and Shauna, and is Gram to Hanna. She graduated with distinction from the University of Regina's School of Journalism and Communications in May 1995.

Cowan was the recipient of numerous awards and scholarships while attending the University of Regina, including the Sir William Stephenson Travelling Scholarship. As a result of winning this scholarship, she worked at the Gemini News Service in London, England for three months.

Following her return from England, Cowan freelanced for numerous publications before accepting a position at the *Leader-Post* as staff writer for the *Regina Sun*. She also researched and wrote the text for *Cornerstones 1* and *2 – An Artist's History of the City of Regina*. In the spring of 2000, Pamela began working as a general assignment reporter for the *Leader-Post* and was recently assigned to the education and health beat.

Balancing reporting, home responsibilities and writing *Cornerstones 1* and *2* was challenging, but the challenge was made much easier because of the support she received from her daughters, her parents, Joyce and Ian Cowan, and her partner in life, Bill Busby.

ACKNOWLEDGEMENTS

Regina Leader
Leader
The Morning Leader
Leader-Post
Standard
Regina Sun
Archdiocese of Regina – A History, Regina, 1988
A Brief History of Regina: Over A Century of Prairie Progress, City of Regina
The City of Regina, Saskatchewan – W. P. Stewart, Maple Creek, Saskatchewan: Butterfly Books, c. 1979
From Tent to Cathedral: A History of St. Paul's Cathedral, Regina – Trevor Powell, Regina, St. Paul's Cathedral, 1995
Heartland Tradition – Saskatchewan Curling, W. P. Argan
Heritage Tours Booklets, Regina, Saskatchewan: City of Regina, 1985
History of the Diocese of Qu'Appelle – Jean T. Embury, Regina, 1958
A History of the Provincial Laboratories – H. E. Robertson, W. A. Riddell, Regina, 1986
A History of Wascana Country Club, R. N. Reid
Let the Bells Ring, Knox-Metropolitan Church – Dorothy Hayden, Regina, Saskatchewan: 100th Anniversary Committee, Knox-Metropolitan United Church, 1981
Ninety Years of Golf, Mickey Boyle
The Origin and Development of Wascana Centre – W. A. Riddell, Regina: s.m., 1992
Our Heritage: The History of the Regina and Region Jewish Community, Regina, Beth Jacob Congregation, 1989
Regina : A City of Beautiful Homes, Margaret Hryniuk and Meta Perry, Regina, 1994
Regina, An Illustrated History – J. William Brennan, Toronto: Lorimer, 1989
Regina Before Yesterday – A Visual History 1882 to 1945 – J. William Brennan, Regina: Centax of Canada Ltd.
Regina from Pile O' Bones to Queen City of the Plains – W. A. Riddell, Burlington, Ontario: Windsor Publications, 1981
Regina: Pride of the Prairies – Carol Bentley, Regina, Saskatchewan: Windsor Publications, c. 1991
Regina, The Queen City – Earl Drake, Toronto: McClelland & Stewart, 1955

ACKNOWLEDGEMENTS

Regina, The Street Where You Live – Lillian Mein/Stewart Mein, Regina, Saskatchewan: Regina Public Library; Saskatchewan Department of Culture and Youth, 1992
Saskatchewan: A Pictorial History, Saskatoon: Western Producer Prairie Books, 1980
A Souvenir of Regina; Queen City of the Plains, Regina, Saskatchewan: Western Printers, 1953
Spirit of Patriotism, W. P. Argan, Regina, 1998
Wetmore – Reunion '85, W. P. Argan, Regina, 1985
Regina Board of Trade Publications

Campion College
City of Regina Archives – Ivan Saunders
City of Regina Transit
Government House Historical Society
Leader-Post staff – Will Chabun, Susan Marshall, Gloria Moor
McMasters Photographers – W. P. Argan Photograph
Prairie History Room, Regina Public Library – Ken Aitken, Sharon Maier, Brenda Laliberte, Beth Ellsworth, Inge Hunt
Regina Plains Museum
RCMP Museum – Malcolm Wake, Curator
Saskatchewan Archives – Tim Novak, Jean Goldie
Saskatchewan Publisher's Group
University of Regina Archives
Wascana Centre Authority

Thank you to the following individuals:

Aussie Alzomal
Doug Archer
Glen Argan
Helen Argan
Laura Argue
Kay Banda
Lloyd Begley
Carol Gay Bell
Dick Bell
Murray Bercovich
Lorraine Birstein
Frank Boldt
Kevin Boyle
Peter Bresciani
Grace Brown
Clarence Brown
Joan Brown
Raoul Burchi
Steve Burchi
Jacqui Campbell
Will Chabun
Warren Champ
Don Chatwin

Joan Church
Jill Collins
Keith Critchley
Ray Crone
Joni Darke
Francine Deiana
Deanna Elias-Henry
Eyton Embury
Rose Engelhardt
Donna Evans
Cec Ferguson
Doreen Fisher
Doug Folk
Murray Forbes
Jean Freeman
Iona Glabus
"Red" Glasser
Shirley Good
Doreen Hamilton
Wayne Hellquist
John Hudson
Liz Hugel
Brian Hugel

Harry Jedlic
Steve Jerkovits
Bruce Johnston
Patricia Johnston
Daisy Junor
Pamela Kendel-Goodale
Ed Klopoushak
Don Kramer
Patricia Lines
Grace Lipinski
Penny Malone
George Mario
Jim McCrum
Kelly McLintock
Barb McWatters
Marnie McWatters
Rod Milic
Barbara Neil
Jean Owen
Marion Paterson
Dwayne Pearce
Reid Peterson
Trevor J. D. Powell

Ross Reibling
Candas Resch
Keith Rever
Bill Rudichuk
Margie Sandison
Bonnie Schaffer
Larry Schneider
Allan Shore
Jacqui Shumiacher
James K. Struthers
Heather Turner
Merrill Weicker
Gerry Welsh
Gord Wicijowski
Marcia Wickenheiser
Ruth Whitmore
Victoria Whitmore
Tracy Wilson
Ken Yee
Vas Zaharik

Project Coordinator: Dan Marce, Director of Marketing, Publishing Solutions, a Division of PrintWest/PW Group

INTRODUCTION

*O*ne hundred years ago, as the first settlers crossed the vast prairies, who would have dreamed that a city of close to 200,000 would some day rise from the horizon of flat, barren land? It was men and women with vision, who could see beyond the horizon and dream dreams that others would someday come to enjoy. The people of vision saw to the establishment of churches, schools, hospitals, streets, transportation and communications. One family with such a vision was the Sifton family which, in 1928, purchased both the *Regina Leader* and the *Saskatoon Star Phoenix*. The patriarch of the Sifton family, Michael C. Sifton, believed in giving back to the community and, with leadership from his son, Michael C. Sifton Jr., they enabled the *Leader-Post* to establish the Leader-Post Carrier Foundation.

The Foundation had its beginnings in 1986, when a group of visionary people from both the *Leader-Post* staff and the community, led by Jim Struthers, was invited to establish the workings of the Foundation. After several months of deliberation, the Leader-Post Carrier Foundation came into existence, its stated purpose being to honour past and present paper carriers by responding to educational and humanitarian needs in the *Leader-Post* market area.

At the time of publication of this legacy book, the Foundation has awarded 180, $1000.00 scholarships in its 18 years of existence. Today the Board is anxious to pursue its second objective, answering humanitarian needs. With the approach of the City of Regina's 100th anniversary, led by the Chair, the Foundation felt that a legacy book, built on the success of its *Cornerstones 1 and 2,* could offer a significant boost. Bill Argan, the artist for the two earlier books, was commissioned to provide additional new drawings to help build an abridged architectural history of Regina's first 100 years. An individual with experience and knowledge of Regina buildings and builders was needed to research and write the history that was to be included. This person was Gordon Staseson, long-time community builder. Dan Marce of Publishing Solutions, and a Carrier Foundation Board member, was the coordinator of the sponsorship for this book and of the myriad details required for the realization of this project. After three years of research, hundreds of drawings, plus hours of editing by Margo Embury, formatting and indexing by Iona Glabus, this book is now in your hands. It represents the Leader-Post Carrier Foundation's contribution to the celebration of Regina's first 100 years.

This book is intended to pay tribute to the people, organizations and businesses that have contributed to making Regina the vital community it is today. Omissions and errors are inevitable in a project of this magnitude, and we apologize in advance to the many deserving individuals and groups that have not been included.

Regina – The First 100 Years will assist the Foundation in responding to the humanitarian needs of the people of southern Saskatchewan. All of the profits from the sale of this book will be given to the Hospitals of Regina Foundation. In this way, the Sifton vision of giving back to the community will continue to live as the Foundation contributes to the wellness of people in southern Saskatchewan.

Thank you for purchasing this book, and thank you for helping the Foundation's dream come true. The past and future of Regina is now in your hands.

Jim Toth
Chair, Leader-Post Carrier Foundation

LEADER-POST CARRIER FOUNDATION BOARD MEMBERS

* **Jim Toth – Chair**

* **Bob Hughes – Vice Chair**	**Barbara Pollock – Director**
* **Bill Johnson, QC – Secretary**	**Gerry Krochak – Director**
Vern Fowke – Treasurer	* **Wayne Kuss – Director**
John Grossman – Director	* **Joe Laxdal – Director**
Janice Dockham – Director	**Dan Marce – Director**

* **Founding Directors**

COMMUNITY PARTNERS

*T*he Leader-Post Carrier Foundation would like to thank the following Community Partners for their financial support of this legacy to the City of Regina's first 100 years. Their support is typical of their leadership in our community.

In addition to committing the seed money to proceed with this project, this contribution will greatly add to The Foundation's objective of donating $100,000 toward a mutually agreed upon capital expenditure for the Hospitals of Regina Foundation, which will benefit everyone in southern Saskatchewan.

REGINA – HISTORICAL OVERVIEW

*T*he Queen City's origins were far from regal. When Regina was chosen as the site for the new North-West Territories capital in 1882 by Lieutenant-Governor Edgar Dewdney, it was merely a point on the dry, bare, treeless plain, distinguished only by a pile of buffalo bones. Only three settlers lived at the point where the CPR railway survey crossed Pile of Bones Creek on May 13, 1882.

In the second half of the 19th century, buffalo were slaughtered in large numbers. The bones of the slaughtered animals were placed symmetrically on top of a cylindrical pile, and as time passed the mound grew in size.

The name "Pile of Bones" arose in the early settlement days for a location on Wascana Creek near the present site of the city. It was called Tas d' Os, Pile of Bones, Manybones and Bone Creek. The word for bones in Cree is "oskana". Captain Palliser, leader of an expedition commissioned by the British government to report on the area's potential, misunderstood the Cree word and recorded it in his diary as "Wascana", the name by which the creek has since been known.

The Government of Canada and the Canadian Pacific Railway were responsible for choosing the Territorial capital. CPR General Manager William Van Horne was so busy completing the railway that the decision rested solely with Territorial Lieutenant-Governor Dewdney.

Regina 1882

On June 30, 1882, Dewdney posted a notice on a tent pole pitched on the banks of Wascana Creek. On the notice Dewdney announced the government's decision to reserve the land for later use.

The new settlement was formally named when the first passenger train arrived on August 23, 1882. The Governor General's wife, Princess Louise, suggested the name Regina in honour of her mother, Queen Victoria.

W. C. Van Horne and the dignitaries were taken to the end of the rail line, near the RCMP barracks, and the place was christened with champagne poured over a pile of railway ties.

Queen Victoria

The railway from Winnipeg to Regina had been built by Montreal sub-contractor Pascal Bonneau, who settled in Regina. His daughter Marie, at age 4, was the first settler's child in Regina in 1882.

The Assiniboia Club, Western Canada's oldest men's club, was organized in Regina in 1882.

Marie Bonneau

Regina was officially confirmed as the site of the new Territorial capital on March 27, 1883.

Soon after the capital's transfer from Battleford to Regina, the North-West Mounted Police also relocated to Regina from Fort Walsh in the Cypress Hills.

"During the fall of 1882, the Manitoba *Free Press* reported: 'the town has not yet assumed any degree of regularity and tents and houses alike have been put down promiscuously without any regard to geometrical precision. It is now, for the most part, directly south of the CPR station. . . . Six weeks ago the town was established on open prairie. Today it contains 8 hotels, 18 stores, 2 blacksmith's shops, 1 saddler's shop, 2 livery stables, 2 tin shops, 2 laundries, 3 billiard halls, 2 bakeries, 1 drug store, 1 jeweller's shop, 2 doctors, 6 lawyers, 4 lumber yards and a population of between 8-900 souls.'" – Drake, *Regina*

There were many critics who harshly condemned Regina as the site for the capital because there was insufficient water, poor drainage, no sheltering hills, and no timber for fuel, lumber or shade. However, Dewdney defended his decision, saying Regina was centrally located and surrounded by fertile farmland.

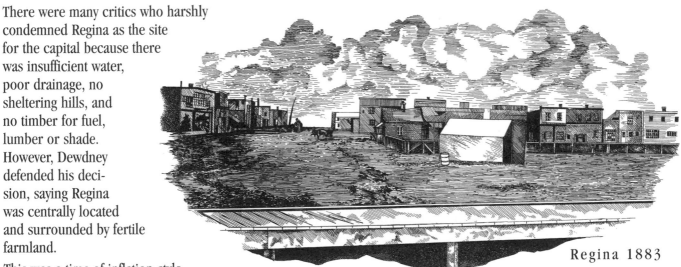
Regina 1883

This was a time of inflation-style prices. Creek water sold for 50 cents a barrel, bread for 25 cents a loaf, and wood for $12 a load.

The trustees were responsible for the subdivision of the townsite. Initially, development spread southward from the CPR station. The territorial government buildings and the NWMP barracks were situated further to the west.

The streets were laid out perfectly straight and intersected each other at right angles. All east-west thoroughfares were labelled avenues and were numbered 1 to 16, from north to south, except for Dewdney, South Railway and Victoria Avenues. The north-south arteries were labelled streets and named after townsite trustees, their friends and Canadian cities.

Fire was a constant hazard for the new settlement because the wooden structures were built close together and there was a water shortage. A volunteer fire brigade was formed in December 1882, and an earth and wooden dam was built across Wascana Creek to improve the water supply. The dam created the original Wascana Lake, a reservoir that covered more than 200 acres.

The first private school opened in March 1883 and, two months later, the first free public school was begun in the Methodist Church. Educational services were limited by funding because there was no council with authority to levy a school rate. However, when the North-West Council passed a School Ordinance, the situation improved and the Regina Protestant Public School District No. 4 was proclaimed on December 20, 1884.

Reverend W. J. Hewitt was the CPR's unofficial padre. He arrived in Regina on August 23, 1882, and four days later he conducted Regina's first religious service from a tent pitched on the station grounds.

The first church was built in 10 days by the Methodist congregation. The building was finished on November 17, 1882, and served as church, court room, school house, town council chamber and public lecture hall.

A week after the first Methodist service, the local Presbyterians started worship services. The first St. Paul's church was built in 1883, several months after the arrival of the first resident Anglican clergyman, Reverend Alfred Osborne.

Regina was predominately Protestant. There was a group of Roman Catholics, but they had no resident priest or church until Pascal Bonneau and Charles McCusker raised over $1,000 to build a small church, in 1884, near Cornwall Street and 12th Avenue.

St. Paul's Church

Louis Riel

Most of Regina's citizens came from quiet respectable Ontario and Manitoba homes and were church members. Indeed, Regina had a reputation for being peaceful and law-abiding.

On December 1, 1883, Regina was proclaimed the first organized town in the Territories, with a population of 1,000.

The town's early tranquillity was shattered by the trial of Metis leader Louis Riel. Regina became famous as the trial attracted hordes of newspapermen and spectators. The first day of Riel's trial, 650 guards were present. Riel, accused of treason, was dressed in a Mounted Police uniform so he could be safely escorted from his barrack cell to the Regina Courthouse. Despite his bushy black beard protruding from beneath his helmet, Riel arrived at the court house virtually unrecognized and unharmed. The jury deliberated for 65 minutes before returning the guilty verdict with a recommendation for mercy. Riel was hanged at the barracks on November 16, 1885.

Although early Regina had few physical attributes, its citizens' hardy spirit was an asset, overlooked by critics, which more than compensated for the townsite's shortfalls.

There was a magnificent celebration for Dominion Day 1886, with horse racing and a concert at the new town hall. There was also a billiard tournament at the Palmer House and a torchlight parade. On July 1st the first train to the Pacific went through Regina, arriving at Port Moody, British Columbia on July 4th.

Regina people showed their enterprise when Sir John A. and Lady Macdonald visited the town July 6, 1886. Reginans went beyond decorating with the traditional red, white and blue flags. To camouflage the town's barren appearance, residents cut green trees from the creek and planted them in the ground along the procession route.

In his address at Government House, Sir John A. Macdonald said: "It has given me great pleasure to visit Regina. I had something to do with the selection of it as the capital of the Northwest and the future capital of Assiniboia. After my visit today and notwithstanding that I have seen other locations to the south and east of you, I am clear that the selection was a wise one. There is everything to make you a great city. Situated as you are in the centre of this continent, with a fertile soil, destined to be a great railway centre, I don't see that there can be any hindrance to your future progress." – *Leader,* July 20, 1886.

In 1887 the first telephone switchboard was established, as was the Musical Ride of the NWMP.

Fire was a constant enemy. Early in the morning of March 15, 1890, an entire business block on South Railway was destroyed in spite of the fire-fighting efforts of the fire brigade, 80 Mounties and most of the townspeople.

A happier occasion occurred that year when the town was lit, not by fire, but by the first electric lights. Eventually 10 street lights were turned on, but only for Saturday nights.

The NWMP football club sponsored the first football tournament in the territories in 1891. The Regina Curling Club hosted the first bonspiel in the Territories in 1892 – Regina won two first prizes; Calgary won a second.

It was the pioneers' enduring spirit which helped them cope through the drought of 1894. There was only 8.05 inches of precipitation (including snow) in 1893 and 6.25 inches the following year. As a result, the crop was almost a total failure. Two years previously the homesteaders had battled a typhoid fever epidemic. The epidemic and the depression forced the Territorial Government to provide relief aid.

The first ladies' hockey club in the North-West Territories was organized in Regina in 1896.

In 1898 Government House opened as a residence for the lieutenant-governor.

WILLIAM ARGAN

JAS. GRASSICKS CARTER & FEED AND SALE STABLE

MUSIC

CARETTE

Regina, with a population of 3,000, was incorporated as a city on June 19, 1903. J. W. Smith was the first mayor of the newly incorporated city. That year two important bylaws were approved. One involved bringing in spring water from Boggy Creek, several miles away. The other allowed for municipal ownership of an electric light plant. Tenders for the water project were awarded by December and a year later the project was completed.

Saskatchewan became a province on September 4, 1905. A cairn in Victoria Park marks the occasion. After Saskatchewan attained provincehood, debate erupted again over the location of the province's capital. A number of centres, including Saskatoon, lobbied hard to be selected as the capital. The matter was finally decided after the first provincial election in 1905. The new Premier, Walter Scott, a former Member of Parliament for Regina, convinced the Legislature that Regina should remain the capital.

By 1906, at least $5 million worth of implements was shipped out of Regina. The Queen City was Saskatchewan's financial centre, with most major trust and insurance companies moving in and five more banks opening branches.

In this year the cornerstone was laid for the grand new city hall on 11th Avenue, and the first street paving and construction of concrete sidewalks began.

A swell of immigrants caused Regina's population to explode, reaching more than 30,000 by 1911. The 1905 statistics break the year's immigrants into ethnic categories: 971 Britishers, 967 Germans, 495 Americans, 355 Canadians, 239 Norwegians, 79 Austrians, 68 Galicians, 51 Romanians, 31 Russians, 18 Swedes, 14 Icelanders and 12 Swiss.

As a result of the influx of new settlers, land prices soared. In February 1907 an American paid $30,000 for six lots, at the corner of Hamilton Street and 12th Avenue, which had been purchased seven months earlier for $22,000.

The Regina Orchestral society held its first concert in City Hall in December 1908.

In 1909 Governor General Earl Grey laid the cornerstone for the Legislative Building; the first public library was opened in City Hall, and the first Saskatchewan Music Festival was held.

Regina's rapid expansion posed many problems. According to 1910 statistics compiled by the Trades and Labour Congress, Regina had the lowest average wages and the highest cost of living in Western Canada. Unskilled laborers were paid 20 cents an hour and worked 10-hour days. Overcrowding was also a concern. A local newspaper of the day, *The Standard*, reported that one March night there were 400 people walking the streets because they had no accommodation.

Mother Nature also created havoc for Reginans. In May 1909 a mild earthquake shook the city. The quake caused minimal damage.

The Regina Rugby Club, the forerunner to the Saskatchewan Roughrider football team, was formed in 1910. In the same year, the first permanent Regina Public Library building opened on Lorne Street, and Regina's street cars had their inaugural run.

On Sunday afternoon, June 30, 1912, a cyclone ripped through Regina, killing 30 people, injuring 200 and leaving 2,500 homeless. Property damage was more than $4 million. Some of Regina's finest buildings suffered heavy damage, including the Methodist, Baptist and Presbyterian churches, the YMCA and YWCA, the Central Telephone Office and the Public Library.

Mulligan's livery stable, complete with 50 horses, was lifted from South Railway and set down on the CPR tracks. None of the horses were injured.

Despite the widespread devastation, Regina citizens rallied to rebuild, with the help of trainloads of carpenters from Winnipeg and elsewhere. Within a year there was little physical evidence of the destructive storm, but it took the city 46 years to repay a $500,000 loan from the provincial government.

The Regina Roughriders played their first game in 1912 at Dominion Park, located at 7th Avenue and Broad Street.

WILLIAM ARGAN

Opening of the Provincial Legislative Building

On October 12, 1912, the Duke of Connaught dedicated the Provincial Legislative Building at the official opening, and on October 14 he officially opened Regina College on 16th Avenue (now College Avenue). Union Depot (Union Station) was also completed in this year.

The outbreak of WW I virtually halted European immigration. Between 1911 and 1916 Regina's population dropped from 30,213 to 26,127.

Reginans also had a brush with death in 1917, when a crowded grandstand on the Exhibition grounds caught fire during the fair. Within seven minutes, the 3,000 occupants emptied the stands without a fatality. Seconds later, flames engulfed the stands and the building. Despite the fire, the fair continued. The debris was cleared and a new stand for nearly 6,000 people was constructed by the next day, just in time for the first race.

The war period ended with the influenza epidemic that lasted from 1918 to 1920. On October 6, 1918 the first "flu" death occurred. All public gatherings, such as church services, were banned and anyone caught coughing, sneezing or spitting in public could be fined $50. The epidemic claimed 330 lives, with the greatest mortality among males between the ages of 20 and 40.

In spite of the epidemic, Reginans celebrated continuously in the streets for 24 hours when the armistice was announced. About 8,000 revellers gathered at Wascana Park to hear dignitaries speak and to pay tribute to the dead.

Union Station greeted many important dignitaries, including the future King Edward VIII who visited as Prince of Wales in 1919 and again in 1927.

By 1920, grain prices had dropped sharply, so farmers took matters into their own hands and formed the Saskatchewan Co-operative Wheat Producers Limited, the forerunner of the Saskatchewan Wheat Pool. The large Sherwood Department Store at Albert Street and Victoria Avenue was purchased as a head office.

The first licensed aerodrome in Canada was built in Regina, and Regina pilot Roland Groome became Canada's first licensed commercial pilot in 1920.

In 1922 CKCK Radio, Saskatchewan's first station, was established by the *Leader-Post*.

The Regina Capitals professional hockey team played in the Western Canada Hockey League in the 1920s. The team, owned by hotelier Wes Champ and his brothers Dave and Stewart, won the Western Canada Hockey League Championship in 1922. Eddie Shore of Cupar started his pro career with the Caps as a forward in 1922. Shore went on to become a Hockey Hall of Famer with the Boston Bruins. In the mid-twenties western professional hockey could no longer compete economically and the Regina Capitals were relocated to Portland to become the Portland Rosebuds of the PCHL. Moving with the team were future NHL stars Dick Irvin, Johnny Gottselig and "Mush" March. The entire PCHL was sold to the NHL for $272,000 in 1926 and the Regina Caps, that had moved to Portland, became the Chicago Blackhawks.

On Dominion Day in 1927, Regina celebrated the Diamond Jubilee of Confederation. Led by the RCMP, 38 floats depicted Canada's history and her achievements since Confederation. 160 Indians on prairie ponies also participated in the parade and four Indian tepees were erected in Wascana park. A special reviewing stand was erected at the corner of Albert Street and College Avenue. Premier James Gardiner, whose home can be seen below on the northeast corner of this intersection, was part of the reviewing party, which included Lieutenant-Governor H. W. Newlands and Mayor James McAra.

Diamond Jubilee Parade

College Avenue at
Albert Street

Al Ritchie

Coached by Al Ritchie, in 1928 the Regina Pats Junior Hockey Club won the first of three Memorial Cups.

In 1928, Jimmy Trifunov won a bronze medal in wrestling for Canada at the Olympics. He was Canadian amateur champion ten times and an Olympic participant in the 1924, 1928 and 1932 Olympics. He coached Canada's Olympic wrestling team in 1952, 1956 and 1960. Trifunov is a member of five Halls of Fame, including the Saskatchewan and Canadian. He also received the Order of Canada.

In 1929, the year Darke Hall opened, there was more construction in Regina than in any other Canadian city. Then the stock market crashed. Grain prices fell to record lows and industries closed. By the end of the year, there were over 1,200 unemployed and, by October 1932, 20 per cent of Regina's population sought relief. Extreme drought and the grasshopper plagues of 1933 and 1934 added to the devastation brought by the world-wide Depression. The City set up relief projects to employ as many men as possible. The Winnipeg Street subway, the Albert Street reservoir and bridge, and the improvement of Wascana Lake were some of the make-work projects for over 2,000 men.

Gorgeous Displays and Attractions From Many Far-Off Land

One of Regina's most notable landmarks, the Albert Memorial Bridge, was constructed at a cost of $230,000. Opened in November 1930, it is said to be the longest bridge over the shortest span of water in the world.

Despite the pessimism the depression brought, the World Grain Show, with exhibits from around the world, was held in 1933. Also in this year, the Sherwood Co-operative Association, the Co-op Refinery and the Co-operative Commonwealth Federation (CCF) were formed, and Regina College became a branch of the University of Saskatchewan.

Gaston (Gas) Eichel won the first of two Canadian Light-Heavyweight Championships. In his 14-year career he fought 47 bouts and lost only three. He won 12 by knockouts.

Walter Martin, who later became a judge (son of Premier W. M. Martin) was named Canada's top tennis player in 1933 and 1934. Martin was a Canadian Davis Cup team member four times.

Ken Goff advanced to the Featherweight Dominion Championships in 1934, but lost in the semi-final. He organized the Olympic Boxing Club in 1936.

Reginans weren't alone in their economic misery. In 1935, hundreds of unemployed men, travelling chiefly by box-cars, from as far west as Vancouver, planned to converge on Ottawa to present their concerns. By June 14, when the train reached Regina, the number of men had risen to about 1,800. Prime Minister Bennett issued orders to stop the trekkers in Regina.

The desperate men, frustrated by unemployment, rallied in Market Square on July 1. The peaceful meeting was disrupted when RCMP and Regina police arrested seven men. Violence erupted. Detective Millar of the Regina City Police was killed in the riot.

Stones and other missiles were thrown, and hundreds of glass windows in businesses, cars and streetcars were broken. Aside from the single fatality, 39 Mounties were injured and 40 trekkers and local citizens were hospitalized. The Mounted Police converged on the area and rode down one business block after another until the streets were cleared. Tensions abated after a few days, with no charges laid regarding the police officer's death. The remaining trekkers returned to British Columbia by train.

In 1935 the first Community Chest drive (now the United Way) raised $35,000 and the organization became an enduring Regina agency.

The MacKenzie Art Gallery had its beginnings in 1936 when Norman MacKenzie bequeathed his art collection to the university.

Regina fireman Vern Pettigrew was a member of the Canadian Olympic Wrestling Team at the 1936 Berlin Olympics. He won five Canadian Amateur Wrestling Championships in 1933, 1935, 1936, 1937 and 1940.

Flags were flying at Union station on May 25, 1939 when the royal train pulled in with King George VI and Queen Elizabeth. Queen City residents were thrilled. Six Regina groups, joined by nine out-of-town bands, provided music for the 100,000 people who lined the 14-mile procession route.

But the optimism generated by the royal visit and recent good crops died with the onset of WW II.

Queen Elizabeth

King George VI

During the war years, Regina was an intensive training centre for all the services. The General Motors assembly plant, which was closed in the depression, was taken over by the Dominion Government, retooled and renamed Regina Industries Limited. The business became the province's largest munitions plant and provided work for over 1,000 people at the peak of wartime production in 1943. The war contracts ended shortly after the war ended and the staff, who had been working on a secret weapon, were dismissed (see page 225).

Coached by Ken Goff, Claude Warwick won the Canadian Featherweight Boxing Championship in 1940. The Regina Rangers "Cinderella" team, coached by Freddie Metcalfe, won the Allan Cup in 1941, defeating the Sydney Millionaires in the seventh game at Queen City Gardens (Exhibition Stadium). Ranger players included "Sugar" Jim Henry, Al "Bud" Sandelack, Garth Boesch and the "kid line" of Scotty Cameron, Grant Warwick and Frank Mario.

In 1945, Government House was leased to the Department of Veteran's Affairs to be used as a convalescent and rehabilitation centre for servicemen. It was later used as a home for handicapped and unemployable veterans of both wars.

There was little building activity in Regina during the war years, and R. H. William's department store remained the city's economic centre.

Adam Faul won the Canadian Heavyweight Boxing Championship in 1947 and 1948. Faul's unbeaten record ended in his second bout at the 1948 Olympics when an accidental hit resulted in a severe eye injury, which prevented further competition in the games.

Don Hodges won the Western Canada Tennis Championship in 1948, one of many tennis and badminton championships he would achieve in later years. In the same year, Bill Ebbels won the Saskatchewan Men's Singles Tennis Crown. He went on to later win the championship a record of eight times, and was runner-up on seven other occasions.

The highly touted Regina Capitals hockey club lost the controversial "egg-shaped" rink final in Ottawa to the Ottawa Senators in 1949. The Capitals team included "Sweeney" Schriner, Mel Hill, Vic Myles, Gus and Bill Kyle, Chuck McCullough and Ab McDougall.

Bill Clarke

In 1950, Bill Clarke, later of the Saskatchewan Roughriders, won the first Canadian Junior Curling Championship.

Prince Philip

Queen Elizabeth II

There were cheers at Union station when Princess Elizabeth and the Duke of Edinburgh arrived in 1951 and when they arrived again as Queen and Consort on July 23, 1959. The monarch's second visit to Regina was greeted by a 21-gun salute, band music, and the cheers of some 2,000 people packed along South Railway.

Prosperity returned in the post-war years. Relief numbers were small, civic finances were sound, employment widespread and crops were good in the 1950s. As times improved, the birth rate increased and people moved to Regina from the country. Postwar residential expansion in Regina was primarily to the east, southeast and to the north. The new subdivisions featured neighbourhood shopping facilities, spacious lots and parks.

Along the city's main thoroughfares, shopping malls were erected. The Golden Mile Plaza opened in 1955, the Northgate Mall in 1965, the Midtown Centre in 1968, the Southland Mall in 1975, the Cornwall Centre in 1981 and Victoria Square in 1983. The Normanview Mall and Sherwood Mall were opened in northwest Regina. The Midtown Centre, renamed the Galleria, reopened in 1989. This shopping centre, located on the site of the original city hall, is connected to the Cornwall Centre by a pedestrian walkway.

The rapid population growth had drastically changed the Queen City. Private developers turned vacant land into residential subdivisions and shopping centres. The provincial government and private developers also reshaped the downtown area with the addition of new department stores and office towers.

In 1954 CKCK became the first licensed television station in Western Canada. The Museum of Natural History opened in 1955.

1956 saw the formation of Prairie Pipe Manufacturing Co. Ltd. followed by the creation of Interprovincial Steel Corporation Ltd. in 1957.

Wascana Centre Authority was created in 1962. Administered jointly by the city, the province and the university, Wascana Centre provides a beautiful setting for the University of Regina, the Museum of Natural History, the

Saskatchewan Centre of the Arts, the MacKenzie Art Gallery, the Legislative Building and government offices.

Frederick G. Todd, a Montreal landscape architect, had been appointed in 1906 to plan Wascana Park, even before the Legislative Building was constructed. Although most of his plans were never implemented, his suggestions about the provision of trees were acted upon. Mature trees were expensive so Todd recommended that a large quantity of seedling trees should be purchased and grown, for a year or two, on soil that was similar to Regina's, until ready for transplanting. By May 1913, almost 11,000 trees and shrubs were transplanted, according to Todd's plan, on the grounds surrounding the Legislative Building.

It was the careful planning of generations of Reginans, beginning in 1907, that spurred Regina's transformation from barren prairie to fertile oasis. Today Regina boasts a quarter-million trees, which is testament to the citizens' commitment to beautify their city. Each of those trees was hand-planted.

Anton "Red" Glasser won the Canadian Ten Pin Bowling Singles Championship in 1962 and, with his partner Joe Most, won the Canadian Ten Pin Bowling Doubles Title in 1964.

Ron Lancaster

Led by quarterback Ron Lancaster and running back George Reed, the Saskatchewan Roughriders won their first Grey Cup in Vancouver in 1966, defeating the Hamilton Tiger-Cats 29 to 14. The junior Regina Rams won the Canadian Junior football title, defeating Montreal's Notre Dame de Grace Maple Leafs by the same score.

A major step forward for the performing arts was the opening of the Saskatchewan Centre of the Arts in 1970.

The worst flood in Regina's history occurred in April 1971, when Wascana Creek overflowed its banks. In the same year the Canadian Western Agribition agricultural exhibition was established.

Harvey Mazinke and his team of Bill Martin, George Achtymichuk and Dan Klippenstein were undefeated in 1973 when they went on to win the Men's Canadian Brier Curling Championship (see page 292).

Harvey Mazinke team

The University of Regina was established as an independent university in 1974. In the same year, coached by former Pat and Montreal Canadien's NHL player Bob Turner, the Regina Pats won the Memorial Cup in Calgary. Players included Ed Staniowski, Clarke Gillies and Dennis Sobchuk.

In 1978 Regina celebrated its 75th anniversary as a city. On July 29 of that year Queen Elizabeth and Prince Philip unveiled a bronze plaque in front of City Hall, officially naming the area Queen Elizabeth II Court.

The first Western Canada Farm Progress show was held in Regina, and the city's anniversary was also marked by the construction of the new Police Headquarters Building, officially opened on December 14, 1978.

In 1979, the C. M. Fines Building, head office for Saskatchewan Government Insurance was opened as part of the $100-million Cornwall Centre. Also opened that year was the T. C. Douglas Building, a provincial government building located in the southwest corner of Wascana Centre.

Construction of the Saskatchewan Telecommunications Tower in the Cornwall Centre and the decision by Sears to locate in the Cornwall Centre aided downtown rejuvenation in 1980. That year, after extensive renovations, the former City Hall (formerly the Post Office Building) became the permanent home of the Globe Theatre and the Regina Plains Museum.

Marj Mitchell team

In 1980, Marj Mitchell's curling team of Mitchell, Nancy Kerr, Shirley McKendry and Wendy Leach won Canada's first Women's World Curling Championship (see page 295).

Also in 1980, Regina hosted the Memorial Cup in the new Agridome. The Regina Pats' star player was Doug Wickenheiser.

Rejuvenation of the downtown area continued when the McCallum Hill Building was imploded in 1982 to make way for new twin office towers on the Scarth Street Mall. The mall was renamed the Frederick W. Hill Mall in 2001 and the Twin Towers (McCallum Hill Centre) were featured on Regina's 100th anniversary logo.

Claire (Ehman) Lovett, winner of 13 city and seven provincial badminton and tennis championships, and two world titles, won the 1983 World's Intersport Invitational Veterans' Championship in Taiwan.

In 1984, Regina's world class distance runner Lynn Ann (Kanuka) Williams won a bronze medal in the 3,000 metres at the Los Angeles' Olympic Games.

Regina's Stacy Singer was eight years old when she won the gold medal in the junior (under 14) division at the World Baton Twirling Championships in Germany in 1985. She won the gold again at age eleven in the freestyle event in Japan. She went on to win six consecutive gold medals and one team medal as a member of the Buffalo Gals baton twirling team that won the world team championship in 1991 (see page 322).

Stacy Singer

The Ramada Renaissance Hotel (later Delta Hotel) and Saskatchewan Trade and Convention Centre complex officially opened in February 1988. The Queensbury Centre opened on the Exhibition Grounds in the same year.

The new Wascana Rehabilitation Centre, the province's largest and best-equipped facility for long-term care of the disabled, became operational in January of 1989. In the same year, the Duke and Duchess of York officially opened the Saskatchewan Science Centre in the old power station.

Also in 1989, the Regina Economic Development Authority, under the chairmanship of Gordon Staseson, was established by the city as an independent body with a mandate to promote business opportunities for Regina. The name of the authority was later changed to the Regina Regional Economic Development Authority, to include the areas surrounding the city.

The Saskatchewan Roughriders won their second Grey Cup in 1989, before 54,000 fans in Toronto's Skydome. With a thrilling last-play field goal, from 26 yards out, by Dave Ridgway, they defeated the Hamilton Tiger Cats 43 to 40. Fans across Canada voted the game the best played and most exciting in Grey Cup history.

In 1990 the MacKenzie Art Gallery moved into superb new quarters in the T. C. Douglas Building in Wascana Centre, at Albert Street and 23rd Avenue. The Kramer IMAX theatre opened in the Saskatchewan Science Centre in 1991.

Regina's downtown skyline changed dramatically with the completion, in 1992, of the Crown Life Building on Scarth Street, to accommodate the head offices of Crown Life, relocated from Toronto. The Farm Credit Corporation head offices were also relocated from Ottawa to the new FCC Agriculture building at the corner of 11th Avenue and Hamilton Street. The Crown Life Building was renamed the Canada Life Building in 1999. Casino Regina opened in the former Union Station building on Saskatchewan Drive in 1994, and the $26-million Riddell Centre (fine arts building) opened at the university.

In the early 1990s the CFL adopted a policy of the annual Grey Cup game being played in various CFL cities. Regina won the right to host the game in 1995. $1 million was spent to erect 20,000 temporary seats in Taylor Field, increasing capacity to 54,000. The game was a sellout, and on November 19th the Baltimore Stallions won their first Grey Cup, defeating the Calgary Stampeders 37 to 20. CFL Officials considered the festival hosted by Regina as the "best ever".

In playoff upsets, the Saskatchewan Roughriders defeated the Calgary Stampeders and the Edmonton Eskimos to earn a berth in the 1997 Grey Cup played in Edmonton. Half of the the fans in the stands came from Saskatchewan. The Riders lost to the Argonauts 47 to 23.

Sandra Schmirler team

At the 1998 Winter Olympics in Nagano, Japan, the Sandra Schmirler curling team, with Jan Betker, Joan McCusker and Marcia Gudereit, won the first Olympic gold medals ever awarded to women's curling. They had won their first Saskatchewan Women's Curling Championship in 1991, and went on to win a record three Canadian Women's Curling Championships and three World Curling Championships.

In 1998 the Regina Airport became locally operated. The Government of Canada transferred the airport to the Regina Airport Authority, headed by President R. P. (Dick) Rendek.

The turn of the century signified a milestone for the University of Regina sports' program. After dominating the Canadian football junior ranks from the mid-1960s through the 1990s, under the guidance of the legendary Gordon Currie and, later, Frank McCrystal, the Regina Rams left junior football to join the Canadian Intercollegiate Athletic Union (CIAU). In 2000, only their second year in the college ranks, they were finalists in the Vanier Cup, losing to the University of Ottawa Gee-Gees 42 to 39. Also in 2000, the University of Regina Cougars Women's Basketball team won the Canadian University Women's Championship, and the Cougars Women's Hockey Team lost in the National final. 2000 was a great year for the University of Regina sports' program.

Prince Charles

The Prince of Wales visited Regina in 2001. His Royal Highness presented Saskatchewan Volunteer Medals to sixteen citizens. He also toured Scott Collegiate and visited the well-known "Chili For Children Lunch Program" started by Theresa Stevenson in 1985. Stevenson, a status Indian, saw children in her own community going hungry and was so moved she started a hot lunch program with money out of her own pocket. She was awarded the Order of Canada in 1994. The program continues, operated by Regina Indian Community Awareness Inc. and serves nutritious meals to approximately 400 children, three days a week, at three locations.

Regina hosted a well-organized week-long Memorial Cup Celebration in 2001. Games were played before capacity crowds at the Agridome. The Regina Pats played well but were eliminated in the semi-finals, losing 5 to 4 to Val d'Or in overtime.

The Galleria Shopping Centre on 11th Avenue, between Rose and Hamilton Streets, was closed in 2002 to undergo extensive renovation for the centralization of Government of Canada offices in downtown Regina.

The RCMP announced plans in 2002 for a new museum, estimated to cost $25 million, to be located at the RCMP Training Depot and federal cabinet minister Ralph Goodale announced an expansion to the RCMP forensic laboratory in Regina.

Regina was named host city for its second Grey Cup Game in 2003, as part of the city's centennial celebrations.

On August 11, 2002, the North Regina All-Stars won the Canadian Little League Championship. Led by pitcher Eric Bryce, the All-Stars became the first Regina team ever to win the Canadian Little League title and compete in the World Series Little League tournament in Williamsport Pennsylvania.

The Saskatchewan Federated Indian College building, designed by internationally renowned architect Douglas Cardinal, on the University of Regina campus, is scheduled to open in the spring of 2003. Cardinal is best known for his design of the Museum of Civilization in Hull, Quebec.

When driving through Regina in 2002 with its population of 190,000, it is difficult to visualize the Regina of 1883 with its canvas tents mired in mud and a population of 1,000. The initiative, endurance and courage of the people of Regina played a vital role in overcoming storms, fires, droughts and depressions. Their spirit, foresight and creative planning makes Regina deserving of the name Queen City.

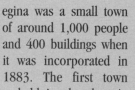egina was a small town of around 1,000 people and 400 buildings when it was incorporated in 1883. The first town meetings were held in churches, in stores or wherever there was room.

Regina's first town hall was built in late 1885 and early '86 on the northeast corner of Scarth Street and 11th Avenue. The first Town Council meeting was held in the building on February 15, 1886.

It was a wooden structure which housed the Council Chambers, the police station and the town's fire engine. The upstairs was used as a school during the day and as a public meeting room in the evening and on weekends. It also functioned as a banquet hall. An addition to house the fire engine was built in 1887. The town soon outgrew the building, which briefly housed the Bijou Theatre where hand-cranked movies were shown.

When Regina became a city in 1903, the lieutenant-governor of the North-West Territories, Amédée Forget, rode in a carriage to Town Hall with a Mounted Police escort.

The cornerstone for Regina's second City Hall was laid by Mayor McAra in 1906 and two years later, in March 1908, the new City Hall was open for business. The building was built by Smith Brothers and Wilson. It was considered to be the finest building of its kind in the west and, in some respects, superior to anything found in Toronto.

In its heyday, Regina's City Hall was more than just the seat of municipal government; it also served as a "centre for fine arts, music and literature." The facility included an auditorium which was a combination ballroom and lecture hall, with seating for 1,000. This facility was available for public as well as civic use and, as such, it witnessed everything from company Christmas parties, dances,

Town/City Hall – Scarth Street and 11th Avenue
1886 to 1908

City Hall – 11th Avenue between Hamilton and Rose Streets
1908 to 1962

REGINA

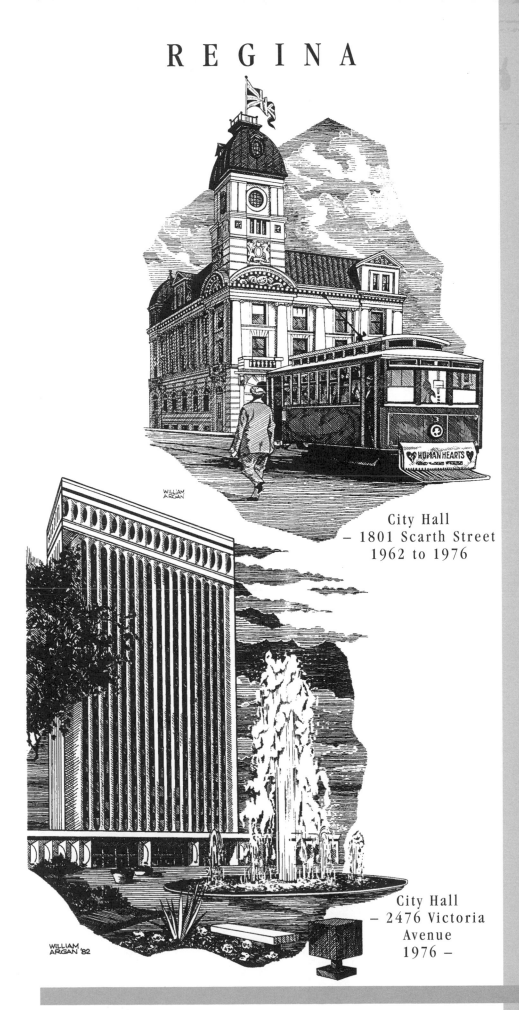

City Hall
– 1801 Scarth Street
1962 to 1976

City Hall
– 2476 Victoria
Avenue
1976 –

WILLIAM ARGAN

WILLIAM ARGAN '82

wedding receptions, political meetings and boxing matches.

When the cornerstone was lowered into place, tucked into a specially chiselled compartment in the centre was an iron strongbox containing souvenirs of the occasion. Fifty-eight years later, in February 1965, when the building was demolished, the strongbox was removed from the cornerstone and opened in Mayor Baker's office. The box contained four newspapers, seven coins, eight postage stamps and a half-dozen photographs. All were mementos of a time when Regina was young, and her City Hall was the pride of the west.

In 1962, the municipal government moved into what had been the old post office on the southeast corner of 11th Avenue and Scarth Street. The building was soon too small and it needed extensive renovation. It is now called the Old City Hall Mall and houses a number of businesses and the Globe Theatre.

The present 16-storey City Hall was built in 1975/1976 and was officially opened on December 14, 1976. It is named Queen Elizabeth II Court in honour of the Monarch. Joseph Pettick, the Regina architect who also designed the SaskPower building, designed City Hall.

The City Hall is a distinctive part of the downtown skyline. The ring of bright high-pressure sodium lights around the top floor are a symbolic crown which welcomes people into the Queen City.

The Council Chamber is officially named Henry Baker Hall, after Regina's longest-serving mayor. He was mayor during the time the present City Hall was built.

An arch from Regina's 1908 City Hall has been installed horizontally in the lawn in front of the present City Hall.

TOWN TRUSTEES

*T*he Canada North-West Land Company, in co-operation with the CPR, played a role in promoting new townsites. The CPR was faced with a shortage of working capital. It sold 2.2 million acres of its land grant, and all of the townsites to be laid out along the main line west from Brandon to the Rockies, to the Canada North-West Land Company. Four trustees were appointed to advertise and sell the lots. Donald A. Smith and R. B. Angus represented the CPR; E. B. Osler and W. B. Scarth represented the Canada North-West Land Company.

Edmund B. Osler

*S*ir Edmund Boyd Osler helped to finance the founding of the Dominion Bank and served as its president from 1901 to 1924.

Osler was a member of Parliament from 1896 to 1917 and a governor of the University of Toronto.

Richard B. Angus

*R*ichard Bladworth Angus was chosen by the CPR to represent them as a trustee.

Donald A. Smith

*D*onald A. Smith was present at the christening of Regina on August 23, 1882. Smith was not formally a member of the syndicate formed in 1882 to build the CPR, yet he risked his personal fortune to keep the venture afloat.

On November 7, 1885, he was honoured by being chosen to drive the last spike to complete the Canadian Pacific Railway that now stretched from coast to coast.

William B. Scarth

*W*illiam B. Scarth was the only trustee residing in Regina when the railway reached the Queen City in 1882, so he was responsible for developing the townsite. In February 1883, Regina citizens became discouraged because of rumours about the capital being moved, a water shortage and general neglect of the town by the Government and the Railway. Scarth called a public meeting to assure residents that a test well would be sunk, streets graded, public buildings erected, a bridge and reservoir built, and water would be brought from Boggy Creek.

The morning after the meeting, over seventy-five lots were sold to Regina businessmen.

Scarth fulfilled his promises. Four miles of streets were graded and, on April 24, 1883, a test well sunk on South Railway resulted in a good water supply.

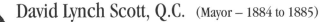

REGINA MAYORS

David Lynch Scott, Q.C. (Mayor – 1884 to 1885)

David L. Scott studied law in Brampton, Upper Canada (now Ontario). He moved to Regina in 1882. Life was primitive, most people lived and worked in tents, so Scott pitched a tent and hung out a tin sign to advertise his name and profession.

Regina was proclaimed the first organized town in the Territories on December 1, 1883. A month later, Scott became mayor by acclamation and served two years.

The first municipal election was a quiet affair. The January 17, 1884 *Leader* reported: "The election for the civic council passed away without riot or bloodshed. There were polled in all 213 votes which is a good number." Council meetings were held on the first and third Monday of each month. At the February 2, 1884 meeting, Dr. Cotton offered to rent his hall on Broad Street for council meetings for five dollars per month which included fuel and light. That offer was accepted.

During the Northwest Rebellion in 1885, Scott organized volunteers, known as the Regina Blazers, for home defence. Although the company had rifles and belts, they did not receive uniforms or ammunition until just before Riel's capture so they played no role in the Uprising. The only service the Blazers saw was to present arms to General Middleton at Riel's trial. After the Rebellion was crushed, Scott was one of the prosecutors during Riel's trial – a position which advanced his career. Later that year he was appointed a Crown prosecutor for Assiniboia and was designated a Queen's Counsel. In 1894 he was appointed judge of the Supreme Court of the North-West Territories. He and his family moved to what is now Alberta where he died in 1924.

Daniel Mowat (Mayor – 1886 to 1887)

Daniel Mowat was the first merchant to open a store in Regina in 1882. Originally from Ottawa, he came west in 1879 and opened a store at Shoal Lake, Manitoba. A year later he opened another at Fort Qu'Appelle. In partnership with his brother, Alex, he constructed a substantial retail establishment.

Mowat was elected mayor in 1886 – the year the town hall opened. The opening was a memorable event in Regina's history. The *Leader* reported: "We have now a town hall finer than Winnipeg had so recently as 1879; in fact we have a better town hall than Toronto today. This speaks well for the spirit and prosperity of the town and reflects credit on Mr. Scott, Mr. Martin, Mr. McCusker, Mr. Mowat and Mr. Sibbald. The acoustic properties are all that could be desired."

On March 23, 1886, Mowat called merchants together to discuss organizing a Board of Trade. Presiding over the meeting in the town council chamber, he stated: "Union was strength, and the merchants if united in an association, could do more for the trade and commercial prosperity of Regina than by working singly for their own success." The motion to organize a Board of Trade in Regina was carried unanimously. Mowat was one of several prominent local businessmen who founded the Regina Creamery Company in 1896. This firm aggressively looked for outside markets to buy their surplus. In 1898 more than half of the company's butter was sent to British Columbia customers.

William Cayley Hamilton, Q.C. (Mayor – 1888)

William Cayley Hamilton studied law in Ontario and graduated at the head of his law class. Arriving in Regina in August 1882, he was among the earliest settlers. He began practising law immediately and soon became a partner with David L. Scott. Hamilton had many prestigious clients over the years, including the Bank of Montreal. Once his career was established, Hamilton branched out into politics. During 1886 and 1887 he was a town councillor and was elected mayor in January 1888.

After the election, The January 3 *Leader* reported: "It was a difficult thing to choose between Mr. Smith and Mr. Hamilton and it is quite clear the town was pretty evenly divided on their merits, the temperance question turning the balance in favor of the latter. Regina has the largest temperance vote of any town on the line of the Pacific, and this election shows that the towns would vote against prohibition, while in the country districts prohibition would carry." Following his one-year term as mayor (the usual term at the time), Hamilton rekindled his political ambitions and ran for MLA in 1891. He was defeated by the incumbent, Mr. Jelly.

In June 1890 Hamilton was created a Q.C. When Scott left Regina in 1894, Hamilton became head of their law firm. Regina's third mayor died on October 21, 1901 from kidney disease. His popularity in the community was evidenced by the massive turnout of rich and poor citizens at his funeral, held at St. Paul's Church.

Jacob W. Smith (Mayor – 1889, 1902, 1903, 1907)

*P*rior to winning the mayor's seat, J. W. Smith served as a councillor in 1884 and 1887. Regular council meetings were often lively, especially when building sidewalks was on the agenda, because of Regina's gumbo soil and lack of funds.

"Councillor Smith accused Councillors Martin and McCannel of laying their heads together to keep a sidewalk away from Rose Street and run it nearly past their own doors." notes Earl Drake, historian.

When Regina became a city on June 1, 1903, Mayor Jacob Smith declared a half holiday and everybody celebrated the civic inauguration. The Union Jack was hoisted on the city hall by the Lieutenant-Governor, the new city band made its first public appearance and prominent men delivered glowing addresses. Afternoon ceremonies were followed by a concert, speeches, songs, recitations, bagpipe music and an impromptu dance after midnight.

During 1903 two important by-laws were passed with Mayor Smith's support – municipal ownership of an electric light plant and a project to bring spring water from Boggy Creek.

The J. W. Smith Block, 1755 Rose Street, designed in the Edwardian Classical style by Storey and Van Egmond, was built by the Saskatchewan Building and Construction Company in 1907.

James A. McCaul (Mayor – 1890)

*J*ames McCaul was elected the Regina Board of Trade's first president on April 6, 1886, and the town of Regina's mayor in 1890 with "a substantial majority of thirty seven" reported the *Leader*. The paper's January 7th article continued: "We hope our new Mayor will apply himself at once to the sanitary question. He follows a man who proved himself zealous and successful and we believe he will display a like zeal and will face with courage the pressing problems of the town. . . . A discussion arose last night on the question of a steam fire engine, and although we think the retiring Council did not err in going cautiously we believe the time has now arrived when a steamer should be bought. No Mayor and Council can properly fulfill their duties unless they work in the light of the future and under the abiding impression of the imminent (sic) progress and expansion of which the capital of these Territories can certainly count. But the first thing to grapple with is the sanitary question."

In Regina's early days most citizens worked hard for meagre returns, yet social life in the small town was surprisingly varied. Most sports were exclusively for men. English football was popular and crowds would turn out when the town team played the team from the police barracks. Also popular was cricket and shooting. Shots could be heard near the town and both wild fowl and deer were bagged. After Wascana was widened by the dam, James McCaul put the first outrigger on it and boating was added to the list of sports.

Richard Henry Williams (Mayor – 1891, 1909)

R. H. Williams was town mayor in 1891 and mayor of the city of Regina in 1909. During the 1908 mayoralty contest, he won by a scant 19 votes. It was the warmest election Regina had seen in years.

He entered into the lumber and construction business soon after he arrived in Pile of Bones, NWT on August 22, 1882, the day before the town was christened Regina. He describes his arrival to Regina in a story published in the *Regina Saturday Mirror*, October 19, 1912. "It was absolutely bare prairie and I saw the railway laying the first siding in order to shunt off their cars. There was a tent town growing up near the barracks – perhaps there would be a dozen and a half tents altogether. . . . When I came to Regina the meal tents charged 50 cents for a meal, while the tariff at the hotels was $2 a day. . . . During the winter of 1882, the city's meat supply consisted of pemmican and buffalo meat. Water for drinking was brought into Regina from Boggy Creek, which is now the fountain head of the city's water supply. That water cost us 25 cents a pail."

In 1888, Williams, with his son J. K. R. Williams, established Glasgow House on South Railway. It prospered, necessitating the construction of a second, larger store in 1889. In 1910, he built a new, three-storey store on 11th Avenue. Two additional storeys in 1913 made it one of the largest department stores west of Winnipeg. It was later occupied by Simpson's (see page 191).

When the street railway was planned, Williams, as mayor, cast the deciding vote to have the track laid on 11th Avenue rather than on South Railway, the centre of business. Therefore, every streetcar had to stop in front of his store. Williams also owned Regina Lumber and Supply Company – a chain of eleven stores. The Mounted Police enforced the law during Regina's first nine years as a town, but by 1892, Mayor Williams became concerned about the number of misdemeanours and violations of bylaws, so he proposed that city council should appoint a constable. In July of 1892, Jim Williams, an ex-corporal of the Mounted Police, was appointed Regina's constable. After the city charter was granted in 1903, the council established a police force of four men.

John Henry Charles Willoughby, M.D. (Mayor – 1893)

I n the late summer of 1892, a typhoid fever epidemic hit Regina, where sanitation standards were incredibly poor. The first sewers, in 1891 and 1892, drained some of the stagnant cesspools, but excreta of typhoid victims was thrown on heaps in back yards and later transported and dumped at the edge of town with no attempt to destroy it.

The only public hospital was in Medicine Hat and, although Reginans helped to support this institution, few could afford the long expensive trip. Dr. Willoughby was one of the few pioneer Regina doctors who cared for the sick during the epidemic.

The *Leader's* October 5, 1893 edition noted that Willoughby was a hardy soul. "The mayor, Dr. Willoughby, arrived Sunday morning from the World's Fair via the new 'Soo' road. Owing to connections not being very good between Regina and the terminus of that road, our worthy mayor walked the remaining distance home. A comfortable, or we should say uncomfortable forty miles."

In 1894 only 36 doctors lived in the area now known as Saskatchewan. Local midwives and knowledgeable laymen were called on to care for the sick. Medical men needed to supplement their earnings, so they often took part in politics or local businesses. Willoughby was active in politics as an alderman, school trustee and mayor. He also ran a drugstore and edited a newspaper, but it was his real estate transactions that made money.

In 1897 he moved to Saskatoon and started a brokerage business.

Robert Martin (Mayor – 1894, 1913 to 1914)

R obert Martin was the eighth mayor of the town of Regina in 1894 and city mayor in 1913 and 1914. In 1883 he came to Regina as a druggist. In 1887 the Canada Drug and Book Company was formed by an amalgamation of the bookstores of Peter Lamont and Charles H. Black, and the drugstores of Robert Martin and William G. Pettingell.

Under the heading Local News, in the February 24, 1891 issue of the *Leader*, it was reported that "Mr. Robert Martin has received the contract for supplying strychnine to the North-West Government for the use of farmers."

Twelve per cent of Regina's population was of Germanic origin, according to the census of 1911. The war period was exceptionally trying for these citizens. Some patriots tried to burn the home of the printer employed by the local German-language paper, *Der Courier*. The commanding officer of the local military advised the city to place armed guards around public utilities and all explosives as a precaution against disloyal elements.

However, Mayor Martin replied that precautions would be taken but there was no need for a militia guard because "non-English-speaking citizens are as peaceable and anxious for the city's well-being as any."

George T. Marsh (Mayor – 1895)

G eorge T. Marsh was an employee of the Land Corporation of Canada. Prior to his election as mayor he served as a town councillor from 1891 to 1893. The January 10, 1895 *Leader* reported: "On motion of Mayor Martin, seconded by Dr. Willoughby, G. T. Marsh was nominated, and there being no other nomination, Mr. Marsh was declared the mayor elect of 1895. '(cheers)' "

Marsh was town mayor during the Territorial Exhibition – a successful promotional venture with a financial downside. Regina granted 100 acres west of town for exhibition and agricultural purposes. Town council was dismayed that the town was responsible for a half-mile of wooden sidewalk linking Albert Street with the exhibition grounds, but without the sidewalk, pedestrian traffic would have been halted due to Regina's gumbo.

By the time the exhibition opened on July 30, 1895 it boasted a grandstand with seating for 1,000 people, a half-mile track for horse racing and extensive stables. At the exhibition, 900 head of stock was shown with prizes given for livestock, saddle horses, draft horses and thoroughbreds. A $500 prize was also awarded for the best prairie fire extinguisher. Machinery row was a popular stop during the ten-day show. There the newest implements and labour-saving machines were displayed. Spectators had a variety of entertainment to watch, including ploughing matches, bronco busting and the Musical Ride by the Mounted Police.

The number of visitors greatly exceeded the available accommodation, so the town hall and curling rink were used and numerous tents were pitched near the fair grounds.

Although the exhibition incurred losses of $14,000, it did leave Regina with a lasting legacy. In 1896 the town purchased the site from the Townsite Trustees and all subsequent fairs have been held there since. In 1897 Parliament provided additional funds to the exhibition and management was able to satisfy its creditors – many of them local people.

W. F. Eddy (Mayor – 1896 to 1897)

*T*he January 9, 1896 *Leader* read, "All By Acclaim: Noticeable Anxiety to Keep Out of It." It continued, "No contest, No Excitement – The Civic Elections Settled on Nomination Day – School Trustees Re-Elected – W. F. Eddy Becomes Mayor of Regina. Proceedings at the town hall on Monday, the day set for municipal nominations, were of the tamest possible description. A goodly number of the ratepayers of Regina put in an appearance, but the main idea of one and all appeared to be the desire to steer clear of office. At ten o'clock Mr. Secord, returning officer, was in his place to receive nominations. At 11:30, excepting for school trustees, no one had accepted nomination. Mr. Donahue had been proposed for Councillor and had declined. At 11:30 W. T. Mollard's name was received. He did not back out. At 11:45 the name of Hugh Armour was added. At 11:50 Mr. Eddy was proposed for Mayor. He accepted. 'Only ten minutes left, gentlemen,' said Mr. Secord. 'Just five minutes now,' Mr. Secord remarked a little later. 'Two minutes is all we've got,' once more remonstrated Mr. Secord.

"Still the time sped and there was no motion! Eleven fifty-nine! Eleven fifty-nine and a half!! Eleven fifty-nine and three-quarters!!! Ah, at last there is a tumble, and by the time the clock strikes twelve, four names have been added to the paper – R. H. Williams, H. C. Lawson, F. N. Darke (three old councillors) and J. K. McInnis. After some hesitation these agreed to accept nomination, as refusal would have made a muddle." And so it was that W. F. Eddy and councillors were elected for town council in 1896.

W. F. Eddy built the Eddy Block, the YMCA's first home, in 1890. Formally opened on November 20, it was "brilliantly illuminated" by the very first electric lights in Regina.

Francis Nicholson Darke (Mayor – 1898)

*F*rancis N. Darke was born on a farm near Charlottetown and worked there until age 29, before coming west with a group of homesteaders. After exploring the west, he returned to Prince Edward Island and married Elizabeth McKinnon in July 1892.

The newlyweds returned to Regina where Darke bought a small butcher business. By 1900 he was dealing extensively in cattle and swine. In 1906, he sold his butcher business to James Grassick and by 1907 Darke's real estate holdings, which included a five-storey building, the Darke Block, on 11th Avenue and Cornwall Street, were substantial enough to allow him to retire from active business life.

Darke served on city council nine times, becoming Regina's youngest mayor in 1898 at the age of 35. He also served as a Liberal Member of Parliament in 1925.

In addition to providing political leadership, the public-spirited Darke enriched the cultural life of Regina by contributing $85,000 and raising over $40,000 for the establishment of Regina College in 1910. Darke Hall for Music and Art was built in 1929 with money donated by Darke. He also gave Reginans the Darke Memorial Chimes which were placed in trust in Knox-Metropolitan United Church.

Darke's first house was sold to the CPR and the Hotel Saskatchewan was built on the site. For years he lived in an impressive residence on College Avenue and Cornwall Street, now the site of the Helmsing Funeral Chapel (see pages 261 and 283).

In July 1940, Darke suffered a heart attack and died at the age of 77. He was buried in the Darke Mausoleum in the Regina Cemetery.

John K. McInnis (Mayor – 1899)

*J*ohn Kenneth McInnis was an outspoken Scottish-Canadian school teacher who became editor of the new *Regina Standard* in 1891 when its forerunner, the *Regina Journal*, went bankrupt. He later started *The Regina Daily Standard* – the first daily newspaper in the future province of Saskatchewan.

St. Andrew's Society, Regina's first ethnic organization, was organized in 1891. Historian, Earl Drake writes: "This club performed the remarkable feat of bringing together two inveterate newspaper rivals at a memorable haggis feast when John Kenneth McInnis of the new *Standard* performed a sword dance and Nicholas Flood Davin of *The Leader* brought greetings from the Irish."

Shortly after the Territorial Exhibition, the Dominion election of 1896 was held – one of the most exciting elections held in the constituency of Assiniboia West because of the colourful contenders: Conservative MP Nicholas Flood Davin and Liberal candidate J. K. McInnis.

Davin was thought to be impregnable, but McInnis came within one vote of beating him. A recount established the official vote as 1,502 for Davin and 1,502 for McInnis – the returning officer broke the tie. The narrow electoral defeat did not deter McInnis from politics. He was elected to town council in 1896 and elected mayor in 1899.

In 1913 McInnis sold the *Standard*. Although he dropped from public prominence, he and his sons remained in Regina and pursued their extensive real estate interests. In 1918, Imperial Oil Limited began its huge refinery and distributing centre in Regina and purchased fifty-five acres of farm land from J. K. McInnis at the northern outskirts of the city.

William T. Mollard (Mayor – 1900 to 1901)

W illiam T. Mollard was a clerk in the federal government's Department of Public Works. He served three terms on Regina town council, in 1893, 1896 and 1899.

As mayor in 1900, Mollard held the distinction of chairing the first meeting of Regina's town fathers for the closing year of the century.

He also presided over a huge gathering held on January 15, 1900 at town hall to bid farewell to Regina boys heading off to war in South Africa.

The Leader extensively reported on the departure of the Western Battalion of Mounted Rifles and the send-off fund to which citizens contributed. Under the headline, "God Bless Them", the *Leader* provided verbatim accounts of the farewell speeches by dignitaries.

The seats in the hall were removed. A standing audience completely filled the building to honour the departing volunteers who were joined on the platform by Lieutenant-Governor Forget, whom Mollard introduced, Madame Forget, Premier Haultain and N. F. Davin, MP.

Henry W. Laird (Mayor – 1904 to 1905)

T he city's second mayoralty race was an incredibly close contest. Henry Willoughby Laird won the mayor's seat by a slim four votes over J. F. Bole.

During Laird's inaugural address on January 12, 1904, he outlined a lengthy program of civic plans.

He said: "To my mind the city has now arrived at a stage where we should command the entire services of a first class man to perform the duties of secretary-treasurer. The Regina of to-day is not the Regina of old, when those duties could be performed efficiently by one whose time was partially occupied with other duties. With the constructive works before us this year, a great deal of time will necessarily have to be devoted to the public business."

The plan for a new city hall was welcomed by all. In 1905, Laird declared: "If we ever hope to become a centre of influence . . . not only commercially but in fine arts, music and literature, we must equip ourselves with suitable public buildings."

Laird was Mayor of Regina in 1905 at the time of the inauguration of the province of Saskatchewan. In 1917, he was appointed to the Canadian Senate, a position he held until his death in 1940.

Peter McAra, Jr. (Mayor – 1906, 1911 to 1912)

P eter McAra Jr. was born in India. Educated in Edinburgh, he came to Regina with his parents and large family of younger brothers and sister. In Regina, he laid the foundations of the financial business of McAra Bros. & Wallace.

Major civic improvements took place during McAra's term as mayor in 1906. There was a large waterworks and sewer extension and the first permanent street paving on South Railway – the main business street. The first cement sidewalk was constructed, a central fire hall was erected and twenty-four hour electricity was established. There was an extensive street naming and house-numbering plan, a city-wide tree-planting and park-planning scheme and a new Exhibition building. McAra laid the cornerstone for Regina's first city hall at 11th Avenue and Hamilton Street.

During McAra's second term as Mayor, the inauguration of the street railway system took place in front of the City Hall on July 28, 1911. McAra was motorman on Car. No. 2 – the car that carried the city fathers as passengers. The procession proceeded over the entire route – fourteen and a half miles. Upon return to City Hall, McAra suspended all fares for the inaugural day and 7,400 people rode free of charge.

As mayor in 1912, McAra played a major role in restoring Regina after the devastating cyclone of June 30. That day, McAra had driven a visiting group of Grand Trunk Pacific Railway officials around the city to show them what had been accomplished since the town's establishment. The party was sitting on the lawn of the McAra Victoria Avenue home when the storm struck, leaving vast devastation. Following the cyclone, McAra cancelled the Dominion Day holiday, closed the bars, set up district relief committees, designated five emergency surgical stations and requested all men to volunteer to clear debris. The 95th Rifles under Major J. F. L. Embury were ordered back to Regina from Camp Sewell. Efforts to rebuild began immediately and by 1913 reconstruction of homes was well under way.

James Balfour, K.C. (Mayor – 1915, 1931)

*J*ames Balfour homesteaded in the Lumsden area in 1883 and had a varied career as a farmer, laborer, teacher, lawyer. He was the town clerk for several years and Regina's first city clerk.

As a member of the Musical and Dramatic Society, he performed the role of the Pirate King in the 1899 first annual light opera, the Pirates of Penzance with Alexander F. Angus, Manager of the Bank of Montreal; A. L. Gibbons, choirmaster of Knox Church, and Robert Martin, a former mayor. Balfour also sang for many years in an outstanding male quartet.

When Cornelius Rink made a bid for the mayoralty in 1914, he lost decisively against Balfour. In 1930, there was dissatisfaction with governing bodies. Balfour replaced James McAra as mayor in 1931, but McAra regained the mayor's seat for the 1932 to 1933 term.

The Balfour apartments were built on the site of Mr. Balfour's home on Victoria Avenue (see page 286).

Balfour Technical School was also named after James Balfour, in recognition of his 20 years of service on the Regina Collegiate Board.

Walter D. Cowan, D.D.S. (Mayor – 1916 to 1917)

*T*wo silk hats were known to exist in Regina in the early days. One belonged to Mr. Davin, the other to Dr. Walter D. Cowan. The August 31, 1918 edition of the *Leader* reported he wore it with "no coyness about its display. . . . " "He wore it settled rakishly on his poetic locks on all and every occasion that summoned him out of doors. When he was engaged in his dental practice, it reposed on a table in his consulting room where it could be regarded with respect by his admiring patients. Dr. Cowan was indissolubly associated with that hat – or its successor – for years."

One of Saskatchewan's first graduate dentists, Cowan came to Regina with his bride in 1889. He took an active interest in the city's life and in a number of organizations, including a debating society. Many men who became prominent citizens made their first public speaking foray in the dentist's office.

But Cowan's many public activities did not interfere with his profession. He became recognized as one of the leading dentists in western Canada and was president of the Saskatchewan Dental Association almost from its inception.

He served on Regina town council in 1891 and city council in 1907 before becoming mayor in 1916.

Henry Black (Mayor – 1918 to 1919)

*A*n early building contractor in Regina, Henry Black was one of two occupants in the Black Block in 1909 – the other occupant was J. C. Black, a physician. Henry Black served five terms as alderman and was active on the Regina Hospital Board and the Collegiate Board.

The WW I era and immediate postwar period was marked by tense relations between organized labour and business across Canada. Mail service was disrupted for nine days during the first nation-wide postal strike in July 1918, and in October 1918 provincial telephone workers went out, but local and long-distance service was not disrupted. This tension was also reflected in Regina where there was talk of a strike during a dispute involving Regina's building trades.

The most dramatic manifestation of labour unrest occurred in Winnipeg when 35,000 workers left their jobs on May 15, 1919. City council authorized Henry Black to take whatever steps necessary to maintain order and continue the operation of the public utilities. However, this was not necessary as the Winnipeg strikers lost the support of the Regina Trades and Labour Council in early June.

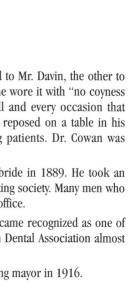

James Grassick (Mayor – 1920 to 1922, 1940 to 1941)

*J*ames Grassick came to the district in 1882 with his father to select land near Pile of Bones. As a youth, he did a man's work so he had little time for formal education. He broke land, clerked, acted as ranch foreman, and drove an army transport during the Northwest Rebellion from Fort Qu'Appelle to Battleford, before establishing his draying, livery and feed business, which he later sold to Capital Ice Company. The owner of Capital Ice Company for nearly 50 years, Grassick hauled ice from Boggy Creek and Wascana Lake to sell to hotels and butcher shops. He later built a reservoir at his farm and filled it with city water every fall, to provide ice to his customers.

Grassick devoted much time and energy to public life. He served as board chairman of Knox Church for 45 years, as a director of the Regina Exhibition Board from 1907 to 1932, as local Conservative MLA for four years, and as mayor in 1920, 1921, 1922, as well as 1940 and 1941.

While he was mayor during the forties, two police cars equipped with two-way radios were purchased, the speed limit was increased from 15 to 20 miles per hour, and the bobby helmets worn by local constables were replaced by ordinary caps.

In 1955, Jubilee year, he was initiated as Chief Strong Heart by Chief Harry Ball (Sitting Eagle) of the Piapot Cree Reserve. In 1956, while walking across Highway 1, two miles east of Regina, Grassick was hit by a car. He died of his injuries two hours later at the Regina General Hospital. He was 88 years of age. To recognize his many contributions, a park, a street, a playground and a northern lake were named after him.

Stewart Coulter Burton (Mayor – 1923 to 1924)

"*R*egina loses a brilliant businessman", read a December 31, 1941 *Leader-Post* article. The written tribute was for former mayor, Stewart Coulter Burton, who had died at the age of 64.

In 1907, Burton came to Regina from Ontario as a store manager. He became president of the Regina Board of Trade in 1915, was a member of the Regina Public Library's first board and chairman of the Regina General Hospital board. After serving on council for four years, Burton was elected mayor in 1923.

In 1929 the provincial government invited him to take over management of the Saskatchewan Co-operative Creameries which was in the red. The company was put into receivership and Burton was appointed receiver and manager in 1932. The article reported: "His was the brain-fagging job of getting the business back to normal. How he did it is looked on as a feat of sheer business ingenuity plus hard work."

When the business was taken over in April 1939 by the provincial government, J. G. Taggart, minister of agriculture, said: "During the years of his management, Mr. Burton built up an efficient staff and generally managed the business with such care that when the government took title to the property in 1939, the business was well-organized, well-managed and had the confidence of its patrons to a very marked degree."

William E. Mason (Mayor – 1925 to 1926)

*W*illiam Mason opened a branch of the Canada Permanent Mortgage Corporation in Regina in 1905 and became manager of the W. E. Mason Discount Company and the Prudential Trust Company fifteen years later (see page 274). A civic-minded individual, he helped raise public funds for the reconstruction of the Metropolitan Methodist Church and the YMCA following the 1912 cyclone.

Elected mayor in 1925, Mason drew on his five years of experience as an alderman in the early 1920s. Following his term as mayor, he was a member of the board of trustees for the city's sinking fund. In that office he was regarded as an individual who remained patient, no matter how stressful the circumstances.

James McAra (Mayor – 1927 to 1930, 1932 to 1933)

*A*s a small boy, James McAra moved to Regina with his family from Edinburgh. His first taste of public office was at the age of ten when he was a pageboy for the North West Council of 1886. He later became the lieutenant-governor's secretary, a newspaper publisher, and partner with his brother Peter in an insurance and real estate business.

McAra went overseas with the 28th Battalion in 1914. When he returned to Regina, he organized a local unit of the Military Hospitals Commission, was the initiator of the Regina soldiers' cemetery and honourary Dominion President of the Canadian Legion.

In 1930, McAra lost his bid for the mayoralty, but he regained the position easily in 1931. The 1932 election was much closer – he beat Cornelius Rink by a mere 19 votes.

By the end of the decade, with his fourth win at the polls, James McAra was Regina's longest-serving mayor at that point in the Queen City's history. His brother Peter had previously served as mayor in 1906, 1911 to 1912.

Cornelius Rink (Mayor – 1934 to 1935)

*B*orn in Holland in 1871, Cornelius Rink went to South Africa at the age of twenty and fought with the Dutch against the British in the Boer War. At the end of the war, Rink returned to Holland briefly before moving to the United States where he lived for several years.

He immigrated to Regina in 1907 and was involved in real estate and, later, in a bottle exchange.

Rink was active in local organizations, including the Boer War Veterans' Association where he was the only member who had fought against the British.

During his career in municipal politics, Rink served as alderman for the years 1911 to 1914, 1925 to 1926 and 1932. He entered the mayoralty race in 1933 and lost by 19 votes to James McAra, but clinched the mayor's seat for the 1934 and 1935 terms.

Rink was a colourful and witty mayoral contender. When a prominent brewery director and an established civic leader, known to be a tippler, suggested that an ordinary bottle collector like Rink was not distinguished enough to run as mayor, Rink retorted that not only was he an equal of the other two, but he was in partnership with them.

"I collect bottles; my first opponent, he fills them; and my second opponent, he empties them."

Rink died in 1949 at the Grey Nuns Hospital. To honour his many years of public service, the City of Regina named Rink Avenue after him.

Alban C. Ellison (Mayor – 1936 to 1939)

*A*lban C. Ellison, a popular English-born lawyer, was a Labour alderman in 1932, 1934 and 1935. Elected mayor for the 1936 term, his labour associates gained control of city council at the same time.

During 1935 and 1936, a yearly average of 5,000 transient unemployed passed through the Salvation Army men's hostel in Regina. Men were arrested for begging and sentenced to ten days in jail.

Unparalleled crop failures took place in the disastrous year of 1937 – the same year Ellison beat former mayor Henry Black by more than 8,000 votes. In 1938, Ellison won the mayor's chair by acclamation.

Regina's bleak economic times brightened after 1937 when General Motors local plant reopened. Although there were layoffs between production periods during 1938 and 1939, the large factory's operations eased unemployment.

In 1939, as in 1936, there were allegations of undue communist influence in the selection of the Labour slate and Ellison lost to James Grassick. All of the Labour aldermen who sought re-election were defeated.

Ellison served in both world wars and was the first commanding officer of HMCS Queen, earning him the title of Regina's sailor mayor.

Charles C. Williams (Mayor – 1942 to 1944)

*A*rriving in Regina in 1931, Charles Cromwell Williams was almost a permanent fixture in civic and provincial politics.

He served as alderman in 1938 to 1939, and as Regina's chief magistrate for three years in the early forties.

In the years 1944 to 1961, Tommy Douglas and the CCF won five successive June elections. C. C. Williams was appointed Minister of Telephones and Telegraphs and Minister of Labour – a post he held for 20 years, the longest time period in Saskatchewan's history for a cabinet minister to hold one post.

He was responsible for the 1944 Trade Union Act which ensured the right of collective bargaining. Saskatchewan's minimum wage became one of Canada's highest during his term of office.

In the 1952 provincial election, Williams set a record when he received the highest vote ever gained by a Saskatchewan candidate at that time.

Williams was born in Moosomin in 1896 and spent his boyhood at Wapella, where he received his public and high school education. He later attended Brandon College. He served overseas during WW I and was wounded at Amiens on August 8, 1918.

A labour man, Williams joined the Canadian National Railways as a train dispatcher in 1919. He served in Winnipeg, Dauphin, Calgary, Edmonton, Biggar, Melville and Prince Albert before coming to Regina.

At the age of 79, he died in his sleep in 1975 in Vancouver.

Thomas G. McNall (Mayor – 1945 to 1946)

A s a salesman for the George Weston Limited biscuit company, Thomas George McNall came to Regina in 1907. He bought the Regina office of the Weston business in 1914 and renamed it McNall and Co. Ltd.

He was president and manager of the business until 1950, when he sold it to the Hudson's Bay Company. He continued as director of the company until his death.

From 1926 to 1944, McNall was a city alderman. While in office, he introduced the five-cent street railway fare. It came into effect in 1943 and continued until June 1948. He served as mayor of Regina from 1945 to 1946, McNall started the Regina Citizens Band in 1946, and was its president. For two years, the 40-piece band gave numerous concerts and received grants from the city, but it was unable to make ends meet.

In April 1949, the Regina branch of the Canadian Legion undertook sponsorship of the band, which was renamed the Legion Band. McNall was named honourary president.

On his election, McNall was described in the *Leader-Post*: "He seldom gets into the discussions in the city council, although he pays close attention to everything said. And when he does say something, his remarks contain a lot of merit. Jovial and good-natured, he takes the interests of Regina to heart."

Hugh McGillivray (Mayor – 1947 to 1948)

H ugh McGillivray was one of Saskatchewan's early pioneers.

The youngest of a large family, McGillivray came west with his widowed mother and family in 1884 and homesteaded north of Pense. In the spring of 1882, his oldest brother Archie reached Pile of Bones Creek where three tents were pitched on the future site of the Queen City.

McGillivray homesteaded before establishing a hardware store in Pense. After serving as the first reeve of Pense municipality, he moved to Regina in 1920. He served on city council from 1940 to 1946 and was elected mayor for the term of 1947 to 1948.

McGillivray's term as mayor coincided with the return of WW II veterans.

For his work as chairman of the South Saskatchewan Regional Dependents Advisory Committee, McGillivray was made a Member of the Order of the British Empire.

His other community activities included service as chairman of the Community Chest and director of the Regina Welfare Bureau. He was on the executive of the provincial Red Cross Society, on the executive of the provincial Boy Scouts Association and a board member of the Canadian National Institute for the Blind and the Saskatchewan Wheat Pool.

In addition, he was a member of the Regina Old Timers' Association, the Regina Historical Society, president of the Regina Exhibition Association and active in the Regina Board of Trade.

He died in 1959 at the age of 84.

Garnet N. Menzies (Mayor – 1949 to 1951)

A headline in the November 5, 1949 *Leader-Post* read: "He knows his own mind".

The article was devoted to Mayor Garnet Menzies who had just been re-elected and was still on a "mayoralty honeymoon".

"During his first 10 months in office, the mayor has commanded a growing respect from civic employees, department heads and citizens in general.

"When he came into office they said he was too quiet and lacking in force. Yet before many weeks went by they learned Garnet Menzies was a man who made up his own mind, who knew how to say 'Yes' and, more important, 'No.' They also found he would do so only after he heard the whole background in a situation."

Described in the article as one of Regina's fairest mayors, the mayor's formula for amicable relations was: "Give city employees all that's coming to them and no more."

As 1949 opened, Menzies identified the problems the city would face that year: water, housing and the rising mill rate. The *Leader-Post's* Robert Moon remarked that Menzies "called the shot on all but one – the disastrous street railway barns' fire."

Gordon B. Grant (Mayor – 1952 to 1953)

*G*ordon Burton Grant was Regina's first "native-born son" to become mayor. He had been a city alderman for six years prior. When the insurance agency executive took over as mayor, he was Regina's 50th chief magistrate and the 19th person to hold the job. The position carried a salary of slightly more than $5,000 a year, plus a car allowance of $30 a month and a small additional allowance for incidental expenses.

In his inaugural address, Grant identified the Buffalo Pound project, housing and street improvements as major problems facing the new council. Speaking of the Buffalo Pound project, he said contractors had made reasonable progress and that the intake at the lake was 80 per cent completed, the lake pumping station 90 per cent completed and the below-ground work on the filtration plant "well under way".

He further noted that while 354 houses had been built in the city during the past year, more were needed. Local improvements were a major problem as a result of "the holiday that had been forced in this department by the 20 years embracing the depression and WW II."

In 1964, Regina South Liberal candidate Gordon Grant became his party's advance guard in the provincial election when he was the first candidate in the province to be assured a seat in the Legislature. Grant defeated the only other contestant, George Bothwell, CCF candidate, 7,683 votes to 3,496. Grant's win robbed Bothwell not only of the election, but of his election deposit as he lost to Grant by more than half the votes.

During his three terms as MLA, he served as provincial minister of telephones, public health, highways and transportation, and industry and commerce.

In 1975, as the Opposition Whip, Grant reflected on the future of Saskatchewan and said: "I'm not optimistic that Saskatchewan will become a densely populated country and I don't think that's important. I can't see it becoming highly industrialized either unless there's a major oil find, in which case the situation would be similar to Alberta."

Leslie Hammond (Mayor – 1954 to 1956)

*B*orn in Saskatoon and raised on a farm near Elrose, Hammond obtained a degree from Toronto University and then worked as an accountant for various corporations. He served as alderman from 1947 to 1952 before becoming mayor in 1954. He served as alderman again from 1971 to 1973.

In the fall of 1955, Hammond and a group of aldermen met with provincial government officials to solve an existing housing crisis for the city's seniors. WW II veterans had recently returned and required much of the rental housing; the baby boom had begun and seniors desperately needed good, affordable housing.

The meetings resulted in the construction of 100 cottages reserved specifically for seniors. The cottages were a first in Saskatchewan and one of Hammond's many civic ventures.

Hammond challenged hundreds of volunteers, service clubs, churches and government agencies to develop what has become Regina Pioneer Village. By the end of the 1980s, Pioneer Village had grown to become one of the largest special care homes in North America.

Hammond also served his community as a member of the Chamber of Commerce, Royal Canadian Legion and Masonic Lodge.

Thomas H. Cowburn (Mayor – 1957 to 1958)

*T*homas H. Cowburn exchanged his seat on city council for the mayor's chair in 1957 to 1958.

Cowburn was involved in Regina's educational system for years. In 1927 he taught mathematics and science at Central Collegiate and transferred to Balfour Technical School in 1930. He became principal of Balfour in 1947 and retained that position until he retired in 1954.

Mayor Cowburn declined to seek re-election in 1958, citing health reasons.

"A younger more vigorous man with extra pep should be mayor," he said in an interview in the May 29, 1958 *Leader-Post*.

The interview was held on his first full day back in his office since suffering a severe heart attack while washing his car.

The 68-year-old mayor said: "Doctors want me to go slow for awhile and they have urged me not to go back to my former 16 hours an office day routine."

Henry H. P. Baker (Mayor – 1959 to 1970, 1974 to 1979)

*H*enry Harold Peter Baker was born to politics. With his sixth win at the polls in 1968, Baker became Regina's longest serving mayor.

Born in 1915 on his family's farm near Lipton, Baker grew up in an atmosphere of municipal politics as his father was a municipal councillor.

Baker went to Teacher's College in Regina and began teaching when he was 19 years of age. During WW II, he joined the RCAF and taught air crew personnel. After the war, he studied business engineering and personnel administration in Chicago.

When he returned to Regina, he served as Secretary of the Public Service Commission where he remained until December of 1958. He became mayor in January of 1959.

Baker's relationship with city council was often stormy, but he had a reputation for being sensitive to the wishes of ordinary citizens, particularly those who lived in the city's older neighbourhoods.

Defeated in 1970, he returned in triumph three years later and held the mayoralty until 1979.

For 10 years, Baker had the unique distinction of being the city's mayor and an NDP member of the provincial legislature at the same time.

Over the years, he oversaw the building of the Ring Road, the Centre of the Arts and the current City Hall, which opened in 1976.

In 1997, city council paid tribute to the former mayor by naming the council chamber at City Hall and a city scholarship program after him.

Harry G. R. Walker (Mayor – 1971 to 1973)

*H*arry G. R. Walker was mayor of Regina from 1971 to 1973. He graduated from Regina Normal School in the early 1930s and taught in a rural school near Rouleau before teaching in several Regina elementary schools.

During WW II, Walker served overseas and was principal of a Department of National Defence school in Germany from 1958 to 1961. When he returned to Regina he was principal of Massey School – a position he held while mayor of the city.

As mayor, Walker proposed that Regina build a new city hall on the outskirts of the downtown area, to replace the city hall on Scarth Street and 11th Avenue.

A September 14, 1972 *Leader-Post* article reported: "The mayor said he envisaged a civic complex between Smith and McIntyre where an expanded civic administration could be brought together to work in one site instead of being spread around the city as it is now. 'Whatever happens, it won't be done overnight,'" observed Walker. The new city hall on Victoria Avenue opened in 1976. Most civic departments have offices located there.

Larry Schneider (Mayor – 1980 to 1988)

*H*arry Schneider never planned to be Regina's mayor. "I certainly had no intention of going into a political life at all," he said in an interview with the *Leader-Post* after he stepped down. In spite of his original intentions, Schneider served as Regina's mayor for nine years.

He recalls a highlight, "The date was November 1, 1979. I assumed that this was the day that I should show up for my new job. The October 24 newspaper said that I had been elected. I found my way to the clerk's office. The receptionist asked if she could help me. I replied that I would like to speak to the City Clerk, Fred Howard. She asked me to wait for a moment. I did and then she indicated that he would see me. I asked Mr. Howard what it was that I should be doing. He responded by saying, 'Here is a copy of the Urban Municipality Act, read it and you will know.'

"Two major positive issues stand out in my mind during the nine years I spent in City Hall.

"The first was the drive to remove the tarnished image of our city, the reputation of us having water that 'was a meal unto itself.' We acquired federal funding to put into place a granular activated charcoal filtration system. This funding was matched by the province and the city, equally. The $15-million project has now functioned for 15 to 20 years and has proven to be cost effective for the problems facing us at that time.

"The second accomplishment is Canada's Infrastructure program. I was elected to the executive of the Federation of Canadian Municipalities and in that position was chosen to make the case to the federal government and the other two (at the time) political parties to convince them to contribute one-third of the cost to repairing the deteriorated condition of Canada's streets, roads, bridges, water supplies and sewers."

Schneider resigned in 1988 to run as the federal Progressive Conservative candidate in Regina Wascana. Appointed to cabinet in 1993, he was defeated when he sought re-election.

Doreen E. Hamilton (Mayor – October, 1988)

*H*istory was made in 1988 when a woman sat in the Mayor's chair for the first time. Doreen Hamilton, a first-term councillor, served a one-month term when Larry Schneider resigned to run in the November 1988 federal election. She handled the mayor's duties until the civic election was held on October 26.

Recalling her brief stint as mayor, she says: "It began at an executive committee meeting of city council where Larry Schneider tendered his formal resignation to seek a federal seat as a Conservative. This was September with about a month and a half to a civic election. It was decided that anyone not running for the mayor's position in the election was eligible to enter a draw. The winner would serve as Interim Mayor. The clerk, George Day, collected the ballots, placed them in an empty stationary box and my name was chosen. . . . "

"The two things I am especially proud of are having my name as a link in the Mayor's official Chain of Office and having my caricature done as Mayor by Bill Argan. It hangs with all the other portraits in City Hall."

Doreen Hamilton also served as an NDP MLA in the Saskatchewan Legislature.

Douglas R. Archer (Mayor – 1988 to 2000)

*E*lected in 1985 as councillor, Doug Archer became mayor in 1988. His priorities have been economic development, community development and sound management at City Hall. He established and chaired the Mayor's Board of Inquiry into Hunger, served as a member of the Mayor's Task Force on Women and chaired the Mayor's Task Force on Accessibility.

As a member of the Regina Regional Economic Development Authority, established in 1989, Archer worked to build a positive economic climate and actively promoted Regina's tourism industry. He was elected to the Board of Directors of the Federation of Canadian Municipalities for nine years and served on the executive.

Archer was born in Winnipeg and raised in Saskatoon where he received his Bachelor's Degree in Economics. He moved to Regina in 1971. An experienced administrator, Archer worked for 12 years in the provincial civil service. In 1983, he became a partner in Knight-Archer Insurance Services.

He recalled: "There have been many special reasons to celebrate what has happened in Regina and reflecting back on the last 12 years, I have been very fortunate to work with some very dedicated people in our community, on City Council and in the City administration. There has been a very significant improvement in the way Regina people view their own city. As an example, the 1999 Tourism Awareness campaign results indicated 65 per cent of Regina residents rated their city as a better place to live than any other western Canadian city . . . up from a low of 26 per cent after the first campaign in 1991. . . .

"In the last three years, we have demonstrated our commitment to making Regina a competitive city to do business through the elimination of the business tax. This was done without transferring taxes to the residential taxpayer or reducing services. By the year 2003, the City of Regina's 100th anniversary, we will have eliminated our tax-supported debt, a further indication of our determination to deliver services in the most efficient manner possible."

Pat Fiacco (Mayor – 2000-)

*W*hen Pat Fiacco was elected Mayor he had no previous experience in municipal politics, but his passion and dreams of success for his hometown have made him one of Regina's best ambassador's. His pride and positive attitude are helping to change Regina's image, at home and across the country.

Fiacco was born in Regina and has lived here throughout his life. His father, mother and oldest brother left Italy in 1957 and moved to Regina to take advantage of the many opportunities. He says; "My family has lived in Regina for nearly fifty years. They have made a home here and believe in this city just as much as I do. The Fiacco family is positive proof that an immigrant family can enjoy a quality life in Regina, now and into the future."

Before being elected mayor, Fiacco was Director of Strategic Business Development at DirectWest. He also held other sales and managerial positions during his career. He served on the Sask Sport Inc. board of directors and was a Hockey Regina coach. Active in Kinsmen, he has worked on Telemiracle and the Queen City Kinsmen Big Valley Jamboree. He is also co-founder of the Ken Goff Memorial Boxing Classic, a renowned international boxing competition held in Regina each spring.

Fiacco served as the National Chief Official for Boxing Canada, and as a Canadian official for the 2002 Commonwealth Games in Manchester, England. He served as a Canadian Boxing Official for the 1999 PanAm Games, and is also a former provincial and Canadian amateur boxing champion.

"Sport has been very important to my life," Fiacco says. "It taught me fair play, helped me to set goals, and showed me that working together as a team is the best way to get things done. Our city is like a team and I ask that everyone work together to make our city better. I ask that every Regina resident become an official ambassador, be proud, let the world know just how great Regina is.

"The 100th anniversary of our city is a time for us to reflect on our accomplishments and to set goals for the future of Regina. We enjoy an exceptional quality of life, with beautiful parks, excellent schools, sports, arts and culture. Regina has all the amenities of a big City with a small town heart. Dare to dream out loud, I did. It's time to tell the world about Canada's greatest city. I love Regina!"

TOWN
MAYORS

CITY
MAYORS

WILLIAM ARGAN '82

TOWN WELL

Northwest corner of South Railway and Broad Street

*U*ntil the Municipal Water Supply Project was undertaken in 1904, three local wells, placed at strategic corners throughout the community, served the population.

The first test well, located on South Railway, struck a good water supply on April 24, 1883. Before the wells were dug, pioneers relied on snowbanks for water. A Winnipeg paper wrote: "any resident of Regina that has a snow bank [sic] on his lot is said to possess a 'bonanza'."

WILLIAM ARGAN

REGINA POST OFFICE

12th Avenue and Scarth Street

*R*egina's first postmaster got the job from Sir John A. MacDonald.

In 1882, the Queen City's first post office was a crude packing box that traveled from store to store. Each storekeeper would remove mail for himself and his customers.

Settlers protested the lack of postal service to the Inspector in Ottawa so J. J. Campbell, who had a big tent, took over mail distribution. However a more permanent location and postmaster were necessary.

John A. MacDonald offered the position of postmaster to Joseph Irvine, one of his supporters. Irvine was appointed in 1882 and he held the position until 1888.

The post office, first located on South Railway, moved several times until a permanent post office opened in January 1886 in this new two-storey brick building at 12th Avenue and Scarth Street. The post office remained at this site for over 20 years.

POST OFFICE

1801 Scarth Street

*C*onstruction of this Post Office began in 1906. It was designed by David Ewart with an addition in 1929 by architects Storey and Van Egmond. The building functioned as a post office from 1907 until 1956. City administration offices moved into this structure in 1962, but vacated the premises when the new City Hall officially opened on December 14, 1975.

The building, renamed the Old City Hall Mall, currently houses the Globe Theatre and the Regina Plains Museum on the upper floors. Commercial office and retail outlets occupy space on the main floor. In February 1982, the old Post Office was one of the first two buildings in Regina to be designated as a Municipal Heritage Property.

WILLIAM ARGAN

REGINA POWER PLANT

2903 Powerhouse Drive

*I*n 1890, the Regina Light and Power Company was established by local entrepreneurs. It survived privately until 1904 when it was purchased by the city.

Regina's first power plant was at Smith Street and Dewdney Avenue. In 1914 the city built this coal-fired generating plant. Streetcars hauled coal on tow-cars through Regina's streets at night. In the 1940s, a conversion was made to burn fuel oil and in the 1950s, natural gas.

The old power plant used five steam boilers, operating at 800°F, passing steam through three turbines. Water from Wascana Lake was pumped as coolant and condensed steam was restored to storage tanks. The warmed lake water flowed back to where it came from. This helped to keep the plant's machinery warm, but it also encouraged the Canada geese colony on Wascana Lake to remain over winter.

The building underwent extensive reconstruction and opened in 1989 as the Saskatchewan Science Centre. The five-storey-tall Kramer IMAX Theatre was added in 1991. In 1999, the Centre opened the SaskTel 3D Laser Theatre, one of only ten 3D theatres in the world (see page 149).

Buildings in the fledgling community of Regina were made mostly of wood, brought in by rail. Heated by wood or coal, they were all too prone to fire. It was feared that a blaze in one building could spread to much of the town. Several devastating fires and other problems led to the first meeting of concerned citizens on December 5, 1882. They discussed fire fighting, sanitation, water supply, law and order, and other issues.

A few days later several men were appointed to take charge of the community. Money was collected to buy fire fighting equipment. John Cottingham was named the town's first fire chief. He immediately began organizing a volunteer bucket brigade. The brigade held its first official meeting on February 27, 1883, at which time the members adopted the name Regina Pioneer Brigade.

Regina's first paid employee was Fire Inspector Joseph W. Smith. He was paid $25 a month to inspect all stovepipes and chimneys.

Three years later a horse-powered pumper – Regina's first fire engine – was purchased. The engine was housed in the Town Hall. The first self-contained fire station, Central Fire Hall, opened in 1894 and closed in 1907.

Fires periodically destroyed businesses and claimed lives. In 1890 a fire destroyed an entire block of twelve businesses on South Railway. Three years later another twelve businesses disappeared in flames on the 1700 block Broad Street.

William A. White became the volunteer Fire Chief in 1900. Six years later White was appointed Regina's first paid (and longest-serving) Chief. The fire hall on Albert Street at 13th Avenue is named after him. That same year the Fire Department purchased its first horses to aid in fighting fires. The last horses were retired in 1939.

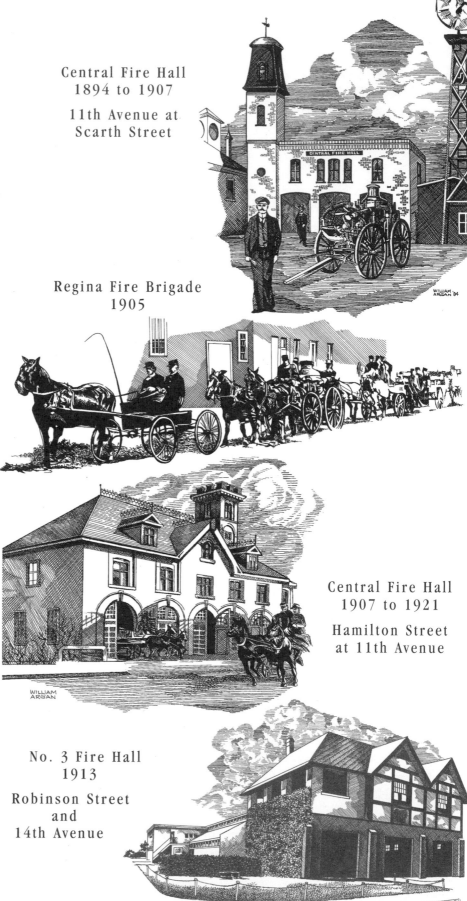

Central Fire Hall
1894 to 1907

11th Avenue at
Scarth Street

Regina Fire Brigade
1905

Central Fire Hall
1907 to 1921

Hamilton Street
at 11th Avenue

No. 3 Fire Hall
1913

Robinson Street
and
14th Avenue

FIRE DEPARTMENT

Central Fire Hall
1920 to 1988

11th Avenue at
Osler Street

WILLIAM ARGAN

No. 1 Fire Hall
Albert Street and 13th Avenue

The years of White's service as Chief were marked by rapid growth of the Department and of the City. Central Fire Hall was replaced by a larger building in 1907. Another fire hall was added in 1911, and two more in 1914.

In 1906 the phase-out of volunteer firefighters began. The last volunteer was replaced by a paid employee in 1913. In the same year the first four motorized vehicles were purchased and 25 fire-alarm boxes were installed on city streets.

The Fire Department served proudly during the flu epidemic following WW I, moving the sick to hospital, hauling wood and coal, and assisting the ill with daily chores.

In 1921 the Fire Department moved to the reconstructed 1908 Market Building at 11th Avenue and Osler Street. It served as No. 1 Fire Hall until it was vacated in 1988. Now called the Old No. 1 Fire Hall, it is a municipal heritage building housing a community association and various organizations and businesses.

Probably the most spectacular and dangerous fire in the city's history occurred in July 1925. The Canadian Oil Company plant, along with several other oil companies' buildings and inventory, was destroyed by fire. Spectacular explosions could be seen as far away as Moose Jaw. Forty-five gallon gasoline drums rocketed into the air in high elliptical trajectories, landing several blocks away as firefighters vainly battled to douse the flames. Two firefighters were hospitalized after being blown across the street by the force of the explosions. Miraculously, neither they nor any citizens suffered life-threatening injuries.

When Chief White retired in 1938, a divided City Council chose to close two fire halls and retire the last two horses, instead of granting firefighters a day of rest in each seven days.

Two new fire halls opened in 2001, one in east Regina on Arens Road, and the other in the north on 9th Avenue North. The Ross Avenue fire station is now an education and training centre. Five other stations are located throughout the community. The total number of firefighters is 253.

Police Officer
1903

Traffic
Police Officer

Black Maria

During the late 1890s, Regina, the capital of Canada's North-West Territories, was little more than a collection of frame buildings and tents. In 1891, citizens lobbied Town Council to appoint an individual to maintain sanitation laws and help keep livestock off the street. By 1892, Mayor Richard H. Williams was concerned about the increase of petty crime in the town, a concern that turned to annoyance when the North-West Mounted Police refused to enforce town bylaws. Finally, on July 19, 1892, Council approved the appointment of James Williams as Regina's first Town Constable. He was sworn in on July 23, 1892 and worked out of the first City Hall on 11th Avenue and Scarth Street. He earned a monthly salary of $50 and a free uniform to wear while on duty. He supplied his own gun. Williams' duties included impounding stray animals, preventing street obstructions, keeping the town "toughs" under control, ringing the town bell four times daily, waiting on Council, enforcing sanitation laws, controlling roaming livestock, licensing transient traders, billiard rooms and refreshment houses and issuing dog tags. Williams' successors were Tom Hitchcock (1895 to 1899) and Neil McInnis (1899 to 1903).

The first form of the "paddy wagon" was a wheelbarrow supplied by Neil McInnis. McInnis' duties expanded to include dogcatcher and firefighter. In 1903, R. J. Harwood became the first Chief Constable and the first to command a police force consisting of four men. By 1908, the Regina Police Department moved to the new City Hall at Hamilton Street and 11th Avenue.

1909 saw the establishment of the first organized patrol system, Traffic and Detective Divisions, and the utilization of fingerprints and photography. By 1913, the first motorcycle and auto patrol (paddy wagon) were acquired.

Regina City Police Headquarters
1930 to 1978
Halifax Street and 11th Avenue

POLICE SERVICE

Whistling Willie Greer

Motorcycle
Police Officer

Regina Police Service Headquarters, 1978 –
1717 Osler Street

The paddy wagon, dubbed "the Black Maria", doubled as a makeshift ambulance. The creation of a Morality Section in 1915 directed efforts toward the control of prostitution and pool halls.

In the days before traffic lights, the Hamilton Street and 11th Avenue Street intersection was the busiest street corner in downtown Regina. To control pedestrian traffic the city police stationed a constable during busy periods at the southwest corner of the intersection, just outside the old Royal Bank.

People were allowed to cross only on the signal of a whistle. If pedestrians did not comply they had to brave the scolding of Constable Willie Greer who was always assigned to that corner. Constable Greer was a popular figure in the downtown and became known as "Whistling Willie".

During the thirties the Regina Police Department employed extensive use of motorcycle policemen. Every kid in Regina knew who they were because the cops made a point of stopping off at playgrounds and street corners to talk to them. Among the most popular were Constables Richardson, Apps and Hopkins.

By the 1920s, the home of the Regina Police Department was the basement of Alexandra School. This provided more space to accommodate additional equipment and personnel. In 1931, the police finally acquired their own building at Halifax Street and 11th Avenue, at a cost of $113,000. The building was considered to have all the conveniences necessary for the operation of a modern police force. December 1978 marked the opening of the present Regina Police Service Headquarters, 1717 Osler Street, at a cost of approximately $6 million.

Since the humble beginnings of the Regina Police in 1892, the Police Service has expanded, in 2002, to an authorized strength of 338 sworn members, 4 special constables and 138 civilian employees.

The impact of the Mounted Police on the Canadian identity is obvious. It has become a national symbol. Incorporated in 1873 and sent west the following year, the NWMP marched into the hearts and minds of Canadians and the world. Through most of these nearly 130 years one thing has remained unchanged – Regina was and is the home of the Royal Canadian Mounted Police.

In 1882 Regina replaced Battleford as the seat of Government of the North-West Territories. During this time Regina was a product of competing real estate interests. Lieutenant-Governor Edgar Dewdney, in the summer of 1882, along with Commissioner A. G. Irvine and Inspector S. B. Steele, selected the site for the new permanent North-West Mounted Police headquarters located one and one-half miles west of the territorial capital in what was known as the "Dewdney Section". It was Lieutenant-Governor Dewdney's plan to shift the new capital westward through the placement of various public buildings. The Mounted Police have occupied this site since July 1882. The first buildings were shipped in prefabricated sections in 1883 from Eastern Canada over the newly completed railway. Gracing the southwest corner of the Parade Square stands the spiritual home of the Mounted Police. Built in 1883, this building, which originally served as a beer canteen and mess hall, was converted into a chapel in 1895.

The site chosen by Irvine was also to serve a second purpose. It was to be the location for the force's primary "depot of instruction", and was so named in the fall of 1885 – due in part to the doubling of the force to 1,000 men in the aftermath of the North West Rebellion. The training depot remains on the same site today, adding to the image of security and safety in Regina.

NWMP Regina Barracks, c. 1895

Louis Riel

NWMP Guard Room, c. 1890

NWMP Town Station, c. 1890

MOUNTED POLICE

RCMP Depot Chapel
1883

NWMP Riding School
1888

WILLIAM
ARGAN

RCMP Museum

Very few of the original, pre-WW II buildings remain, but the two that do serve an important role in preserving the history and image of the present-day force. The RCMP Chapel is the oldest building in the city. The A. B. Perry Administrative Building, built on the southwest corner of the barracks square, is architecturally significant because of its Tudor Gothic styling which directed the look of the entire depot. Local architect Neil R. Darrach designed the building. Today these two buildings, the RCMP Centennial Museum, the sprawling complex of contemporary buildings, the Sunset Ceremony, and the mystique of the force itself draw thousands of tourists to the city each year.

"There's a proud tradition in the museum," says Bill MacKay of the RCMP Centennial Museum. "The RCMP are a Canadian icon, recognized around the world, glamourized in some places, respected in all." When training in horsemanship was a requirement, the Regina depot was the headquarters for many years for the world-famous RCMP Musical Ride.

Canadians from all corners of the country and people from all over the world come to the barracks and grounds and are impressed. Since the depot houses the only training academy in Canada, every member must come to Regina for his or her training, "contributing to the variety of the community," says MacKay.

"There is a social and economic benefit to the barracks' location in Regina other than tourism. With a permanent staff of approximately 450 it is one of the largest employers in the city. As members of the community, as well as of the RCMP, the staff gets involved in many ways," explains MacKay. "From hockey coaches to the Knights of Columbus, from charity balls to the Alzheimer's Society, our members/instructors are community-minded.

"They do their bit economically, from owning homes to buying groceries. Our members are woven into the fabric of Regina society."

RCMP CHAPEL

6101 Dewdney Avenue

*K*nown as Chapel on the Square, the chapel on the RCMP grounds is the oldest and most historic building remaining among those erected by the mounted police in the early days. Originally, the chapel was built as a mess hall, with the materials cut and partially assembled in the east and transported to Regina in 1883 by steamer and ox team. In 1889, an L-shaped addition was built to serve as a canteen.

Mrs. Herchmer, wife of the police commissioner, wanted a chapel for force members, who were largely a separate community from the town, two miles to the east. Carpenters of the NWMP converted the mess hall to a chapel and fashioned the altar and pews themselves. The building was dedicated on December 8, 1895.

Two stained-glass memorial windows on either side of the altar portray a member of the force. On the left, a constable is portrayed standing in the attitude of mourning; on the right, a trumpeter is portrayed sounding reveille. The Memorial Project came about following the shooting of Constable Willis Edward Rhodeniser on the White Bear Reserve near Carlyle, Sask. on August 26, 1939. A small mural tablet in scarlet, blue and gold accompanying the windows is the work of J. H. Lee-Grayson.

Two other stained-glass memorial windows, one on each side wall near the front, were dedicated on November 4, 1951. The west window "The Resurrection" honours serving members and the east window "The Nativity" was presented on behalf of relatives and friends of the sons of members and ex-members of the Force who gave their lives in WW II.

Other tributes to the past include the Union Jack and Red Ensign which flew over Fort Walsh between 1875 and 1880, a chair upholstered in blue which was used at the coronation of King George VI, and an organ which was dedicated on April 27, 1941.

King George VI and Queen Elizabeth visited the Chapel in 1939, as did their daughter Princess Elizabeth (Queen Elizabeth II) and the Duke of Edinburgh in 1951.

The Chapel on the Square is one of the oldest Anglican houses of worship in the Northwest

NORTH-WEST TERRITORIAL GOVERNMENT BUILDINGS

3304 Dewdney Avenue

*I*n March 1883, the government seat for the North-West Territories was transferred from Battleford to Regina. The Government Buildings were built by October 1883, and were used until the new Legislative Building was completed in 1912. The building in the foreground, the North-West Territories Administrative Building, was designed by Dominion architect Thomas Fuller. The design is in the Second Empire style as shown by the Mansard roof. Built in 1890/1891, it housed the offices of the North-West Territorial Government from 1891 to 1905.

This building served the provincial government from 1905 to 1910. The Finance Department occupied one main floor room and the Public Works and Education Departments occupied single rooms on the second floor. The Provincial Laboratories and Diagnostic Laboratory were located in the basement of the building until 1911, when they were moved into the new Legislative Building. Dr. George A. Charlton, a bacteriologist and pathologist, whose work came under the Department of Agriculture, did tests for the Province of Saskatchewan and, for two years, for the Province of Alberta. By 1909, over 57 per cent of all samples submitted came from physicians and over 80 per cent of Saskatchewan physicians were using the laboratory's services. – Robertson, Riddell, *Provincial Laboratories*

WILLIAM
ARGAN

From 1910 to 1922 it housed the Ruthenian Training School for immigrants from eastern Europe.

Nearly destroyed by fire in 1922, the building was repaired and leased from 1922 to 1971 by the Salvation Army as Grace Haven, a Salvation Army Hospital and home for unmarried mothers.

The building was restored in 1979 by the provincial government and served as the North Central Community Centre. It is a designated Provincial Heritage Property.

Famous people who began their careers at this historic site include R. B. Bennett, former prime minister of Canada; A. C. Rutherford and A. L. Sifton, premiers of Alberta; R. S. Lake and G. W. Brown, lieutenant-governors of Saskatchewan; and A. E. Forget who was lieutenant-governor of the Territories from 1898 to 1905 and Saskatchewan's first lieutenant-governor.

REGINA'S FIRST GOVERNMENT HOUSE

Dewdney Avenue at Royal Street

*I*n 1883, Regina's first Government House was erected on Dewdney Avenue where Luther College presently stands.

The wooden structure was composed of two portable houses built in Ottawa and Montreal and transported to Regina. Although the building was a makeshift dwelling, it was the hub of activity for the social elite of the Territories, particularly Regina.

There was much controversy surrounding the decision to build a new Government House in Regina. Sir John A. Macdonald defended the decision in the House of Commons saying: "It is a wretched place, and I do not see how the Governor's family live there during the winter. I have occasion to know that their sufferings from the cold in winter are very great. There were 17 stoves going continually, and the inmates could not keep themselves warm."

Edgar Dewdney

WILLIAM ARGAN

Although the Government of Canada and the CPR were responsible for choosing the site of Regina, the first lieutenant-governor of the North-West Territories, Edgar Dewdney, influenced the choice more than anyone else. Acting primarily on Dewdney's advice, the Government also made Regina the headquarters of the North-West Mounted Police.

Regina's first Government House was demolished in 1910. The new Government House was built east of the Mounted Police barracks in 1889.

REGINA'S SECOND GOVERNMENT HOUSE

4607 Dewdney Avenue

*T*he second residence of the lieutenant-governor of the Territories was constructed between 1889 and 1891 under the direction of Dominion architect Thomas Fuller. The first lieutenant-governor in residence was The Honourable Joseph Royal.

Until 1945, Government House played host to countless ceremonial functions and was the social hub of Regina. Six lieutenant-governors lived and entertained in the building. The Honourable Amédée Forget, George W. Brown, Sir Richard S. Lake, Henry W. Newlands, Hugh E. Monroe, Archibald P. McNab.

McNab, the ninth and last lieutenant-governor to live in Government House, 1936 to 1945, was a very popular and colourful individual. As an MLA and Minister of Public Works for 13 years, he oversaw the building of two sanatoriums and provincial jails, plus court houses, telephone buildings and land titles offices across the province.

As lieutenant-governor, he kept the traditional New Year's Levées, dances and other social events. Although he was 72 when he assumed office, McNab "probably attended more functions in his official capacity than any other representative of the crown." – *Leader-Post* obituary Particularly fond of children, he once encountered a group of small boys off to snare gophers. He joined them and purchased ice-cream cones for all of them when the hunt was over. Stories of his good nature and unpretentious manner abound. When Lord Tweedsmuir, the Governor General visited in 1938, McNab said, "Call me Archie, I've been called damned near everything but that's the name I like best."

A friend of the Indian people, he was made an honourary chief (Chief Kind Heart) of the Piapot Reserve in 1938.

During WW II he was honourary president of the Mayor of London's Distress Fund and spoke at numerous fund-raising and related events. In 1939, he hosted a state dinner at the splendidly redecorated Government House for King George VI and Queen Elizabeth, Prime Minister King, Premier Patterson and Mayor Ellison. When the king dropped his spoon during the dinner, the solicitous McNab said, "Don't bother to pick it up; we've got lots of spoons." As the royals departed, McNab invited, "Bring the kids next time." He was remembered by Queen Elizabeth as "one of the dearest old men I have ever met."

In the mid-1940s, Government House became a veterans' hospital and later a school. Restorations begun in 1978 returned the historic building to its earliest elegance. In 1984, the lieutenant-governor's office was returned to Government House, allowing the building to reacquire its official status.

Government and charitable organizations hold dinners and receptions in the beautifully refurbished ballroom. Since 1990, The Government House Historical Society has held Victorian Teas in the ballroom of Government House, serving 110 to 120 people every weekend throughout the year, except in January and February. Expansion plans to move the office space out of the second floor of Government House will provide a space for an interpretive historical gallery in the House.

Government House has 2.5 hectares of beautifully landscaped gardens.

PROVINCIAL LEGISLATIVE BUILDING

2405 Legislative Drive

*T*he provincial government purchased 168 acres of land south of Wascana Lake from McCallum Hill and Company, at a price of $96,250, on which to build the new Legislative Building. Construction of the largest public works project undertaken in the city at that time began on August 31, 1908.

In 1909 Governor General Earl Grey came to Regina to lay the cornerstone.

Thirty-four types of marble were used to finish various sections of the building. At the end of 1912, the total cost of the building, furnishings and site improvements totalled $2,350,000.

The official opening of the Provincial Legislative Building took place October 12, 1912. The building was formally dedicated by the new Governor General, the Duke of Connaught. This occasion was the season's social highlight as the Duke and Duchess and their daughter were welcomed by a royal salute and a guard of honour.

Regina's elite, dressed in their finest, celebrated the building's dedication that evening against a background of outdoor fireworks.

WILLIAM ARGAN

DOMINION LANDS OFFICE

1975 Scarth Street

*T*he Dominion Lands Office was built in 1900 on the site of Regina's first courthouse, where Louis Riel was tried in 1885. The Lands Office moved into the new Land Titles Building on Victoria Avenue around 1908. After the Dominion Lands Office relocated, this building was used by several business tenants. In 1935 this building was demolished and the Federal Building was erected on this site (see page 62).

LAND TITLES BUILDING/ SASKATCHEWAN SPORTS HALL OF FAME

2205 Victoria Avenue

*T*his building, built in 1907/1908, served as the Land Titles Office until 1977.

The structure was designed by Darling and Pearson and was the first public building constructed for the Province of Saskatchewan. It became the first provincially designated Heritage Property in Saskatchewan in 1977, and now houses the Saskatchewan Sports Hall of Fame.

It is also the Administration Centre for Sport, Culture and Recreation and the offices of the Sports Governing Associations.

REGINA COURTHOUSE

2002 Victoria Avenue

*T*his courthouse was erected in 1894 to replace Regina's first courthouse which was located on Scarth Street at Victoria Avenue, the later site of the Federal Building. It was later enlarged.

The building was demolished in 1965 and the Avord Towers building was constructed on the site. In 1961 the new courthouse was built at 2425 Victoria Avenue.

THE REGINA COURTHOUSE

2425 Victoria Avenue

*T*he new courthouse was built in 1961 and was designed by Portnall and Grolle architects. It was constructed for the Province of Saskatchewan by Poole Construction Co. Ltd.

This building houses the Court of Queen's Bench for Saskatchewan which hears civil, family and criminal matters. The Saskatchewan Court of Appeal is also located in this building as is the Federal Court of Canada.

DOMINION GOVERNMENT (FEDERAL) BUILDING

1975 Scarth Street

*T*he Regina Federal Building, originally known as the Dominion Government Building, was built between 1935 and 1937 as a relief project. It was erected on the site of Regina's first courthouse, where Louis Riel's trial took place.

The building was constructed according to plans conceived by Francis B. Reilly, a Regina architect, and completed by Francis Portnall. In 1987, the Federal Building was placed on the National Registry of Historic Properties. Between 1988 and 1990 the structure was renovated, but care was taken to ensure the changes reflected the original heritage design.

PROVINCIAL COURTHOUSE

1815 Smith Street

*T*his building was built in 1985 to house court proceedings formerly held in the municipal court house located on the second floor of the former police station at 11th Avenue and Halifax Street.

Activities in this courthouse relate to municipal and RCMP matters, including traffic offences, small debt court, initial hearings and other local matters which may be raised to a higher court at a later time.

The building was designed by Building Design 2 Architects and built by Tricor Construction for the Province of Saskatchewan.

CENOTAPH

Victoria Park

*I*n November 1925, the City of Regina held a design competition for a Cenotaph as a monument to Regina's citizens who were killed in WW I.

"The over-whelming majority of Regina recruits entered the Army, especially Saskatchewan's own 95th Regiment . . . At the outbreak of hostilities, the current CO, Lt.-Col. J. F. L. Embury was authorized to recruit a unit for overseas, the 28th Battalion CEF . . . The battalion was recruited from all over Saskatchewan . . . but many volunteers, and nearly all the Headquarters staff, were local men and the capital always proudly called the unit 'Regina's Own'. . . . Among the early recruits was Ben Allen, who later became the end man on the famous 'Dumbells' army concert group.

"The 28th Battalion" as Max Aitken, Lord Beaverbrook, wrote, "throughout the fighting, set a notable example of gallantry and endurance. . . they became the first Canadian unit to enter German territory, all without ever surrendering a foot of ground. At the armistice this great battalion was occupying the most forward Canadian position. Before the war ended it had supplied two general staff officers, two Brigadier Generals (J. F. L. Embury and Alex Ross, both Reginans) and a future Major General (H. N. L. Salmon). It had also won over three hundred decorations for valour.

"The prairie city, which was devoid of military tradition or inclination, produced many heroes. Some of its best athletes were lost: Captain Clarrie Dale who, after being wounded and invalided home, had then re-enlisted only to be killed at the front; Captain E. L. "Hick" Abbott, M. C., of whom his CO wrote, "by his death the battalion has lost the most gallant officer it ever had"; and Flight Lieutenant Sam Taylor, who participated in the conquering of Baron Von Richthofen, destroyed thirteen planes, and won the Croix de Guerre, before being shot down. Regina mourned many other brave sons who had been less widely known. A local carpenter, Sergeant Arthur Knight, was posthumously awarded the Victoria Cross, because 'he displayed the greatest valour under fire at very close range and by his example of courage, gallantry and initiative, was a wonderful inspiration to all.' About six hundred Regina men were killed and over two thousand wounded." – Drake, *Regina*

R. W. G. Heughan of Ross & Macdonald, Montreal, won the design competition for the Cenotaph and F. H. Portnall, a Regina architect, aided him in the creation of the gray granite monument. The Cenotaph was erected in the centre of Victoria Park and unveiled on Armistice Day 1926.

Each year hundreds of people gather at the Cenotaph on November 11 to lay wreaths and pay tribute to Regina citizens who gave their lives during war. In the summer of 1995, extensive renovations to Victoria Park enhanced the area surrounding the Cenotaph.

REGINA ARMOURY

1600 Elphinstone Street

Erected by the Regina Armoury Association in 1928, the Regina Armoury was later turned over to the Canadian Government. The members of the Association included Col. J. S. Rankin, Lt. Col. A. C. Styles, Lt. Col. R. H. Matthews, Lt. Col. H. L. Jackes, Lt. Col. J. W. Wickward, Lt. Col. S. R. Parker, Lt. Col. F. J. James and Lt. Col. A. P. Lintong.

Designed by architect Stan. E. Storey, the building was constructed by Poole Construction Co. Ltd. and is 258 feet long and 158 feet wide on the 9th Avenue side. The roof was considered to be of "peculiar" construction and the only one of its type in the province. The roof is entirely of steel plate on heavy steel trusses, insulated on top and covered with asbestos roofing. The underside is covered with sound-absorbing material to enhance the building's acoustics. The two-storey structure is heated by two smokeless boilers, and there are four miniature rifle ranges in the basement.

Until 1939 the Armoury was the headquarters for the Canadian Army and the Royal Canadian Navy Volunteer Reserve. After the outbreak of WW II, the navy headquarters and training centre were relocated to the Wascana Winter Club, which was called The HMCS Queen. In 1954, the Naval Headquarters moved to their own building on 2800 Broad Street in Wascana Park.

In addition to being headquarters for the Armed Services, the Armoury was also used for social activities, sports events, entertainment programs and political events.

In the 1930s through the 1950s New Year's dances were held there because the hardwood floor in the drill hall, used for training, was ideal for dancing. The indoor Pollack Bros. Circus performed in the building on many occasions. It was also the venue for touring bands, entertainment groups, boxing matches, bazaars and even a bowling tournament.

Prime Minister MacKenzie King held a giant political rally in this building in 1935. Premiers Douglas, Thatcher and Blakeney used the Armoury for major election campaign rallies on a number of occasions.

In 1966, the City of Regina staged a huge "Welcome Home" rally here in honour of the Saskatchewan Roughriders on their return from Vancouver after winning their first ever Grey Cup.

The Regina Armoury is home to four army reserve, or militia, units of 38 Brigade Group which is headquartered in Winnipeg, Manitoba. These units are 10 Field Regiment RCA, The Royal Regina Rifles, 16 (Saskatchewan) Service Battalion and 16 (Regina) Medical Company. In addition to these units the Armoury also accommodates the Garrison HQ, the Saskatchewan Military Museum, the Militia Support Section (vehicle mechanics), the Clothing Stores for southern Saskatchewan, the Domestic Operations Detachment (Saskatchewan) for Land Force Western Area, and four cadet units – 155 and 2370 Royal Canadian Army Cadets and 34 and 41 Royal Canadian Air Cadets.

ROYAL CANADIAN LEGION MEMORIAL HALL

1820 Cornwall Street

"*I*n 1926, the Legion's Regina branch received the first charter to be issued by what was then known as the Canadian Legion British Empire Service League. This building was designed by Storey and Van Egmond and was built in two phases between 1947 and 1951. The future Queen Elizabeth and Prince Philip were among those present at the official opening of the Memorial Hall in October of 1951. In its exterior design, architectural detailing and interior decoration, the building constitutes a relatively late, but highly representative example of the Modern Classical style (a variant of the Art Deco movement). It was designated as a Municipal Heritage Property on September 21, 1992.

"The stepped, symmetrical and horizontally oriented composition of the building in general is contrasted with the strong verticality of the Memorial Peace Tower. The tower is capped with a large entablature of Tyndall stone, "supported" at each corner by squared, fluted stone cantons (i.e. corner pilasters). In turn, the entablature is decorated with a "zig-zag" band course and features an engraved dedication to those who lost their lives in WW I and WW II. Directly above the entry doors is an elaborate stained-glass window, presented to the Legion by the Saskatchewan government and unveiled by Governor General Vincent Massey in 1952. Two pairs of smaller stained-glass windows are situated on either side of the tower.

"Inside, the auditorium foyer (known as the Memorial Chamber) features a number of elements of architectural, artistic and historic significance. Of general interest is a series of eight murals executed by noted Canadian artist Kenneth Lochhead, and installed in 1956. The murals depict important events and images of Canadian military history, the theme of remembrance and the ongoing objectives of the Legion. Lochhead, a member of the "Regina Five" group of artists, was appointed Director of Regina College's School of Art in 1950." – City of Regina, *Heritage Tours*

With the passing of the years and the inevitable aging of our veterans, the Royal Canadian Legion has found it beneficial to "open the doors" to many other sectors of the population beside the ordinary military members who have a relationship to a veteran.

The expansion of eligibility for membership has grown over the past five years to include: non-voting affiliates being allowed to apply for voting privileges after two years of continuous service to the Legion; police service members; RCMP officers; firefighters.

These changes to membership eligibility will ensure that the future of the Legion in Canada is continued and that its reason for being – Remembrance – will carry on for generations to come.

The functions of the Legion remain much the same, poppy sales, Remembrance services and programs, Literary and Essay Contests for young people. The education of young people in these areas is the most important function of all Legions across the country.

KNOX PRESBYTERIAN CHURCH

Scarth Street and 11th Avenue

*I*n June 1882 the Fort Qu'Appelle area was white with tents belonging to prospective settlers and land speculators. They were waiting for an announcement from Lieutenant-Governor Edgar Dewdney, who was visiting the Fort, about the location of the new site of the future capital of the North-West Territories. On June 30, Dewdney travelled to Pile of Bones Creek, now known as Regina, and posted a notice that this would be the capital's new site.

Reverend J. W. Mitchell was in the vicinity and wrote: "I conducted the first Presbyterian service in the new city on the second Sabbath after it was named, the first Sunday in September. The service was conducted in a livery stable tent normally occupied with buckboards and ponies. The audience consisted mostly of the crowd that was following up the railway construction."

The Presbyterians claim to have had the first formal place of worship in Regina, a portable structure sent out by the Board of Home Missions in the fall of 1882. The building soon became too small for the congregation so various makeshift buildings followed, including McCusker's Hall, quarters above Charles McCusker's blacksmith shop, and a rented building at South Railway and Scarth Street.

On July 26, 1885, Knox congregation finally put down roots at its new church at Scarth Street and 11th Avenue. The 54- by 42-foot brick-veneer building was erected at a cost of $5,500.

The *Leader*, June 30, 1885 reported: "The opening of Knox Church, Regina is one of the noted events in the history of the town. The builders, Reilly & Reilly, deserve great credit, as does Mr. Eddy who put in the brick work. The church is indeed a beautiful one and throws nearly every building in Regina into the shade."

The Scarth Street site was later sold to the Dominion Government as the site for a new post office. A permanent church building was erected at 12th Avenue and Lorne Street in 1905 (see page 72).

ST. PAUL'S CATHEDRAL

1861 McIntyre Street

S t. Paul's Cathedral (Anglican) is the oldest church in continuous use, and the oldest remaining building in downtown Regina. The original portion of the church building (now the nave) was erected in 1894/1895 to a design by Frank H. Peters in the Gothic Revival style. It replaced the first St. Paul's Church built on this site in 1883. William Reilly designed the transepts and chancel of the present building, which were added in 1905/1906. Notable features include the distinctive corner tower, fieldstone foundation walls and stained glass windows, particularly the rose window at the west end of the church.

On December 27, 1882, the parish of St. Paul's was officially formed. Anglican services had been conducted earlier in 1882, but the first resident priest, Alfred E. Osborne, arrived in November of that year.

As recorded in the "Book of Remembrance" at St. Paul's Pro-Cathedral: "In the year 1883, two years prior to the time of the N.W. Rebellion of 1885, a little red church was built in Regina, on the present site of the Pro-Cathedral of St. Paul. The Parish of St. Paul had been formed the previous year as part of the Diocese of Saskatchewan. In 1884 it became a part of the newly created Diocese of Qu'Appelle. In 1889, St. Paul's became a self-supporting Parish. In 1895, the Nave of the present Church was constructed, the cornerstone being laid by Officers of the Grand Lodge of Manitoba. The old Church was moved to nearby Smith Street where it was used as the Sunday School, until the Parish Hall was built in 1911. During the First Great War 1914 to 1918, the Parish Hall became a hospital for wounded soldiers. In 1905 to 1906 work was commenced on the present chancel and north transept. For many years the transept was occupied on Sunday by members of the Royal North West Mounted Police. Now it is occupied each Sunday by the girls of the Q.D.S. In the year 1944, St. Paul's became the Pro-Cathedral of the Diocese. For many years it had been used as the meeting place of the Synods of the Diocese." – Embury, *History*

WW I saw a serious depletion of the membership of St. Paul's as over 150 men volunteered for service, including Lieutenant-Colonel J. F. L. Embury and choirmaster Franklin Laubach, who was also the founder of the Regina Symphony. In November 1921, 40 parishioners who had died in service during the War were remembered by the unveiling of a plaque by General Embury, dedicated by Archdeacon G. F. Davidson.

St. Paul's choir was well known throughout Regina. Franklin Laubach, who had returned from the war, was instrumental in its accomplishments. He retired in 1922, after 18 years as choirmaster.

Under the leadership of Bishop E. H. Knowles, St. Paul's was designated Pro-Cathedral of the Diocese of Qu'Appelle on May 18, 1944. A post-war renovation project included a Memorial Chapel, donated by Mrs. D. McNiven and designed by F. H. Portnall. The organ, which had been installed in 1907, was rebuilt. It was played by Bernie Laubach, son of Franklin Laubach, at the dedication ceremony in 1951. A new parish hall, designed by F. H. Portnall, was built on the site of the old rectory, at a cost of $160,000. It was dedicated by Bishop Coleman on January 19, 1958.

In 1979, St. Paul's Cathedral became the church of the Royal Regina Rifle Regiment. In 1970 and in 1982, St. Paul's was honoured in having Bishop Frederick Jackson and, subsequently, Bishop Michael Peers elected to the office of Metropolitan of the Ecclesiastical Province of Rupert's Land. St. Paul's was designated as one of Regina's first two Municipal Heritage Properties in 1982.

ST. MARY'S ROMAN CATHOLIC CHURCH/ BLESSED SACRAMENT

1863 Cornwall Street/2049 Scarth Street/2030 Winnipeg Street/2026 Winnipeg Street

S t. Mary's Parish is known as the "Mother Church" of Regina. Mass was first said on a little field altar in a prairie democrat by Father Joseph Hugonard in April 1882. The earliest recorded history of the parish begins December 3, 1883 with Reverend L. N. L'Arche as pastor. For his first year he celebrated mass in Charles McCusker's blacksmith shop.

The first Catholic church was built in Regina in 1883/1884, on the later site of Burns-Hanley Church Supplies at 1863 Cornwall Street. It was dedicated on August 3, 1884, as St. Mary's Church by Archbishop Taché (1) and was known for its fine acoustics. The 300-pound bell in the steeple, the first in Regina, could be heard for miles over the Regina plains.

In 1903 the parish was entrusted to the Oblates of Mary Immaculate. Father Augustine Suffa was one of the first Oblates to arrive. He remained pastor until 1918, when he died after tirelessly caring for victims of the influenza epidemic.

In 1905, a new St. Mary's Church (2) was built at 2049 Scarth Street. This church carried the name until 1935. It was used mainly by Regina's Catholic German-speaking congregation. An addition to the church was blessed on October 19, 1913 and the old Cornwall Street church was torn down. By 1930 there were 1,100 families in St. Mary's Parish.

In 1933, the Oblate Fathers turned St. Mary's Church over to the diocesan clergy and it was given the name Blessed Sacrament (2). The name "St. Mary's" was kept by the Oblate Fathers and assigned to St. Joseph's Hall (3), 2030 Winnipeg Street, which was converted into a church.

On March 7, 1959 fire damaged St. Mary's Church (3) and it was decided to rebuild on an adjacent site. On December 18, 1960 the new church (4) at 2026 Winnipeg Street was blessed.

Stations of the Cross, entirely composed of Italian mosaic – with thousands of pieces and at least 120 colours – were installed. It was one of the first instances where all 14 stations were displayed along one wall. In August 1963, another new piece of mosaic, "The Resurrection", was added to complete the Stations on the east wall of the church. In 1961 a new pipe organ was installed in the back gallery. In 1976 the old St. Mary's church (3) at 2030 Winnipeg Street was torn down.

ST. MARY'S CHURCH/
BURNS-HANLEY CHURCH SUPPLIES

1863 Cornwall Street

*R*egina's first Catholic church, St. Mary's, illustration (1) on page 68, was originally located at 1863 Cornwall Street, the site where Louis Riel's body was hidden.

When Riel was hanged in Regina in 1885, his body was guarded in a grave under the altar of St. Mary's church for three weeks before it was moved to St. Boniface, Manitoba for burial.

At this site on April 7, 1913 "a merry crowd of 200 or more gathered" when the Catholic Club block was opened. The *Leader* reported: "The club now has rooms of which it may well be proud. The auditorium is situated on the third floor and extends the entire length and width of the building, while the second floor is used as the club rooms, with pool and billiard apartments at the rear. These rooms are a good size and neatly finished in brown with dark trimmings. Beautiful pictures adorn the walls, which add greatly to the homelike appearance of the apartments. A writing desk and an extensive library are at the disposal of the members.

"As luck would have it the new furniture for the rooms has not arrived yet, and consequently the furniture in use in the old hall had to be pressed into service for the accommodation of the guests. When the new furniture has been put in place the Catholic Club will have one of the coziest apartments in the city." The ground floor was rented and the remainder of the building was used by the club with the exception of one small room set aside for the Knights of Columbus.

The Catholic Club quarters were described by the *Leader* as "the finest building in Western Canada, costing as it did $40,000 and being exquisitely appointed throughout."

By 1948 the building was referred to as the Burns-Hanley Building. Church supplies were sold here until the 1980s, when the business moved to 13th Avenue in the Cathedral district.

SALVATION ARMY CITADEL

*I*n June 1895, two young women, Captain Isaacson and a lieutenant, brought the Salvation Army to Regina. Their first congregation numbered only four. As part of the great Territorial Fair, also in June, other Army officers came to help hold open-air services at the fair, which helped to create more interest in the Army.

The Salvation Army Citadel was constructed in 1902 at 1738 Broad Street. The building was acquired by the congregation of the Christian Apostolic Church in 1918 and moved to 1772 Montreal Street. It is still in use as the Apostolic Christian Church.

In 1913, the Salvation Army erected the Citadel at 1740 Broad Street. In the early years, beginning in the late 1920s, the Salvation Army Band was a major part of the "Sally Ann" program throughout the world. Whether you were in downtown Regina, or on the streets of New York, in Times Square, it was a common occurrence to see and hear the band performing on a street corner and preaching the gospel and peace making.

The Salvation Army became famous for its dedicated support to the troops in the armed services and became known as "the friend of the soldier" in both WW I and WW II.

1738 Broad Street

Towards the end of 1929, City Council gave a $500 grant to the Salvation Army to work with Regina's 600 unemployed single men. These funds only stretched to provide "a bed, two bowls of soup and four slices of bread" for 40 to 50 men daily.

"During 1935 and 1936, a yearly average of five thousand transient unemployed passed through the Salvation Army men's hostel in Regina." – Drake, *Regina*

In 1936 the Army bought the former residence of R. H. Williams and turned the 14-room house into the Eventide Home for elderly men. They also purchased the old North-West Territories Administrative Building on Dewdney Avenue and opened it as Grace Haven, a home and hospital for unmarried mothers.

In the 1930s the Army began a successful Christmas Kettle campaign, to provide food and help for needy families. This campaign has continued with the help of other organizations and service clubs.

The Regina Citadel relocated on March 17, 1973 to 2012 McIntyre Street.

1740 Broad Street

The Salvation Army maintains two Worship Centres in Regina. They also have an Emergency Disaster Services program to provide immediate survival needs to victims. The William Booth Special Care Home, at 50 Angus Road, provides residence to 88 seniors, an adult day support program, respite care, a Palliative Care unit and a convalescent care program that offers recuperation time for patients.

Waterston Centre
1845 Osler Street

The Community and Family Services program at 2240 13th Avenue works with people to encourage self sufficiency, develop domestic and budgeting skills, and offers a summer camp program for children of low-income families. Grace Haven offers support for pregnant teens, while Gemma House has programs for girls 12 to 16, to help them work through severe behavioural/emotional problems. The Waterston Centres care for the needs of homeless men, providing accommodation for 125 men. In September 2002 a renovation project was announced to add 25 more beds and a youth wing. The House of Concord program works with boys sentenced under the Young Offenders Act, and Correctional and Justice Services supports the prison system with a Salvation Army chaplain working with inmates and officers, offering counselling to victims and to inmates' families.

Waterston Centre
1865 Osler Street

ST. NICHOLAS ROMANIAN ORTHODOX CHURCH

1770 St. John Street

*R*omanian immigrants first settled in Regina in the 1890s. In 1902 they joined together to build St. Nicholas Romanian Orthodox Church. It was the first of its kind in North American, and is now the oldest Romanian Orthodox church in North America.

The main entrance is located at the rear of the building in keeping with a tradition that requires the altar to be placed at the east end of the church.

A highlight for the Romanian community was a visit to the church in 1963 by Mother Alexandra, a former princess of Romania.

Renovations in 2002, for the 100th Anniversary celebrations, include new hand-painted pictures of icons and a hand-carved oak iconostasis to replace the originals.

KNOX PRESBYTERIAN CHURCH

12th Avenue and Lorne Street

*T*he "new" Knox Presbyterian Church was built in 1906. The cornerstone was laid in 1905 by Reverend Dr. John A. Carmichael who had been pastor at the first church at Scarth Street and 11th Avenue for 12 years. It was damaged in the 1912 cyclone, but repairs were effected within a year.

The Knox Church congregation joined the United Church of Canada in 1925, but there was organized opposition to the union. The vote was 544 for union, 286 against. The dissidents under Judge W. M. Martin left to form First Presbyterian Church.

In 1951, Knox Church's congregation merged with the Metropolitan Methodist Congregation to form Knox -Metropolitan United Church. In 1952, Knox Church was demolished and the site became the location of SaskTel's Telecommunications Centre.

METROPOLITAN METHODIST CHURCH/
KNOX-METROPOLITAN UNITED CHURCH

2340 Victoria Avenue

*T*he original Metropolitan Church was designed by the Toronto firm of Darling and Pearson, and was constructed in 1906/1907 at a cost of over $100,000. The 1912 cyclone destroyed the building and it was rebuilt eleven months after its destruction to a revised design by Francis Portnall and James H. Puntin.

In 1925, when the United Church of Canada brought together Methodist, Presbyterian and Congregational churches, both Metropolitan and Knox became United Churches, but maintained their separate buildings. In November 1951, both congregations joined to form Knox-Metropolitan United Church, in the former Metropolitan Church building.

The Darke Memorial Chimes were donated to the citizens of Regina by F. N. Darke and placed in the care of Knox-Metropolitan Church.

Knox-Met is home to the annual Rotary Carol Festival which, since 1941, raises funds to assist needy families and provides a venue for 90 plus local choirs and singing groups.

The church was designated as a Municipal Heritage Property in April 1986.

TRINITY EVANGELICAL LUTHERAN CHURCH

Ottawa Street between 12th and Victoria Avenues

*T*he first Evangelical Trinity Lutheran Church was constructed and dedicated in 1907.

This building was erected on the same site in 1913 and served the congregation until 1960, when a new church was constructed at 1909 Ottawa Street. The old building was subsequently demolished.

1913 to 1960

WILLIAM ARGAN

The "new" Trinity Evangelical Lutheran Church was erected in 1960 to accommodate the ever-growing congregation. At that time it had increased to over 2,500 members. The design chosen was an "A" frame which forms a triangle and also represents the Holy Trinity. In later years stained-glass windows were added as well as a free-standing bell tower which still supports the original bell. Every Sunday morning the church bells ring out clearly calling the community to worship.

Since its first organization, Trinity Evangelical Lutheran Church continues to serve the community and the wider world community through its ministry.

1960 –

FIRST BAPTIST CHURCH

Victoria Avenue at Lorne Street

*T*he Baptist Church in Regina was organized in 1891. This building, designed by local architect William W. Hilton, was erected in 1911/1912 by Smith Brothers. & Wilson.

The church's interior fittings included an organ with gold pipes and a large chandelier which hung from the domed ceiling. The 1912 cyclone extensively damaged the roof, the auditorium and the organ, but repairs were quickly completed.

In the spring of 1992 a $1.3 million restoration of First Baptist Church was completed. The restored church was designated as a Municipal Heritage Property on March 9, 1992 and received the 1993 Municipal Heritage Award for its excellent exterior and interior restoration.

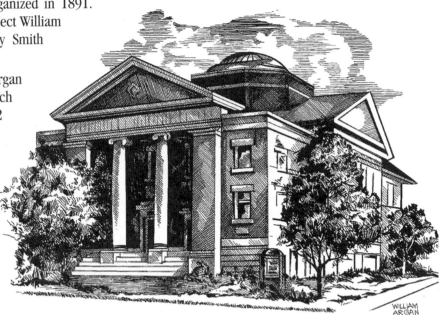

ST. CUTHBERT'S HOUSE

1501 College Avenue

*S*t. Cuthbert's House was built in 1912 by the Archbishops' Western Canada Fund to house the members of the Railway Mission. Founded in 1910, the mission helped to establish Anglican parishes and construct churches in settlements along the rapidly expanding railway network.

The building was designed by Brown and Vallance of Montreal, the firm responsible for the original University of Saskatchewan campus.

Plans were made for a major addition to the building, but those plans were permanently scrapped with the onset of the depression.

When the Mission closed in 1920, the house was given to St. Chad's Theological College which remained here until 1952.

The building currently accommodates the offices of the Anglican Diocesan Synod.

ST. CHAD'S COLLEGE

1601 College Avenue

*I*mmigrants moved west in large numbers after 1900 and the Anglican church had difficulty ministering to them with the men and money available at the time.

In 1906, while on his annual trip to England, Bishop Grisdale of Qu'Appelle sought funding from a variety of sources to train churchmen, since all local resources were required for the pastoral needs of the settlements. As a result, the Shropshire Mission to North West Canada was formed and, in 1907, St. Chad's Hostel was built at its first location on the south side of the 3000 block of Dewdney Avenue. At St. Chad's, four students spent half of their time in mission work and the other half studying.

Soon the hostel doubled as a training school and a church. Recognizing this location would not be adequate for long, 15 acres of land were bought from the province in 1911. The new training college was completed in 1914 and the hostel changed its name to St. Chad's Theological College.

When the WW I broke out, the student body decreased substantially. The Diocese offered the main part of the building to the government in 1916 as a convalescent hospital for veterans. In the last year of the war, another Diocesan institution came into being – the Qu'Appelle Diocesan School for Girls founded by the Anglican Sisters of St. John the Divine. It outgrew its original quarters on Albert Street and moved to St. Cuthbert's House. This was to be a temporary move, but the girls' school remained and, in 1965, the name officially became the St. Chad's Girls' School. In June 1970, when the school could no longer support itself, the doors were closed.

In 1975, the Saskatchewan government paid an undisclosed sum for 20 acres of land, including Harding House, Bishop's Court, Anson House, St. Cuthbert's House and St. Chad's Girls School. In 1980, the province designated the Diocesan property a Provincial Heritage Property and, in 1992, the City of Regina awarded it a Municipal Heritage Award for the exterior restoration.

ANSON HOUSE

1611 College Avenue

Bishop A. J. R. Anson

*A*nson House was named after the first Bishop of Qu'Appelle, Adelbert John Robert Anson, and was the official residence of the Diocesan secretary until 1979. Canon Anson was a graduate of Oxford University and the second son of the Earl of Lichfield. He resigned a comfortable rectorship in England to come to the Canadian northwest as an unpaid missionary.

In August 1883 the Synod of the Ecclesiastical Province of Rupert's Land approved the creation of the Diocese of Assiniboia (later changed to Qu'Appelle). Its establishment coincided with the arrival of Canon Anson who came to assess the state of Anglican mission work.

Impressed with Anson's dedication in advancing the Church of England's position, he was appointed Commissary for Assiniboia by the Metropolitan of Rupert's Land, with powers to raise money in England for the endowment of the see and to procure clergy there. Anson was so successful that he was offered the bishopric of Assiniboia and was consecrated Bishop in Lambeth Palace Chapel on June 24, 1884.

To ensure that places of worship were accessible to everybody, he forbade the introduction of pew rents. During his episcopate, Anson tried to make the church self-supporting, however, a series of poor harvests and little money among incoming settlers made regular giving difficult. In 1892, having established 24 Anglican churches in the Diocese, Anson resigned as Bishop of Qu'Appelle and returned to England, where he died in May 1909.

Brown and Vallance prepared plans for this 1913 building, but in the end a design from Edgar M. Storey and William Van Egmond was chosen.

In 1928, the single-storey addition to the east end of the house was completed.

HARDING HOUSE

1731 College Avenue

*H*arding House was originally known as the Maple Leaf Hostel when it was erected in 1925. The Fellowship of the Maple Leaf was a society formed in England to send British teachers to schools in western Canada. Established in 1918, the hostel was a residence for British students attending Normal School.

During the Depression, there was a surplus of teachers so the hostel provided accommodation for Anglican teachers in training and business girls coming to the city for training or work.

During WW II, Harding House was rented to the RCAF for $300 a month. Following the war there was a dire lack of housing, so it was used for the housing of women, particularly those who had returned from war service, under the supervision of the YWCA.

Harding House served as the fourth home of St. Chad's Theological College from 1952 until 1964.

Saskatchewan Social Services currently maintains offices in this building.

BISHOP'S COURT

1701 College Avenue

A single anonymous donor from England paid for the construction of Bishop's Court in 1926. Designed by Francis H. Portnall, a prominent Regina architect, this building was the official residence of the Bishop of Qu'Appelle.

Right Reverend E. H. Knowles was the first bishop to live in Bishop's Court. He became bishop in the depths of the depression and guided the church through very difficult times, which only improved after the country had again gone to war.

Under Bishop Knowles' direction the diocese had succeeded in climbing out of debt by 1949.

On Bishop Knowles' retirement, the synod of the diocese elected Canon Michael Coleman, who was subsequently consecrated as the sixth Bishop of Qu'Appelle.

CARMICHAEL PRESBYTERIAN/UNITED CHURCH

1431 15th Avenue

WILLIAM ARGAN

*C*armichael Presbyterian Church was established in 1912 by the congregation of Knox Presbyterian Church to serve its members on the southeast side of the city. It was named after Reverend Dr. John A. Carmichael, pastor of Knox Church for 12 years prior to his appointment in 1902 as the superintendent of Presbyterian Missions for the North-West Territories. The church was originally on 2200 block Halifax Street. The cornerstone of the present Late Gothic Revival building was laid in 1920.

In February 1923, CKCK Radio aired the first live broadcast of a church service in the British Empire from this location. "Rev. J. W. Whillans of Carmichael Church had been a chaplain with the air force in France; he was already aware of radio's significance when it arrived in Regina, and CKCK had carried some religious programs from the studio before Mr. Whillans broached his novel idea for a direct broadcast of a church service. With the co-operation of announcer-operator-engineer Bert Hooper and the Government Telephones, a special line was strung to Carmichael Church in preparation for the broadcast of the evening service. However, on February 11, 1923, the morning service came in so well that Bert Hooper decided to put it on the air without the knowledge of the minister or the congregation." – Drake, *Regina*

In 1925, when Presbyterian and Methodist congregations across Canada voted in favour of union, to form the United Church of Canada, the Carmichael congregation joined the unionists.

The addition on the west side of the church was completed in 1957. The last service at Carmichael was held on June 15, 1995.

WESTMINSTER PRESBYTERIAN CHURCH/ WESTMINSTER UNITED CHURCH

3025 13th Avenue

*A*s early as 1912, two of the largest churches in Regina, Knox Presbyterian and Metropolitan Methodist, realized new churches were needed to serve the growing city. The Presbyterians held a meeting on March 28, 1912. Thirty-eight people were present. The congregation that formed was known as Westminster Presbyterian congregation. The following Sunday the first Sunday school was held in the Arena Rink on Robinson Street.

The first service was held on September 1, 1912, in Victoria School. Further services were held at St. Paul's Anglican Church until December 15, when the south section of Westminster Church was ready for use.

Shortly after the cyclone of 1912, construction began on Westminster Presbyterian church at 3025 13th Avenue. The first service was held on May 11, 1913.

Members of the Methodist Church living west of Albert Street organized a new congregation, Fourteenth Avenue Methodist. The church building was located on 14th Avenue at Retallack Street. The congregation worshipped there until 1925, when Fourteenth Avenue Methodist and Westminster Presbyterian became Westminster United Church – a part of the union of Methodist, Presbyterian and Congregational churches which took place across Canada.

On May 31, 1925, the congregation of Fourteenth Avenue Methodist Church, led by the Salvation Army band playing "Onward Christian Soldiers", marched west on 14th Avenue to Cameron Street and north on Cameron Street to 13th Avenue. The members of Westminster Presbyterian Church were lined up on either side of the street outside of the church. As the Methodists approached, the Presbyterians joined arms with them and escorted them into the inaugural service as members of Westminster United Church.

In 1963 an addition to Westminster United Church included the Pioneer Memorial Chapel.

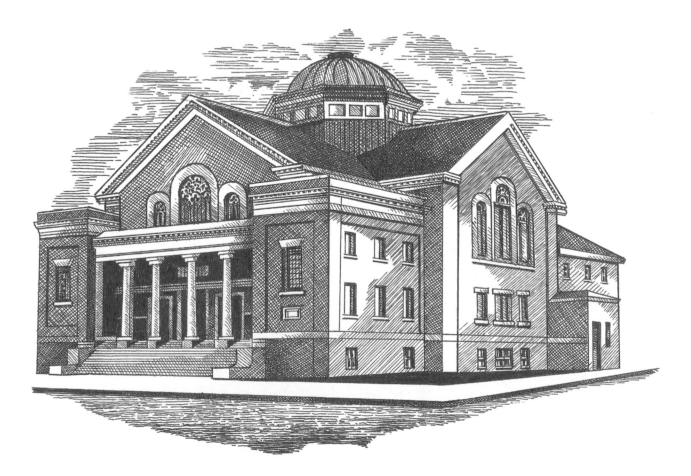

HOLY ROSARY CATHEDRAL

13th Avenue and Garnet Street

*B*etween 1,500 and 2,000 people attended the blessing of Holy Rosary Cathedral, dedicated to Our Lady of the Rosary, on June 29, 1913. Some crowded the steps while others watched from the streetcar tracks in front of the church.

The designer of the cathedral was Montreal architect J. E. Fortin and the general contractor was the Regina firm of Smith Brothers & Wilson.

Construction of Holy Rosary Cathedral had been under way for only one month when the June 30, 1912 cyclone left much of Regina's downtown area in a shambles. The area about the cathedral was left relatively intact. Bishop Mathieu celebrated the first mass in the cathedral on November 23, 1913 and greetings were given by three prominent Catholic laymen: J. O'Connor in English, Attorney General W. F. A. Turgeon in French and Frank Brunner in German.

The cathedral's interior was redecorated in 1928, 1951, 1968 and 1977.

In February 1949, thirty-three stained-glass windows, most of which were donated by parishioners, were added to the cathedral's interior at a cost of $28,500. The windows were created and installed by world-famous artist M. Andre Rault of Rennes, France.

One of the windows was donated by Mrs. A. E. Forget in memory of her husband, Saskatchewan's first lieutenant-governor.

BETH JACOB SYNAGOGUE

1913 to 1946
Ottawa Street between Victoria
and 13th Avenues

*T*he first Jewish settlements in Saskatchewan were rural. It wasn't until about 1900 that Saskatchewan's first significant urban Jewish community arose in Regina. In 1905 there were sufficient members to form a minyan or quorum for complete worship services. From 1905 to 1909, Jewish people held religious services in private homes or hired halls during the High Holy Days. They introduced weekly services in 1910. A building committee was organized in 1912 and there was a successful canvass of all Jewish citizens, so that the new synagogue was built free of all debt or encumbrance.

In the spring of 1913, the foundation stone was laid for the Beth Jacob Synagogue on Ottawa Street. The building was a modest brick structure with a ladies' gallery and a full basement.

During the opening ceremonies, a procession bearing an ancient Hebrew scroll and other insignia marched to the new building and addresses were delivered. Once the procession reached the synagogue, Sam Pearlman announced that he had a golden key for auction. The winner would use it to open the building. Mr. M. Prosterman of Moose Jaw won the auction by bidding $100 for the key. He presented it to his father, one of the first Jews in Regina, and Mr. S. Prosterman opened the new synagogue. When the door was open, over 200 Jews from the city and area entered to celebrate the new facility which had a mikva (ritual bath). Following the formal ceremonies, everyone went to the basement to eat, sing and dance.

With the completion of the synagogue shortly before Rosh Hashanah in 1913, negotiations began with the City of Regina for the formal transfer of title of the two acres of land already in use as a Jewish cemetery. The arrangements were completed two years later and resulted in the official consecration of the Broad Street cemetery, still in use today.

Regina's second permanent synagogue was located at 1640 Victoria Avenue. The building's cornerstone was laid by Mrs. F. Silverman on November 20, 1949 and construction was completed less than ten months later. To signify spiritual continuity, 100 bricks from the old synagogue were incorporated into the structure of the new one.

With a change in the population size and the move by members to the south and southeast parts of Regina, the local Jewish community opened a new synagogue and the Victoria Avenue building was sold.

1640 Victoria Avenue

BETH JACOB SYNAGOGUE

4715 McTavish Street

O ver time, the local Jewish community has decreased in size and dispersed, primarily into the south and southeastern part of the city. In response to these trends, a new synagogue was opened at 4715 McTavish in 1993, in what was formerly St. Leo's Catholic School.

The synagogue at 1640 Victoria Avenue was sold in 1992 and subsequently became a print shop. The only remaining vestige of its former use is the cast-concrete menorah, a branched candelabra which is a traditional symbol of Israel, on the west wall of the building. The rest of the religiously significant ornamentation, including 12 stained-glass windows (representing the 12 Tribes of Israel), was removed and most of it reinstalled in the new synagogue.

HEBREW SCHOOL/TALMUD TORAH

2060 Halifax Street

R egina's Jewish community opened a Hebrew School in 1913 in rented quarters on 11th Avenue with 40 children and two teachers. By the early 1920s, a new facility was required to meet the growing student population.

Reverend Rabbi Kahanovitch, Chief Rabbi of Winnipeg, assisted in the laying of the cornerstone for the Talmud Torah (Hebrew school), on May 11, 1924. The community treated the event as a Jewish holiday, complete with a parade led by the Scouts' band. Another impressive ceremony was held when the new building was completed in September 1924. At the opening were several dignitaries, including the Chief Justice of Saskatchewan, the Attorney General, the Minister of Education and the Mayor of Regina.

The total cost of the building was estimated at $55,000, of which $45,000 was raised during the construction process. The architectural designs were prepared by Storey and Van Egmond. The two-storey building contained four classrooms, cloak rooms, a recreation room, kitchen and an auditorium.

Classes began on October 22, 1924 with three teachers and 150 students. Jewish children attended public schools in the city so classes took place after school and on Sundays. Hebrew lessons supplemented their education in the Hebrew language and literature, as well as Jewish history, culture and religion.

When the Ottawa Street synagogue was condemned as unsafe in October 1946, services were transferred to the Talmud Torah until Beth Jacob Synagogue on Victoria Avenue was opened in 1950. The Hebrew School building was sold in 1954 and classrooms were added to the new synagogue. The new synagogue wing was officially opened on April 18, 1955.

CKRM Radio, a component of the Harvard Communications group, has been in the Halifax Street building since 1954.

ST. GEORGE ROMANIAN ORTHODOX CATHEDRAL

2005 Edgar Street

*R*omanians were among the pioneers who settled Canada's prairie provinces. Initially, in the Regina area, they worshipped at the little St. Nicholas Church, built on St. John Street in 1902. After two decades of steady immigration, there were too many Romanians in the Regina area for St. Nicholas Church to accommodate.

Built of wood, at a cost of $24,000, St. George Romanian Orthodox Church was erected in 1914 at Edgar Street and Victoria Avenue. In 1928 a fire destroyed part of the church.

St. George took on a new look after this, renovations included a lofty Byzantine onion dome which replaced the peak of the former tower. The onion-shaped dome was popular in Ukraine and the rest of northeastern Europe because of the weight of snow that accumulated on church domes. In order to make the snow slide down easily, to avert collapse, church architects began to build domes with pointed peaks. Thus the onion-shaped dome was born.

1914 to 1928

1928 to 1959

As a preventive measure against fire, the church was eventually faced with imitation brick, placed over tin squares, reinforcing the weakened structure. Further improvements and changes came with the years. Beginning in 1950, the church's interior was lined with veneer and chandeliers were added. Most revolutionary was the installation of pews. Three-and-one-half-hour services with everyone standing became a thing of the past, even though for a while some of the old-timers refused to use the pews.

Construction of a large brick church started in 1959. The cathedral was finished in 1960 at a cost of $189,000.

The new structure was the largest Romanian Orthodox Church in Canada — capable of housing up to 500 people. The basement was divided into a banquet hall, kitchen and classrooms.

1960 –

HOLY TRINITY SERBIAN ORTHODOX CHURCH

1775 Winnipeg Street

*B*uilt in 1916, the church was originally located at 1844 McAra Street. In 1933 the building was moved to 1775 Winnipeg Street, at 11th Avenue.

This basilica-plan church was completed in 1933 for Regina's small Serbian community. It replaced the McAra Street church.

The building features gothic windows and a bull's eye window above the arched entrance. The tiered bell tower is topped with a cross. Previously faced with stucco and wood, the exterior of the church was totally refinished with brick and stone in 1992.

Holy Trinity Church has close ties to the Serbian Canadian Cultural Club (see page 345).

GRACE LUTHERAN CHURCH

1037 Victoria Avenue

*I*n 1924 Grace Lutheran Church was organized. A building located in the 1800 block of Winnipeg Street was bought to accommodate the church membership at Victoria Avenue and Quebec Street. By 1954 the congregation had outgrown the quarters so this building was demolished and a new church was built in 1955.

Henry P. Baker, the city's longest serving mayor, was secretary of Grace Lutheran Church's board for more than 25 years.

Henry P. Baker

FIRST PRESBYTERIAN CHURCH

2170 Albert Street

A meeting of the General Assembly of the Presbyterian Church, in 1916, led to the union of the Presbyterian, Methodist and Congregational Churches as the United Church of Canada. In 1925, those opposed to this policy organized throughout the country.

Judge W. M. Martin, later Chief Justice of Saskatchewan, had called upon all of the Knox Presbyterian members dissenting from the union vote to organize a new Presbyterian congregation for Regina.

First Presbyterian Church was founded early in January 1925, to continue Presbyterian witness and tradition at the time of church union.

Services were held in the City Hall auditorium on January 11, 1925. The congregation worshipped here until First Presbyterian Church was built. The auditorium of First Baptist Church was made available on certain occasions.

A building site was donated by Mr. and Mrs. M. E. Gardiner at the corner of 14th Avenue and Albert Street. F. H. Portnall was the architect. The first sod was turned by M. E. Gardiner on May 31, 1926.

Mr. W. H. Duncan laid the cornerstone of First Presbyterian Church on August 18, 1926. He had been a member of the group that had prepared a livery stable tent for the first Presbyterian service held in Regina on September 3, 1882.

The building was dedicated upon completion on January 9, 1927, by Dr. A. S. MacGillivray, Moderator of the General Assembly, just two years after the congregation had been formed.

The Christian Education Centre was added to First Presbyterian Church in 1959.

ST. MATTHEW'S ANGLICAN CHURCH

2165 Winnipeg Street

An Anglican Sunday School was organized in 1907 by people living on the east side of the city. Classes were initially held at the Broder farm, located south and east of Winnipeg Street and Victoria Avenue. A small wooden church, named Grace Church in memory of their daughter, was erected on four lots donated by George Broder. Broder had immigrated to Canada from Ireland in 1855 and came to the North-West Territories in 1883. While delivering supplies during the Northwest Rebellion he was held prisoner for 3 weeks. Broder moved to Regina in 1886 and operated a dairy farm on land east of Regina, later known as Broder's Annex. He also built the Broder Building (Medical and Dental Building) and owned the Champlain Hotel building (see page 174).

Between WW I and WW II, the congregation moved to the corner of Winnipeg Street and 14th Avenue. They worshiped in the church basement until the church was completed in 1926. At that time, the name of Grace Church was changed to St. Matthew's. Canon Basil Prockter wrote: "One suspects that some of our Victorian church leaders felt that Grace was not sufficiently dignified. Women were very secondary to men in those days, and especially in church."

The church basement was also the headquarters of the Fifth Regina Scout Troop.

In 1961, Grace Broder's three sisters paid for the finishing and furnishing of the Grace Broder Memorial Chapel.

In February 1986, 16 historical stained-glass windows were installed in the church. All of the scenes tell of how a multi-cultural congregation came to be housed at 2165 Winnipeg Street

In September 1987, a nine-foot circular window was installed at St. Matthew's to replace one that was destroyed by 11 shots from a high-powered rifle in August 1985. Reverend Bernard Shaw said that church members were happy the window was replaced, "It's been very dark at that end of the church and now we'll have light again."

ST. MICHAEL'S UKRAINIAN ORTHODOX CHURCH

McDonald Street and 13th Avenue

S t. Michael's Ukrainian Orthodox Church officially opened on November 21, 1926. At the dedication ceremony, a list of donors to the church fund, members of the church, the bishop and clergy, as well as a copy of the *Morning Leader* and information about current government officials, was secreted in a small receptacle which was later placed under the altar. The exterior of the church was refinished in the late 1960s.

1821 Winnipeg Street

UKRAINIAN ORTHODOX CHURCH OF THE DESCENT OF THE HOLY GHOST

1821 Winnipeg Street/1305 12th Avenue

S ometime after WW I, a stream of first and second generation Ukrainians moved to Regina where they formed a substantial colony. By 1927 the colony had grown so much it could afford to build two churches. This church was dedicated to the Descent of the Holy Ghost.

The consecration of this Ukrainian Greek Orthodox Church took place on April 1, 1928.

In 1960 the sod was turned on the site of the new Church of the Descent of the Holy Ghost at 12th Avenue and

Toronto Street. The first service in the new church was held January 6, 1961 – Christmas Eve, as observed by Orthodox Ukrainians.

On June 4, 1978, His Beatitude Metropolitan Wasyly raised the status of the church to that of a Sobor (Pro-Cathedral). This recognized the church's prominence in the diocese, its historical background and its location in the capital city of the province.

The church completed a new auditorium at 1625 Montreal Street by May 1981. Adjacent lots were purchased by the Society of Prosvita and were donated for additional parking. An adjacent Prosvita building serves as a general office and meeting place.

In 1991, the church officially opened its seniors' complex, Selo Gardens, at 1106 McNiven Avenue. Sixty-eight suites are available for seniors of the church community and others who wish to enjoy retirement in a pleasant setting.

The congregation of the Descent of the Holy Spirit Church (Sobor) recently celebrated the 75th Anniversary of its establishment in Regina.

1305 12th Avenue

SACRED HEART ROMAN CATHOLIC CHURCH

1380 Elphinstone Street

S acred Heart Church was formally erected on September 25, 1927, but its history as a mission of Holy Rosary Cathedral began with religious services in 1923.

The original Sacred Heart Church, often referred to as "the Chapel of Ease", was located on the corner of Elphinstone Street and 8th Avenue. It was only 25 by 50 feet, but it served parishioners' needs at the time. The Redemptorist Fathers of the Cathedral parish served there from 1923 to 1927. That building later became the rectory.

Before 1923 there were few homes located within the city limits north of the CPR tracks. With growing development of the city's north side, the number of Catholics also increased. At the first meeting of the Board of Trustees, on October 10, 1927, plans were discussed for providing accommodation for the parish. At that time it was necessary to have four masses a Sunday to meet parish needs.

The church hall, erected in the 1300 block Elphinstone Street, was used as a parish hall and church until the new church was built in the 1950s. In September 1928, the new hall and Sacred Heart School were completed. Archbishop Mathieu, then a patient at Grey Nuns Hospital, attended a parish supper at the hall on September 25, 1928 – it was his last public appearance.

The third decade of Sacred Heart Parish was a time of rapid expansion, marked by growing enrollment at Sacred Heart School and the construction of the new Sacred Heart Church, which was blessed on November 11, 1956.

The *Leader-Post* reported: "It will have a room with a soundproof window from which mothers with crying infants can see the altar or hear over a loud-speaker what is going on in the church."

The church, designed by Lithuanian architect Jonas Labenskas of Regina, took a year and a half to build. It could seat 600 and cost $260,000.

ST. MARY'S ANGLICAN CHURCH

3337 15th Avenue

S t. Mary's Anglican Church came about in stages. In 1912 the parish of St. Mary the Virgin was established in the west end of the city. In 1913 two lots were purchased on which to build a church for the newly formed parish and a frame church was built.

In 1921 the first Girl Guide company in Regina was organized at St. Mary's Church.

The foundation stone of the church shown here was laid in June 1927 and the new building was dedicated on October 27 of the same year.

When the church was completed, permanent furniture was installed in the nave, but further progress was delayed because of the depression and drought.

In January 1945 it was voted to raise funds to purchase a two-manual, 15-stop pipe organ which was installed in time for Easter services. The organ was dedicated April 25, 1946. The guest organist was Arnold Goldsborough, assistant organist at Westminster Abbey, London.

In 1954 the church was enlarged 32 feet at the west end. A gothic-style stained-glass window, depicting Christ in three stages as Saviour of the world, was installed in 1958. The window arrived from England, carefully packed in sections. A cutter had to be brought from Winnipeg to fit it into the rear church wall.

CATHOLIC YOUTH CENTRE

2030 Hamilton Street

t. Mary's Hall was erected in 1911 at 2030 Hamilton Street, east of what was St. Mary's Church on Scarth Street, now known as Blessed Sacrament Church.

The hall served as a social centre for the parish. It became the headquarters for various organizations including the Knights of Columbus.

The meeting hall for the Knights was located in the Burns-Hanley building on Cornwall Street. In 1934, St. Mary's Hall became the centre for the Catholic Youth Crusade and it was renamed the C.Y. Centre.

The hall was demolished after it was condemned in 1985.

SETTLEMENT HOUSE

1876 Wallace Street

At the beginning of the 20th century, the Dominion government adopted a vigorous colonization policy, bringing an influx of settlers from countries where the English language was not spoken. As the immigrants settled they continued to use their own languages and follow their native customs.

In 1916, three of Regina's Methodist churches founded Settlement House as a mission to help the newcomers learn the Canadian way of life.

Miss Nellie Forman set up night classes in English and taught immigrant children the English language, Canadian customs and Sunday School lessons. She provided instruction in homemaking and other practical subjects, and organized a variety of social and recreational programs.

The first Settlement House was rented at 1848 Toronto Street where Miss Forman lived and worked. When quarters became cramped Settlement House moved to 1032 Victoria Avenue. Once again space became an issue.

New and larger facilities, including a gymnasium, were opened on Wallace Street in 1927. Programs continued until 1956, when Settlement House was closed. The building was sold to the Knights of Columbus who used it until 1986. It was vacant until 1991 when the location became home to the Serbian Club.

ST. BASIL'S UKRAINIAN CATHOLIC CHURCH

1733 Toronto Street/1757 Toronto Street

*U*krainian settlers first arrived in Regina about 1890, and by 1925 Ukrainian Catholics constituted a sizeable group in the city. However, there were no facilities in the city for their spiritual needs, which had to be met either in Roman Catholic churches or in centres outside Regina.

The first mass at St. Basil's Ukrainian Catholic Church, 1733 Toronto Street, was celebrated on April 28, 1929. This building was demolished when the new church was completed.

1733 Toronto Street

1757 Toronto Street

In 1960 this new St. Basil's Church was constructed at 1757 Toronto Street to replace the older St. Basil's Church that had become too small for the congregation.

ST. ANTHONY'S ROMAN CATHOLIC CHURCH

2235 Atkinson Street

*O*riginally, the Polish people of Regina belonged to St. Mary's Parish. However, many of them couldn't understand the services at St. Mary's as they were conducted in German.

After the WW I, Polish immigrants started organizing a church, but it wasn't until June 1930 that St. Anthony's celebrated its first mass. The delay was due to lack of money. In 1930 only 18 men in the Polish community, which comprised 130 families, were employed. The 18 pledged $450 toward the building of the church and everyone who was able donated their time, committing to at least 92 hours of labour each. A considerable number of people each put in over 500 hours of work.

In 1931 Monsignor Anthony Gocki came to Regina full time and, with the families of his parish, built St. Anthony's. Gocki points out, "We didn't pay five cents for labour outside of the plumber and the electrician. There's not a single shingle on the rectory roof that I did not nail myself."

Gocki was involved in many community and church activities in his lifetime of service. He organized the first Roman Catholic scout troop in Regina. A scout camping trip in 1945 took him to a piece of pasture land in the Qu'Appelle Valley where he founded Camp Monahan. He spoke Czechoslovakian, Ukrainian, Serbian and French as well as Polish. Pastor of St. Anthony's from 1931 to 1974 and from 1981 to 1983, he was a missionary, "immigration officer", hockey coach, scholar, carpenter, recreation director and parish priest during his career.

In 1980, on the occasion of Monsignor Gocki's 80th birthday, the Government of Saskatchewan named a lake after him, in the Macoun Lake area north of La Ronge, to honour his 58 years of unselfish and devoted service to the community as a priest and his work on countless public community projects.

ST. ANTHONY'S PARISH HALL

1825 Winnipeg Street

*S*t. Anthony's Parish Hall was designed and built by Steelcon Construction Co. in 1963 to serve the Polish community living east of Broad Street.

Monsignor
Anthony Gocki

The hall is the direct result of Monsignor Gocki's leadership. He became known as "the baseball priest" while serving as an assistant at St. Joseph's Catholic Church in Moose Jaw. "Do you play baseball?" he was asked by the priest who interviewed him. When Gocki answered "Yes," the priest said, "Then you are just the man I wanted!" His love of sports and young people became one of his chief interests. Gocki (pronounced Goskey) said, "They called me the baseball priest because they couldn't pronounce my name."

This hall is one of the most popular stops in Regina's Mosaic celebrations as the Polish community showcase their cultural, culinary and dance traditions.

LITTLE FLOWER CATHOLIC CHURCH

Many members of Little Flower Roman Catholic parish were of German descent, the children of pioneers who came to Saskatchewan from Hungary, Austria and Russia. In December 1930 it was decided to detach the eastern portion of St. Mary's Parish to establish Little Flower Parish. Monsignor F. Gerein was appointed to organize the parish and Father A. J. Janssen was the first pastor.

Architect Puntin O'Leary designed a two-story stucco building, with the upper floor as the church and the lower portion serving as the parish hall. Work on the church began during the Depression and was mainly completed by volunteers. The church was blessed by Archbishop McGuigan on April 12, 1931. The cost was $21,809.43.

College Avenue between
Edgar and Elliott Streets

Loretto Convent played a major role in the life of Little Flower Parish. In 1932, at the request of Father Janssen, the Sisters of Loretto opened a house at 526 College Avenue, for social work in Regina East and to house the sisters teaching at St. Augustine School (named after Father Augustine Suffa), located just north of the church. They also taught at Loretto High School, which was opened in 1937. In 1954 the name Loretto High School was changed to St. John Bosco High School. Sisters, lay teachers and assistant Fathers taught at the school until 1966, when the new Regina Roman Catholic High School District was established and Miller High School opened.

By the early 1950s the Little Flower congregation had outgrown their original church. Five masses were being celebrated every Sunday to standing-room-only attendance. Sod was turned for the second Little Flower church on April 18, 1955. The architect was H. K. Black, and the church was constructed by Hilsden and Company, at a cost of over $200,000, to hold 700 people. The first mass was held on August 26, 1956. For many years, four masses were celebrated each Sunday with a total attendance of 2,400 people.

St. John Bosco High School was accommodated in the basement of the church, which was designed with six classrooms, a library, and an office built around a large assembly area.

420 College Avenue

ST. STEPHEN'S CATHOLIC CHURCH

Reynolds Street between 14th and 15th Avenues

S t. Stephen's church, built in 1932, was demolished in 1986. The congregation of St. Stephen's Catholic Church was largely Hungarian. The church's origins can be traced back to about 1910 when a few Hungarian families settled in Regina. As their numbers grew they held services in the basement of St. Mary's Church, which was located in the 2000 block of Scarth Street. This arrangement, using Hungarian-speaking priests, continued until 1932 when St. Stephen's Parish was established with Father Robert Koch as its first pastor.

The church was named in honour of St. Stephen (c. 975 to 1038), the first king of Hungary, who turned Hungary into a largely Christian country.

The first church was situated on the 2200 block Reynolds Street. The congregation purchased the German-Canadian Hall. Using volunteer labour, they converted it into a church and added a hall.

German-Canadian Hall/
St. Stephen's Church

The church was raised and moved onto another lot in 1951, and a full basement was added. The church was expanded and both the interior and exterior were remodelled.

From the 1930s to the 1950s the grey-shingled church housed a congregation of about 500. In 1956, when Hungarian immigrants fled the revolution in their homeland, the parish numbers increased for several years, but membership gradually decreased and the church was forced to close in 1986, having served the Hungarian population of Regina for 54 years.

Father Michael Vezer, who had come to Regina in 1933 from Hungary, served as pastor of St. Stephen's from 1939 until his retirement in 1986.

ST JEAN-BAPTISTE (LA PAROISSE ST JEAN BAPTISTE)

Regina Cleri Seminary, 1932 to 1953
2445 13th Avenue

*T*here has always been a French Catholic presence in Regina. However, until recently, it has not been practical for the French to have their own parish. From 1932 to 1953, the Franciscan Fathers provided special masses for the French in their chapel at the Regina Cleri Seminary, which had been the Archbishop's Palace from 1912 to 1932.

At Christmas in 1953, Archbishop M. C. O'Neill decreed the erection of the St Jean-Baptiste Parish for the French-speaking Catholics of Regina and instructed the Franciscan Fathers to organize the parish.

Under Father Sylvestre Beaudette, O.F.M. about 60 parish families got together and bought the old Odd Fellows Hall on Lorne Street. They converted it into a church, which Archbishop O'Neill blessed on March 28, 1954.

Father Sylvstre was assisted by Fathers Kemble, O.F.M.; Lajoie, O.F.M. and Chabot, O.F.M. He was succeeded by Father Amédée Houle, O.F.M., in 1955. Illness forced Father Amédée to retire, so Father Sylvestre continued the pastoral ministry until 1956, when Father Rufin Turcotte, O.F.M., became pastor.

In 1962, the parish purchased two lots just south of 25th Avenue and a new parish centre was inaugurated in December 1963.

The Franciscans looked after St. Jean-Baptiste until 1974, when the Oblates of Mary Immaculate assumed charge. Father Albert Gervais, O.M.I., followed by Father Benoit Paris, O.M.I., were pastors until 1985, when Father Louis Philippe Jean from the Archdiocese of St. Boniface, Manitoba, assumed charge.

1954 to 1964
Lorne Street

The parish has been very active over the years and has been very involved in the development of the francophone community. Classes in French, for both children and adults, have been offered. Before the establishment of French immersion schools, the parish was involved in the teaching of French in Regina. L'Ecole Mathieu was even part of the parish centre. Various parochial societies, such as the Conseil Langevin (French council of the Knights of Columbus), Les Dames de L'Autel and Le Club d'Age d'Or have been set up and are still active. For many years, a French credit union or caisse populaire operated out of the church on 25th Avenue. Other groups, such as the French Scouts and l'Ecole Monseigneur de Laval, benefit from a close association with the parish.

The parish is soundly organized and has a very active parish council.

St Jean-Baptiste continues as Regina's only French parish.

1963 –
2517 25th Avenue

LAKEVIEW UNITED CHURCH

3200 McCallum Avenue

A new pastoral charge was formed in the Lakeview district of Regina in 1946. It was the first church of any denomination in the rapidly developing Lakeview area. Worship services began in Lakeview Public School in 1948. A church hall building committee, headed by C. E. Hird, was formed in 1949, and a major building campaign was organized under the leadership of Dr. H. M. Graham, with the assistance of architect H. K. Black. The church hall was built by Poole Construction and was opened in 1951.

The Building Committee for Phase 2 Lakeview United Church was headed by Chairman J. D. Rowand and committee members, F. M. Froom, Dr. W. A. Riddell, Mrs W. S. Allan, J. E. Beamish and Reverend J. R. Hurd. The building was designed by H. K. Black and built by Piggott Construction Co. Ltd.

The dedication and opening services of Lakeview United Church were held on October 10th, 1956.

CHRIST THE KING CHURCH

3239 Garnet Street

*B*y the early 1950s, residential building in the Lakeview area experienced rapid growth and development. Catholic residents of this area formed part of the parish of Holy Rosary Cathedral. This was soon to change.

On September 3, 1955, Archbishop M. C. O'Neill appointed Father Emmett Mooney as pastor of a new parish south of Wascana Creek. The first Mass was held in the St. Pius X School basement and Father Mooney performed his pastoral duties out of the rectory of Holy Rosary Cathedral. Numerous names were considered for the new parish, including St. Pius X, St. Patrick, St. Joseph and Christ the King. Parishioners voted for the name Christ the King.

Fundraising began and E. J. McCudden was retained as architect, with Poole Construction Ltd. as the contractor. On the evening of December 24, 1956, Father Mooney celebrated Midnight Mass in the new Christ the King Church. The cost of the church and rectory was $152,000. It accommodates between 500 and 600 people.

Archbishop O'Neill formally blessed the church on January 13, 1957. The tower at the front of the church was not part of the original construction, but was built later.

The wood carving of Christ the King, on the wall behind the altar, came from Italy. The Stations of the Cross were carved by J. Guardo, an Italian sculptor living in Montreal. The marble statues of Our Lady and St. Joseph, purchased through Mr. Guardo, are thought to be carved in Italy. Antonini and Sons Ltd. supplied the baptismal font and constructed the Botticinium marble altar from a design provided by Father Mooney. The altar is one of the few in the city that is consecrated. The consecration ceremony was performed by Archbishop O'Neill on November 3, 1957, with relics of the Holy Martyrs Speciosa and Beata deposited in the altar.

In 1962 the parish had grown to approximately 470 families, much of it due to the residential growth in the Hillsdale and Whitmore Park communities. Accordingly, the Archbishop established the parishes of St. Anne and St. Martin.

WILLIAM P. ARGAN

REGINA CHINESE ALLIANCE CHURCH

3010 Arens Road East

*T*he first Chinese Alliance Church in North America was officially formed on January 29, 1961 in Regina, and was headed by Reverend Augustus Chao, formerly of Hong Kong.

Before the church's formation in 1961, Ruby Johnston began an outreach program, in 1932, for the Chinese in Regina. At that time there were only about two Chinese families, but a number of Chinese men worked in restaurants, laundries and shoe repair shops.

In 1945, students from Western Canadian Bible Institute (now Canadian Bible College) gave Chinese men lessons in English and the Bible. With the change of immigration laws in 1947, women and young people were permitted to come to Regina and families were established.

In 1955 the Regina Chinese Christian Fellowship was formed and, in 1956, Sunday worship took place in the afternoon at the Alliance Church on Osler Street and 13th Avenue. There was an adult ladies' English class and a Sunday School was organized for children.

At the 1964 Provincial Exhibition, $2,000 was raised for the church building fund by selling Chinese food. In 1967 the Alliance Tabernacle was built in another part of the city, so the Chinese purchased the previous Alliance Church building for $50,000. On July 2, 1967 the building was dedicated. By 1977 the church had witnessed conspicuous growth, with Sunday worship attendance averaging 191. By 1984 Sunday School attendance reached 200. To accommodate the increase, a nearby elementary school was rented.

During the church's silver jubilee in 1986, it was decided to purchase 1.56 acres of land and build a new church. On September 6, 1987 the sod-turning ceremony took place, and on October 9, 1988 the first worship service was held at 3010 Arens Road East.

In 1995 Ken Yee was appointed pastor for the English-speaking ministry. In 1999 the old building was sold.

ST. MARTIN DE PORRES CHURCH

4720 Castle Road

*T*he parish was first formed in 1962 with 175 families. The congregation originally assembled in the gym of St. Matthew's School, until St. Martin's Hall was completed in December of that year. St. Martin's Church Hall then became the chapel and centre for all activities until the church proper was completed.

The church was designed by Black, Larson, McMillan and Partners and built by Bird Construction Co. Ltd. Construction was completed and the first mass was held on June 24, 1966.

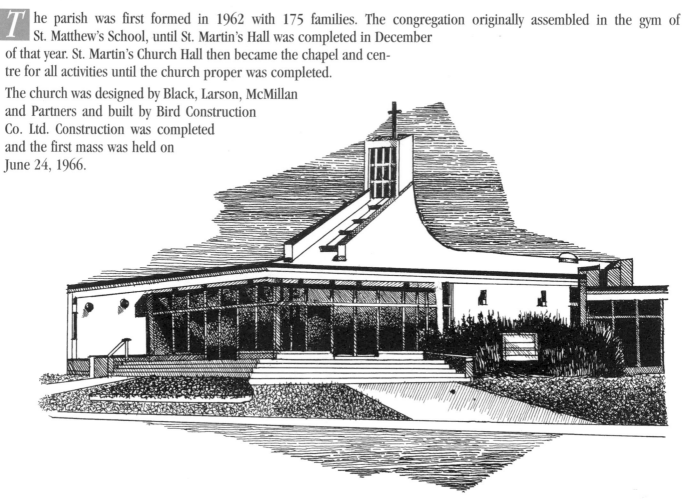

In the early 1960s, when the parish was being formed, a small baseball league began to take shape in Whitmore Park. Carl Mazzei, a member of St. Martin's Parish, ran the league and it became known as the "Mazzei League".

By 1967 the league had grown and Carl Mazzei had left the parish. The St. Martin's Men's Club accepted responsibility for the organization and management of the league, including the purchase and maintenance of equipment. The league was renamed Whitmore Park Baseball League. Games were played on three diamonds at three locations: in the park behind St. Martin's; the park on Norris Road; in Richardson Park on Shannon Road. The championship games, always held in the park behind St. Martin's, attracted large crowds for the games, trophy presentations and the festivities that followed.

St. Martin's has supported the Consuelo mission in the Dominican Republic since 1973. The project was initiated by former pastor, the late Father John Reidy. Since that time an annual collection, ranging between $4,000 and $5,000, has been forwarded directly by St. Martin's to the Grey Sisters in Consuelo. The money has been used for the first van for the medical clinic; assisting with training support services at the Womens' Centre; providing financial assistance to the multi-purpose centre, and a senior's centre for Haitian men who formerly worked in the sugar fields. St. Martin's has also provided funding for development of 150 homes for school personnel, and assistance for students wanting to continue their education at university or technical school. Teachers anxious to upgrade their qualifications have also benefited. There are no administrative costs associated with the program. Every dollar received from St. Martin's is used for direct assistance. Since the project was initiated in 1973, every December is "Consuelo" month at St. Martin's.

ST. ANNE'S ROMAN CATHOLIC CHURCH

1701 Cowan Crescent

S t. Anne's Roman Catholic Church, designed by Etienne Gaboury of St. Boniface, and built in 1967, rises in copper-sheeted blocks to a tower with inset stained-glass windows. The stained-glass windows are abstract designs in gold, purple and white, suggesting religious themes, but not detailing them.

From the outside, the lower walls of the building are textured white stucco, with the copper sheeting rising above the white base and soaring upwards to the tower.

The baptismal font and the circular confessional are placed in front of the sanctuary space. The elevated black opalescent granite altar, beneath the 64-foot tower, is the focal point of the church. Arranged in five rows, the pews will accommodate 500 people at a time. In an unusual arrangement, the only entrances to the church are to either side of the altar, a situation that has latecomers facing the congregation as they enter.

Natural lighting above the altar flows in through stained-glass windows, which portray in abstract symbols, doves, water, crosses and rugged lines.

WILLIAM
ARGAN

ST. ATHANASIUS UKRAINIAN CATHOLIC CHURCH

55 McMurchy Avenue

U krainian people began to arrive in Regina about 1890. They organized their first church, St. Basil's, in 1925. The second Ukrainian Catholic parish in the city, St. Athanasius Parish, began in May 1966 when property was purchased at McMurchy Avenue and Sheppard Street. The plans called for a multi-purpose centre to be constructed first, with a church built later. St. Athanasius was established in 1972, within a parish centre designed for spiritual, cultural and social use.

Construction of the church and administrative areas began in June 1977. The Divine Liturgy was first celebrated in the church on February 26, 1978.

The church, built along modern lines, offers a blend of traditional Byzantine Ukrainian architecture in the design of the sanctuary and its fixtures. On the exterior it is expressed in the tower dome. Constructed at a cost of $32,000, the tower rises to a height of 55 feet.

In the sanctuary, two pillars are anchored and two are exposed. The interchanging arch, spanning a diameter of 16 feet and rising an additional ten feet, caps the four pillars. It is tied together with a two-foot quartz ring, painted black. The pillars are painted white. A hollow five-inch black metal cross is 30 feet long. The arms of the cross are three feet. Rising an additional ten feet above the arch, it gives the tower a height of 65 feet.

The dome symbolizes the sacred utensils used in the Ukrainian Catholic Church at the celebration of the divine liturgy.

WILLIAM ARGAN

ST. PAUL'S GREEK ORTHODOX CHURCH

3000 Argyle Road

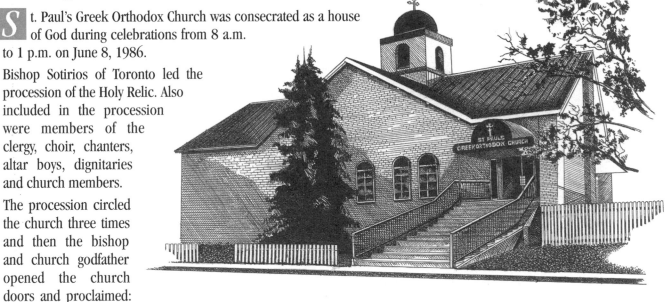

S t. Paul's Greek Orthodox Church was consecrated as a house of God during celebrations from 8 a.m. to 1 p.m. on June 8, 1986.

Bishop Sotirios of Toronto led the procession of the Holy Relic. Also included in the procession were members of the clergy, choir, chanters, altar boys, dignitaries and church members.

The procession circled the church three times and then the bishop and church godfather opened the church doors and proclaimed:

"Open your gates, open wide the ancient doors and the King of Glory will enter."

The service, steeped in centuries-old tradition, calls for the Holy Relics of the Martyrs to be placed in the crypt of the altar.

The bishop washed, anointed and sanctified the holy altar with rosewater and blessed oil from the Ecumenical Patriarchate in Constantinople. Concluding the consecration, the bishop anointed all of the Byzantine-style icons and the narthex of the church.

Returning to the nave, the bishop lit the eternal light and invited the faithful to add a drop of oil to the altar's eternal lamp.

HINDU TEMPLE

3702 Pasqua Street

I n the late 1980s, the number of people who emigrated from India had increased to the point that there were enough Hindus living in Regina to enable the building of a Hindu temple.

A temple committee was organized, and by 1990 sufficient funds were pledged for the construction of a Temple. It is supported by approximately 100 families.

Hinduism differs from Christianity and other Western religions in that it does not have a single founder, a specific system of morality, or a central religious organization. It consists of thousands of different religious groups that have evolved in India since 1500 BC.

Hinduism has grown to become the world's third largest religion, after Christianity and Islam. It claims as members about 13 per cent of the world's population and is the dominant religion in India, Nepal, and among the Tamils in Sri Lanka. It is estimated there are about 157,000 Hindus in Canada.

REGINA'S FIRST HOSPITAL

McIntyre Street and 11th Avenue

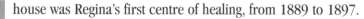

A house was Regina's first centre of healing, from 1889 to 1897.

Scarlet fever, diphtheria, typhoid fever and smallpox were major causes of illness and death in the Queen City during the last two decades of the 19th century and well into the 20th century.

Although the town began laying sewer lines in 1891, Regina was served by one trash collector who dumped his cart, filled with debris and excreta, at the town's edge.

From the founding of Regina until 1889, the closest hospital was in Medicine Hat. Recognizing the critical need for a local hospital, Mrs. Mary E. Truesdell, a teacher, opened a private hospital in her two-storey home on the corner of 11th Avenue and McIntyre Street in 1889.

The hospital accommodated four men and two women and served Regina's citizens for eight years. Over the next few years, Mary and her staff assisted at operations and births, and nursed many patients, including victims of the typhoid epidemic of 1892.

COTTAGE HOSPITAL

Southeast corner of Hamilton Street and 13th Avenue

I n 1895, a group known as the Regina Local Council of Women started campaigning for the building of a public hospital. Support was poor, partly because Regina was in the midst of a depression.

Despite the poor response, the women raised funds through public subscription, and a grant from the Cottage Hospital Fund of the newly established Victorian Order of Nurses.

Regina's Cottage Hospital opened in a rented house in 1898. Staffed by the Victorian Order of Nurses, this new hospital had beds for seven patients. In charge was Miss Mary McCullough, one of the first to be trained in Victorian Order work.

Within two years, the hospital could not meet the community's needs, and in 1901 the Victoria Hospital was erected at Hamilton Street and 14th Avenue.

VICTORIA HOSPITAL

Southwest corner of Hamilton Street and 14th Avenue

*T*he Victorian Order of Nurses contributed $1,500 toward the $9,000 cost of Regina's new hospital on the understanding that it would be named the Victoria Hospital, which it was until 1907.

Opening in 1901 on Hamilton Street and 14th Avenue, Victoria Hospital had beds for 25 patients, its own water supply and sewage system, central heating, electric lights and telephone. It was Regina's hospital when Regina became a city in 1903.

Although health-care facilities had improved, some patients still had to be turned away from Victoria Hospital, which was dependent largely on public donations.

The government grant, in 1901, of 25 cents per day for each patient did not cover the costs. The responsibilities of caring for the sick, 40 per cent of whom were charity cases, plunged the hospital into debt by 1903. That year, the hospital board asked city council for a grant of $400, but they were refused.

On December 1, 1907 the city took over the Victoria Hospital, at the request of its overwhelmed board of directors. The name was changed to the Regina General Hospital. The hospital was moved to its present site in 1909.

Regina became a healthier city when comprehensive health bylaws were passed that made water and sewer connections obligatory, where available. The number of reported typhoid cases fell from 71 per 1,000 of population in 1906 to 3 per 1,000 in 1911.

REGINA HOSPITAL

14 block Angus Street

*R*egina's health-care conditions improved in June 1907, when the Order of Grey Nuns opened a hospital in the existing Park Sanitarium, located on 14 block Angus Street. The Sisters began caring for the five patients who were already there on June 26, and two days later the Regina Hospital was officially opened by Lieutenant-Governor Forget.

The *Leader* reported that Forget referred to the work which had been done in Canada by the Order of Grey Nuns: "Long before railroads had been laid across the prairies the Grey Nuns had come and had faced all descriptions of dangers and difficulties. They had been attending to the sick and suffering wherever humanity had been found from the boundary line to the Arctic Ocean."

The hospital's three floors could accommodate 30 patients in a pinch and "in case of an epidemic probably a number of tents could be erected on adjoining lands."

There was a great demand for the Sisters' services, but when they asked the city for $20,000 in 1907 taxpayers defeated the motion. By April 1909, the Sisters began refusing patients. A committee met with city council and council voted unanimously to offer the Sisters a site for a new hospital building. While waiting for the new building, the Sisters added a section to the old building. This was opened on September 13, 1909. By March of the next year plans were drawn up for the new hospital. They moved to the Grey Nuns Hospital on September 12, 1912.

REGINA HEALTH

egina's first hospital was a private hospital created in 1889 in a two-storey home located on the corner of 11th Avenue and McIntyre Street.

In 1898, the Cottage Hospital, a rented house on the southeast corner of Hamilton Street and 13th Avenue, opened as Regina's first public hospital. Health-care demands soon exceeded hospital capacity and three years later, in 1901, the Victoria Hospital opened on Hamilton Street and 14th Avenue.

The Victoria Hospital was named in recognition of the Victorian Order of Nurses' financial and nursing contributions. Subsequently, in December 1907, the City of Regina took over the Victoria Hospital and the name was changed to the Regina General Hospital.

In 1909, the Regina General Hospital moved to its present location at 1440 14th Avenue as a 100-bed, state-of-the-art facility. It was completed in 1911 at a cost of $100,000.

Additions to the south and north ends of the original building were completed in 1913 and in 1927, respectively, bringing the hospital's capacity to 410 beds. By 1949, capacity was increased to over 800 beds, with subsequent additions. The McPherson wing was completed in 1966.

Meanwhile, in June 1907, the Order of Grey Nuns opened the Regina Hospital on the 14 block of Angus Street to accommodate 30 patients. After outgrowing a 1909 expansion of the hospital, the Grey Nuns built a new facility on Dewdney Avenue, between King and Pasqua Streets. On October 6, 1912, the Grey Nuns Hospital was blessed by Bishop Mathieu and one week later it was officially opened by the new Governor General of Canada, the Duke of Connaught. It had a capacity of 80 beds, which could be extended to 100 for emergencies.

A west wing was added in 1914, a nurses' home was added in 1915 and in 1926 the hospital was again enlarged by the addition of the east wing and a new wing on the nurses' home.

Regina General Hospital
1909 –

Nurses' Residence –
General Hospital

General Hospital
2002

DISTRICT

Grey Nuns Hospital
1907 –

Pasqua Hospital
2002

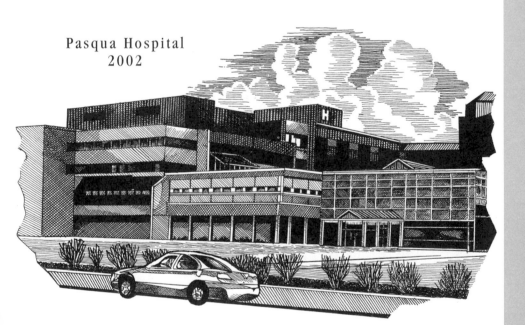

In 1939 a $150,000 cancer clinic was opened. In 1942 a new south wing was added to the hospital at a cost of $150,000. A new four-storey cancer clinic was built in the shape of a cross in 1945. That year a power house was also built and a new laundry was completed.

In 1951, the hospital's appearance was changed with the completion of a three-storey addition along Dewdney Avenue, across the front of the building.

The Grey Nuns Hospital was sold to the provincial government in 1972 and renamed the Pasqua Hospital. In 1974, the Regina General Hospital was also sold to the government. Both of these tertiary acute-care facilities continued to operate under separate boards.

In 1974, the Plains Health Center opened as an additional tertiary care hospital for the people of southern Saskatchewan. Along with the Pasqua Hospital, it was operated by the South Saskatchewan Hospital Board. As part of the government's health services reform initiatives, and the formation of the Regina Health District in 1993, the decision was made to consolidate acute-care services in two facilities – the Pasqua Hospital and the Regina General Hospital. The Plains Health Care facility closed in November 1998.

Improvements at the Pasqua included an expansion of the Allan Blair Cancer Centre, an improved emergency department, enhancement of the Palliative Care Unit, a Native Healing Centre and a new service known as ambulatory care to handle non-urgent scheduled treatments and ease the emergency department's workload.

The General Hospital was expanded by 410,000 square feet and the Pasqua Hospital was enlarged by 70,000 square feet.

Equipment additions to the General Hospital have included a Spiral CT Scanner in November 1998 and a MRI machine in 1999. Wasakaw Pisim Native Counselling Services, a native healing centre, opened on December 10, 1999 to offer counselling, cross-cultural training and referrals to other agencies for aboriginal people. The opening of a new renal unit in February 2000 provides highly specialized dialysis treatment to more than 140 patients.

EARL GREY MILITARY HOSPITAL/EARL GREY SCHOOL

12th Avenue and Ottawa Street

N amed after the Governor General, Earl Grey School opened in 1909, but closed in 1916 when the building became the headquarters for the 77th Battery.

In 1917, "H" unit of the Military Hospitals Commission was established in Regina and Earl Grey School was converted into a military hospital.

Under the supervision of Major E. James Ashton and Major James McAra, "H" unit coordinated all civilian and military efforts toward the rehabilitation of invalided veterans.

In 1921, after one year as a military barracks and four years as a military hospital, Earl Grey Hospital was demobilized. Almost 2,000 patients had been cared for during that time period.

The school reopened for elementary school classes in 1923. It was closed in 1933 and demolished in 1937 (see page 118).

First Hearse/Ambulance

PLAINS HEALTH CENTRE/SIAST – WASCANA CAMPUS

4500 Wascana Parkway

*P*lanned by Premier Ross Thatcher in 1969, the Plains Health Centre was opened in 1973, by Premier Allan Blakeney. It was intended to be a teaching hospital serving all of southern Saskatchewan The hospital was designed by architects Kerr, Cullingworth, Riches, Ramsay and Ramsay, and built by PCL Construction at a cost of $18 million. The building was eleven storeys high and contained 302 beds.

The Board of Governors was chaired by Dr. W. A. Riddell, first principal of Regina Campus, University of Regina.

However, the concept of a teaching medical centre serving the southern half of the province was never fully achieved as rural communities continued to build local hospitals. Upon regeneration and expansion of the Regina General and Pasqua Hospitals, the Plains Health Centre was closed in 1998.

The building was redesigned and it reopened in 2000 as the Saskatchewan Institute of Applied Science and Technology (SIAST). Formed in 1988 to amalgamate Saskatchewan's technical colleges and community colleges, SIAST is a post-secondary education institution that specializes in skills training and technical education.

The Regina facilities and classrooms were spread among several local venues, but the availability of this building made it possible to centralize the Regina (Wascana Campus) SIAST programs.

CANADIAN RED CROSS BUILDING

Southeast corner of Victoria Avenue and Smith Street

*T*he first Junior Red Cross children's hospital opened in Regina in 1924. In 1949, the Junior Red Cross raised funds to equip a new wing of the Regina General Hospital. Blood transfusion services began in Saskatchewan in 1952 and in 1964 Red Cross started a "Candy Striper" program, a volunteer program for young women to help in hospitals.

Red Cross has a long history in offering first-aid training, swimming lessons and water-safety programs. First-Aid classes began in Regina in 1934, and 1946 saw the beginning of swimming and water-safety programs.

The Regina Red Cross office opened on January 7, 1913, in the Regina General Hospital. Lieutenant-Governor G. W. Brown was president and Premier Walter Scott was vice-president. The building pictured here was used from 1922 to 1957, when it closed. Before 1922 it was the home of Senator Laird, a former mayor of Regina.

The Red Cross was founded in 1859 as an international humanitarian movement. The Canadian Red Cross Society was established in 1909 by an official Act of the Canadian Government. The Red Cross began by providing emergency services to veterans and victims of natural disasters.

As community needs have changed, so have the services offered by the Red Cross. Examples of this include an arts and crafts program for senior citizens, which began as a pilot project in 1971. Red Cross Youth began offering babysitting courses for students aged 12 and over in 1976.

Building on decades of experience in prevention education and community-based safety programs, the Canadian Red Cross has been helping to break the cycle of abuse, harassment and interpersonal violence since 1984. "RespectED: Violence and Abuse Prevention" programs promote safe and supportive relationships and healthy communities through on-going partnerships across Canada. In 1998, Canadian Blood Services was established to oversee management of the country's blood system. Canadian Red Cross moved from its familiar office location at Broad and Broadway to its current offices at 2050 Cornwall Street.

Over the years, Regina citizens have donated their time, talents and treasure in vast quantities to support Red Cross programs and services. Today, Red Cross continues to assist the most vulnerable members of our society, both here at home and around the world.

EMBURY HOUSE

2134 Winnipeg Street

N ow the location of Embury Heights, this building was named Embury House after J. F. L. Embury, a WW I Brigadier-General and King's Bench judge. He was also a founding member of the Wascana Country Club and a member of Regina's first Public Library Board.

Early in 1915, Embury took the 28th Battalion overseas where he distinguished himself in the Canadian Corps. He was decorated Commander of the Order of the Bath and Commander of the Order of St. Michael and St. George. On his return in 1918, he was immediately appointed to the bench. Upon his death, the August 16, 1943 *Leader-Post* noted: "Judge Embury, by nature, made an excellent judge, being endowed with a fine mind and a great heart. He was quick to discern and eager to rectify any semblance of injustice wherever he found it. He was simply incapable of knowingly doing an injustice to anyone and any person who thought otherwise simply did not know the man."

Judge Embury's son and grandson followed him into the practice of law and community service. Alan W. Embury went overseas in 1939 with the Saskatoon Light Infantry and was its commanding officer in Sicily and Italy. He was elected to the Saskatchewan Legislature in 1944 as the serviceman's representative for the Mediterranean Theatre. He was honourary aide-de-camp to Governor General Viscount Alexander of Tunis and was the first president of the United Services Institute after WW II. He also served on the board of the Regina Public Library and the Salvation Army. Grandson John Embury was the first third-generation lawyer in Saskatchewan and president of the Saskatchewan Liberal Party.

WILLIAM ARGAN

Embury House was also known as the Children's Aid Home. The Children's Aid Society was formed in 1910. The November 19, 1917 *Leader* reported the home was expected to be ready for occupancy by January 1, 1918. The two-storey structure "will accommodate some forty children without any crowding.

"Sleeping accommodation is furnished on the upper floor by two large dormitories, one for boys and one for girls, with washrooms, toilets and wardrobes adjoining. There is also an attendant's room in connection with each dormitory. On the same floor there is an isolation department consisting of three rooms and a toilet, with dumb waiter service to the kitchen. Opening off this floor there is a large screened balcony which will be enclosed with glass sash in the winter time. On the ground floor there is also a large verandah. The main entrance opens into a large reception hall which leads to the upper floor. Opening from the reception hall are the living room, nursery, dining room, board room and juvenile court department comprising court room, two cells and toilet. The main kitchen is also located on this floor with the necessary pantries, etc. and matron's room with bathroom adjoining."

The total cost of the building was estimated at $20,000. The building was erected by the City of Regina with the assistance of the provincial government. This location is now the site of Embury Heights and the Regina Senior Citizens' Centre (see page 347).

REGINA PUBLIC SCHOOLS

The history of Regina Public Schools has been intertwined with the development of the province and the city for over 117 years. Since the establishment of Regina as the capital of the North-West Territories in 1883, the organization of the first school in 1883, and the election of the first school trustees in 1885, Regina Public Schools has encouraged strong local support for high-quality publicly funded education.

The first school opened by the then-named Regina Protestant School District No. 4 was in 1885, in a building on Scarth Street owned by D. S. McCannell, the teacher of the school. In February 1890, the first school was built in Regina on the corner of Hamilton Street and 11th Avenue. Named the Union School, it became known as the White School because it was built of solid white brick. In 1903, when the City of Regina was incorporated, the White School had 10 teachers and approximately 500 students. A Normal School program, to train new teachers, was opened in one of the attic rooms in 1903.

Today, Regina Public Schools serves more than 22,000 students, from Pre-Kindergarten to Grade 12, in 51 elementary and 10 high schools, with approximately 1,450 teaching and 520 non-teaching staff members. We provide comprehensive educational services to students of all backgrounds and abilities. Within each school is a team of professionals including administrators, assistants, maintenance staff, resource centre personnel, special services staff, support staff and teachers. Our employees work closely with parents/guardians and members of the community to provide high-quality educational opportunities for students.

Regina Public Schools has developed statements of shared values that reflect and affirm our commitment to our mission: *to instill the value of knowledge, the dignity of effort and the worth of the individual.* Our value statements are *I Belong, I Want To Know, I Respect,* and *I Am Responsible.* The expression of these shared values confirms and guides the delivery of successful educational experiences for all children and young people attending Regina public schools.

Our schools continue to grow with Regina, providing an education that emphasizes high academic standards within a safe and caring environment.

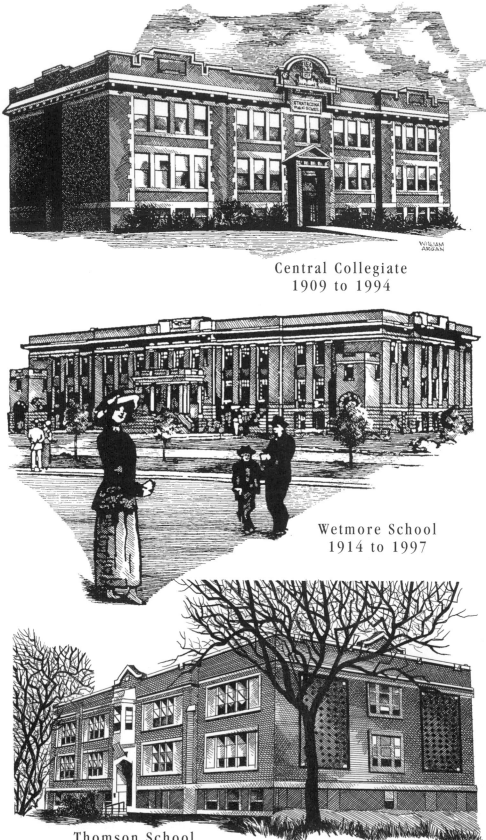

Central Collegiate
1909 to 1994

Wetmore School
1914 to 1997

Thomson School
1927 –

REGINA CATHOLIC SCHOOLS

Sacred Heart
Academy
1910 to 1969

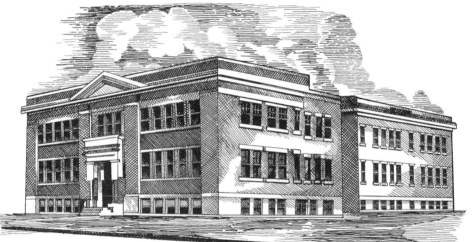

St. Joseph School
1913 to 1989

Campion College
1918 to 1975

Sponsored by Greystone Managed Investments

*I*n Regina Catholic Schools, faith is our foundation. It should not be surprising, therefore, that the birth of our school system was inspired more than 100 years ago by a man of great faith – Father Damien Gratton.

Father Gratton came to Regina from the province of Quebec to serve as the pastor of St. Mary's Church. He earned the love and respect of his parishioners and was well known for his commitment to providing quality education for Catholic children and youth. His dedication and care touched the lives of all members of the Catholic community.

Sadly, however, Father Gratton's life came to a tragic end when, upon returning to Regina from a school inspection in Wood Mountain in 1891, he was caught in a prairie blizzard and froze to death. Father Gratton was just 33 years old.

In honour and memory of Father Gratton, when the Catholic ratepayers of Regina decided in 1899 to establish a separate school district, they named it the Gratton Roman Catholic Separate School District. Likewise, when the first school opened in 1900, it was also named the Gratton School. The first Catholic school in our city featured one teacher and one teacher assistant – the total annual expenditure of the division was a whopping $355.76!

Eight years later the original Gratton School was closed in favour of a larger school constructed on what is today the site of the SaskPower building. This new school, St. Mary, was staffed by seven teachers.

From that time forward, ours became a story of growth. Today, Regina Catholic Schools consists of 29 schools, over 10,000 students, 1,000 teachers, support and administrative staff, and an annual budget exceeding $65 million.

But while the division has become larger, and has changed in many ways, one thing has always remained the same: our devotion to the Catholic faith. Our mission today, to provide "Quality Catholic Education", is no different now than it was in 1900. Thus, as we enter our second century of service, Regina Catholic Schools will continue to protect, preserve and promote the faith for the greater glory of God.

UNION SCHOOL/WHITE SCHOOL

Southeast corner of 11th Avenue and Hamilton Street

*T*he Union School, built in 1890, served as both an elementary and high school. Built of white brick, it was also called the White School. Three of the eight rooms formed the high school, while the other five served as elementary school-rooms. The lab was in the dormer-windowed attic room. A kindergarten class was added in 1892.

The first school in Regina had been started by Miss Fanny Laidlaw, as a private school, in March of 1883. The first free public school was opened two months later, in the Methodist Church, with a Mr. Schaffner as the teacher. Voluntary contributions were solicited to keep the school open. In the spring of 1884, Donald S. McCannel, a local pioneer, taught 38 students in a succession of improvised schoolrooms, for a very modest salary.

The school situation improved when, on December 20, 1884, the town proclaimed Regina Protestant Public School District No. 4 after the North-West Council passed a school ordinance. In 1885 McCannel opened the first school in the new school district in a building he owned on Scarth Street.

In 1888 the NWMP established Herchmer Public School, named after NWMP Commissioner Herchmer, at the barracks.

In 1903, in one of the attic rooms in the White School, a Normal School (teacher training program) was started. White School was demolished about 1905 when the land was sold to R. H. Williams for the erection of R. H. Williams department store, "Glasgow House", which subsequently became the Robert Simpson Company department store.

ALEXANDRA SCHOOL

East side of Hamilton Street between 12th and Victoria Avenues

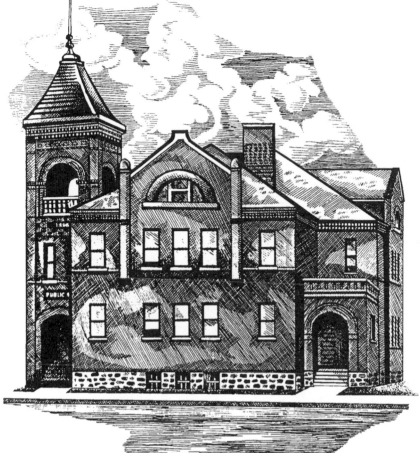

*T*his red brick building, built in 1896, was initially named Red School. In 1906 it was renamed Alexandra School. The building functioned as a school until 1910 and later housed the Normal School (Teachers' College) for some years.

From 1921 to 1931, the school served as a police station and jail. Later, in the 1930s, it became a relief office. Prior to being demolished in 1955 it was used as a youth centre. The Georgia Hotel was later erected on this location (see page 176).

VICTORIA SCHOOL

McIntyre Street between Victoria and 13th Avenues

*B*uilt in 1905, Victoria School was opened in 1906 with a capacity of 200 students. It was considered the very latest in school design. Victoria School was demolished in 1958 and the YMCA was built in its place.

The school board salvaged the cornerstone, the Tyndall stone "Victoria School" carved above the main door, and a beaver crest, also in Tyndall stone. These were incorporated on the grounds of the new Victoria School situated at 12th Avenue and Retallack Street.

GRATTON CATHOLIC SCHOOL/ST. MARY SCHOOL

Cornwall Street and 13th Avenue

Regina's Roman Catholics organized a separate school district in 1899. The first Gratton School was at 12th Avenue and Cornwall Street. Charles McCusker was chairman of the Regina Catholic School System for nine of its first ten years.

A new Gratton School, located immediately north of the original school, formally opened on October 29, 1900. By 1905 the attendance was 120 boys and 101 girls. In 1908, during the Thanksgiving break, the contents of the school were moved to the new St. Mary School.

Damien Gratton

Gratton School was named after Father Damien Gratton, the local parish priest, who died an untimely death in March 1891 while returning from Wood Mountain where he had been conducting services. Following a heavy snowfall, Father Gratton attempted to snowshoe 25 miles into Regina after his team and driver had become exhausted. Losing his way in the deep snow he succumbed to a heart attack. All of Regina mourned the popular young priest's death.

In the 1880s, Father Gratton started a small circulating library in Regina. He brought 150 books from Montreal and charged the modest fee of ten cents per person per month.

ST. MARY SCHOOL

Southeast corner of Scarth Street and Victoria Avenue

t. Mary, the second Catholic school constructed in the City of Regina, opened its doors in September 1909 at its original Scarth Street and Victoria Avenue location.

St. Mary school fared well until the 1930s, when the Great Depression wreaked havoc on the prairies. Although the teachers willingly accepted drastic reductions in pay, this gesture was not enough to keep the financially strapped school open.

In 1939 St. Mary was forced to close its doors. In 1945 the building and school property were sold to the Government of Saskatchewan. The Saskatchewan Transportation Bus Terminal and Reliance School of Commerce occupied the building before it was replaced with the SaskPower building in 1963.

WILLIAM ARGAN '84

In 1962, a newly-constructed St. Mary school was built at 140 McIntosh Street North. From that point onward the school experienced an incredible period of growth, culminating in an enrollment of 701 pupils in 1974.

As more schools were constructed to the north and west, the population of St. Mary began to decline. However, the availability of more space in the school facilitated the establishment, in 1978, of a French Immersion Program. The program continues to flourish and is home to 306 students and 21 staff members.

EARL GREY SCHOOL/EARL GREY MILITARY HOSPITAL

12th Avenue and Ottawa Street

*E*arl Grey School opened in 1909, but closed in 1916 when the building became the headquarters for the 77th Battery. From 1917 to 1921 the school served as a military sanitarium. It reopened for elementary school classes in 1923. The school was closed in 1933 and demolished in 1937 (see page 108).

WILLIAM ARGAN

STRATHCONA PUBLIC SCHOOL

Rose Street between 14th and 15th Avenues

*S*trathcona School opened in 1910 and closed in 1984. The school was located in the Transitional Area, one of the city's first residential neighbourhoods, dating back more than 100 years. The name of this neighbourhood relates to its ongoing transition from largely residential to a mix of commercial and residential development. It was the city's most prestigious neighbourhood prior to the development of the Crescents' area and Lakeview.

WILLIAM ARGAN

With a substantial number of Jewish students attending Strathcona, no new lessons were begun on Jewish holidays as so many students were absent.

Graduates of Strathcona School who went on to make significant contributions to the community include retired Chief Justice of the Court of Queen's Bench Donald K. MacPherson, Gordon Staseson, Paul Pearlman, Clarence Brown, Judge Howard Boyce, actress Frances Hyland, Judge Isadore Grotsky, Dr. Mitch Finklestein, John Rowand, Howard Rennebohn, Donald Hipperson, Murray Bercovich, Oscar Abdoullah, Vic Young, Dr. Jack Gitterman, Shirley Bergman-Bell, Reverend Walter Krenz.

The school was demolished in 1990.

SACRED HEART ACADEMY

13th Avenue and Garnet Street

*T*here were no blackboards or proper desks for the ten students, boys and girls, at Sacred Heart Academy when it was opened by the Sisters of Our Lady of the Missions in 1905 at 2059 Scarth Street. Father Augustine Suffa had invited the sisters to come to Regina and teach in St. Mary's parish.

Later that year the sisters moved to a house at 1866 Albert Street, the former residence of Mayor Laird, because the Scarth Street house was needed as a rectory for the newly completed St. Mary's Church. The Albert Street location had room for two classrooms and a small chapel. It was palatial compared to the Scarth Street school. However, the sisters continued to be tested as stovepipes collapsed, water pipes burst and a chimney caught fire.

As the student population increased, it was obvious that Sacred Heart Academy was bursting at its seams. As early as 1906, the sisters purchased land far out on the prairie, in the "slough". In September 1910 the new school, a fine three-storey building, built by Smith Brothers and Wilson, opened at 13th Avenue and Garnet Street. The new school had a chapel, classrooms, music room, art room, dining room and dormitories. From then on Sacred Heart Academy was to be a boarding school for girls only. By 1913 the private school had 80 students, necessitating the addition of the middle annex, the second part of the building, in 1914.

There were also academic additions. Beginning in 1915, high-school exams could be written at Sacred Heart Academy. Commercial classes were opened in 1917. In 1920 home economics was added to the curriculum and, in 1924, the Academy became a junior college of the University of Saskatchewan, offering first-year university classes. Students could now get their schooling from kindergarten to first-year university at Sacred Heart Academy and College. Florence Honan and Kathleen McGuiness were the first students to do so. A west wing was added to accommodate the increase in students. A large chapel with a domed ceiling and gallery and a gymnasium were notable features of the new addition. In the 1930s the elementary grades were discontinued.

In 1926 the Sisters at the Academy opened Sacred Heart College at 3625 Albert Street. It served as a novitiate and as the new location for the Academy's university program. By the late 1950s Sacred Heart College was offering a full high-school program and, in 1964, an expansion, Marian High School, was added.

In 1965 Regina Catholic Schools took over the private school. By then the school lacked modern facilities and required repairs. At the end of June 1969, after 63 years of service, the school closed due to low enrollment.

Since then the building has housed nuns, several archdiocese offices and condominium apartment units.

CENTRAL COLLEGIATE

The corner of Scarth Street and 15th Avenue

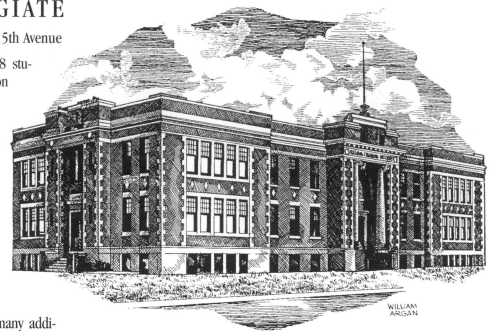

WILLIAM ARGAN

Central Collegiate opened to 138 students under Hector Lang, B.A., on November 15, 1909, as Regina Collegiate. It was the first school in Regina to be dedicated solely to secondary education.

Designed by Storey and Van Egmond architects, it was constructed by Smith Brothers and Wilson. The cost of the original west block was $108,322.

The name changed to Central Collegiate in 1924 when Scott Collegiate opened. Throughout the school's 76-year history it saw many additions, including a commercial department, new classrooms, a gymnasium, manual training room and art room. From 1909 until June 1985 when the school ceased operation, its average enrollment fluctuated between 600 and more than 1,000 students.

Known for high academic standards, Central Collegiate produced nine Rhodes Scholars, believed to be a North American record. Students of Central Collegiate had an outstanding record of academic and sports achievements. Central Gophers teams included athletes: hockey players George Beach, Gord Staseson, Jim Fairburn, Del Wilson, Jim Owen, Mo Young, Ed Litzenberger and Billy Hay; football players Fred Young, Howie Milne, Bill Traynor and Al Ford; basketball star Ross Upshall; tennis champions Don Hodges and Bob Fuller; pairs badminton champions Ted and Pat Child; figure skaters Barry Green, who skated professionally with Ice Capades, Margie and Joan Penfold, Margie (Sandison) went on to become an international figure skating judge, the DeWitt twins, Joan and Jean (Owen) became professional figure skaters with Sonja Henie's Hollywood Ice Revue. Del Wilson owned the Regina Pats and became a professional golfer.

Business leaders were: Bob Fuller, vice-president S. C. Johnson & Sons in Newark; Warner Cudmore, vice-president Western USA, Sun Oil in Chicago; Arden Haynes, CEO, Imperial Oil; Ward Longworthy, IOL Regina refinery plant manager; Reg Rideout, president Aluminum Co. of Jamaica; Charlie Pike, CPR western Canada vice-president; George Pike with Air Canada; Ross Sneath owned the Trianon; John Green, president of SGI; Gene Ciuca, president of Gene's Ltd.; Graham Bradley, SaskTel innovator in Fiber Optics; Frank Degenstein, CEO SaskTel; John Konoff, engineer; Frances Mitchell (Olson) started the first all-female realty company; Linda Barber (Jacobson) and Joan Hudson (Wilson), Best of Bridge series authors and publishers.

Media personalities include: Dick Irvin, Hockey Night in Canada sportscaster; Bob Bye, voice of morning radio in Vancouver; Roy Brown, CKRM radio; Bill Walker, CJRM radio and CTV; Ross McRae, Canadian Press World News Correspondent.

Jack Milliken taught medicine at Queen's University; Paul Schwann, Paul Good and Bill McRae became doctors. Campbell Dixon, Gord Schwann, Alf Geisthardt and Mel Nattrass became dentists. Brian Dickson was Chief Justice of the Supreme Court of Canada; Ted Hinkson was a B.C. Supreme Court Judge; "Sandy" MacPherson, Murray Forbes, Larry Kyle and Grant Armstrong, Saskatchewan Court of Queen's Bench judges; Donald K. MacPherson, Chief Justice, Court of Queen's Bench. Jim Balfour and Simon DeJong became MPs and Balfour was later a Senator. Elected officials include: Mary Hicks, Public School Board; aldermen Stan Oxelgren, George Bothwell and Fred Clipsham. Myrtle Bainbridge Surjik was the first Miss Grey Cup in 1950. Doreen Stimpson (Fisher) was the first female president of the Central Student's Council.

Architects "Bud" and Don Ramsay designed the Plains Health Centre. In the arts: Herb Spanier became a famous jazz musician; Chris Gage a professional pianist; Paul Brodie, a world-class saxophonist. Pat Blair (Krause) became a writer; Lynn Goldman, actress and television writer; Carol Gay Bell, a television writer, founded "Saskatchewan Express"; Shirley Douglas (Sutherland), Canadian and Hollywood film star; Barbara Franklin and Frances Hyland, Canadian stage and film actresses. Artists Art McKay and Victor Cicansky are internationally recognized.

Central Collegiate was demolished in 1994.

CENTRAL COLLEGIATE FACADE

*T*he facade of Central Collegiate was dismantled, catalogued and turned over to the Public School Board to be rebuilt brick-for-brick as the entrance to Winston Knoll Collegiate, a new high school in northwest Regina which opened in the fall of 1997.

COLLEGE GARDENS/COLLEGE COURT

College Park 2300 block Scarth Street

*B*uilt between 1995 and 1999, in three phases, by Frank Remai, P.R. Developments, Saskatoon, on the old Central Collegiate site, this luxury condominium development consists of 101 units. It is three and four storeys high and covers an entire city block.

The design by architect Brian Saunders, of Saunders Evans Architects, is in keeping with the aesthetics of the original Central Collegiate building. It blends well with the transitional setting which surrounds it, including the Nicol Court heritage building on the west side on Scarth street, University of Regina heritage buildings on College Avenue in Wascana Park to the south, and a redeveloped park on the old Central Park site to the north.

The condominium development complex received the 2001 Municipal Heritage Award for new design and sensitive infill.

ST. JOSEPH SCHOOL/PRINCIPAL MIKE KARTUSCH

13th Avenue and Toronto Street

B uilt in 1912, St. Joseph was the third school constructed in the Regina Catholic School Division. It was built to serve students in the east part of the city. During the school's early years, St. Joseph was recognized for its compassionate response to the Spanish flu epidemic which ravaged all of Europe after WW I, and which was brought to Canada by Canadian troops returning from the war overseas.

In 1918, to assist in the fight against the flu epidemic, St. Joseph School was transformed into a secondary hospital to provide space for the overflow patients Regina's two existing hospitals could not accommodate. In the face of severe nursing shortages caused by the war and the flu epidemic, hundreds of volunteers offered their time, talents and energy to provide care for the more than 3,000 patients who were treated at St. Joseph. One of these dedicated volunteers was Father Augustine Suffa who for more than 15 years had been pastor of St. Mary's Church. Sadly, after working tirelessly in the service of the sick, Father Suffa himself fell victim to the dreaded disease.

Father Augustine Suffa

In 1929 St. Augustine School, located just north of Little Flower Church at 2343 Edgar Street, was named after Father Suffa.

While the early years of St. Joseph were marked by the community's response to a world-wide tragedy, in later years the history of the school became inextricably linked with one particular principal, Mike Kartusch. After serving for three years in the Canadian Armed Services, Mike became principal of St. Joseph school in 1944 – a position he would hold for the next 30 years!

Mike Kartusch

As St. Joseph principal, Mike Kartusch was involved in almost every school activity – but there is little doubt that his first love was the game of hockey. In fact, many Reginans will remember Maple Leaf Rink, situated just east of St. Joseph school, as the winter home for Mike and for hundreds of young people in the area. During the peak years, Mike coached and supervised as many as 18 teams per season. According to Mike, at times it was so cold that when the puck hit the goal post, it would literally split in two!

In 1947 Mike Kartusch began his association with the Montreal Canadiens and the Regina Pats minor league system. The "barn on Pasqua Street" (Exhibition Stadium) became another winter home during Mike's 30-year association with the Pats.

Mike Kartusch received many honours in his lifetime, including being awarded the Coronation Medal, Canadian Decoration, Kiwanis "Dad of the Year", Knight of the Holy Cross, the Regina Pats Hall of Fame, the Saskatchewan Sports Hall of Fame.

After a lifetime of dedication to children and youth, Mike Kartusch passed away in 1996, seven years after the doors of St. Joseph school closed for the last time.

HOLY ROSARY SCHOOL

3118 14th Avenue

Bishop O. E. Mathieu

H oly Rosary School, like the Cathedral after which it is named, has played an important role in the history of our city and of Regina's Catholic community.

In 1911, His Excellency, Bishop O. E. Mathieu was appointed to establish his see in Regina. He organized Holy Rosary Parish and built the present Cathedral. His Excellency was a great apostle of education and was well known for his commitment to the well-being of children. His dream was to provide a quality education for Catholic children in the Cathedral area.

Bishop Mathieu's dream had humble beginnings. In January 1913, thirteen pupils were assembled in one room in the basement of Holy Rosary Cathedral under the guidance of Sister Mary St. Germaine of the Congregation of Our Lady of the Missions.

In 1914, a four-room school, Holy Rosary School, was built on the same block as the Cathedral. Sister Mary St. Germaine became the first principal. After several additions and renovations Holy Rosary School features nine classrooms and is home to 170 students and 20 staff members.

In 1980 Holy Rosary was designated as a "Community School". According to Principal Richard Kusiak, this designation was significant in that it linked the community and the school in order to improve the educational experience for children and to strengthen the community.

Much has changed since Bishop Mathieu's dream and its inception, but one thing has always been a constant in the history of Holy Rosary School – the commitment of the community to educating children in the Catholic faith.

WETMORE SCHOOL/PRINCIPAL NORMAN DETWILER

Wallace Street between 14th and 15th Avenues

Edward Ludlow Wetmore

Wetmore School opened its doors on January 5, 1914, to educate children of predominately immigrant parents. The school helped first-generation Canadians, from 22 ethnic groups, assimilate and share a sense of community.

Wetmore School is named after Judge E. L. Wetmore, one of the first judges of the Supreme Court of Canada. He was named to the bench in 1887, and appointed commissioner for consolidating the statutes of the North-West Territories in 1898 and of Saskatchewan in 1908. Wetmore was the first chancellor of the University of Saskatchewan, from 1907 to 1912.

Norman Detwiler was born in 1883 in Roseville, Ontario, and joined the Regina Public School staff in 1913 as vice-principal of Victoria School. He was principal of Benson School from 1915 to 1919, and served as principal of Wetmore School from 1919 to 1948.

As a multi-cultural school, Wetmore benefited from Detwiler's ability to read in five languages and speak fluently in German, French and English. In total, Detwiler taught in Regina for 35 years.

Wetmore School was isolated in an eastern corner of the city, with a majority of non-English-speaking families and pockets of extreme poverty. Under Detwiler's principalship, the students excelled in sports, music and scholastics.

In striving to excel the students gained a self-esteem and determination that bonded them and developed a strong sense of loyalty and school spirit that was still apparent at the 1985 reunion. Wetmore graduates came from around the globe to honour Detwiler and celebrate this outstanding school.

Many graduates from Wetmore went on to make great contributions in the areas of community service, sports and the arts. In sports there were: Harold (Mush) March, Mary (Bonnie) Baker, Jimmy Trifunov, Willie Francis, Ken Charlton, Daisy Junor, George Chiga and Duncan Fisher.

Well-known figures in the arts include: Vicky Bodner, June Kowalchuk, William Argan, Carol Phillips, George Babu and Victor Cicansky.

In community service there were Senator Earl Hastings and Fire Chiefs Omar Dixon and Louis Yanko.

Outstanding business leaders included Gene Ciuca, George Solomon and Victor Ursaki.

The school closed in 1997.

LAKEVIEW SCHOOL

3100 20th Avenue

Lakeview School began in 1918 as a two-room cottage for two teachers and 60 students. Increasing population in the Lakeview area necessitated the erection of a new school in 1922. Increasing school enrollment led to the addition of a wing in 1930.

The August 30, 1930 *Leader-Post* reported: "A new heating system has been installed, with two new boilers. Fresh air will be thrown into all classrooms, passing first through large fans, being heated and humidified by thin sprays of water passing, heated again, and forced through the building. Slate blackboards are provided throughout the new section of the building. New wash fountains, for boys and girls, unusual in schools throughout the west, have been installed, to be used instead of wash bowls. It is considered an economical addition to the school equipment, saving water and plumbing upkeep." The contract price of the new wing was $113,407 and the installation of plumbing by the Acme Plumbing Shop cost approximately $28,964.

James Grassick, MLA and chairman of the Regina Public School Board presided over the opening program on October 30, 1930. The October 31, 1930 *Leader-Post* reported: "The school now contains 17 classrooms with separate lockers for each child, basement playrooms for boys and girls, lunch room, household science and manual training rooms and the auditorium which is equipped with a booth for a moving picture machine."

The *Leader-Post* also included a lengthy description of "Round-eyed little boys and girls of the primary grade age," who were chief contributors to the program. "Unabashed by the rows of faces watching them, the youngsters went through their drills and folk dances with the solemn gravity of young children."

Extensive renovations were undertaken at Lakeview in the 1980s. In October 1983 an open house marked the completion of a $1.47-million renovation project. The work included a science room, a music room, a resource centre, a lunch room and upgraded electrical and mechanical systems. The building now met the present-day National Building Code standards and was accessible to the handicapped.

CAMPION COLLEGE

A rchbishop O. E. Mathieu and Father George Daly, rector of Holy Rosary Cathedral, were instrumental in establishing Campion College. Archbishop Mathieu asked the provincial legislature to pass an act of incorporation for a "Catholic College of Regina".

Opened by the Jesuits in 1918, Campion College was originally situated in a classroom in the basement of Holy Rosary Cathedral. In September 1918 these two houses were leased across the street from the Cathedral. There were six students and faculty was one priest, one scholastic and one lay brother. By New Year's Day 1919 there were 22 students. The first rector was Thomas MacMahon, S.J. Campion College was named after Blessed Edmund Campion, an Oxford scholar and Jesuit martyr.

13th Avenue between
Garnet and Cameron Streets

A three-storey building on 23rd Avenue, including boarding facilities, was Campion's new home in 1921. The Knights of Columbus had raised funds in southern Saskatchewan to purchase the property and build. In 1923 a new wing was added. The majority of students attended high school, but Campion, as a junior college of the University of Saskatchewan, had the privilege of teaching first-year arts, the first college in the province to achieve this status.

During WW II, enrollment in the high school continued to increase. Many of the high-school graduates joined the armed services and by the end of the war over 1,000 former students had entered the services, of whom 110 lost their lives.

In 1957 Boyle Memorial Gymnasium opened. It was named after Rector Francis Boyle, whose vision added recreation and drama facilities to the college. In 1960 the arts program became coeducational. Under Rector Peter Nash, S.J., Campion was granted federation with the Regina Campus of the University of Saskatchewan in 1964. In January 1968 classes began in the new college building on the Regina campus. Campion students may choose classes from the entire university spectrum and use all campus facilities while enjoying the intimacy of a small college.

The former college building became solely a high school until 1975, when students were transferred to nearby Dr. Martin LeBoldus High School. The building was then used as part of SIAST Wascana Campus.

Many Campion high-school and university students went on to become great athletes, professionals and prominent businessmen. In sports: Dr. Bill Orban, U of S, developed the 5BX and 10BX training programs for the RCAF; Mike and Wayne Kartusch, educators and hockey officials; Frank McCrystal, Rams coach; Greg Feiger and "Sully" Glasser, Roughriders; "Red" Glasser and Joe Most, Canadian Bowling Champions; Fran Huck, NHL player; Frank "Sully" Sullivan, Regina Aces, Yorkton Terriers and Kimberley Dynamiters; Ross Mahoney, NHL scout. Dr. Jack Alexander, Joe Kanuka, "Red" Glasser, Joe Most and Mike Kartusch were inducted into the Saskatchewan Sports Hall of Fame; "Sully" Glasser, Saskatchewan Roughrider Plaza of Honor.

In the professions and business: principal of Queen's University and renowned economist John Deutsch; Queen's Bench judges, Ted Malone and Ellen Gunn; Appeal Court judge Stuart Cameron; lawyer Joe Kanuka; Dr. Martin LeBoldus, physician and long-time school board member; aldermen Greg Ryan and Gerry Kleisinger, also a school board member; Greg White and Jack Neidermeyer, dentists; Doug Martin, Jack Alexander, Peter Gorman and Mark Ogrady, medical doctors; In business, Paul Hill, president of the Hill Group of Companies; Tim Kramer, president of Kramer Ltd.; Gord Wicijowski, CA and community worker, Honourary Doctorate U of R; Fred Wagman, CEO of Cable Regina and a Roughrider president; Norman Achen, senior vice-president Royal Bank; Adam Neisner, realty developer; Brian Galon and Mark Glabus, insurance brokers; Kevin Boyle and Gerry Welsh, businessmen and school board members.

In the arts and media: actor John Vernon (Vern Agopsowicz); Fred Kanuka, writer; Roy Malone, CKCK radio; Frank Flegel, radio and print journalist; Terry Rigelhof, author and literary critic.

2505 23rd Avenue

SCOTT COLLEGIATE

3350 –7th Avenue

W W I postponed the building of Scott Collegiate, named for the province's first premier – Walter Scott. In the early 1900s, the city required a collegiate in the northwest, so the Collegiate Board purchased a block on 7th Avenue for the new school.

Scott Collegiate was built in 1923 and officially opened in 1924, with nine classes in operation. Soon students exceeded the space available and for some time classes were held in Benson School. In 1927 another wing was added to Scott, but by 1945 the auditorium, labs and 17 classrooms were overcrowded.

Walter Scott

In response to public pressure, Balfour Technical School was built by the city, provincial government and the federal government under a federal government plan to aid vocational and technical education. When Balfour opened in 1930, this eased the pressure on Central and Scott classrooms for a while. In 1949 a $450,000 addition, including a gymnasium, was constructed at Scott Collegiate.

Scott, as one of the first three Regina collegiates, had a proud sports tradition and captured a major share of intercollegiate championships, particularly in football and hockey. During the 1930s, 1940s and 1950s, Scott produced many outstanding hockey players: Bill Hicke, Harvey Bennett, Grant Warwick, Scotty Cameron, Andy Mader, Jack Wilkie, Abe and Red (Bill) Tilson, Lorne Davis, Garth Butcher, Bob Turner, Red Berenson, Dr. Gordon Knutson, Terry Harper, Bev Bell and John Hudson, who went on to play junior, university and professional hockey.

Students who went on to CFL football careers included Roughriders Bill Clarke, Ted Urness, Roy Wright and Bill Baker. Norm Fieldgate played for the B.C. Lions. Bill Clarke also won the first Canadian Junior Curling championship. Millie Warwick played softball with the All-American Girls Professional League. Baker, Clarke, Urness and Fieldgate were inducted into the CFL Hall of Fame. Millie Warwick, Clarke and Baker were installed into the Saskatchewan Sports Hall of Fame and Clarke, Urness and Baker were inducted into the Roughrider Plaza of Honor.

In that same period Scott was a "hotbed" for aspiring radio and television personalities, including CKCK Radio's "Morning Mayor" Johnny Sandison, Ken Compton, Howard Langdale, Don Slade and Garry Miles. Barry Dunsmore became a World News Correspondent for CBS Television; Jim Grisenthwaite was vice-president of Armadale Communications Ltd.

Successful business and professional leaders: radiologist Bill Brown; CA Rand Flynn; Don Stankov, president of Thiessen Mining; Fred Button, vice-president SaskPower; Dr. Louise Forsyth Barton, Dean of Women (Grad Studies) U of S; Arnie Floyd, Honeywell Controls; "Scotty" Cameron, vice-president Pan American Oil; Les Court, Co-op Refineries; Wayne Steadman, Gene's Ltd., all got their start at Scott Collegiate.

As Regina enters the 21st Century, the student enrollment at Scott is predominately aboriginal, with low student-teacher ratios and a focus on aboriginal culture. Prince Charles visited Scott Collegiate during his visit to Regina in 2001 and observed the success of Scott's specialized programs.

Scott Collegiate is proactively addressing the challenge of keeping young aboriginal students interested in learning and staying in school. The *Leader-Post* April 27, 2002 quoted Principal Maureen Johns Simpson: "The First Nations' culture is our specialty . . . while other schools might offer special academic or sports programs, Scott focuses on the culture in activities, curriculum and everyday learning . . ."

LUTHER COLLEGE

1500 Royal Street

Established by the Lutheran community that had settled in southern Saskatchewan, Luther Academy opened in 1913 in Melville. In 1926 the school moved to Regina and became a junior college offering full high-school and first-year university courses. The name was changed to Luther College.

Luther is located on Dewdney Avenue immediately west of Government House, the residence of the Lieutenant-Governor of the Province of Saskatchewan, and east of the RCMP barracks. Built on 18 acres of prime land secured from the provincial government, it was later found that the school's gym is on the site of the first Government House in Saskatchewan. Mr. Dewdney was governor at the time, and the street which is now Dewdney Avenue was part of the trail used by Indians when they came from the west for their treaty money.

The first principal at Luther was Dr. Rex Schneider, who came to Regina from Wisconsin. Principal Schneider's style of leadership established an atmosphere which made Luther College unique. From the beginning, the warm relationship between students and staff became a part of the school spirit that still exists. Over 10,000 students have graduated since the school first opened.

During the 1930s and 1940s, Luther actively participated in athletic events and competition was keen between other schools and colleges. Over the years, Herc Meyer, William Assman, Henry Ast and John Chomay had created championship teams in baseball and track. In 1951 the new gymnasium was completed in time for the 25th anniversary.

The new gymnasium suddenly heralded the development of a sport which has since become almost synonymous with Luther College, basketball. John Chomay was the teacher who conceived the idea and organized the first Luther Invitational Tournament, an event which is to Western Canadian basketball what the Grey Cup is to football. Every year the "LIT", an annual competition of the best high-school basketball teams, draws thousands of fans and players, although Luther itself has only won three times since 1953, the first year of organization.

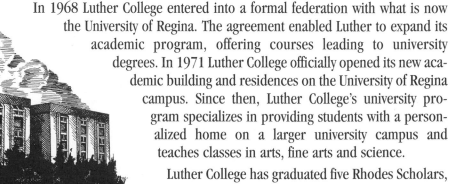

In 1968 Luther College entered into a formal federation with what is now the University of Regina. The agreement enabled Luther to expand its academic program, offering courses leading to university degrees. In 1971 Luther College officially opened its new academic building and residences on the University of Regina campus. Since then, Luther College's university program specializes in providing students with a personalized home on a larger university campus and teaches classes in arts, fine arts and science.

Luther College has graduated five Rhodes Scholars, three presidents of Canadian universities, a winner of the Nobel Prize in Science, and many leaders for the church, professions, business and other areas of service.

THOMSON SCHOOL

2033 Toronto Street

*T*homson School was opened in 1927. Designed by Francis Portnall in a Late-Gothic-Revival or Modern-Gothic style, it is faced with brick and decorated with Tyndall-stone trim and detail work. Above the main entrance is a distinctive oriel window, which incorporates datestones on either side of a relief carving of the school's name. Other decorative features include the crenellated roof parapets and the Flemish diaper on the north and south sides of the building. The original multi-pane windows, removed in recent years, have been replaced with windows and stone panels that are sympathetic to the original building design.

The school was named in honour of Dr. William Alexander Thomson, a distinguished local physician. As a member of city council in 1907 and 1908, he spearheaded construction of Regina's first incinerator and milk pasteurizing plant, and encouraged the adoption of a bylaw requiring the pasteurization of milk and its sale in sealed glass bottles. Thomson ran unsuccessfully for mayor in 1908, against R. H. Williams, he also served on the Public School Board and played a leading role in the establishment of western Canada's first school hygiene program.

Major James Coldwell was Thomson School's first principal. Although regarded as one of the province's best educators, he was better known for his contributions to local and federal politics. During his tenure as a city alderman (1922 to 1925 and 1927 to 1932), he was also active in provincial and national teachers' organizations. A founding member of the CCF, the forerunner of the New Democratic Party, Coldwell was elected as an MP for Rosetown-Biggar in 1935, a seat he held until 1958. He succeeded J. S. Woodsworth as national leader of the CCF from 1942 to 1960.

Another principal of Thomson School who contributed to civic politics was Harry G. R. Walker, mayor of Regina from 1972 to 1973.

Thomson Community School services students from areas throughout Regina. These students are bussed to Thomson to receive special programming in English Second Language and Adaptation Programs. Thomson celebrates the multi-cultural nature of the students. It welcomes children from nations around the world that have come to Regina to start a new life. Nine languages are represented in the school.

The school offers students a daily breakfast program and classes in nutrition. The school also has an education partnership with the Regina Firefighters, the Regina Aboriginal Professional Association and the Royal Bank. These groups give students an opportunity to expand their education beyond the school itself.

DAVIN SCHOOL

2401 Retallack Street

*D*avin School was built in 1929 on land previously owned by Tommy Watson, a dairy farmer who became Regina's first milkman. Prior to the 1900s the land was a racetrack. Designed by Francis Portnall in the Collegiate Gothic style, the building was constructed by Bird, Woodall and Simpson. It constitutes a valuable legacy of Regina's institutional development prior to WW II.

The school was named for Nicholas Flood Davin, a very prominent and colourful individual in the early history of Regina. Davin, who came to the city in 1882, founded two Regina newspapers, the *Regina Leader*, now the *Leader-Post*, in 1883 and *The West* in 1899. He was the first person to hold the federal seat of Assiniboia West, from 1887 until his defeat by Walter Scott in 1890.

"The school was to contain fourteen classrooms which was to be adequate accommodation for 448 students. However, statistics show that at one time there were 470 students accommodated in twelve classrooms. Two classrooms were later designated for Home Economics and Visual Education. The Home Economics Room was to provide laboratory instruction for the girls from Connaught, Lakeview, Victoria and Davin Schools."

The total cost of the building and equipment was $203,000.00. The official opening took place on November 15, 1929.

"The total cost of the land acquired for the Davin School property was $64,100.00 and [it] was assembled over a period of two years. In the early years of settlement the property was owned by the Canada North-West Land Company (see page 32), but as the city grew, lots were sold to individuals.

"Names of previous owners for the lots that now comprise the school site were George Terry Marsh, Thomas Watson, Richard B. Angus, Sir Donald A. Smith, Edmund Boyd Osler, William Bain Scarth, Aleck Clark, Frank R. Debolt, Dixie Watson, Dava Bodgamon, Simion Eisnasu, James W. Milligan, Charles W. Anderson, Laura Edna Philip, Hattie Evaleen Milligan, Andrew Thompson, The Western Trust Company, James Elliott, Lena T. Cross, Lena Haseltine, Mary Elizabeth McGregor, Alfred Anderson, Charles Mann, James Balfour, A. M. Ranney, Johannah Sud, these between the years 1906 and 1928. – Sask Land Titles" – *Davin Memories*, 1989

The gymnasium at Davin School is a unique design and it is said to be the first school in North America with an indoor gym.

The first principal of Davin School was Charles P. Geake. He left Davin in 1931 to become principal of Victoria School where he remained until 1947.

In the summer and fall of 2001, major structural renovations took place to ensure that this historic school, which celebrates its 75th Anniversary in 2004, will be in good shape for another 75 years. The principal in 2002 is Pamela Kendel-Goodale.

BALFOUR TECHNICAL SCHOOL/COLLEGIATE

1245 College Avenue

James Balfour, K.C.

By the end of WW I, the Regina Collegiate Board recognized the need to provide technical instruction as an option in secondary education. In 1920 a vocational education committee was established, with representation from the Regina Trades and Labour Council, to develop training programs in this area. Classes were initially held in the former Victoria Hospital building at the northeast corner of what is now Central Park.

Balfour Technical School opened in September 1930 with an initial enrollment of 810 students and a staff complement of 16 teachers. It was named in honour of James Balfour, a locally prominent lawyer and politician who served as Regina's first city clerk, as mayor in 1915 and in 1931, and on the Collegiate Board for over 20 years. In addition to its core and vocational curricula, the school included a commercial component that offered secretarial and accounting courses and industrial courses for unemployed adults. With the closure of Central Collegiate in 1985, Balfour was given collegiate status in 1986.

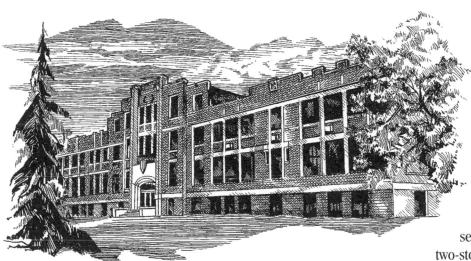

Designed by Storey and Van Egmond (who also designed Central and Scott Collegiates) the building was constructed and equipped entirely with Canadian-made products, at a cost of $485,000. The exterior design is Modern-Gothic style, faced with Fort William brick, with detail work in stone. Decorative embellishment is concentrated around the centred main entrance, framed with a broad segmental arch. Above the entrance is a two-storey bank of multi-pane windows, separated by mullions that are topped with pinnacles. The Collegiate Board crest is topped with a raised stone panel embossed with the original name of the school.

In 1995 Balfour was selected by the Canadian Education Association as one of 21 Exemplary Secondary Schools in Canada. Balfour has always had a strong sports program and the Balfour Redmen won many city and provincial championships in football, hockey and curling. In recent years the Balfour girls' basketball teams won many city and provincial championships.

Students who went on to greater sports achievements include: Dunc Fisher, Bill Giokas, Eddie Boychuk, Lloyd Ailsby, Tony Schneider, Danny Wong and Orville Off in hockey; Paul Dojack, a CFL football referee; Doug Killoh, Danny Banda and Gary Brandt with the Roughriders; Gordon Currie, coach of the Regina Rams; Tom Shepherd, long-time Roughriders' treasurer and a Rider president, as was John Lipp, also a city alderman and School Board trustee. Betty Lou Bingham (Dean) was a world-class swimmer. Jana Schweitzer and Lara Schmidt became star players with the University of Regina Cougars.

Principal T. W. Cowburn was a Regina Mayor, as was Larry Schneider, also an MP and cabinet minister. Don McPherson was an alderman, MLA, Rider president, and a Regina General Hospital wing was named after him.

Other Balfour graduates include Joseph Pettick, SaskPower building and City Hall architect; television personality Murray Westgate, famous for his Imperial Oil commercials on Hockey Night in Canada; Jim Toth, long-time teacher, Rotary International District Governor and Leader-Post Carrier Foundation chair.

Betty Lou Bingham, Paul Dojack and Gordon Currie were inducted into the Saskatchewan Sports Hall of Fame; Don McPherson, Tom Shepherd, Doug Killoh and Gary Brandt were inducted into the Roughrider Plaza of Honor. Dr. Peter Larkin was a Rhodes Scholar.

PAUL DOJACK YOUTH CENTRE

Ritter Avenue and Toothill Street

Paul Dojack

Born in Regina, Paul Dojack lost both parents when he was six years old. He was raised during the depression by his seven brothers and sisters.

Paul was an impatient and determined youngster who grew up hobnobbing with youths who were close to being in serious trouble. He spent many afternoons in front of Dale's Tea Room at 14th Avenue and Broad Street

Dojack helped found the Dale's Athletic Club, which resulted in the formation of the Regina Dale's Junior Football Club. He started as a diminutive quarterback; because of an injury he later became a coach. With Paul's leadership the Dale's won three western titles and, in 1938, the Canadian Junior Football title.

By 1941, Dojack was refereeing in the CFL, where he worked 14 Grey Cups and participated in league history. He was the game official who decided what to do when a fan on the sidelines tripped "Bibbles" Bawel of Hamilton in the 1957 Grey Cup. He was referee for the first tie game in league history in 1961. A year later Dojack, in a game dubbed the "fog bowl", halted the game because of poor visibility. He refereed 546 CFL games from 1947 to 1970.

Paul Dojack entered the Saskatchewan Sports Hall of Fame in 1971. He was recognized as both an individual and as a member of the 1938 Dale's. In 1978 he was honoured by the Canadian Football League Hall of Fame. He later became a member of the Selection Committee. In 1995 he was inducted into the Canadian Sports Hall of Fame.

Considered the most fair and respected official in CFL history, Dojack's accomplishments transcended sport. Recognized for his ability to work with young men, he was appointed Director of the Saskatchewan Boy's School, where he worked with troubled youth for 37 years, until he retired in 1975. Ten years later the school was renamed the Paul Dojack Youth Centre in his honour.

WILLIAM ARGAN

MILLER COMPREHENSIVE HIGH SCHOOL

1024 College Avenue

*D*esigned by architects McCudden and Goldie and built by Smith Brothers and Wilson, Miller High School opened in 1966.

Miller was the first high school in Regina built specifically for the Separate School System. This permitted Catholic families in the city to send their children to a publicly funded school which would provide the distinct atmosphere and religious study previously limited to private denominational schools.

The school was named after Joseph Peter Miller, a former teacher, principal and superintendent for the Department of Education. From 1948 to 1961 he was a member of the Regina Catholic Separate School Board as superintendent and secretary-treasurer. He was also a member of a federal committee that made recommendations regarding education in the Yukon.

In 1963, Pope John XXIII commended Mr. Miller for his services to Catholic education by conferring on him the title of Knight Commander of Saint Sylvester.

Miller was designated a comprehensive (formerly composite) high school to affirm its combination of academic and technical-vocational courses. It was the first school in Canada to make full use of an Educational Television System. This ETV system, computer programming and several other outstanding space-age features made Miller a school of special interest in the 1960s. The primary purpose of Miller Comprehensive High School was to activate an educational philosophy able to meet the new and complex demands of a dynamic society in a scientific age.

Joseph P. Miller

The original school housed a gymnasium, theatre, cafeteria, library, automotive, woodwork, welding and electrical labs, drafting, typing rooms, science labs and 23 classrooms. A short while later, an IBM1130 computer was added to the school equipment, necessitating some remodeling within the school.

In 1970 another expansion took place to accommodate the growth in student population, various new rooms were added including another gym, art room, a new theatre and relocation of the resource centre.

Miller Comprehensive High School offers an academic program, a modified program, classes in automotive, construction, cosmetology, commercial cooking, information processing and welding as part of the Core Curriculum for Saskatchewan Education. In addition, Miller houses the Instructional Media Centre and the Technology Services for the school division.

REGINA COLLEGE
College Avenue

*R*egina College, established by the Methodist Church in 1911 in a 23-acre free site granted by the City of Regina, originally functioned as a residential and day school for high-school students. The college was open to both men and women and all denominations. On opening day 22 students were enrolled.

In 1911, classes were held in the old City Hospital building on the southwest corner of Hamilton Street and 14th Avenue. Dr. W. A. Andrews was appointed as the first principal. This site was inadequate, so it was exchanged, through negotiations with the provincial government, for 13 acres on 16th Avenue (now College Avenue) where the provincial jail had been located.

In October 1912, the Regina College building was officially opened by the Governor General, the Duke of Connaught. The main building included a men's residence, and four years later, in 1916, a women's residence was added.

In 1925 Regina College was affiliated with the University of Saskatchewan and was able to offer first-year university classes.

During WW II, the Canadian Army occupied the Regina Exhibition Grounds as a manning depot, the Navy (RCVNR) headquarters was located in the Wascana Winter Club, and the RCAF used Regina College for recruitment and classroom training. Throughout the war Regina College conducted classes from the upper floors of the Regina Trading Company Building on Scarth Street and 12th Avenue.

From 1934 to 1974, Regina College was part of the University of Saskatchewan in Saskatoon. Only in 1959 did the College become a full degree-granting institution. In the 1960s the University of Saskatchewan, Regina Campus, moved to new quarters south of Wascana Creek.

In 1974 the University of Regina was established as a separate institution. For many years the College Avenue Campus housed the College of Fine Arts, including the Regina Conservatory of Music and the University Extension programs. Today it houses offices for several university organizations, including the University of Regina Rams, the Regina Conservatory of Music and the Senior's Education Centre.

NORMAL SCHOOL

1955 College Avenue

*T*here were several Normal School locations before the new Normal School was built on College Avenue. The cornerstone was laid by Chief Justice F. W. G. Haultain on May 30, 1913 and it was ready for classes in 1914. The building was designed by the architectural firm of Edgar M. Storey and William Van Egmond and built by Parsons Construction and Engineering Company at a cost of $300,000.

In 1916 the Provincial Museum of Natural History moved from the Legislative Building into the Normal School (see page 143).

Normal School classes moved to Lakeview School when the Normal School building was utilized as a training facility for the Royal Canadian Air Force from 1940 to 1944.

By 1944 enrollment in the provincial Normal Schools had dropped sharply, and the Regina Normal School was closed at the end of September 1944. At that point, schools in Saskatoon and Moose Jaw took care of teacher training.

In 1959 the Teachers' College was transferred to Regina from Moose Jaw. Meanwhile, programs at Regina College, a Junior College of the University of Saskatchewan, had expanded; degree-granting status was granted to Regina College. It became Regina Campus of the University of Saskatchewan on July 1, 1961. The two former Teachers' Colleges at Regina and Saskatoon became part of the University of Saskatchewan on July 1, 1964.

The College Avenue property was occupied by the College of Education until 1969. At that time, it was renovated to meet the needs of the College of Fine Arts, until the new Fine Arts Building, the Riddell Centre, opened in 1997.

The north facade of this building has been maintained, but the building itself has been redeveloped and reconstructed as a Sound Stage Production Centre – Canada/Saskatchewan Production Studios for the developing movie and television industry in Saskatchewan. It is now physically connected to the adjacent CBC building to the south (see page 358).

UNIVERSITY

he University of Regina traces its history back to 1911 when the Methodist Church established Regina College to educate young people in an atmosphere of academic excellence and Christian citizenship. The board of governors chose a 23-acre site on College Avenue and arranged for the construction of the main building. The architects were Brown and Vallance of Montreal; R. J. Lecky of Regina was the contractor. Though not quite finished in the fall of 1912, the building was used for classes, the students moving through hallways filled with planks and sawdust. In 1913 tenders were put out for the tower and the girls' residence on the west side of the tower. Although the outbreak of WW I slowed construction, the buildings were finally completed in 1916.

Beginning in 1925, Regina College offered first-year university in addition to high school courses. Then the Great Depression of the 1930s brought severe financial hardship, and in 1934 the University of Saskatchewan assumed control of a near-bankrupt institution. The college enjoyed modest growth until the early 1960s, when enrolment sky-rocketed with the arrival of the baby boomers. The University of Saskatchewan decided in 1959 to allow Regina to offer a full Arts and Science degree. Accordingly, the college was renamed the University of Saskatchewan, Regina Campus on July 1, 1961.

Since the College Avenue location was too small, the new campus was situated on a large tract of land south of Wascana Creek.

Laboratory Building

Dr. John Archer Library

Campion College

Luther College

OF REGINA

Education Building

Dr. William Riddell Centre

Saskatchewan Indian Federated College
(based on architect's rendering)

Minoru Yamasaki prepared a master plan and designed the first three buildings: the Classroom Building, the Laboratory Building (both completed in 1965) and the Library (1967). Renowned for his imaginative concepts and ability to relate design to the environment, Yamasaki also designed buildings at Wayne State University, Oberlin College and, most famously, the twin towers of the World Trade Center in New York.

A significant milestone was reached in 1974, when Regina Campus achieved independence as the University of Regina. One of the newest buildings is the Dr. William Riddell Centre (1997), which houses the Faculty of Fine Arts, Student Affairs, and the Students' Union. The latter contributed about $4.5 million of the cost through the collection of student fees over many years. Students were finally able to move out of the "temporary" building that had been erected in 1969. Pointing to the future, the new Saskatchewan Indian Federated College Building is located in the northeast corner of the campus. Designed by Douglas Cardinal (famous for the Canadian Museum of Civilization in Hull, Quebec), it has a curvilinear structure symbolic of the Sundance Lodge tradition.

The University of Regina has come a long way since its modest beginnings in 1911. Today it has nine faculties, three federated colleges, and more than 12,000 full- and part-time students. It will continue in the future, as it has done in the past, to strive to meet the educational needs of the community and live up to its motto, "As One Who Serves".

REGINA PUBLIC LIBRARY (CENTRAL)

Northeast corner of Lorne Street and 12th Avenue/Southwest corner of Lorne Street and 12th Avenue

*R*egina citizens, led by Premier Walter Scott, petitioned City Council in October 1907 to establish a free public library. The bylaw was passed in January 1908 and in February the first Library Board was appointed: Chairman, Reverend Canon G. C. Hill, Alderman T. Wilkinson, J. F. L. Embury, A. M. Fenwick, S. C. Burton, John McCarthy, Mayor J. W. Smith, Ex-Officio. J. R. C. Honeyman was the first Chief Librarian.

In January 1909, the first public library opened on the second floor of City Hall. Within a year, library service became so popular that enlarged facilities were required. Construction was soon under way with the purchase of the Lorne Street site and a $50,000 grant from Andrew Carnegie. Lieutenant-Governor G. W. Brown officially opened the new Central Library building, designed by Storey and Van Egmond, on May 11, 1912. It received extensive damage when the cyclone struck six weeks later. Carnegie came to the rescue and paid the reconstruction costs, $9,500.

In 1913 two branch libraries were opened, Albert and Prince of Wales. Eastview (originally Scott) branch was opened in 1918. A new Albert branch was opened in 1927. Connaught branch, at Elphinstone and 13th Avenue, was opened in 1931. Designed by Joseph Warburton, both Albert and Connaught branches were designated as heritage properties in 1984.

**Central Library
1912 to 1961**

In 1948 Marjorie Dunlop was appointed Chief Librarian. She began a program of exhibiting artworks in the periodicals reading room.

Starting in 1954, book trailers were used to supplement library services and service the rapidly expanding population of Regina.

City Council, in 1960, submitted a money bylaw to the people of Regina to build a new Central Library. It passed by a large majority. In 1961 the original Carnegie building was demolished. The new building, designed by Izumi, Arnott and Sugiyama and built by Smith Brothers and Wilson, opened on December 2, 1962.

The new Central Library had a designated art gallery, with a curator, Bruce Parsons, and a theatre space which was used by Globe Theatre for the next four years. In 1972, after Marjorie Dunlop had retired as Chief Librarian, the Library Gallery was officially named the Dunlop Art Gallery in her honour.

The Prairie History Room and Learning Centre in the Central Library were opened in 1973.

In 2002, the Regina Public Library has eight branches throughout the city and over 200 full- and part-time employees. Stonework from the original Central Library has been preserved and placed in the entrance to the new building. The motto reads: *"Qui Legit Regit"* – He who reads, rules.

**Central Library
2311 12th Avenue
1962 –**

SASKATCHEWAN AND REGINA ARCHIVES

3303 Hillsdale Avenue

*I*n 1945 legislation established the Saskatchewan Archives as a joint university-government agency. As early as 1909, the Legislative Library had collected and preserved historical documents. In 1938 the University of Saskatchewan and the Government of Saskatchewan officially joined forces to transfer government records to the newly-created Historical Public Records Office on the University campus.

The Archives Act expanded archives' activity beyond its primary responsibility for the official records of the Government of Saskatchewan to include acquisitions of documentary material from local government and private sources "having a bearing on the history of Saskatchewan". Saskatchewan's archival legislation was largely based upon the following principles: it was important to document the lives of ordinary Saskatchewan people as well as those of the political, social and economic elite; all points of view regardless of affiliation or persuasion must be respected and documented; politics must be removed from the appraisal, selection and access process.

The Saskatchewan Archives provides records-management services for the provincial government. The Information Management Section researches, develops and disseminates records/information management standards for government.

The Saskatchewan Archives is also a public-service institution dedicated to encouraging and assisting everyone who is interested in exploring Saskatchewan's history and/or pursuing genealogical information. The Regina Archives branch has homestead files, school, church and Rural Municipality records, manuscripts, photographs, newspapers and oral history tapes relating to the history of Saskatchewan. The varied sources available at the Archives are best consulted by a personal visit to the reading rooms.

Since 1948 the Saskatchewan Archives has published *Saskatchewan History*, an award-winning magazine dedicated to encouraging both readers and writers to explore the province's history. The magazine has established itself as a valuable source of information and narration about Saskatchewan's unique heritage. Every issue contains both scholarly and general articles, as well as book reviews, heritage and archives news, illustrations and photographs.

Noted historian Dr. John Archer served as Saskatchewan Provincial Archivist as well as Saskatchewan Legislative Librarian and Assistant Clerk of the Saskatchewan Legislature. He was also an associate history professor at Queen's University and Director of Libraries at McGill University. He has authored numerous books and articles, including contributions to the *Encyclopedia of Saskatchewan*.

In 1970 Dr. Archer was appointed principal of Regina Campus and in 1974 he was appointed the first president of the University of Regina. The Library Building at the University of Regina was named after him in 1999.

KLEISINGER HALL

1745 Ottawa Street

*K*leisinger Hall was the first dance hall in Regina. A native of Gyorghyhaza (Georgshausen), Banat, in what was then Austria-Hungary, Josef Kleisinger came to Regina, Saskatchewan in 1903 with his wife, Barbara Steiger, and two children. He left his native homeland by ship, arrived in Halifax and travelled by train to Regina. He was a noted musician who passed on his musical talent to most of his 14 children.

Josef's gift for music was developed in his native Banat. He also played with the Austro-Hungarian army when he was in Vienna. He played most instruments and taught music to his children and to many others.

His trades were as varied as his musical talents. He began work in Canada on the railroad, then worked on a farm outside of Regina, at Markinch. He then became a carpenter and built his own home in Regina. He also built the first dance hall in the city, just to the left of his home. The two buildings were attached by an underground tunnel. A talented musician, he wrote and composed most of his music. He had a family orchestra consisting of himself on the accordion, his daughter Frances on the piano and sons, Joseph Jr. on clarinet, Michael and Peter on violin, Kaspar on the base violin and, later, Andrew on drums or clarinet, Anne on drums and John on clarinet and saxophone.

Kleisinger Hall at 1745 Ottawa Street was the epicentre of German-Canadian culture as it also housed the German-Canadian Club for a time. Dances there were a highlight for many pioneers, with the Kleisinger family orchestra performing and playing the German and Banat folk tunes they so dearly loved. Admission to the dance hall was 25 cents for gentlemen; ladies were free. If you were not satisfied your 25 cents would be refunded.

The dance hall survived WW I and remained a dance hall until 1926. Around the time of the Great Depression it was renovated into suites.

In 1974, Mayor Baker's "Street Name Committee" requested names of pioneers who had made a positive contribution to the City of Regina. The family submitted Josef Kleisinger's name and Kleisinger Crescent was named after him.

Kasper   Peter   Michael   Joseph Jr.   (unknown)   Josef

REGINA SYMPHONY ORCHESTRA

Franklin A. Laubach
Regina Philharmonic
Society
1904 to 1922

Dan A. Cameron
Head of the
Conservatory of
Music

W. Knight Wilson
Conductor
1924 to 1955

Howard Leyton-Brown
Conductor
1960 to 1971

Victor Sawa
Conductor
1997 –

*D*ecember 3, 1908, in the city hall auditorium, the Regina Orchestral Society held its inaugural concert. Reserved seats were $1.00 and general admission was 50 cents. Patrons included Lieutenant-Governor Forget; Hon. Walter Scott, MLA; F. W. G. Haultain, MLA; Mayor Jacob W. Smith. The orchestra played works by Hermann, Wagner, Brahms, Haydn, Thome, Czibulka and Amers. One of the soloists was Mrs. W. M. (Violette) Martin, a soprano gold medalist graduate of the Toronto Conservatory of Music.

Franklin Laubach, founder of the orchestra, arrived in Regina from Scotland in 1904. He organized the Regina Philharmonic Society in 1904 and the Orchestral Society in 1908. Classical works and light operas were included in the society's repertoire. Laubach also conducted a massed chorus of 600 school children at a fund-raiser early in WW I, before he enlisted. After the war he returned to Regina and was the conductor of the Choral and Orchestral Society until 1922.

Leader-Post April 28, 1979: "A rather painful development period ensued as the Regina Choral and Orchestral Society evolved into the Regina Symphony Orchestra, the Regina Choral Society and the Regina Male Voice Choir, led respectively by Knight Wilson, George Coutts and Dan Cameron." Cameron, head of the Conservatory of Music and *Leader-Post* music critic, publicly christened the Regina Symphony Orchestra in 1924, in accordance, however, with the Society's minutes, it was not until 1976, 52 years later, that the program masthead was changed to the Regina Symphony Orchestra.

W. Knight Wilson, symphony conductor from 1924 to 1955, established a reputation of well-disciplined performances and a good rapport with first-rate guest artists.

When Darke Hall opened in 1929, with a seating capacity of 750, the symphony orchestra was delighted to accept the offer, for a nominal fee, to use it as their practice and performance hall. It was their home for 41 years.

In 1931, a Canadian radio concert broadcast by the Regina Symphony was described as "the finest piece of advertising Regina has ever had." At that time the orchestra had 34 professional and 14 amateur players.

In 1959, with the elevation of Regina College to the status of university, the music department was expanded and the instructors, first-rate musicians, contributed their talents to the Symphony. Public funding became available to the orchestra in the late 1960s, from Canada Council and the Saskatchewan Arts Board. This led to greater emphasis on professional musicians.

Once the Centre of the Arts was completed it became the new home of the symphony. With the Centre's capacity to seat 2,029 people, the symphony faced increased opportunities and increased costs. In 10 years, costs of running the orchestra went from $50,000 to $430,000. Sponsors and donors became increasingly important to symphony operations.

From 1960 to 1971 Howard Leyton-Brown was the symphony conductor. He was the last conductor to have an affiliation with the Regina Conservatory of Music.

In 1997 Victor Sawa became the symphony conductor. He has maintained the excellent quality of symphony performances and has encouraged the use of the symphony as a major resource for Opera Saskatchewan, Regina Philharmonic Chorus, South Saskatchewan Youth Orchestra, University of Regina Music Department, etc. He has also initiated successful outdoor performances, Mozart at Mission Ridge and Beethoven at Buffalo Pound, with attendance figures of over 7,500.

DARKE HALL

College Avenue

F. N. Darke

*O*riginally known as Darke Hall for Music and Art, Darke Hall was designed by J. H. Puntin. It was named after Francis N. Darke who had given $100,000 for its construction, and had donated the building to Regina College to be used for music and arts.

Francis N. Darke came to Regina in 1892 and established a retail and wholesale meat business. In 1906 he disposed of the business and devoted his time to his extensive real estate holdings in Regina and vicinity. Darke served on the town and city council for seven years and in 1898, at the age of 35, was Regina's youngest mayor. In addition to Darke Hall, he gave Reginans the gift of music, the Darke Memorial Chimes that were placed in trust of Knox-Metropolitan Church.

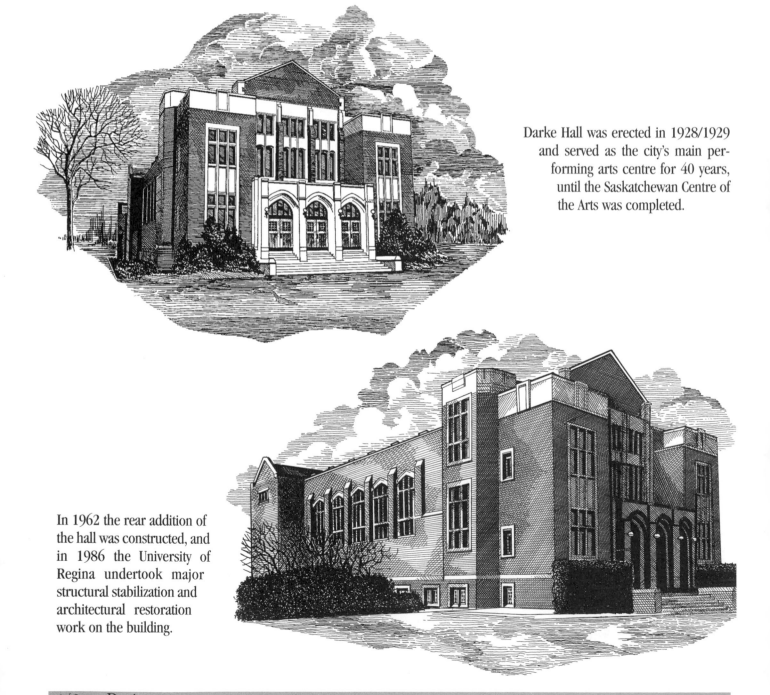

Darke Hall was erected in 1928/1929 and served as the city's main performing arts centre for 40 years, until the Saskatchewan Centre of the Arts was completed.

In 1962 the rear addition of the hall was constructed, and in 1986 the University of Regina undertook major structural stabilization and architectural restoration work on the building.

ROYAL SASKATCHEWAN MUSEUM OF NATURAL HISTORY

2445 Albert Street

THIS MUSEUM OF NATURAL HISTORY IS DEDICATED TO THE HONOUR OF ALL THE PIONEERS WHO CAME FROM MANY LANDS TO SETTLE IN THIS PART OF CANADA A TRIBUTE TO THEIR VISION TOIL AND COURAGE WHICH GAVE SO MUCH TO SASKATCHEWAN AND THIS NATION

*I*n 1906 Saskatchewan was only a year into Confederation but already it was taking steps to preserve its own heritage. The Provincial Museum of Natural History was formed to "secure and preserve natural history specimens and objects of historical and ethnological interest."

The first artifact donated to the Museum was the Beaver Hills Petroglyph. The Museum's first location was in the Regina Trading Company Ltd. (see page 192).

The museum's first specimens were prepared for an exhibit of Saskatchewan's wildlife at the 1906 Dominion Fair in Halifax. The display was set up in the Legislative Building in 1911, but suffered considerable damage in the 1912 cyclone. It was moved in 1916 to the Normal School, where it was eventually expanded into a major diorama display. After several attempts by the Natural History Society to establish a proper facility, the province agreed to construct this building in 1953.

The current museum was constructed on the site of the ill-fated Chateau Qu'Appelle Hotel project of the Grand Trunk Pacific Railway (see page 154). It was opened in 1955 as the Saskatchewan Museum of Natural History, the province's principal project for the commemoration of Saskatchewan's Golden Jubilee year. The museum was dedicated by Governor General, Vincent Massey, as a monument to the pioneers of the province and a symbol of their appreciation of the natural environment within which they settled. In 1959 Queen Elizabeth and Prince Philip visited the museum. It received its "Royal" designation in 1993.

Designed by a former provincial architect, E. J. McCudden, the massing of the building is intentionally low and extended, to emulate the predominant topography of the prairies. The open siting of the building also serves this symbolic function. The building exterior is faced with Tyndall stone. The tops of the exhibit wing walls are decorated with an elaborate series of bas friezes, executed by the artist Robert Garner, that depict the diverse wildlife of the prairies. The building dedication is also inscribed into one of the front exterior walls.

In 1986 the museum welcomed Megamunch, a half-sized robotic Tyrannosaurus rex. His "friendly" roar has greeted thousands of school children, and while the Life Sciences Gallery was being constructed he resided at the Regina Airport and loudly greeted visitors to the city.

In 1991 the bones of a Tyrannosaurus rex were discovered in the Frenchman River Valley by Robert Gebhardt, and in 1994 paleontologists from the Royal Saskatchewan Museum began excavating "Scotty", Saskatchewan's first T. Rex. In May 2000 the RSM began operating a paleontological lab at the T. Rex Discovery Centre in Eastend.

The Royal Saskatchewan Museum offers educational programs for Kindergarten to Grade 12 students in the areas of First Nations, Life Sciences and Earth Sciences. Programs, including the Paleo Pit, are interactive and include hands-on activities and a visit to Museum galleries.

THE MACKENZIE ART GALLERY

3475 Albert Street

*T*he MacKenzie Art Gallery had its beginnings in 1936, when Norman MacKenzie, KC, a Regina lawyer and art collector, bequeathed a major portion of his collection and residual estate to the University of Saskatchewan for use at Regina College.

"MacKenzie had been a member of the Board of Governors at Regina College for many years and was probably the first serious art collector in Western Canada." – Riddell, *Regina* It was his wish that his collection be used for the promotion of art and the appreciation and study thereof in the Province of Saskatchewan and particularly the City of Regina.

Gus Kenderdine, a prominent Saskatchewan artist and member of the University of Saskatchewan Art Department was the first curator of the MacKenzie collection in Regina. He was also the director of the newly-formed School of Art/College of Fine Arts.

In 1950 Ken Lochhead was appointed director of the School of Art and curator of the MacKenzie Collection. He revitalized the school, which had been closed during the war years, and the gallery, which had suffered from lack of display space. Lochhead gathered a group of young artists who became known as the "Regina Five": Ken Lochhead, Art MacKay, Ronald Bloore, Doug Morton and Ted Godwin. All taught at the University and went on to earn national and international reputations.

In 1953 the MacKenzie Art Gallery opened on the College Avenue Campus. Expansion took place almost immediately, with the enlarged gallery being completed in 1957. At that time Alan Jarvis, Director of the National Gallery of Canada, pronounced that the MacKenzie was the finest gallery between Toronto and Vancouver!

Those following Lochhead as directors have included: Richard Simmons, Ron Bloore, Terry Fenton, Nancy Dillow, Carol Phillips, Andrew Oko and Kate Davis. Each, in their own way, has developed and maintained a strong exhibition program, in-house and outreach programs, as well as building the permanent collection.

The permanent collection of the MacKenzie Art Gallery numbers more than 3,500 works of art. The major collecting focus is on Canadian historical and contemporary art, with a special interest in the work of western Canadian artists. Major exhibitions of contemporary and historical Canadian artists, as well as international artists, are organized by the MacKenzie Art Gallery.

In the mid-1980s it became clear that the MacKenzie Art Gallery needed a new home. It had been a department of the University of Regina, and in 1984 the MacKenzie Art Gallery was incorporated to plan for new facilities, and for the transfer of responsibilities to the new organization. The Board's mandate was to build a new community gallery and assume control of the gallery from the University when a new building was ready for occupancy. The new Board would be responsible for raising capital funds to augment those secured from federal, provincial and city sources. It would also be responsible for raising the necessary operating funds. In 1990, after some controversy, the MacKenzie Art Gallery moved into the T. C. Douglas Building in Wascana Centre. The new gallery facility, designed by Willem (Bill) de Lint, encompasses 100,000 square feet on three levels. The exhibition level includes eight environmentally controlled galleries totaling 24,000 square feet. The Gallery boasts state-of-the-art technical areas including conservation lab, workshop, preparation rooms and vault. Other facilities include a 185-seat theatre, public resource centre, gift shop and conference rooms.

The Gallery is visited by approximately 100,000 visitors a year. In addition, 14,000 people are served through the gallery's Outreach Program; in-house school and community education programs reach 25,000.

The MacKenzie Art Gallery is recognized as one of the top galleries in Canada and continues to be an active participant in Regina's vibrant arts community.

THE REGINA LIONS BAND/THE MOSSINGS

2272 Pasqua Street

S tarted in wartime 1943 by Marion Mossing, while her husband, Alexander Bernard Mossing, was away in the armed services, the original band practiced in the Mossing home. After discharge from the army, A. B. Mossing became director of the band and it was renamed the Queen City Band.

While A. B. directed the band, Marion canvassed the city relentlessly for a sponsor. The only organization that would listen to her was the Lions Club, and the band officially became The Regina Junior Lions Band in 1946.

A. B. Mossing
Founder
Lions Band

Marion
Mossing
Founder
Lions Band

Bob Mossing
original band
member and
Director for
over 30 years

The band started as a single band, with 45 members. It has grown to four bands, with over 500 members, and an adult band of 150 members. The band soon became a travelling marching band. In the early days they made an annual trip to Williston. Soon the band developed a strong reputation and began to travel and compete extensively around the world. The band makes a major trip every four years. Band trips have included Europe, the Pasadena Rose Bowl Parade, Disneyland, Disneyworld, Hawaii, the Miami Orange Bowl Parade and Japan.

Annually, the band travels extensively in the North American midwest and has brought world-wide recognition to Regina. The band relies heavily on community support from bottle drives, almond drives, concerts and the help of its many volunteers. Over 8,000 young men and women have played in the band, many of whom carried on with musical careers. The Band moved to a new permanent home at 2272 Pasqua Street in 1993.

The Mossing family, with the help of the Regina Lions Club, has made a great contribution to the youth and music culture of Regina. A. B. Mossing was Director until 1970, when his son Robert took over the band. Robert's brother Darcy was also a band director. Robert Mossing has received many awards, including the Larry Schneider Leadership and Communication Award, Lion's International President's Award, Regina North Rotary Heritage Award, SBA District Band Director Award, National Band Award, Canadian Band Association and the Order of Canada, as well as numerous others.

Robert (Bob) retired in 1999 and was replaced by Tim Michaels, who was replaced as Director in 2000 by Michael Alstad.

GLOBE THEATRE

Old City Hall Building – 1801 Scarth Street

G lobe Theatre, Saskatchewan's first professional theatre company, was founded in 1966 as a children's touring company by Ken and Sue Kramer, at the invitation of the Saskatchewan Arts Board. In 1967 the theatre performed its first adult play, and in 1973 the company took up residence in its first mainstage theatre space. Today, the Globe is housed in the Old City Hall building, a designated heritage site.

Globe Theatre's productions are presented in a theatre-in-the-round configuration. Some of Ken and Sue Kramer's founding principles for Globe Theatre were: to present plays on an open stage, playing to small audiences in an intimate environment; to challenge the audience socially, politically, morally, emotionally, intellectually; to involve as wide a spectrum of the population as possible as an audience; to de-mystify the theatre, returning to theatre as a part of daily life; to present great works of the past and present, and seek out new work from Canada and abroad; to take this work to as many communities as possible.

Susan Ferley began her tenure as artistic director of Globe Theatre in 1990. Under her leadership, the theatre expanded its subscription base, eliminated a significant accumulated deficit and, in 1998, launched the Imagine This! million-dollar capital campaign to refurbish the theatre's facilities.

Ruth Smillie began work as artistic director of Globe Theatre in 1998. As part of the renovations undertaken as a result of the capital campaign, Globe Theatre created a cabaret studio space in the summer of 1998 and produced its first Studio Cabaret Series (SandBox Series). Also in the summer of 1998, Globe Theatre produced the first Lanterns on the Lake festival in collaboration with eight other professional arts organizations.

WILLIAM
ARGAN

THE SASKATCHEWAN CENTRE OF THE ARTS

200 Lakeshore Drive

*T*he Saskatchewan Centre of the Arts was officially opened by Governor General Roland Mitchener on August 24th, 1970, with a grand opening program featuring world-renowned tenor Jan Peerce.

The Centre had been eight years in the making and had encountered many difficulties before it was completed. The first Auditorium Planning Committee meeting was held in 1962 under the leadership of Justice M. A. MacPherson Jr.

The original plans were to have the proposed building completed as part of the 1967 Canadian Centennial, qualifying for federal and provincial financial support as part of Canada's 100th Birthday Celebration. Progress was slow and tedious, and the structure of the organizing committee was changed several times in order to achieve agreement respecting a site and financing. In 1964 the Board of the Diamond Jubilee and Centennial Auditorium Committee was told that a final building program had to be in place by June of that year if the auditorium was to be completed in 1967.

The building project proceeded, with additional delays. The decision was made to divide the tendering into two parts so that structural steel could be awarded and erected while the remainder of the building plans were being completed. It was pointed out that because of many other centennial projects underway in Canada, structural steel was in great demand.

Foundation work and the erection of the structural steel began, however, when tenders were received for the balance of the project. The cost of the building was double the original estimate, due to an overheated construction industry, caused by centennial project demands and the requirement of a 1967 completion date. In a state of shock, with additional finances unavailable, the project was halted and the steel skeleton stood starkly against the sky. It was dubbed by University of Regina engineering students as "the largest monkey bars in the world".

It took almost two years, a reorganization of the board, revisions to the original plans, and agreement by the Government of Saskatchewan to take over responsibility for the project before construction commenced again in July of 1967. The project was completed in 1970. The Chairman of the Board when the "Centre" opened was Mr. H. W. Padwick.

Architects Izumi, Arnott and Sugiyama stayed with the project throughout and contributed countless hours of their time in an effort to achieve success. The fine building that resulted is a tribute to their dedication. The "Centre" has received world-wide acclaim from visiting artists and performers and is a facility of which the citizens of Regina and southern Saskatchewan can be proud. For a number of years Harry Belafonte premiered his annual Las Vegas show in Regina because of the Centre's excellent facilities and acoustics.

Once the Saskatchewan Centre of the Arts was completed, the Regina Symphony Orchestra gave up its Darke Hall location and made the Centre its home. Globe Theatre also relocated to the Centre, but left to take space in the Old City Hall because they could not afford the Centre's rental fees.

In recent years, Centennial Theatre has been renamed Shirley Bell Theatre, and Hanbidge Hall has been renamed Doris Knight Hall, in honour of their family contributions.

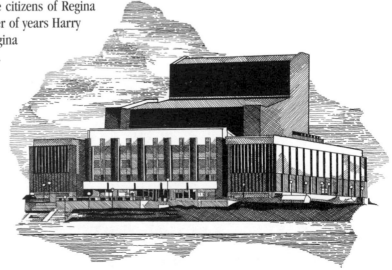

SASKATCHEWAN EXPRESS

2300 7th Avenue

S askatchewan Express originated in 1980 as a project of the Diamond Jubilee Corporation, which was responsible for the 75th Anniversary celebrations of the province. Saskatchewan Express was founded through the vision and dedication of Carol Gay Bell. The group was designed to showcase talented young Saskatchewan performers and give the people of the province the opportunity to see and take pride in what can be accomplished here in Saskatchewan.

The troupe was called "Saskatchewan's Greatest Travelling Birthday Party". Initially sponsored by the provincial government, in 1983 Saskatchewan Lotteries became a funding partner and the group was renamed Saskatchewan Express.

Saskatchewan Express has performed for more than two million people and travelled more than 250,000 kilometers across Canada, from Vancouver to Cape Breton, as well as the United States. The group appeared in the Saskatchewan Pavilion at Expo '86 in Vancouver. They toured British Columbia for "Music '91" and have appeared at the Calgary Stampede; Edmonton Klondike Days; on Parliament Hill in Ottawa; The Brier in Chicoutimi, Quebec; Festival by the Sea in Saint John, New Brunswick; Canada Games in Kelowna, and in Saskatoon, St. John's, Newfoundland and Cape Breton.

Saskatchewan Express was featured during the halftime show of the 1995 Grey Cup in Regina and has appeared at the Buffalo Days Exhibition each year since 1980. Thousands of young Saskatchewan performers have auditioned for Saskatchewan Express and hundreds have had the opportunity to tour the province and the country with the group. Many have gone on to successful professional careers around the world, on Broadway, in stage and musical productions, in film, on television and on cruise ships.

Carol Gay Bell is not only the founder of Saskatchewan Express, as Artistic Director/General Manager, she is also its heart and soul. Saskatchewan Express continues to grow and flourish because of her leadership and perseverance.

She is a person of irrepressible effervescence and commitment to youth. Carol Gay Bell has been described as a friend, a teacher, a den mother and a shining example for the fortunate young people who have received her stimulating artistic direction.

Carol Gay Bell founded The Saskatchewan Roughrider Cheerleaders in 1960 and was the director for 17 years. She directed the halftime show for Grey Cup 1995.

Born and raised in Regina, she has been one of Regina's greatest ambassadors. She has received a number of awards of recognition, including the Ryerson Silver Medal for outstanding female graduate; YWCA Woman of the Year – professional category, 1985; Larry Schneider Communications and Leadership Award, 1986 and the Saskatchewan Order Of Merit in 1997.

Carol Gay Bell

SASKATCHEWAN SCIENCE CENTRE

2903 Powerhouse Drive

When the Saskatchewan Power Corporation purchased the Regina Power Plant (see page 49) from the City of Regina, SPC made a commitment to financially support an alternative community use for the building.

Negotiations with SPC, Wascana Centre, federal and provincial governments, and the City of Regina began in 1979. The Saskatchewan Science Centre Inc. was incorporated in 1981. The next six years were spent obtaining grants from both levels of government and organizing fund-raising programs.

In 1987 Arnott, Kelley, O'Connor & Associates were named architects and Bird Construction was appointed construction manager. The building underwent extensive reconstruction and the Science Centre was completed in April 1989. It was officially opened in July of that year by Their Royal Highnesses the Duke and Duchess of York.

The five-storey IMAX Theatre was opened in 1991 by Lieutenant-Governor Sylvia Fedoruk, and named The Kramer IMAX Theatre, in honour of Donald and Claire Kramer who gave the largest private non-corporate donation to the project. The Kramer IMAX Theatre presents science and nature films in giant-screen format.

In 1999 the Science Centre opened the SaskTel 3D Laser Theatre which is one of only ten 3D theatres in the world.

The Science Centre has 250,000 visitors annually to its two facilities, the interactive Powerhouse of Discovery and The Kramer IMAX Theatre.

The Powerhouse of Discovery is laid out on four levels covering nearly 7,000 square metres of floor space. It is divided into six exhibit areas, each representing a different branch of science; Patterns Around Us focuses on physics; The Living Body covers genetics and human life; The Living Planet deals with biology and ecology; Our Planet Earth looks at geology and meteorology; Beyond Earth covers space. The Discovery Lab houses a variety of reptilian and amphibian species. Visitors can also enjoy live demonstrations on static electricity, cryogenics, lasers, sound, ecology and anatomy.

REGINA RAILWAY STATION (1882-1892)

Broad Street and Dewdney Avenue

With the coming of the railway to Regina in 1882, the CPR depot was built at the end of Broad Street. All roads led to the station, so Broad Street and South Railway were the hub of the early business district.

Pascal Bonneau, a Montreal contractor, built the CPR railway from Winnipeg to Regina and became one of the city's first merchants. His business and home were located at Broad Street and 12th Avenue.

Along with Charles McCusker, he raised money to build the first Catholic church in Regina.

An interesting anecdote in the *Archdiocese of Regina* book involves Bonneau: "During the night before Riel was to be hanged, a North-West Mounted Police officer came to Pascal Bonneau's home with a message from Lieutenant Governor Dewdney. The letter asked for an interview with Bonneau. Pascal was to organize a plot to free Riel from prison and escape. Swift horses were to be posted every ten miles between Regina and the American border. Bonneau hired a number of Metis from Willow Bunch to assist in the execution of the plan. One well-meaning Metis, innocently spoke of the plan to someone not so friendly toward Riel. As a result, the plot failed.

"Riel's body was delivered into the care of Pascal Bonneau, Sr., where Riel's wife and mother took their last farewell. Owing to threats that had been made and the strong feelings engendered over this unfortunate affair, Pascal and his son Treffle placed the body under the floor of St. Mary's Church and set up a guard day and night, to prevent anyone from stealing the body.

"After a few weeks Governor Dewdney sent a message to Pascal Bonneau that a railroad car was stationed at the city limits to receive Riel's corpse. The Bonneaus took advantage of a blizzard and the darkness to dig up the body and transport it to a nearby cart and then to the railroad car. To protect the body against threatened desecration at the hands of bitter partisans, Treffle traveled with the corpse to St. Boniface where he proudly handed it over to Riel's family for decent burial near St. Boniface Cathedral."

Pascal Bonneau

REGINA RAILWAY STATION (1892-1911)

South Railway and Hamilton Street

Regina's second railway station was erected in 1892 and stood at the foot of Hamilton Street, immediately west of the later Union Station. This station was replaced in 1911.

By 1912, 32 passenger trains arrived and departed daily from the city. In 1924 there were 22 lines radiating from Regina with up to 50 arrivals and departures a day.

UNION STATION – 1911

Broad Street and South Railway

*D*espite labour disputes, derailments and avalanches in the Rocky Mountains, southern Saskatchewan had uninterrupted daily passenger service for over a century. On June 28, 1886, Canada's first prime minister, Sir John A. Macdonald, came to Regina to mark the new service.

Union Station was built in 1911 when the newly-formed Canadian Northern Railway (later Canadian National) and the CPR combined their passenger facilities into Union Station. The station replaced the Queen City's second station that had been built in 1892, and stood at the foot of Hamilton Street, immediately west of the current building.

The new building would be "very large and imposing, with commodious waiting rooms on the main floor, lavatories, smoking rooms, two ticket offices – one for each rail company, and lots of baggage room in the east wing of the building." – The *Leader*, May 13, 1911

This heritage building played a vital role in the history of Regina. In the city's infancy, most newcomers' first glimpse of Regina would have been through Union Station. Thousands of immigrants from Ukraine, Poland, Scotland, Germany, Ireland, the United States and Lithuania came to Regina via rail. Regina promised a new start for many who had left behind poverty, famine, revolution and persecution.

For decades, it was at Union Station that almost everybody visiting Regina arrived, where everybody leaving departed, and through which passed all arriving and departing goods. Later, as war threatened the world, men marched through the station to clamber onto troop trains, to fight for freedom. When they returned in 1918 and 1919, family and friends greeted them at the station with tears of joy. In 1939 and 1940, again there were tearful farewells as Saskatchewan boys left the prairies to halt Hitler's aggression in Europe. As they trickled back, bands played and flags fluttered at the station.

In 1921, a substantial extension was added to the west wing of Union Station, and in 1927 the waiting room was expanded and food services were added.

The 1931 expansion cost nearly $1,250,000. It included a major southward projection of the three-storey central section to create the grand concourse. This necessitated the complete removal of the 1911 facade and part of the old offices.

Bas relief pilasters, lacy iron canopies, medallions and stone detailing gave the building a simple elegance. The grand concourse, with its high arched ceiling, bas relief medallions and finely carved stonework, featured contemporary art deco light fixtures manufactured entirely in western Canada by Canadian Electric Plating Company.

The seats in the waiting room, specifically designed for the station, were manufactured in Regina. The flooring in public areas was done in terrazzo, and marble was installed in high-traffic areas such as entrances and stairways. Marble-surfaced counters, brass fixtures and lettering also added to the station's stateliness.

A staircase of white marble connected the main passenger lobby to the offices above. This area featured an interesting central octagonal ticket office. The waiting rooms were finished with white polished oak. Centered on the east wall of the main lobby, between the restroom doors, was an ornate drinking fountain, surmounted by a bronze plaque commemorating CPR employees who had died in the Great War.

At this time, the trackage was re-laid to provide five station tracks, each with a concrete platform. New heating and lighting service was also installed and the passenger car yard facilities were renovated.

Surrounding Regina's CPR station was an elaborate formal garden that dated back to 1910. For many years, this garden's grounds were joined to Stanley Park, Regina's first park. The dryness and dust storms of the Great Depression and the construction of the 1931/1932 addition nearly destroyed the gardens. However, they lasted until the 1960s, when the park gave way to parking.

One of the more unusual events at Union Station was the passage of the Silk Train across Canada. The silk was loaded in Japan and brought by ship to Vancouver where it was loaded onto the train and headed across the country to the east. Travelling at over 100 miles an hour, the train crossed Canada in fewer than five days. When the train went through Union Station the station was locked so no one could get onto the platform.

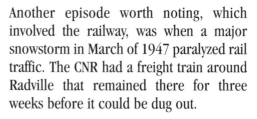

Another episode worth noting, which involved the railway, was when a major snowstorm in March of 1947 paralyzed rail traffic. The CNR had a freight train around Radville that remained there for three weeks before it could be dug out.

There was an attempt to convert Union Station into a multi-modal centre which would serve trains, buses, taxis and airport limousines, but in 1983 the provincial government abandoned a funding proposal which halted discussions between the provincial government, VIA Rail and the Saskatchewan Transportation Company.

In 1984 VIA Rail bought Union Station from CP Rail and in 1991 Union Station was designated an official Federal Heritage Site. However, the Station's days as a rail depot were numbered. Many options were proposed for the continued use of Union Station and, in 1996, after extensive redevelopment, it reopened as Casino Regina.

CASINO REGINA AND CASINO SHOW LOUNGE

1880 Saskatchewan Drive

T he establishment of Casino Regina in Union Station on Saskatchewan Drive was an important boost to the redevelopment of the northeast corner of downtown Regina. $37 million was spent on the creation of a modern casino, without sacrificing the heritage history of the Union Station site.

Designed by Gordon Arnott and Associates, Casino Regina was the largest most modern casino in western Canada when it opened in 1996. It has become an extremely popular entertainment centre which attracts visitors from all parts of western Canada and the northern United States.

After five years of steady growth Casino Regina undertook a major $22-million expansion program to provide necessary parking and a new entertainment centre, the Casino Show Lounge.

In keeping with the desire to retain the existing heritage streetscape of Saskatchewan Drive, the original CPR telegraph building was salvaged and incorporated into the design of the new complex, to be used as a staff training centre.

As part of a major expansion of Casino Regina in 2001, overhead skywalks were constructed connecting the Delta Hotel to the Cornwall Centre though Sears and to the main Casino through the new Show Lounge at the west end. Visitors and city residents are able to walk indoors via a network of climate-controlled skywalks from the Canada Life Building, and the McCallum-Hill Centre at the south end on 12th Avenue, to the Delta Hotel and Casino Regina on Saskatchewan Drive.

GRAND TRUNK PACIFIC RAILWAY STATION

Corner of Angus Street and 16th (now College) Avenue

*G*rand Trunk Pacific erected a railway passenger station at the corner of Angus Street and 16th Avenue in 1911. Following bankruptcy in 1919, the railway station was abandoned.

The Grand Trunk Pacific and the Great Northern Railway merged to form the Canadian National Railway.

GRAND TRUNK PACIFIC RAILWAY STATION

2720 16th (now College) Avenue

*W*heat and the railways were key factors in Regina's economic growth in the early 1900s. When the 1906 census showed that Moose Jaw's population had surpassed Regina's, business leaders in the Queen City decided to increase business by securing additional rail connections.

In November 1910, the city gave the Grand Trunk Pacific Railway (GTP) land for spur tracks and freight sheds, and agreed to close a number of streets so that the company could build a short line along 16th Avenue to Albert Street, where it proposed to build its own passenger station. The GTP agreed to build a first-class hotel in the vicinity of the station, to make Regina a divisional point (see page 171).

The railway station was located in the second block on 16th Avenue, west of Albert Street. The line ran east/west down 16th Avenue, between Albert Street and Elphinstone Street, where it connected with a north/south line.

In 1912 council agreed to lease part of Wascana Park and provide tax and other concessions for the construction of a lavish GTP hotel on the corner of Albert Street and 16th Avenue.

The Grand Trunk Pacific Railway went bankrupt in 1919 and the station was removed about 1924.

CANADIAN NORTHERN RAILWAY FREIGHT SHEDS

Albert Street and Dewdney Avenue

*T*here was a flurry of railway building in 1906, the year the Canadian Northern Railway entered Regina. That year it acquired the line running from Regina north to Prince Albert, and completed another line from Brandon to Regina in 1908.

In 1911, the Grand Trunk Pacific Railway (GTP) built a line from Yorkton and Melville, and the city provided land for the construction of new terminal facilities for the Canadian Northern and the GTP. Each railway built additional lines. By 1913 a total of 12 railway lines radiated out of the city.

New freight sheds and offices of the CNR were built at Albert Street and Dewdney Avenue in 1912.

"Watch the Smoke . . . Not ours, but that of the hustling, bustling activity now underway in northwest Regina. Beginning at Albert and Dewdney there are the Canadian Northern Freight Sheds, Regina Street Railway Barns, Railway Tracks, Spurs, Extensions, Trunk Sewer Line, Street Car Extensions, Mills, Oil Distributaries, Building Supplies, Coal Yards, Foundries, Canadian Northern Yards, Shops, Coal docks, Scales, Stockyards and ditto for the Grand Trunk." – March 2, 1912 *Leader*

GALLOPING GOOSE/NO. 340

*U*nion Station, Regina's major link with the outside world, flourished from its inception until after WW II.

During that period, Regina was terminal for the fastest train in western Canada, making the run to Moose Jaw in less than 55 minutes, and doing it up to four times a day.

The No. 340 was a sleek maroon gas/electric unit which combined engine, baggage, express, mail and passenger coach in one.

Affectionately known as "The Galloping Goose", the No. 340 operated on short runs to give frequent local service where the service of heavy steam trains was not economical.

Throughout the summer months the commuter train made regular weekend trips, taking passengers to and from Regina Beach and surrounding resorts.

Although the train was known as the "Galloping Goose", it was better known as the "Skunk" because of odour from the fumes of its diesel.

REGINA TROLLEY CARS AND STREETCAR BARNS

*P*lans were made for a municipal transit system in 1911. Early that year construction of trackage was started and the first streetcar ran on July 28, 1911. Wooden streetcars, built in England, initially travelled three routes, each route having two cars. They operated Monday to Saturday. An adult fare in 1911 was five cents; in 1920, ten cents. In the depression years fares returned to five cents to encourage usage.

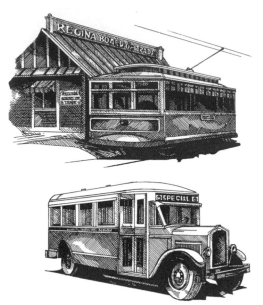

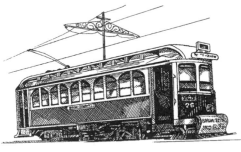

1911 Regina streetcar

One of Regina's first gasoline buses, used during the 1930s

Streetcars were noisy. During the war years, city council considered switching to diesel-operated buses; they didn't because rubber and gas were rationed.

Old No. 46 travelled Regina streets during the 1940s

Trolley coaches, rubber-tired buses run by electricity, were introduced on September 8, 1947. Two long poles came up from the back of the roof and connected to the wires strung along the route. These coaches were utilized until a disastrous fire on January 23, 1949. The fire raced through the streetcar barns and destroyed the major portion of the building and three-quarters of the rolling stock. Lost in the fire were 14 streetcars, 17 trolleys and 9 diesel buses – $1 million damage in total. The transportation system was momentarily crippled, but enough gas buses were rented to continue.

Trolley coach used by Regina
Transit in 1950

The old transit system was replaced on September 11, 1950 by power-driven trolleys, supplemented by gas-powered buses. To mark the change, the name of the public transport department changed from Regina Municipal Railway to Regina Transit System.

GOOD LUCK - GOOD BYE

Regina's last streetcar says
"Good-bye" on
September 11, 1950

From 1950 to 1955, the trolleys were the city's only form of public transport. Eventually they were phased out and replaced with diesel buses.

Transit diesel bus used during 1950s

In March 1966, the last trolley ran from Scarth Street and 11th Avenue, and Regina became the first Canadian city to completely convert from trolleys to diesel buses.

Transit diesel bus in 1961

Moving into the 21st Century!

*R*egina Airport has come a long way since a handful of barnstorming aviators first flew an aeroplane into the city's summer skies. The history of aviation in Regina boasts many "firsts".

In 1919 three Royal Flying Corps veterans, Lt. Roland J. Groome, Edward Clarke and Bob McCombie, formed the Aerial Service Company in Regina and built an airfield that became Canada's first licensed aerodrome on April 22, 1920. The first Canadian aircraft registration letters, G-CAAA were issued to one of the Aerial Service Company's Curtiss J N-4 biplanes on April 20, 1920. At the same time, Bob McCombie, the company's engineer, received the first Engineer's Certificate. Lastly, Lt. Roland Groome was issued the first Commercial Pilot License (No. 1) by the newly formed Canada Air Board on July 31, 1920.

The prairie provinces settled into a depression in 1923 and most of western Canada's aviation ventures folded. Two new airfields opened in 1927, and the one established by the Regina Flying Club was purchased by the City of Regina in 1928. Following three years of development, the Regina Municipal Airport was officially opened on September 15, 1930. In 1939 Canada went to war and the federal government took over operation of Regina Airport.

The Department of National Defence built three hangars, ancillary buildings and equipped the airport as a British Commonwealth Air Training Plan base. The training program ended in 1945 and the Department of Transport resumed operation of Regina Airport until 1955, when it was turned back to the municipal government.

Hill Avenue and
Cameron Street

Roland Groome

AUTHORITY

Airport operations were not financially viable for Regina taxpayers and the airport was sold to Transport Canada in 1972 for $2.3 million. The decade from 1972 to 1982 saw Regina Airport continue to grow and change. Increasing passenger demand and larger aircraft necessitated a $35-million expansion project which commenced in 1982, and saw the Terminal Building more than tripled in size. The architectural design of the new facility is state of the art, earning it many awards, including the Premier's Award for Design Excellence.

A new and exciting chapter in the proud and continuing history of Regina Airport commenced on May 1, 1999. On that date, Regina Airport Authority, a locally represented not-for-profit corporation, assumed managerial, operational and developmental control of the airport from the Federal Government. Dick Rendek, a lawyer and former president of the Saskatchewan Roughriders was the first president and CEO of the Regina Airport Authority from 1999 to 2001.

The transfer enables the community to take greater advantage of an invaluable asset to better reflect and serve community interests. While the mandate of the airport is virtually unchanged with respect to the provision of first-class aviation facilities and services, the Authority is committed to expanding and enhancing these services in a cost-effective manner through partnership with the local community.

www.yqr.ca

Regina Airport Authority

REGINA AIRPORTS

Hill Avenue and Cameron Street/Albert Street and 25th Avenue/Regina Avenue west of Lewvan Drive

*I*n 1911 Bob St. Henry and his Curtiss Pusher biplane made the inaugural flight over Regina from the Exhibition Grounds. The racetrack's infield offered a fairly flat runway surface.

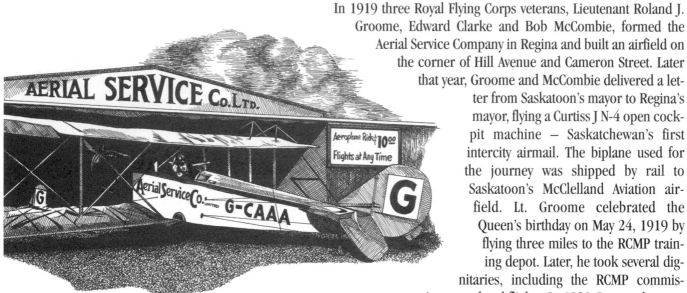

In 1919 three Royal Flying Corps veterans, Lieutenant Roland J. Groome, Edward Clarke and Bob McCombie, formed the Aerial Service Company in Regina and built an airfield on the corner of Hill Avenue and Cameron Street. Later that year, Groome and McCombie delivered a letter from Saskatoon's mayor to Regina's mayor, flying a Curtiss J N-4 open cockpit machine – Saskatchewan's first intercity airmail. The biplane used for the journey was shipped by rail to Saskatoon's McClelland Aviation airfield. Lt. Groome celebrated the Queen's birthday on May 24, 1919 by flying three miles to the RCMP training depot. Later, he took several dignitaries, including the RCMP commissioner, on local flights. In 1920 Groome became Canada's first licensed commercial aviator and McCombie, the company's engineer, received the first Engineer's Certificate.

Early in 1927, Groome and Jack Wight organized Universal Air Industries and opened a second airfield, the "Lakeview Aerodrome" on the present site of the Golden Mile Shopping Centre. They provided pilot training and commercial flights.

Also in 1927, the Regina Flying Club was formed and 160 acres of land was bought, two miles west of the city, to build a modern airport. In 1928, A. E. Whitmore was named the first chairman of the Regina Municipal Air Board, a position he held until 1947. The City of Regina purchased the Flying Club in 1928 and built a hangar and gasoline storage facilities. In the same year, Regina was also included in the regular mail and passenger service initiated by Western Canada Airways, a Winnipeg firm. The Lakeview Aerodrome closed in 1929 and all aircraft moved to the new site. A second hangar, built in 1930, still stands on the present airport site and is the home to the Government of Saskatchewan Executive Aircraft Services.

On September 15, 1930, after three years of development, the Regina Municipal Airport was officially opened.

Air mail contracts were cancelled in the early 1930s because of economic problems brought on by the Depression, and not many machines stopped overnight. However, 1932 saw asphalt runways constructed at Regina so airplanes could taxi from tarmac to runway, safe from the sticky mud so famous in Regina. Regina Airport had the only paved runway system between Montreal and Vancouver.

American pilot Frank Hawks flew non-stop from New York to Regina in a Northrop Gamma monoplane to mark the opening of the 1933 World Grain Fair.

The Regina Flying Club biplanes were maintained in their own hangar up to the beginning of WW II, though Regina Flying Club machines were in and out of the larger hangar up to 1939. On September 20, 1935 tragedy struck when Groome and a student crashed at Regina Airport. The crash was fatal for Groome.

Trans-Canada Air Lines was formed in 1937 and began the first transcontinental airmail and passenger service between Montreal and Vancouver the following year. Prairie Airways of Moose Jaw provided connecting flights for Moose Jaw, North Battleford and Prince Albert to Regina and Saskatoon.

In 1938 Regina's runway system was rebuilt, and in 1939 the Department of Transport completed an administration building and control tower. That year, Canada went to war and the operation of Regina's airport was taken over by the federal government. Three hangars were built by the Department of National Defence and the airport was equipped as a British Commonwealth Air Training Plan base. No. 15 Elementary Flying Training School, a subsidiary of the Flying Club began operations in 1940. The training program ended at the end of the war and the Department of Transport resumed operation of Regina Airport.

This expanded air terminal building was opened in 1960, and seven years later Regina's main runway was extended to accommodate larger aircraft with increased landing speeds.

The airport was sold to Transport Canada in 1972 for $2.3 million. The next decade was a time of growth and renovation. Two loading bridges were added in 1976 and Air Canada constructed a cargo facility. In 1981 Canada Customs moved into a separate customs building. In 1982 a new maintenance garage was built, and in 1983 extensive improvements were made with construction and extension of taxiways.

Arnott, Kelley, O'Connor & Associates Ltd. designed the renovations for the expanded Regina Air Terminal Building. The official opening of the airport took place on September 14, 1986.

A chartered Air France Concorde airliner brought French President François Mitterrand and his official party to Regina for a brief visit to the province. Its landing, late on the afternoon of Wednesday, May 27, 1987, drew thousands of spectators to the vicinity of the Regina airport to watch the legendary supersonic-speed airliner (which had to keep its speed below Mach 1 while over Canada) land in Regina.

BANK OF MONTREAL

Victoria Avenue and Lorne Street/Scarth Street and 11th Avenue /1800 Scarth Street

*T*he Bank of Montreal opened its doors on January 2, 1883, and was the first chartered bank west of Winnipeg. The bank was located where Knox-Metropolitan Church now stands at 2340 Victoria Avenue. In the early days business was often conducted from canvas tents because timber was scarce and there was uncertainty about the town's final location. Reginans knew the Bank of Montreal was permanent when it imported a wooden building from Chicago.

Victoria Avenue and Lorne Street
1883 to 1897

After 14 years in its original office, the Bank of Montreal erected a four-storey building at Scarth Street and 11th Avenue. In 1901 a new bank manager arrived, Alexander F. Angus. For the next 19 years he was a leader in Regina's musical life, including being bass soloist and choirmaster of Knox Church. Fire destroyed this building on February 25, 1905. It was termed the worst blaze in the history of Regina with losses deemed to be $50,000.

Scarth Street and 11th Avenue
1897 to 1905

Scarth Street and 11th Avenue
1905 to 1950

After a fire destroyed the second Bank of Montreal in 1905, this building was erected later in the same year. In 1950 the structure was demolished.

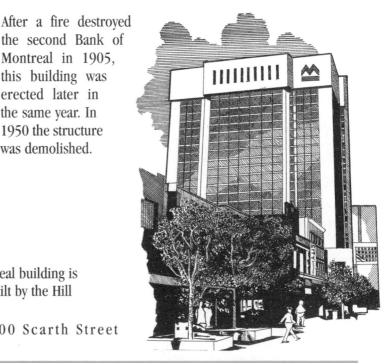

On the Frederick W. Hill Mall, this newest Bank of Montreal building is connected to the Cornwall Centre by a skywalk. It was built by the Hill Group of Companies.

1800 Scarth Street

UNION BANK OF CANADA

Hamilton Street and South Railway

*T*he Union Bank of Canada, constructed in 1903, was located on Hamilton Street and South Railway. It opened in May 1904 and on February 23, 1918 moved to 1822 Scarth Street. The Dominion Taxation Office replaced the Union Bank on South Railway and later Service Printers occupied the building from 1935 to 1959. This building was demolished and the Delta Hotel (initially the Ramada Renaissance) and Saskatchewan Trade and Convention Centre are located on this site (see page 179).

NORTHERN BANK BUILDING

Frederick W. Hill Mall

*T*his building was constructed in 1906/1907 to house a branch of the Winnipeg-based Northern Bank. In 1908, after amalgamation with Toronto's Crown Bank, it was known as the Northern Crown Bank.

In 1918, this institution joined the Royal Bank and the structure was sold. It has since served as a retail and office building and was restored in 1988/1989 by the Fennell Companies.

For many years this building was owned by the Goldman family. Regina-born artist Tony Thorn had his art studio here.

Now owned by Denise and Len Currie of Colliers International, with offices in Regina and Minneapolis, the building is being redeveloped into downtown condominiums. A large condominium on the third floor is the home of Denise Currie's mother, Francis Olson, who was president of Regina's first and only all-female real estate company, Frances Olson Realty.

BANK OF OTTAWA/
BANK OF NOVA SCOTIA

1641 Broad Street/1769 Scarth Street

he first Bank of Ottawa, built in 1907, moved its offices from 1641 Broad Street to 1769 Scarth Street in 1911.

1641 Broad Street
1907 to 1911

Erected in 1911, this Bank of Ottawa building was designed by Storey and Van Egmond. Two large columns, flanking pilasters and egg-and-dart moulding were just a few of its noteworthy architectural features. The Bank of Ottawa, through a merger, became the Bank of Nova Scotia in 1919. The facade of the Bank of Ottawa is now located in the Cornwall Centre.

Bank of Ottawa/Bank of Nova Scotia
1769 Scarth Street
1911 to 1968

IMPERIAL BANK OF CANADA

1775 Scarth Street

*D*esigned by Darling and Pearson, this building was constructed in 1911/1912 and is the only "complete" pre-war bank building remaining in Regina.

From 1886 to 1906, this property was approximately the site of Regina's first town hall. The Imperial Bank of Canada later merged with the Canadian Bank of Commerce to form the Canadian Imperial Bank of Commerce which was located in this building for many years.

In 1962, upon amalgamation of the Imperial Bank of Canada and the Canadian Bank of Commerce, the Saskatchewan regional branch of the Canadian Imperial Bank of Commerce was located in this building. It remained here until a new CIBC tower was built at 12th Avenue and Hamilton Street in 1968.

During the planning stages of the Cornwall Centre there were negotiations between CIBC and the developers of the Cornwall Centre in regard to incorporating the CIBC 11th Avenue and Scarth Street branch into the shopping mall. Negotiations failed to result in an agreement and in 1980 CIBC embarked on a renovation/restoration program for these premises.

In 1984 G. I. Norbraten Architect Limited was awarded a Municipal Heritage Award for Exterior Restoration of the east entrance on the south facade facing 11th Avenue. In 2000 the building was purchased by Fred Soofi. The main floor consists of a retail outlet with the second floor divided into condominiums.

THE CANADIAN BANK OF COMMERCE

1736 Scarth Street

*T*he facade of the Canadian Bank of Commerce (on the west side of the Cornwall Centre's north/south concourse) is all that remains of this building that was moved to Regina from Winnipeg in 1912 and reconstructed at 1736 Scarth Street. The Winnipeg bank had been constructed in 1901.

The Canadian Bank of Commerce later merged with the Imperial Bank to form the Canadian Imperial Bank of Commerce.

The facade was designated as a Provincial Heritage Property in May 1978.

THE ROYAL BANK OF CANADA

1800 Hamilton Street

*L*ocated at Hamilton Street and 11th Avenue, this Royal Bank of Canada building opened in 1917 and closed in 1985.

The Royal Bank was an amalgamation of three earlier banks: Traders Bank, 1906-1912; Northern Crown Bank, 1906-1918 and the Quebec Bank, 1914-1917.

When the building was demolished, a new CIBC office tower was erected by the Hill Group of Companies. The Royal Bank moved its operations across the street.

CIBC Tower was renamed FCC Tower/Agriculture Place when the Farm Credit Corporation moved its headquarters from Ottawa to Regina.

PALMER HOUSE

Southwest corner of South Railway and Broad Street

*P*almer House was constructed in 1883 and renovated in August 1895. The building was destroyed by fire on August 23, 1967.

When the North-West Territorial Council met in Regina, the elected members would meet at the Palmer House Oyster Parlor for an oyster supper.

The Palmer House featured in an early story about Regina's town fathers: "Despite the occasional loss of tempers, the town fathers were often animated by good fellowship and a sense of humour. Town Treasurer Charles Black on one occasion called an unexpected special meeting of the council to discuss 'a weighty financial matter.' The worried members assembled at Black's store where, being only a part-time town official, he kept the town safe and records. After the meeting had been formally opened by the mayor, Black announced with due solemnity that a financial crisis had arisen requiring the assistance of the council. Then, with a wry grin, he explained. 'As you can see I've enlarged my store, so the safe will have to be moved, and I need you fellows to carry that weighty financial matter.' The town fathers moved it, but not before they had carried a motion that Black pay for snacks in the Oyster Parlour for the whole crew, after the job." – Drake, *Regina*

LANSDOWNE HOTEL/ GRAND HOTEL

Southeast corner of South Railway and Scarth Street

*I*n 1882, the McNicol Brothers built one of the first frame buildings that was used as a store.

In 1885 they opened the Lansdowne Hotel located at Scarth Street and South Railway. The Lansdowne provided lodging to a wide variety of groups including, in 1887, the Winnipeg Cricket Club and the Puck Comic Opera Co. and, in 1888, five members of the Princess Theatre Co., all of Winnipeg. The ledger also listed guests from as far away as Montreal, England, Scotland and Holland. In 1910 the hotel was renamed the Grand Hotel.

WINDSOR HOTEL

Broad Street and 10th Avenue

*T*he first Windsor Hotel, owned by Charley Howson, opened in November 1883 and was destroyed by fire during the Regina Curling Club's first bonspiel in 1892.

The new four-storey Windsor, pictured here, reopened in October 1893, complete with a billiard room, oak furniture, a splendid bar and a large wine hall. There was some dissent from the general praise of the new hotel by churchmen who were concerned about the selling of liquor. On November 19, 1906 this structure was also levelled by fire.

CLAYTON HOTEL

Broad Street at 10th Avenue

*T*he Clayton Hotel was built in 1905 by Clayton Peterson. In 1912 James Boyle, who had immigrated to Guelph, Ontario from Ireland, came to Regina to manage the Clayton. His sons Thomas and John worked at the Clayton before they purchased the King's Hotel in 1925.

James Boyle was also known for his harness horses, which he raced on the Western Circuit. The Clayton Hotel was demolished in 1973 to build new quarters for the Army, Navy and Air Force Veterans Association.

WASCANA HOTEL/HAMILTON HOTEL

West side of Hamilton Street between
South Railway and 11th Avenue

*T*he Wascana Hotel was built in 1906. Renamed the Hamilton Hotel, it was demolished in 1979.

ALEXANDRA HOTEL

East side of Hamilton Street between
South Railway and 11th Avenue

*T*he Alexandra Hotel opened in 1907 and closed in 1977. The Alexandra was one of 15 hotels in Regina by the eve of WW I.

CHAMP'S HOTEL

Southwest corner of South Railway
and Rose Street

*O*ne of Regina's earliest store blocks was leased by the Peart Brothers, prominent Regina wholesalers, to the Champ Brothers, Wes, Dave and Stewart in December 1918. It was converted into Champ's Hotel, a modern hotel and restaurant with a pool room and barber shop attached. Located on South Railway at the corner of Rose Street, the hotel was directly across the street from Union Station. Because of its location Champ's was a popular gathering place for business travellers and visitors.

Champ's Hotel was demolished to make way for new development in June 1980.

KING'S HOTEL

Scarth Street between 11th Avenue and South Railway

*E*rected for J. H. Haslam, "The King's Hotel was built in 1907 and enlarged in 1911 and remained for twenty years the most prestigious hotel in the city. Its contrasting strips and arches of stone over brickwork was colloquially referred to as the 'streaky bacon style' similar to New Scotland Yard and Westminster Cathedral in London." – Brennan, *Regina*

The Regina Rugby Football Club held their first Annual Banquet at the King's Hotel on December 8, 1911.

The 1912 cyclone tore away part of the west wing, about 100 windows and frames were blown in. Damage to the brick and stone building was about $1,000.

Thomas and John (Jack) Boyle bought the hotel in 1925. They had come to Regina in 1912, with their father, James, who managed the Clayton Hotel. In the years the King's was owned by the Boyle family, two themes emerged. One was hockey and the other was Liberal politics.

Hockey teams made the hotel their Regina headquarters. In the late 1930s the Chicago Black Hawks of the NHL held fall training camps in Regina and lived at the King's. Junior league teams from Alberta and Manitoba used the King's as their headquarters while they made their Saskatchewan tours. Tom Boyle helped reorganize the Regina Pats in 1946, and the Pats billeted players at the hotel each fall as they held tryouts for the team. Jack Boyle was an owner of the senior pro team the Regina Capitals during their heyday, including 1948, the year they were Allan Cup finalists. He also served as a director of the Regina Pats for a number of years.

Liberal politicians made the King's their Regina home right up to the time when the Boyle family sold the hotel in 1971. Hamilton MacDonald used the King's as the venue to announce his resignation as leader, making way for Ross Thatcher. Hazen Argue chose a function room at the King's as the place to announce that he was leaving the NDP to become a Liberal.

Until he was elected premier in 1964, Ross Thatcher, a resident of Moose Jaw, kept a suite at the King's as his Regina residence while he was leader of the opposition. Kevin Boyle recalled that, "The night before the first session of the new legislature, enough Liberal MLAs had dinner at the King's to allow Mr. Thatcher to suggest that since they had a quorum they might start doing business right at that time."

Thomas Boyle died in 1948 and Jack Boyle died in 1963. Jack's son Kevin Boyle operated the King's from 1961 until it was sold in 1971. The hotel, which changed its name to The Royal International Inn, went into receivership in 1975.

Approval for the hotel's demolition was given in 1978 to make way for construction of the Cornwall Centre.

CHATEAU QU'APPELLE HOTEL

2445 Albert Street

*T*he hotel that never was – Chateau Qu'Appelle, billed as the "palatial million dollar Grand Trunk Pacific hotel," came to a mean end because of the end of GTP means. Designed in the Scotch Baronial style, the Chateau was to have been situated at the corner of Albert Street and 16th (now College) Avenue.

The October 30, 1912 *Morning Leader*: "The turning of the first sod yesterday in the construction of the palatial million dollar Grand Trunk Pacific hotel at Regina marked an event of no small importance in this city's future development. . . . This magnificent hotel will be advertised throughout the world as only a great railway system can advertise it. . . . Regina will be advertised by reason of this hotel as Quebec has been advertised through the Chateau Frontenac and Ottawa by the Chateau Laurier."

WW I halted construction of the hotel. The lavish Chateau Qu'Appelle was unfinished when the company went bankrupt in 1919. There were two sub-stories of reinforced concrete basement under the northwest corner of Wascana Park. The basement was sunk in 1913 to support the 10-storey Chateau Qu'Appelle. The steel structure, towering five stories high, stood as a skeleton for over 10 years. Much of the steel was ultimately used to construct the Hotel Saskatchewan, built in 1927.

The Royal Saskatchewan Museum, built to celebrate the province's 50th anniversary, now stands on the site of the ill-fated Chateau Qu'Appelle Hotel. Partly for aesthetic reasons, and partly to avoid the expensive task of uprooting the pilings, the museum was built on an angle.

HOTEL

Standing tall and proud on the corner of Scarth Street and Victoria Avenue, in the heart of Regina's downtown core, is a symbol representing the prosperity and optimism that filled Saskatchewan hearts during the 1920s. The Hotel Saskatchewan Radisson Plaza represents the wealth and economic opportunity that existed before the great depression. Overlooking scenic Victoria Park, part of the reason the site was chosen, it has had an impact on the Regina skyline since its erection in 1927.

Built on the site of F. N. Darke's first residence, the Hotel Saskatchewan was completed in a short 11 months. Saskatchewan finally had her own grand hotel, the first in the province and only the third grand city hotel built in the West at that time.

Building a structure of this magnitude in less than a year was a monumental task, adding considerably to the economic prosperity of the city. At the peak of construction, 1,000 men worked in shifts 24 hours a day to complete the hotel. Making this task even more daunting was the fact that much of the work was completed during the winter – with temperatures dipping to their normal -20 and -30 degrees. Materials for the hotel were imported from across Canada, including Manitoba Tyndall stone for the outer facade. Tyndall stone is heavily laced with fossil remains, giving it a beautiful effect, especially suitable for the Modernist Classical design of the hotel. The same stone was used in building the Legislative Building and the Royal Saskatchewan Museum.

The hotel's interior was even more magnificent, the epitome of luxury then and now. It was a self-contained building, providing its own power and water. The kitchen was the most sophisticated in the city; it even had an automated vegetable peeler. The foyer had vaulted, decorated and panelled ceilings and marble thresholds. The workmanship was meticulous. Saskatchewan finally had her "Jewel of the Prairies".

Queen Elizabeth
(the Queen Mother)

Prince Philip

Queen Elizabeth II

S A S K A T C H E W A N

Reginans had a hotel of which they could be proud. To most residents it has become "The Hotel". It has long been a place for social and club gatherings, a place to gather for tea, cocktails or dinner. "Long-term residents still consider it their own and are committed to it, concerned for it and love it," says Marla Preston, General Manager.

"Although it's a heritage property," she says, "we're still modern and savvy. The most prestigious hotel in the province, the Hotel Saskatchewan has been Saskatchewan's only Four Diamond property for the last eight consecutive years."

The hotel was declared a Municipal Heritage Property in 1993, ensuring the next generation will appreciate and love the building's unique history and elegance. Preston says people use the hotel as a special place, holding their weddings and anniversaries within its walls. The hotel also has an Old World aura. It is the first choice for any members of the royal family when they stay in the Queen city and, between 1945 and 1984, was the official residence of the province's lieutenant-governor – the royal family's representative. It has played host to many distinguished guests: the Queen Mother, Queen Elizabeth and Prince Philip, Prince Edward, Princess Margaret, Princess Anne, Princess Alexandra and The Honourable Angus Ogilvy, Lord Louis Mountbatten, former French President François Mitterrand and Liberace.

"Probably the most flamboyant, extravagant guest we've had recently was Count Thiessen of Argentina," says Preston.

But being the centre of mystique and gossip for Reginans over the past seventy-plus years isn't the only way it has contributed to the community. Preston is committed to corporate responsibility in the community. The Hotel helps many charity groups through buying tickets and tables at events, and through sponsorships. The Hotel does stay close to the arts community in Regina, including the symphony, galleries and writing guilds.

"The hotel needs to be forward thinking – old isn't good enough," Preston says. "We must be current to the needs and desires of the community."

CHAMPLAIN HOTEL/DRAKE/SHERATON DRAKE/ CHELTON INN

Southwest corner of 11th Avenue and Rose Street

W es Champ left his brothers Dave and Stewart at the Champ's Hotel and opened the Champlain Hotel at the corner of Rose Street and 11th Avenue in 1926. The building, which was designed by Storey and Van Egmond architects, was owned by George Broder, a Regina pioneer who also owned the Broder Building (Medical and Dental Building) across the street and had developed most of Regina's east end (see page 87). The Champlain became the Drake Hotel in 1937, the Sheraton Drake in 1963 and the Chelton Inn in 1984.

Wes, a Regina sportsman, owned the Regina Capitals Professional Hockey Club that played in the Western Professional Hockey League in the 1920s. The Capitals won the Western Canada Hockey Championship in 1922. Players on that team included Spunk Sparrow, Amby Moran, Red McCusker, Johnny Gottselig, "Mush" March and Dick Irvin. Wes signed Eddie Shore, originally from Cupar, to his first professional contract as a forward in 1922. He sold the team for $75,000 in 1926, and they became the Portland Rosebuds. The Rosebuds, named after the Oregon State flower, the rose, played in the Pacific Coast Hockey League. The entire league, consisting of six teams, was later sold to the National Hockey League for $272,000.00. The Rosebuds became the Chicago Blackhawks and the Victoria Cougars became the Detroit Cougars, later to become the Detroit Red Wings.

When Broder and Champ could not agree on the terms of a new lease, the hotel was taken over in 1940 by N. J. (Piffles) Taylor, Broder's son-in-law. Taylor had been a quarterback with the Regina Rugby Club, the predecessors of the Saskatchewan Roughriders, and Taylor Field is named after him. During WW I he served as a fighter pilot as did his brother Sam (see page 63). A city alderman from 1923 to 1928, he was also manager of the Broder Financial Agency Ltd.

In 1946 Taylor was president of the Canadian Rugby Union. He was also a vice-president of the Western Senior Hockey League, president of the Western Canada Interprovincial Rugby Union and of the Saskatchewan Roughriders. He was inducted into the Roughriders Plaza of Honor.

A 1986 *Leader-Post* story titled "Two War Heros" talks about both Sam and Piffles Taylor. Piffles was shot down over France in 1917 and became a German prisoner of war. On his return to Regina, "Piffles continued playing rugby, once stopping play during a game to search for the glass eye he wore to replace one lost during the war. Finding it, he reinserted it and continued the game."

LASALLE HOTEL

Hamilton Street between 11th and 12th Avenues

*G*eorge and Nicholas Kangles were Greek immigrants who came to Regina in the early 1900s. Both brothers operated cafes until 1929, when they went into partnership and built the LaSalle Hotel. The hotel opened July 1929.

In the 1950s and 1960s the LaSalle was the place to go for Regina teenagers. Chips and gravy and lime cokes (or cherry cokes) from the soda fountain were the most popular items.

The LaSalle Cafe, along with the Balmoral (see page 235), became one of the favourite meeting spots of the Roughriders, both players and management, in the 1970s and 1980s.

The LaSalle closed on March 2, 1987 and was demolished a year later.

ARLINGTON HOUSE/HOTEL

Northeast corner of Victoria Avenue and Albert Street

*A*rlington House was built in 1915 on Albert Street at Victoria Avenue. The Arlington Hotel replaced Arlington House in 1936.

Regina lawyer E. W. Hinkson acquired the Arlington Hotel in the 1930s. Along with his son Frank, he demolished the old Arlington and constructed a new hotel called the Plains in 1956. Frank Hinkson and his sons sold the Plains in 1983 to former Roughrider Larry Bird and partners.

Shortly thereafter the Hinksons purchased the Landmark Hotel on South Albert Street.

GEORGIA HOTEL

Hamilton Street between 12th
and Victoria Avenue

*B*uilt on the old Alexandra School site (see page 115) in 1957, the Georgia Hotel was operated by George Kangles and his son Harry. George Kangles was also a co-owner of the La Salle Hotel. The hotel closed in 1989 and was demolished in 1993.

KITCHENER HOTEL/
RADIO STATION CHWC

1763 Rose Street

*T*he Kitchener Hotel, located at 1763 Rose Street, was originally built by R. H. Williams in 1907 as a three-storey department store. In 1918 alterations and additions designed by architect W. G. Van Egmond were made to convert the store into the Kitchener Hotel. The hotel was later owned by George Grant, who was the Executive Director of The Regina Hotels Association. George sold the hotel to Bert Summers in 1962 and retired to Victoria. In later years the hotel was replaced by other commercial development.

Radio station CHWC became the second radio station in Regina in 1926 (see page 354). Also owned by R. H. Williams Department store, the radio station began operating from a room on the top floor of the store where the transmitter was located.

CHWC's studio was eventually relocated to the Kitchener Hotel.

SIESTA MOTEL

641 Victoria Avenue

*B*uilt in 1954, the Siesta Motel was, at that time, the last building on Victoria Avenue east. Located between Embury and Borden Streets, it was the second motel to be built in Regina. The Golden West Motel on south Albert Street was the first.

Designed by architects Izumi, Arnott and Sugiyama. The flat-roofed ranch-style building consisted of 25 units, half containing kitchenettes. The motel complex was complete with a service station and popular, attached family restaurant. The service station enjoyed the second largest daily gas sales in the province.

The motel courtyard featured a swimming pool and, because the owner "Bud" Gamelin was an avid golfer, it included a regulation grass putting green. In 1968 the Hacienda night club, featuring nightly entertainment, was added to the complex. The motel and family restaurant closed in 1970, and the Hacienda night club continued to operate as The Pump.

REGINA INN

1975 Broad Street

*T*he northeast corner of Broad Street and Victoria Avenue was formerly Broad Street Park (playground).

In the 1930s through the 1950s, the playground was turned into an open-air hockey and skating rink in winter. The city boasted that it was the largest outdoor rink in the world.

For many years the Queen City Kinsmen Club held its Annual Kinsmen Karnival in Broad Street Park. The Karnivals were also held at other downtown locations, including on the street on 12th Avenue, north of Victoria Park and south of the McCallum-Hill Building. There were also Karnivals on the open lot north of the Traveler's Building on Broad Street.

Broad Street Park was also used by travelling circuses and by midways as a stopover on open dates.

Broad Street Park was sold by the city to Sam Hashman Construction of Calgary in 1965 for the construction of the Regina Inn.

When the Regina Inn first opened it featured an indoor swimming pool, the Tiki Night Club and Stage West Dinner Theatre. Stage West featured many famous television and screen personalities, including Sid Caesar. Caesar developed severe health problems while he was appearing in Regina, and he credited Dr. Saul Cohen with saving his life.

SHERATON CENTRE/DELTA/
RAMADA HOTEL AND CONVENTION CENTRE

1818 Victoria Avenue

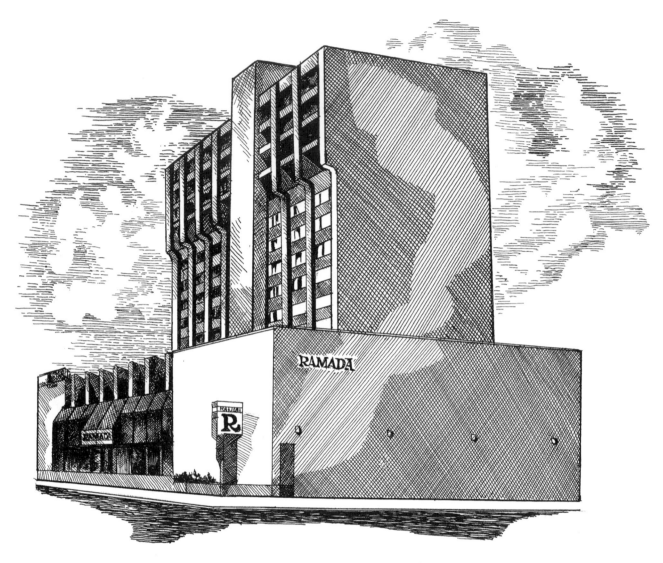

*T*he Sheraton Centre Hotel was built by the Leier Brothers of Cavalier Enterprises Ltd. of Saskatoon in 1977. The 12-storey motor inn and hotel with 209 rooms, convention facilities and underground parking was part of the Leier family chain of Saskatchewan Cavalier Inn hotels.

The hotel was designed by architects Folstad and Friggstad of Saskatoon, and has a business centre equipped by Sasktel with Video Conference facilities.

Originally the hotel operated under the name of the Sheraton Centre Hotel, until it was sold by the Leiers in 1986 to Westwater Industries Ltd. of Vancouver. The ownership changed several times in recent years and it is now the Ramada Hotel and Convention Centre.

RAMADA RENAISSANCE/DELTA REGINA/ SASKATCHEWAN TRADE AND CONVENTION CENTRE

1919 Saskatchewan Drive

*I*n 1903 this was the site of the Union Bank of Canada (see page 163). Originally the Saskatchewan Trade and Convention Centre Ramada Renaissance Hotel, it was built by John Remai of Remai Investment Co. Ltd. of Saskatoon and opened in January 1988. The 25-storey hotel is 280 feet high. The hotel was rebranded in 1998 as part of the Canadian-owned Delta Hotels and Resorts chain and renamed the Delta Regina/ Saskatchewan Trade and Convention Centre.

The hotel/convention complex is a state-of-the-art facility encompassing 28,000 square feet of convention space, 254 elegant hotel rooms and 20 Signature Club one-bedroom suites featuring full parlors and two-person Jacuzzi tubs. The hotel is connected by a skywalk to a 6-storey parkade across Rose Street.

The hotel and convention centre also includes five storeys of office space leased by the provincial government. When the complex was planned, the City and province provided financial assistance to support the Trade and Convention Centre during its initial years, as part of the major downtown core regeneration program which began with the construction of the Cornwall Centre. Upon opening, in excess of 140 national/international conferences and events had confirmed bookings with the facility. Many of these conferences were being held for the first time in the city of Regina.

As part of a major expansion of Casino Regina in 2001, overhead skywalks were constructed connecting the Delta Hotel to the Cornwall Centre, through Sears, and to the main Casino through the new Show Lounge at the west end. Visitors and city residents are able to walk indoors via a network of climate-controlled skywalks from the Canada Life Building and the McCallum-Hill Centre, at the south end on 12th Avenue, to the Delta Hotel and Casino Regina on Saskatchewan Drive.

SHERMAN THEATRE/AUDITORIUM RINK

Corner of 12th Avenue and Rose Street

*T*he Sherman Theatre featured road shows, vaudeville and comic opera stage productions. The theatre opened July 12, 1905 with Roscians Comic Opera Company performing.

During the off season as a hockey rink, it was also used as a roller-skating rink and dances were held here, sometimes with the Kleisinger family band providing the music.

In 1905, the inaugural gala ball, to celebrate Saskatchewan's becoming a province, was celebrated in the theatre/Auditorium Rink. It remained opened during the summer months until 1908.

The building also played host to the 1914 World Hockey Championships and the crowd roared when Regina's Victorias won (see page 314).

Fire destroyed the building in the spring of 1921.

EDISON ELECTRIC FAMILY MOVING PICTURE THEATRE

Northeast corner of Broad Street and South Railway

*B*uilt in 1906, the Edison was Regina's first moving picture theatre. Seating consisted of 165 kitchen chairs held together with planks. The theatre closed in 1911 when the equipment was destroyed by fire.

REGINA THEATRE

12th Avenue between Hamilton and Rose Streets

*T*he old town hall, on the northeast corner of Scarth Street and 11th Avenue, was converted to the Bijou Theatre in 1908. Hand-cranked silent movies were shown with piano accompaniment. Local amateurs and travelling road shows performed on its rickety, sloping stage. When the Bijou Theatre was hauled away in 1909, the Whitmore brothers, A. E. (Bert), George and Dr. Frank, along with Chief Justice J. T. Brown and James Balfour, built the splendid new Regina Theatre which opened February 7, 1910. With 870 seats, including eight boxes, it was able to accommodate the largest travelling vaudeville shows and featured stage plays and concerts.

The Regina Theatre closed in 1929, following a fire. The building remained vacant until 1939 when it was torn down.

The Hudson Bay Company Department Store was built on this site in the late 1960s. The Bay moved to the Cornwall Centre in 2000.

ROSELAND THEATRE

South Railway and Rose Street

*T*he Roseland Movie Theatre opened on December 9, 1910. The theatre closed in 1920.

PRINCESS THEATRE

Scarth Street between 11th and 12th Avenues

*T*he Princess Theatre was built in 1911. This drawing depicts the theatre shortly after the 1912 cyclone. The first talking picture was shown in 1927 at the Princess, but the picture and sound were of poor quality.

LUX THEATRE

11th Avenue between Hamilton and Rose Streets

*T*he Lux theatre opened in 1911 and closed in 1915. The Lux was one of many theatres that were built in Regina during the initial rage for movies. Patrons enjoyed movies featuring stars such as Mary Pickford and Douglas Fairbanks. Admission for an adult was 15 cents and children were admitted for 10 cents.

THE REX/ALLEN/METROPOLITAN/BROADWAY THEATRES

Hamilton Street between South Railway and 11th Avenue

*T*he original Rex Theatre on 1700 block Hamilton Street opened on December 28, 1912. The building was owned by the chief projectionist, Jack Watson.

With the arrival of "talkies" the Rex Theatre was leased by Jack Watson to Harry A. Bercovich. The theatre was operated and managed by Harry, an extrovert entrepreneur who never left a stone unturned to be successful. To attract theatre patrons during the height of the depression the Rex held weekly "bank nights" with door prizes. Items of silverware and a different piece of a china dinner set were given away each week to patrons. However, to obtain a complete set of silverware or a dinner set it was necessary to attend every week.

1912 to 1938
1700 block Hamilton Street

THE REX/ALLEN/METROPOLITAN/BROADWAY THEATRES

1939 to 1959

*O*n Saturday mornings the theatre presented a western movie for the kids. Every Regina youngster knew early cowboy stars such as "Hoot" Gibson, Tom Mix, Ken Maynard, Hopalong Cassidy, Gene Autry, Tim McCoy and Roy Rogers because they saw them all in the movies at the Rex. When the movie ended every kid got a sucker or similar treat, usually doled out by Harry, when they left the theatre.

The Rex Theatre was destroyed by fire in 1938 and reopened in 1939. The lease ran out soon after and Harry left the Rex. The Rex Theatre closed in 1959.

Harry A. Bercovich had come to Regina from a homestead between Lipton and Balcarres in 1905. His first involvement with the theatre industry was with the Allen theatre group. The original Allen (Rose) Theatre was located on the corner of Rose Street and 11th Avenue where the Medical and Dental building was later located (see page 184). At one time or another he ran the Rex, the Rose and the original Allen theatre. He was an original member of the Motion Picture Pioneers of America.

1918 to 1981
Southwest corner of 11th
Avenue and Broad Street

The new Allen Theatre, later the Metropolitan Theatre, at the corner of Broad Street and 11th Avenue, it opened in 1918 and closed in 1923. When the theatre reopened it was renamed the Metropolitan. With the arrival of "talkies" it became part of the Famous Players theatre chain. It also closed its doors in 1981 and was demolished in 1987.

1930 to 1981
Broad Street between South
Railway and 11th Avenue

Harry was also the principal owner of the Broadway Theatre, on the 1700 Block Broad Street, which opened with great success in 1930. The "all talkie" theatre closed in 1931 and remained closed throughout the depression. Apparently there was an agreement between Famous Players and Harry and his partner to keep the theatre closed. When the arrangement ended in 1941, Harry moved from the Rex to the Broadway and the theatre reopened with the Olsen and Johnson movie *Hellzapoppin*.

The Broadway Theatre closed permanently on October 29, 1981.

Harry Bercovich was a popular Regina businessman who was very active in the community. His nickname was "Scotty" and each year he organized the annual Regina Kiwanis Club's Scotchmans' Day Robbie Burns program.

GRAND THEATRE

11th Avenue between Lorne and Cornwall Streets

*O*pening in 1912 and closing in 1957, the Grand Theatre hosted stage productions through the 1920s under the Sherman Theatre banner (see page 180).

During the 1912 cyclone Boris Karloff, who later became a famous Hollywood actor, was appearing in a play at the Grand. Vaudeville shows performed at the Grand were very popular. In February 1926, Peggy Coucher starred in the Layne Players production of "Abie's Irish Rose".

In the 1950s the Roughrider Quarterback Club was hosted from the stage of the Grand each Sunday night by sportscaster Johnny Esaw of CJRM radio. When the Grand closed the Quarterback Club moved to the stage of the Rex Theatre.

ROSE THEATRE

Southeast corner of 11th Avenue and Rose Street

*T*he Rose Theatre opened its doors on July 16, 1914.

It was common in 1915 to see streetcars decked out with poster ads promoting movies at the Rose Theatre.

The Rose theatre's orchestra, which provided musical accompaniment for the silent movies, was also popular as a provider of local entertainment.

The Rose Theatre closed in 1929 to make way for the Broder Building (Medical and Dental Building).

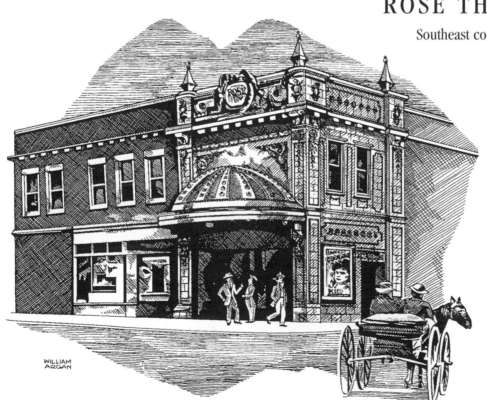

WILLIAM ARGAN

CAPITOL THEATRE

1901 Scarth Street

*T*he Capitol Theatre opened in 1921. At its opening it was touted as "one of the finest theatres in the Canadian West" by the *Leader*. The theatre could seat 1,500 people and had its own 10-person orchestra to accompany silent movies and vaudeville acts.

World Movie Premiere – *North West Mounted Police* in Regina in 1940 directed by Cecil B. DeMille, the movie starred Gary Cooper, Madeleine Carroll, Preston Foster, Robert Preston, Paulette Goddard, George Bancroft, Akim Tamaroff, Lon Chaney Jr. and Lynne Overman. The story is about a Texas Ranger coming to Canada to search for a fugitive. The fugitive happened to be James Stewart, in his first minor role.

The premiere was a gala event with all the pomp, glamour and searchlights that are part of a Hollywood production. The exterior walls of the street sides of the theatre were covered in logs to appear as a stockade. Indeed, Regina was front and centre on a world stage that summer evening

In 1954, the Capitol was the site of another world premiere, the movie *Saskatchewan*, featuring Alan Ladd and Shelley Winters.

Many musical productions and stage shows took place on the stage at the Capitol Theatre over the years. Hypnotist Reveen and the Amazing Kreskin also appeared on the "Cap" stage on several occasions.

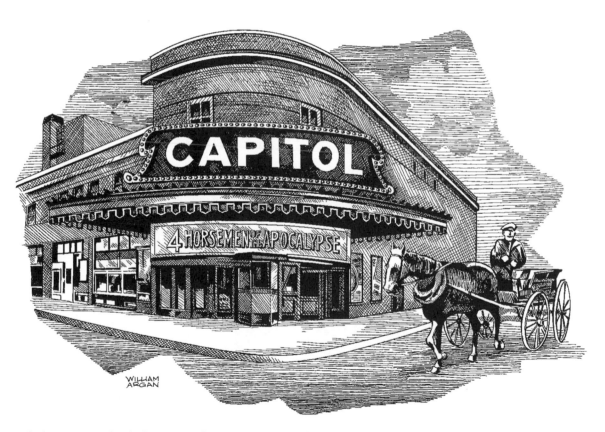

The Capitol Theatre was divided into two theatres in 1975. When it was demolished in 1992, remnants of the movie house were salvaged. The Regina Plains Museum received a wide selection of memorabilia, including seats, uniforms, ticket and cash machines and a seating plan. The City of Regina received the doors, a fireplace and sections of the balcony and ceiling.

This site is the current location of the Canada Life Assurance Company Building.

ROXY THEATRE/NORTOWN THEATRE

12th Avenue between Broad and Osler Streets

*T*his building was erected in 1929 by Lockhart Motors as a sales outlet. On February 9, 1935 Isadore Reinhorn, a Regina businessman, opened the Roxy Theatre in this building.

The Roxy closed on May 28, 1966 and the building was destroyed by fire in December 1977.

In the mid-1950s the Nortown Theatre was built at the southwest corner of Pasqua Street and Dewdney Avenue. It was part of a chain of Saskatchewan theatres, including the Roxy Theatre in Regina, owned and operated by Isadore Reinhorn and his son Leonard. The Nortown was a bit of an experiment in that it was the first theatre to be located in a residential neighbourhood in Regina. Its life as a theatre was short lived, however, as the industry was going through major changes at that time.

With national chains making it harder for independent operators to obtain films, and television and VCRs becoming more commonplace, the Nortown was converted to a bowling centre in 1961, remaining under the ownership of the Reinhorns. In 1983 Leonard's son Arthur joined the family business, and in 1984 Isadore passed away.

In 1991 the Nortown Bowling Lanes was moved to 6831 Rochdale Boulevard, in the Northwest Regina Mall. Leonard Reinhorn passed away in 2001, but the Nortown still remains in the Reinhorn family and is operated by Arthur Reinhorn.

REGINA THEATRES 21ST CENTURY

*R*egina theatres are flourishing despite television, VCR, DVDs and computers. In Regina, as in other Canadian cities, multiplex theatres, often situated within shopping malls, are increasingly popular.

The Cornwall Centre Theatre, Famous Players, opened in 1981 with four screens. In 2002, Regina also has the Coronet Theatre multiplex, Albert Street and 11th Avenue; Southland Mall multiplex, 3025 Gordon Road; Rainbow Cinemas multiplex at Golden Mile Centre, 3806 Albert Street. Other theatres include the Regina Public Library Theatre, the Cinema 6 Drive-In and the Kramer IMAX, for a total of more than 30 theatre screens in the city.

There are plans for two new theatre complexes in the northwest area of the city, Harvard Developments Inc's Galaxy Cinemas, in the Normanview Shopping Centre, starts construction of a ten-screen, 2,200-seat theatre complex in October 2002, for completion July 2003. The Sherwood Mall Theatre will be a seven-screen theatre. Even with the closing of the downtown Cornwall Centre Theatre in August 2002, Regina will have 44 theatre screens in 2003.

McCUSKER'S BLACKSMITH AND IMPLEMENT SHOP

Hamilton Street between South Railway and 11th Avenue

*M*cCusker's Blacksmith and Implement Shop was built in 1883. Charles J. McCusker, a prominent pioneer merchant, had come to Regina in June 1882, when it was still known as Pile of Bones. He was both a blacksmith and a mechanic, so his store carried a stock of carriage and implement supplies.

Before any churches were built, McCusker provided the upstairs of his store, called McCusker's Hall, to Presbyterian and Catholic groups for religious worship.

Catholic masses were celebrated on his premises for one year, from 1883 to 1884. With Pascal Bonneau, McCusker raised funds to build a Catholic church, St. Mary's on the northeast corner of Cornwall Street and 12th Avenue, facing Victoria Park. Before Knox Presbyterian church was completed in 1885, its congregation also used McCusker's Hall for its services.

McCusker was a town council member for six years between 1885 and 1902. He was also a member of the Gratton School Board.

By 1900, McCusker was the Territorial distributor for several farm implement companies, including Deering, John Deere, Advance and Waterloo farm implements.

Charles J. McCusker

McCARTHY DEPARTMENT STORE

Broad Street between South Railway and 10th Avenue

*E*dward McCarthy established this general store on Broad Street in 1883. The store was destroyed by fire 10 years later.

McCarthy maintained his business in several locations until 1900 when he built a large department store at Broad Street and South Railway.

In 1904 a third floor was added. This structure, the first three-storey block in the downtown area, burned down in 1912.

McCarthy also operated a 1,000-acre farm near Regina, and served as an alderman in 1899 and from 1903 to 1904. He and his brother John J. were active in the establishment of the Gratton Separate School District (see pages 116 and 340).

Regina's first movie house, the Edison Electric Family Moving Picture Theatre, was established in this location in 1906 (see page 180), and later the Palace Theatre occupied the premises.

As an alderman McCarthy pushed for the municipal ownership of electric lights, water works and street railways. He arranged the purchase of the privately owned Regina Light and Power Company in 1904 and set up the system of city-owned power.

REGINA BOARD OF TRADE (CHAMBER OF COMMERCE)

South Railway at Rae Street/2145 Albert Street

James A. McCaul

*I*n response to high railway freight charges, Regina merchants decided to unite their strength and form an association to benefit the trade and commercial prosperity of Regina, rather than work singly for their individual success. This association was called the Regina Board of Trade and it held its first official meeting on April 6, 1886.

James A. McCaul was elected the first president. He also served as mayor of Regina in 1890 (see page 34).

A Board of Trade report in 1907 described the city as growing so fast that the publicity pamphlets were out of date before they were all distributed.

For many years a single room served as the Board's headquarters. In 1908 a small building near the train depot was erected on South Railway (now Saskatchewan Drive). Following the traumatic events of the 1930s and 1940s, including the depression, drought and WW II, the Board played a prominent role in setting up committees on reconstruction and rehabilitation of the city.

In 1947 the Regina Board of Trade changed its name to the Regina Chamber of Commerce, to conform to the American and British practice, so visitors would recognize the office and understand its function.

Over the years the office moved to various facilities, including the Bank of Commerce Building, the McCallum-Hill Building and the Regina Trading Company Building, before it acquired a permanent location in 1953 at 2145 Albert Street. Fifty years later, the Regina Chamber of Commerce remains at this address.

Today, the Chamber continues to be an independent, non-profit, volunteer organization dedicated to enhancing the business community of Regina by actively promoting economic growth and providing a collective voice for the benefit of its members. In 2002 the Chamber's membership hit a record high, over 1,000 members.

The Chamber's vision is to lead Regina toward an economic and social environment that fosters wealth creation and economic growth, making Regina the best place to live and do business.

GLASGOW HOUSE

2021 South Railway

*T*his is the original R. H. Williams store, established in 1888. In partnership with Alex Sheppard, Mr. Williams was a general merchant at 2021 South Railway. The following year, Williams bought out Sheppard.

Shortly thereafter, the store was found to be too small and the business moved to new quarters on South Railway between Rose and Broad Streets. One of the principle general stores in the Regina area, it was later enlarged several times and eventually moved to 11th Avenue and Hamilton Street, where it became known as R. H. Williams and Sons Department Store (see page 191). Glasgow House grew with the city and represented the pioneer merchandising family of Regina.

"Mr. Williams, so legend has it, first tasted the fruits of commercial enterprise on the day he reached Qu'Appelle by Red River cart. In his possessions he had half a crate of lemons. Dominion Day was being celebrated at Qu'Appelle where the Hudson Bay Co. had gathered a number of Indians and Mr. Williams used his supply of lemons to make lemonade for the Indians. Never having tasted lemonade, the Indians were good customers and at the end of the day Mr. Williams had made $43." – August 6, 1946 *Leader-Post*

R. H. Williams served as Regina's mayor in 1891 and 1909 (see page 34). He died August 25, 1924.

R. H. WILLIAMS AND SONS DEPARTMENT STORE/ ROBERT SIMPSON COMPANY

11th Avenue and Hamilton Street

W illiams bought this Hamilton Street and 11th Avenue site, the location of Regina's first public school, in 1910, to construct a multi-storied centrally located department store.

In 1911, when the street railway was planned, Mayor Williams cast the deciding vote to have track laid on 11th Avenue, not South Railway, so every streetcar stopped in front of his store.

The Williams store was well known for its award-winning window merchandising displays. The business remained with the Williams family until 1946.

The Robert Simpson Company's mail-order business had been active in Regina at Broad Street and 4th Avenue since 1915 (see page 213), but in 1946, when they decided to open a retail business, they bought out the R. H. Williams store and operated it until 1979.

R. H. Williams

The Simpson's downtown store, like the Williams store before it, was famous for its artistic and detailed window displays which were not limited to its own merchandise but supported community projects and celebrated seasonal events such as Easter, Dominion Day, Remembrance Day and Christmas. Often the elaborate displays covered a number of windows. When shoppers visited downtown, stopping by Simpson's to see the window displays was always a must.

When the Hudson's Bay Company bought out Simpson's in 1979, they operated the Regina store, which was only a block away from their own department store at 12th Avenue and Hamilton Street, until June 1981. The building was demolished in 1982, ending almost 70 years of retail service at this location.

The TD Canada Trust office tower is now located on this site.

REGINA TRADING COMPANY

South Railway and Scarth Street/12th Avenue and Scarth Street

*J*ohn Dawson, one of Regina's first businessmen, and his brother-in-law J. Frank Bole opened the Regina Trading Company, Regina's first real department store, on August 2, 1898.

John M. Young was the general manager and Frank Bole was hardware manager. The store carried dry goods, groceries, hardware, tinware, clothing and prescription drugs. Business was so brisk that the store doubled its space in 1900.

The Provincial Museum of Natural History was housed at first in the Regina Trading Company Building, until it moved into the new Legislative Building in 1911 (see page 143).

The Regina Trading Company grew substantially and further expansion was required, so construction of this four-storey building began in 1920 on Scarth Street at 12th Avenue.

In the basement McBride's Limited, the grocers, opened their first of 17 Regina stores. On the top floor was the city's largest cabaret with dining and dancing.

Throughout WW II, Regina College conducted classes from the upper floors of the Regina Trading Company Building because the RCAF were using the Regina College Building on College Avenue for recruitment and training.

The Regina Trading Company eventually declared bankruptcy and in 1980 the building was demolished.

INTERNATIONAL HARVESTER COMPANY

Broad Street and Dewdney Avenue

*I*n 1903, when special freight rates were allowed on farm implements, International Harvester, J. I. Case and Massey Harris erected warehouses in Regina. By 1906 at least $5 million worth of implements were shipped out of Regina. Consequently, Regina became the largest farm implement distributing centre in the world.

This scene shows the Broad Street subway being erected in 1912. George Silverman Furniture Warehouse occupied the International Harvester building until 1985 when the structure was demolished and a strip mall was built on the site.

J. I. CASE THRESHING MACHINE COMPANY

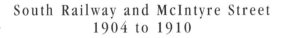

South Railway and McIntyre Street
1904 to 1910

*A*gricultural business was booming in Saskatchewan at the turn of the century.

Frosst and Wood, J. I. Case, Massey Harris and International Harvester, all large implement companies, began construction of warehouses that same year.

The 100-foot long by 100-foot wide J. I. Case warehouse was completed in 1904 under the supervision of L. A. Schlanser, contractor.

The *Leader* noted: "It is a two-storey building complete in every respect and like the American-Abell Co. a full line of repairs is carried in stock. The building is so constructed that an addition can easily be added if business demands it."

This larger warehouse opened on Broad Street six years later and covered a full block between 8th and 7th Avenues. The company operated out of this building until 1977 when several business tenants moved in.

Broad Street between 7th and 8th Avenues
1910 to 1977

H arvard Developments Inc. is the development arm of a group of companies that have, in many ways, grown up with the Province of Saskatchewan. Harvard Developments has evolved from McCallum Hill & Company Limited, one of Regina's oldest and best-known companies. It began quite modestly in 1903, when Walter H. A. Hill, a schoolteacher, and E. A. McCallum, a notary public, shook hands on a partnership to develop a real estate business. 2003 marks 100 years for the company.

The firm's initial purchase was a tract of land on the south side of Wascana Creek. Shortly thereafter, the Province of Saskatchewan was formed and the new government bought a 170-acre parcel from the young entrepreneurs to erect the new legislative building and create Wascana Centre. A year later, the company began subdividing the tract of land west of the new legislative building, the area now known as Lakeview.

In 1909, Saskatchewan Guaranty and Fidelity Company was established. It prospered until it was forcibly taken over by the provincial government in 1949. In response, McCallum Hill formed the Western Surety Company which operates its bonding business, nationally, and is in the top ten of Surety Underwriters in Canada. McCallum Hill continued to sell general insurance, and in 1996 merged with Cook's Insurance.

In 1912, Regina's first skyscraper, the McCallum Hill Building, was built. Ten floors high, it boasted its own well, electrical plant and three elevators.

In 1946, Walter H. A. Hill purchased the outstanding shares from the McCallum estates to become the sole owner of McCallum Hill & Company Limited. A year later, his son Frederick, after returning from WW II as a US bomber pilot and completing his MBA at Harvard Business School, joined the company.

In 1949, Frederick and several business associates founded a contract oil drilling company which became the Canadian Devonian Petroleum Company. It discovered the Stellman oil field in SE Saskatchewan in 1952. This company went public and was taken over in 1953. In the early 80s, McCallum Hill purchased the Canadian subsidiary of Tenneco Oil, which now operates in Calgary as Harvard International Resources.

In 1953, Frederick W. Hill purchased the company from his father. The next year, he embarked on the development of the 600-acre Hillsdale subdivision. Hill notes, "It was the first private residential land development since the war ended in 1945 and it was a real breakthrough, because up until this time the City had

HARVARD

1903 – 2003
100 Years

McCallum-Hill
Building
Scarth Street
at 12th
Avenue

Walter H. A Hill

620 CKRM
104.9 the Wolf
Lite 92 FM

Harvard Broadcasting

Frederick W. Hill

Canada Life Place

McCallum
Hill
Centre

Twin
Towers

DEVELOPMENTS INC.

Paul J. Hill

Bank of Montreal
Frederick W. Hill Mall

Southland
Mall

Normanview
Shopping Centre

handled all infrastructure and residential development". The other major undertaking of the 1950s was the development of the Financial building on 13th Avenue and Scarth Street in partnership with the Black Family and Robert Kramer.

In the 1960s and early 1970s, the company commenced the Normanview subdivision in Regina, followed by Westhill Park. Harvard Developments Limited emerged as the development arm of the business, building multiple residential and commercial properties, including the Normanview Shopping Center.

In 1976, a third family generation joined the company when Fred Hill's son Paul moved back to Regina. In 1978, the City of Regina and McCallum Hill jointly celebrated their 75th Anniversaries, and Paul Hill was appointed President of McCallum Hill. The company embarked on real estate developments outside the province, including two major downtown office buildings in Calgary and developments in the United States.

"The Hill Companies" entered the communications industry with the acquisition of CKCK-TV in 1978 and, later, two Regina radio stations, CKRM and CFMQ-FM. The TV station was sold a decade later but Harvard Broadcasting, a Hill Company Division, currently owns and operates 620 CKRM, 104.9 the Wolf and Lite 92 FM.

The McCallum Hill Building was imploded with much fanfare on October 31, 1982. After a long debate about the building's merits as a heritage site, it was decided the demolition would go ahead. While hundreds watched in awe, it took only six seconds and 200 pounds of explosives to bring down the 70-year-old building, the current site of Tower I.

In the 1980s and early 90s, the company developed five Class A downtown office buildings in Regina, representing approximately 800,000 square feet: The Bank of Montreal, McCallum Hill Center, Towers I and II, CIBC/Agriculture Place (now FCC Tower) and the Crown Life Building (now Canada Life). They also expanded into manufacturing, technology and environment-related companies.

Through Haro Financial the controlling interest in the Crown Life Insurance Co. was acquired in 1991. This precipitated the move of Crown Life's headquarters from Toronto to Regina, bringing more than 1,100 new jobs. "Crown Life had a tremendous impact here. It is estimated that this single transaction, directly and indirectly, increased the gross domestic product of the province by over 2 percent, and that of the City by 10 percent," reported Paul Hill.

The Hill Companies, with their growing diversity and expansion geographically, remain Saskatchewan based. With a strong management team in place, and a fourth generation of the Hill family now in the fold, the company continues to grow and contribute to the community of Regina.

WHITMORE BROTHERS' AND HEINTZMAN BLOCKS

1859 Scarth Street and 1861 Scarth Street

Whitmore Brothers Limited was incorporated in 1904. Shares were owned by Albert E., George R. and Dr. Frank Whitmore. They owned the Whitmore Brothers' Block (the location of Canada Drug and Book) and numerous other Regina businesses, including Regina Steam Laundry, Regina Pharmacy, Regina Theatre Ltd. (see page 181), and Whitmore Brothers – a coal and wood business.

In 1883 J. A. Whitmore brought his family from Ontario to Moose Jaw, where he became the first postmaster. He moved to Regina in 1888 as postmaster of the Territorial capital. As a boy A. E. Whitmore learned to speak fluent Sioux and at one time was the only white person qualified to act as a Sioux interpreter. He managed the family ranch in the Yellow Grass district and was an excellent horseman and polo player (polo was played on a field where the 16th fairway of the Wascana Golf Club is now located).

A. E. Whitmore was a MLA from 1908 to 1912, President of the Board of Trade, President of the Exhibition in 1931, 1932, 1933, and a leader in bringing the World Grain Exposition to Regina in 1933. Some of his other achievements included being named honourary chief of two Indian tribes, being a director of the Bank of Montreal and the Fidelity Life Assurance Company, Dominion Tar and Chemical Company, Western Canadian Collieries Ltd., President of Saskatchewan Mortgage Corp. Ltd., Chairman of the Regina Aviation Board, from its inaugural meeting in 1928 to 1947, and he was instrumental in persuading the CPR to build the Hotel Saskatchewan.

A. E. Whitmore and G. R. Whitmore were founding members of the Wascana Country Club. G. R. Whitmore was also President of Sicks' Breweries from 1947 to 1954 and a founding member of the United Services Institute.

The three-storey Heintzman building served as a music store since its opening in 1908 with manager E. D. Corbeau. This was the Regina home for Toronto-based Heintzman Pianos. The large amount of business transacted by the firm made it necessary for them to employ a staff of 16. The company also had branches in Moose Jaw and Saskatoon. The company carried sheet music and had a gramophone department. They were distributors in western Canada for Berliner Gramophone Company. In the late 1960s, when the Toronto company decided to sell its Regina, Saskatoon, Calgary and Edmonton stores, Jim Atkins, his father, Tom Atkins, and Jack Kimbriel purchased all four western operations. The Regina building was the only real estate they could purchase, so they made Regina the head office for their company, Western Keyboards.

UNITED GRAIN GROWERS (UGG) ELEVATOR

2310 South Railway

*R*egina's only remaining grain elevator, built in 1906, survived the 1912 cyclone but didn't survive the bulldozer in 1996.

After a 14-month campaign, by a coalition of groups, to move the United Grain Growers (UGG) elevator to another location and restore it as a heritage site and tourist attraction failed, the 62-foot elevator was torn down on May 2, 1996.

The campaign started after the owner of the land, Marathon Realty, indicated in February 1995 that it wanted to redevelop the property.

The elevator was one of only five pre-WW I grain elevators in Saskatchewan and the only one in an urban centre. UGG bought the building in 1970; it closed it in 1993.

United Grain Growers paid for the elevator's beams, tin surfacing, weigh scale and other artifacts to be salvaged for use in museums and heritage restoration projects.

United Grain Growers has since merged with Agricore to form Agricore United, surpassing the Saskatchewan Wheat Pool as the largest grain-handling company in Canada.

For many years, as grain companies have consolidated and built massive high-throughput elevators, they have in turn closed hundreds of the traditional prairie sentinels that were the most distinguishing architectural feature of many prairie communities.

The Saskatchewan Wheat Pool has also been under attack for elevator closures. In November 2001, Pool President Marvin Wiens acknowledged that the Pool has closed more than 300 of its traditional elevators and built 30 high-throughput elevators in an attempt to create a more efficient and cost-effective grain transportation system. He then affirmed that ". . . we are now building to the future instead of closing for the future."

SPEERS FUNERAL HOME

1867 Rose Street

*A*rriving in Regina in 1906, George Speers and two other men opened the Speers, Marshall and Boyd Funeral and Furniture Store. A few months later, Speers opened his own funeral home.

Funerals were held every 15 minutes around the clock when an influenza epidemic hit Saskatchewan in 1918. Speers was Regina's only undertaker at the time, literally having buried his competitor earlier in the outbreak. At the peak of the epidemic, 57 corpses laid in the Speers Funeral Home. Almost 4,000 Saskatchewan residents died during the epidemic.

After 10 years on Hamilton Street, Speers moved his undertaking establishment to 1867 Rose Street, where he occupied a house that had been the residence of pioneer Regina businessman Hugh Armour.

Upon the opening of Speers' new morgue, the August 18, 1918 *Leader-Post* reported that the premises were well laid out. "When one enters the well lighted building from the west entrance the reception room is seen. To the right is the office and to the left the room where the remains lie. Relatives and friends of the deceased may remain in this room if they wish or they may retire to a special room on the second floor where they can spend the night. Adjoining the room where the corpse lies is a room where funeral services may be held, connected by a sliding door. There is another entrance to the room, apart from the sliding doors so that close friends of the deceased may have absolute privacy until the services have begun. A display room showing the various kinds of caskets adjoins the service room. . . . The embalming room is immediately under the garage. This is well fitted and furnished in white enamel."

Several months later the June 22, 1918 *Leader-Post* reported: "It is his (Speers) intention to make it as home-like and private as possible, and, to as great an extent as possible, get away from the business of undertaking parlors. The house is a very large one, having ten rooms outside of the first floor in addition to a full basement. The casket car, which Mr. Speers recently received from the east, completes his quota of rolling stock for his business. They include an ambulance, hearse, casket car and private car. The casket car is built on the same lines as the hearse."

In the 1930s, Speers provided an air ambulance service for rural Saskatchewan. The first pilot was Charles Skinner who flew a Waco biplane. Charles was a fearless bush pilot who often landed in farmyards, without navigation aids or landing lights, to pick up his patients. He was considered a hero by the many farm families he helped.

Speers Funeral Home was taken over by Ray Sprowl, George Speers' brother-in-law, in 1949. The chapel moved to the corner of College Avenue and Cornwall Street in 1962, two years before George Speers died at the age of 82.

ADANAC BREWING CO. LTD.

Northeast corner of 4th Avenue and Albert Street

*I*f not for a cinder, the Adanac Brewing Co. Ltd. might not have existed. In the early 1900s, Montague Black (father of Conrad) came to Regina by train. Upon leaving the train at Union Station, he got a cinder in his eye and was referred to the well-known Regina doctor Emmett McCusker. Having removed the cinder, Dr. McCusker informed Black that he owed $10.00 for the treatment. When Black protested, Dr. McCusker said, "Sit down and I'll put it back in."

McCusker and Black got to talking about Regina and local business investment opportunities. Black said that in his opinion Regina could use another brewery. McCusker, with several local businessmen, raised funds to establish the Adanac (Canada spelled backwards) Brewing Co. Ltd.

Dr. McCusker (see pages 271 and 285), a Member of Parliament for Regina, also served with distinction in both World Wars. He won the Military Cross in 1917 and during WW II he served as Deputy Director of Medical Services in England, Sicily and Italy, and was awarded the Efficiency Decoration in 1943. He also attained the rank of Brigadier, was awarded Commander of the Order of the British Empire in 1944 and the Greek Distinguished Service Medal, and was twice mentioned in dispatches. The first chairman of the board of the Medical Arts Council, he was also president of the Saskatchewan College of Physicians and Surgeons, the Regina Roughriders football club, the Canadian Football Union, the Regina Flying Club and the Canadian Flying Clubs Association.

In 1964 Notre Dame College at Wilcox honoured Dr. McCusker by naming a building after him.

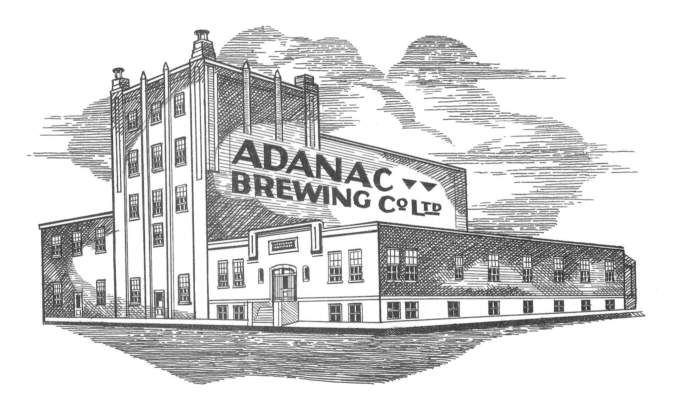

In 1935 a Winnipeg-based company, Drewry's, with Montague Black a major shareholder, bought out Adanac.

Bargain beer was offered in 1935 when Drewry's took over the Adanac plant. "One brand can be bought for 15 cents per bottle or $3.60 a case." The order came from the liquor board to the Regina stores to sell at the lower rate all products bearing the Adanac Brewery labels. "These products are being disposed of to make place for the new products of the Drewry's Regina Ltd., who recently took over the Adanac plant in Regina." March 11, 1935 *Leader-Post*

Drewry's was later bought out by Canadian Breweries Ltd. which established Carlings Breweries in the same location. The Carlings name is retained in a strip mall in this location.

M O L S O N

Fritz Sick

In 1907 three Regina businessmen launched the Regina Brewing Co. Ltd. at 1300 Dewdney Avenue. It remained in operation until the onset of prohibition in Saskatchewan in 1915.

The building also briefly housed the Coca-Cola Bottling Co. in 1917, the Capital Bottling Works in 1918, and the Regina Wine and Spirits Ltd. from 1919 to 1921.

The brewery remained inactive until the repeal of prohibition in 1924 when Fritz Sick of Lethbridge Breweries Ltd. purchased the plant and refurbished it. After extensive rehabilitation the Regina Brewing Company resumed production in 1925. The Regina Brewery continued to prosper into the next decade, acquiring the Wascana Brewery in 1933.

The name was changed to Sick's Regina Brewery in 1944. By this time a new general office was built. In 1948 a 150-bottle-per-minute line was added. Storage capacity was increased in both 1954 and 1956.

After being acquired by Molson in 1959, the brewery had a new million dollar brewhouse added to it, one of the most modern in North America. The brewery went on-line in 1962. Production was boosted to 292 bottles per minute in 1968, and to 700 bottles per minute in 1980, as a result of further expansions which made the Molson's Brewery bottle line the fastest in the province.

With a new production office in 1980, a package warehouse and loading docks in 1981, engineering services upgrading from 1981 to 1983 and a new yeast room in 1985, Molson Saskatchewan Brewery Ltd. continued to dominate the brewing landscape of Regina.

In the early years and later when the brewery was owned by Sicks, several Regina businessmen had shareholder interests. Directors included insurance broker Robert Cook, lawyer Cyril Malone and members of the Whitmore family.

BREWERIES

Although $15 million was spent on upgrading the brewery plant in 1998, making Regina one of the most efficiently operated Molson plants, overproduction and a limited regional market caused the brewery to close in 2002. However, Molson has not interrupted its presence in Saskatchewan as it maintains a provincial sales office in Regina. The Molson commitment to the province and its communities will continue at its highest level of support.

Molson House, the Regina brewery's Hospitality Centre which was constructed in 1965, and opened as the Saskatchewan Sports Hall of Fame, has been the host facility for countless sports and recreational groups over the years. With the closure of the plant it has been turned over to the Queen City Kinsmen. Molson, in concert with the Kinsmen, will renovate and relocate the building which will be used to facilitate the many fundraising efforts generated by the Kinsmen.

Throughout its history Molson has actively supported community activities and amateur and professional sporting groups including: The Saskatchewan Roughriders, Regina Pats, Moose Jaw Warriors, Swift Current Broncos, Regina Rams, Saskatoon Hilltops, Regina Prairie Thunder, University of Saskatchewan Huskie Athletics, University of Regina Cougar Athletics and Saskatchewan's SIAST Campuses. Molson has also been a major sponsoring partner in the Kinsmen's Big Valley and Rock 'n The Valley summer outdoor concerts at Craven.

Molson has also contributed financially to many rural Saskatchewan communities and continues to offer this support through their Local Heroes Program.

Molson's community support programs have benefited the people of Regina and Saskatchewan, including many educational programs and thousands of athletes.

SOUTH RAILWAY

S outh Railway, located between Albert Street and Broad Street, was originally Regina's main street. On May 4, 1981, an order by Regina City Council, changed the name of South Railway to Saskatchewan Drive.

This 1906 scene is looking east to Broad Street.

Two of the businesses shown here, W. G. Pettingell and Robert Martin's Stationary and Drug Store, and Charles H. Black and Peter Lamont's Drugs and Books, joined to form the Canada Drug and Book Company, still active in the Whitmore Brothers' Building on the Frederick W. Hill Mall.

Lamont opened Saskatchewan's first telephone exchange in his bookstore in 1887 and also started Regina's first lending library in his store.

SCARTH STREET

L ooking south from South Railway, this is how the east side of Scarth Street appeared in the early 1900s. St. Mary's (Blessed Sacrament) church steeple is just visible on the southeast corner of Scarth Street and Victoria Avenue.

SCARTH STREET

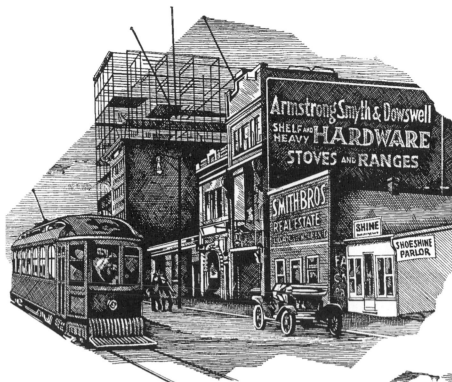

*T*his is a view of Scarth Street in 1912 from 11th Avenue to 12th Avenue. In the background is the McCallum Hill Building under construction.

11TH AVENUE

*T*his is 11th Avenue looking west from Rose Street circa 1920. The R. H. Williams and Sons Department Store is in the centre of the scene.

SCARTH STREET

*L*ooking north on Scarth Street, this view shows the old Post Office/old City Hall/new Globe Theatre building on the corner of 11th Avenue and Scarth Street. The view in 2002 is considerably changed with the development of the Cornwall Centre on the north side of 11th Avenue.

SCARTH STREET

*T*he 1800 block Scarth Street, formerly the Scarth Street Mall and now the Frederick W. Hill Mall. This view is looking north from 12th Avenue.

PIANO

HEINTZMAN & CO

WILLIAM ARGAN

11TH AVENUE AND HAMILTON STREET

RICHARDSON'S AND THE LAST TROLLEY BUS RUN

*T*he north side of 11th Avenue shows the James Richardson & Sons Building. The last trolley ran from Scarth Street and 11th Avenue in March 1966.

MARKET SQUARE BUILDING

Northeast corner of 11th Avenue and Osler Street

WILLIAM
ARGAN

*T*he Market Square Building was constructed in 1908 on a block that had been set aside for use as a public market square. In the beginning, the Square was used as a sports field for baseball, tennis and hockey, as a market and as a place for band concerts and outdoor events. The horses and cattle shown at the first Exhibition were tethered there for the judging.

In 1889 City Council had promised "fifteen dollars a month, from May until the end of October, if the band [the Regina Brass Band] would play weekly in the new Market Square bandstand and at all public occasions." – Drake, *Regina*

The square played an important part in many social, political, joyous and sombre occasions. In 1891 when Sir John A. MacDonald died, Regina politicians, often bitter enemies, put aside their political differences and businessmen of both parties draped their buildings in black. In Market Square the local band played appropriate music at the time appointed for the funeral.

In 1920 the city commissioned Portnall and Clemesha, Regina architects, to renovate the Market Square building and add two storeys to it.

In 1921 the building became Regina's third Central Fire Hall. As part of the renovations, the front of the building was moved out seven feet to accommodate the Fire Department's vehicles.

WILLOUGHBY AND DUNCAN BLOCK

1839/51 Scarth Street

*T*his building was designed by F. Chapman Clemesha and was constructed in 1909. It was built by and named after Charles Willoughby and W. F. Duncan who co-founded the Beaver Lumber Company in 1899. Historically, the building was known as the Wildun Lodge.

The original front facade of the building displayed strong Dutch Colonial influences and was finished with a combination of sand, lime, brick and Tyndall stone. Notable features include the mansard roof, ornate curved pediments above the end dormers and shed-roof dormers between them. Broadly arched ground-floor openings gave the building the appearance of an arcade. However, renovations undertaken in 1951 included refacing of the building and the removal, alteration or sheathing of its architectural detail.

As part of the Scarth Street Mall revitalization project, a climate-controlled pedestrian corridor has been incorporated into the ground floor of the building, directly behind the front facade. Also, the original street-level facade has been exposed to reveal the Tyndall-stone arcade, the original name plate and other decorative features. These elements were incorporated into a redesign of the facade. Scarth Street Mall was renamed the Frederick W. Hill Mall in 1998.

CANADA LIFE ASSURANCE BUILDING

Corner of 11th Avenue and Cornwall Street

*T*he Canada Life Assurance building was constructed in 1912/1913. The six-storey Brown and Vallance design was Regina's second high-rise. Marble and terra-cotta medallions, with the initials C and L (Canada Life) and pelicans, decorate the facade.

From 1945 to 1980, the building served as headquarters for Saskatchewan Government Insurance. In 1980 the provincial crown corporation moved into its present building on the west end of the Cornwall Centre.

Designated as a Provincial Heritage Property in 1978, the building was restored in 1983/1984 by Mark Silver of Toronto.

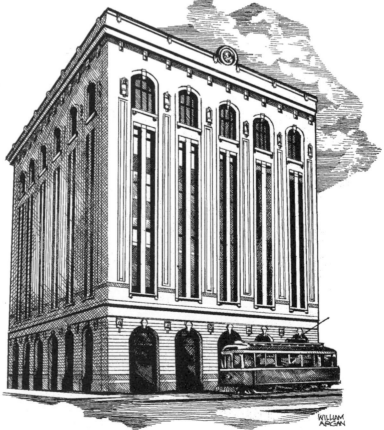

WILLIAM ARGAN

S A S K T E L

S askatchewan Government Telephones (SaskTel) has played a key role in the development and progress of Regina and Saskatchewan for almost a hundred years. SaskTel is the leading full-service communications company in Saskatchewan, offering complete wireline, wireless, Internet and e-business solutions over a state-of-the-art, digital network. Through its subsidiary, SaskTel International, clients around the world benefit from advanced technologies – including fibre optics, digital switching and software systems – that were developed to serve the people of Saskatchewan.

In 1882, less than a decade after Bell invented the telephone, citizens of Regina had the amazing new invention.

In 1887, Saskatchewan's first telephone exchange was opened in Peter Lamont's bookstore on South Railway between Hamilton and Rose Streets. Emily Lander (1869 to 1953) was Regina's (and Saskatchewan's) first telephone operator.

In the early 1900s, Snyder Brothers of Portage La Prairie built Regina's first telephone office at the corner of Lorne Street and 12th Avenue. This building was destroyed in the cyclone of 1912. Architects Storey and Van Egmond designed its replacement, which still stands on the same site, now the head office of Sask Sport Inc. In 1914, the new building housed an automatic dial system which served Regina residents until 1955, when it was replaced by the two-letter, five-digit dialing system.

To accommodate Regina's (and Saskatchewan's) rapidly expanding telephone system, a new three-story administration building was constructed at 2340 Albert Street in 1924. That building is now used for preparation and exhibit storage by the curator of the Royal Saskatchewan Museum which is located just across Albert Street.

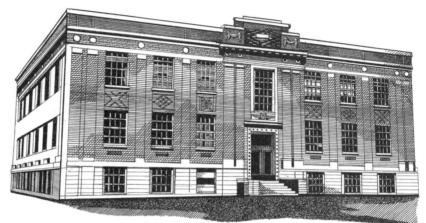

1870 Lorne Street (1914)

2340 Albert Street (1924)

Sculptured Panels – History of Communication

Ralph Vawter

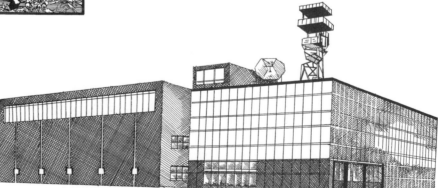

SaskTel Telecommunications Centre
1855 Lorne Street (1955)

2350 Albert Street
(1965)

2121 Saskatchewan Drive
(1981)

When the cross-Canada microwave system was completed in 1955, SaskTel began to construct, in several stages, a telecommunications centre at the corner of 12th Avenue and Lorne Street to receive microwave signals for redistribution throughout the province. In 1958, Regina became one of two regional switching centres in Canada. Further development of microwave and point-to-point radio network occurred in 1960. By 1964, direct distance dialing allowed customers to bypass the operator.

The Lorne and 12th transmission centre was designed by Stock Ramsay and Associates and constructed by Smith Brothers and Wilson. The building's exterior features unique sculptured panels carved by Ralph Vawter, depicting the history of communication from smoke signals to Bell's invention of the telephone, the role of communication workers, the telephone's importance in emergencies, and the worldwide nature of telecommunications.

By 1965, expansion of SaskTel's province-wide network and increasing demand for telephone service made it necessary to construct a new 12-storey head office and distribution centre. The building was designed by McCudden Goldie Architects and built by Bird Construction Co. Ltd. on the corner of College Avenue at 2350 Albert Street, immediately south of the 1924 administration building at 2340 Albert Street.

In 1981, SaskTel's present head office was built at 2121 Saskatchewan Drive, adjoining the new Cornwall Centre. The 13-storey SaskTel Tower was designed by McCudden Goldie and Morley Architects and constructed by PCL Construction Management Ltd.

A century ago, in 1903, there were approximately 2,000 telephones in use in the larger cities of Saskatchewan. In the year 2002, SaskTel has more than 450,000 business and residential customers in this province, linked to the rest of the world through telephone service and Internet access. The next hundred years will be interesting indeed!

SHERWOOD DEPARTMENT STORE/
SASKATCHEWAN WHEAT POOL

2000 block Albert Street

*S*askatchewan Wheat Pool, a unique product of the western prairies, has a fascinating history. The same can be said of the building that houses the company's head office in Regina.

In reality, the head-office building could be described as a complex, composed of a "new" 11-storey west wing and a historic three-storey east wing.

The original building was constructed in 1912 by a Montreal-based firm, architects David Brown and Hugh Vallance, for C. W. Sherwood Company Limited. It was operated as the Sherwood Department Store until 1916, when it was purchased by the Regina Trading Company. It was then used for a variety of purposes, including wartime service as a military supply depot.

"On July 26, 1924, the Saskatchewan Wheat Pool began operating with 6,240,000 acres and 45,000 farmers under contract. The large Sherwood Store at Albert and Victoria in Regina was purchased as a head office. Regina was rightly proud to be made headquarters of this remarkable co-operative marketing institution – the largest in all history." – Drake, *Regina*.

Following the amalgamation of the Wheat Pool and Saskatchewan Co-operative Elevator Company in 1926, the Pool purchased the building, had renovations performed by Hipperson Construction of Regina, and set up offices on the upper two floors. The lower floor was leased to various companies, including Bothwell Motors, the provincial department of Natural Resources and the Bank of Montreal. At one time, a portion of it was even used for an indoor miniature golf course. After WW II, the Pool found it needed more space and occupied much of the first floor as well.

The original building design featured Atlantic terra cotta and decorative gargoyles on the facade. In 1967 and 1968, when the new seven-storey west wing was added, the designers opted for a contemporary facade, leaving the east wing to display the architectural style of the early part of the century. Four additional storeys were added to the west wing in 1981.

Architects for the west-wing addition in 1967, and the additional four-storey expansion in 1981, were McCudden and Goldie Architects, and the contractor was Smith Brothers and Wilson Ltd.

The original east-wing C. W. Sherwood Company Building was declared a Heritage Building on the 60th Anniversary of the Saskatchewan Wheat Pool in 1984.

In 1996, the Saskatchewan Wheat Pool became Canada's largest publicly traded agricultural co-operative, and the 54th largest company in Canada. For the first time in its history, Saskatchewan Wheat Pool had access to public capital markets to help fund the modernization of their grain-handling infrastructure and accelerated expansion into select value-added agri-business.

WILKIE'S GROCERY AND MEAT MARKET

Corner of Winnipeg Street and Victoria Avenue

*R*egina's longest established grocery store, Wilkie's Grocery and Meat Store closed in 1954 when Joseph Wilkie retired. He had been proprietor of the store for 40 years and a Regina City alderman.

After renovation, the building became the Bank of Nova Scotia's second branch in Regina. The bank's main office was located on Scarth Street.

Wilkie started in the grocery business when he was ten years old and left school to work as a messenger boy for a butcher in Perth, Scotland. Ten years later he was manager of the store. He came to Canada in 1911 and worked for a time at Fort Qu'Appelle.

In 1914 he opened his own store at the corner of Winnipeg Street and Victoria Avenue. In over 40 years, he was only away from the store once because of sickness – in 1918 when he caught influenza. The longest period he was away from the business was for a week, when he was out of town on city business.

As alderman for 10 years, he set similar attendance records at council. On council, he was known as the financial expert and had frequent differences of opinion with the city's commissioners over taxation and debt policy.

After his retirement from his business, Wilkie continued to serve on city council.

F. W. WOOLWORTH COMPANY

2007 11th Avenue

F. W. Woolworth opened its first store in Regina in 1914. A new addition built in 1936 doubled the store's size and was described as "the most modern premises of the Woolworth Company in Canada."

"The entire ground floor of the new store is laid out as a sales floor. All sales counters are new. There are 1,200 lineal feet of new sales counters and 250 feet of shelving. There is the latest type of lunch counter and soda fountain equipment, the counter being 100 feet in length and provision being made for 48 stools." – November 5, 1936 *Leader-Post*

Offices were on the second floor, as well as one of the largest and best-equipped kitchens in Regina. The kitchen had "the latest type of automatic dishwasher, potato peelers, cooking units and refrigerator units. Service to the lunch counter is by two electric dumb waiters." Reconstruction of the store took place over a three-month period, during which the store remained open for business, with the exception of three and a half business days immediately prior to its reopening.

"Regina architects Stan E. Storey and W. G. Van Egmond received instructions to complete plans for the new store on August 8 and, the same day, wrecking started on the old buildings, adjoining the old Woolworth store on 11th Avenue. The three-storey Bank of Canada building immediately to the west of the store was completely demolished as was a one-storey billiard room to the east."

This site is now the location of the CIBC Main Branch and Private and Commercial Banking Centres.

ROBERT SIMPSON WESTERN LTD.

1050 Broad Street

WILLIAM
ARGAN

*T*his eight-storey building was constructed in 1915 to house the mail-order operations of Robert Simpson Company and its western headquarters in Regina. Corporate mergers resulted in Robert Simpson Western Limited becoming Simpsons-Sears and then Sears. It is still used as a major call centre for telephone orders and warehousing.

During the 1930s there were three department stores in Regina. The two largest, Simpson's and Eaton's, were located outside the downtown core. Robert Simpson's operated a full retail department store on the first four floors of its Broad Street and 4th Avenue location. In the late 1930s, a special attraction was the children's Toyland at Christmastime. Toyland covered an entire floor and was complete with a miniature children's train ride.

In 1946, Simpson's purchased the R. H. Williams and Sons Department Store at the corner of Hamilton Street and 11th Avenue. Their retail operation was moved there until 1979 (see page 191).

IMPERIAL LTD. REGINA REFINERY

Winnipeg Street North

*L*ocated on 226 acres in northeast Regina, within the city limits, the refinery took less than a year to build. Construction began in February of 1916 and the refinery was in operation eight months later.

To attract the skilled workers required to operate the plant, staff housing was provided immediately south of the refinery on Winnipeg Street North and Wallace Street. The original market area was all of Saskatchewan and western Manitoba.

During WW II, crude came from as far away as Texas. Between 20 to 30 different crudes were processed yearly.

The refinery underwent 11 expansions during its 56-year history. The most major expansion and modernization program was completed in 1954. Crude oil reached the refinery from Alberta by railroad tank cars until 1950, when the first crude oil arrived via Interprovincial Pipeline.

Removal of the bottleneck of moving crude oil immediately increased the refining capacity at the Regina refinery to 20,000 barrels per day.

In 1916 the plant had the capacity to refine 1,500 barrels per day, which increased to 32,500 barrels per day 50 years later when the refinery was in full production. Refined products included motor gasoline, aviation turbine fuel, stove oil, diesel fuel, light and heavy fuel oils and asphalt.

In 1965 the refinery received the Waste Control Achievement Award for water pollution control. The Regina Refinery celebrated its 50th Anniversary in 1966. Production methods, new technology and market centralization caused the plant to close in 1974.

T. EATON COMPANY

7th Avenue at Rose Street

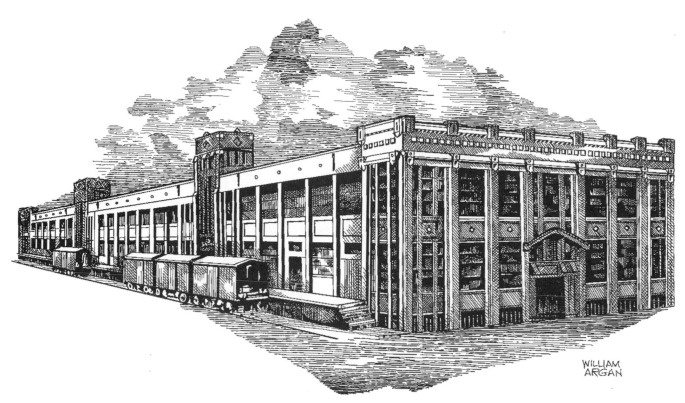

WILLIAM ARGAN

*D*ominion Park, a public reserve with a 600-seat grandstand, built in 1909 to serve Regina's professional baseball, lacrosse and football teams, was sold by the city to the T. Eaton Company in 1917. Sir John. C. Eaton laid the cornerstone of Regina's new mail-order warehouse facility on July 24, 1918. Initially, the store sold heavy hardware, harness, furniture and machinery, but to accommodate the rapid growth of business, Eaton's became a complete department store in November 1926.

During the 1930s Eaton's added a creamery department on the lower floor. It manufactured its own dairy products from milk supplied by rural customers within the Regina area. A complete grocery department was added on the upper floor, adjacent to a restaurant and cafeteria.

At Christmastime, during the late 1940s, Eaton's set up their Toyland on the lower floor, centered around a very large electric train ride. The large rectangular track ran through Christmas Fantasy Land – which changed every year. After two or three rounds on the ride, children disembarked at the station and received a Christmas gift – a game, colouring book or candy.

The addition to the east of the Eaton's store, the Eaton's Dominion Mall, was constructed in 1967. Eaton's remained at this location until 1981, when it moved to the Cornwall Centre downtown. The building on 7th Avenue was renamed the Centennial Mall Shopping Centre. The structure now houses the Sears Clearance Centre, Sears catalogue shopping and a number of retail stores.

In 1999 the T. Eaton Company discontinued operations and The Bay took over the Eaton's retail store location in the Cornwall Centre.

BURNS AND COMPANY LTD.

Northeast corner of Winnipeg Street and Arcola Avenue

*T*he Burns meat-packing plant opened in Regina in 1918.

At its peak the Regina plant served the prairie region and was a complete processing plant. It was strategically located alongside the CPR rail line to receive livestock and to ship finished products.

The Burns plant served as a community clock for northeast Regina neighbourhoods. A piercing blast from the steam whistle sounded the start of the 7:00 a.m. morning shift. Burns provided employment to hundreds of people whose names are part of Regina's ethnic mosaic – Doug Killoh, Bob Yanko, Joe Toth, Pete Nazarchuk, Dave Derges, Wally Kozak, Jess Sidaway, Martin Schaeffer, Murray Massier.

The production line of this plant was extensive. It included smoked hams and bacon, many varieties of sausages, meat loaves, mincemeat, hinds, sides and quarters of beef, cheeses and fertilizers.

A common sight at the plant was a visit by the local rabbi, who came to prepare beef in the proper kosher tradition.

Burns and Company of Calgary discontinued business from the Regina plant in 1973 and the buildings were demolished.

McBRIDE'S LTD. GROCERIES

19th Avenue and Albert Street

Mc cBride's Limited, Saskatchewan's first grocery chain, was formed during WW I. The chain started in Weyburn with five stores and eventually expanded to 65 grocery stores throughout the province, with bakeries in Moose Jaw, Regina and Saskatoon.

This is store #20 located at the northwest corner of the old Albert Street Bridge, later the location of the Wascana Winter Club. James Andrew McBride, the third of eight children of Irish immigrant parents, was born on August 28, 1861, in Iowa. In 1902 he bought farmland north of Weyburn and moved to Canada.

James A. McBride

McBride was involved with several business interests, including the grocery store chain. He and Frank B. Mitchell inaugurated McBride's Limited in the early 1920s. McBride eventually disposed of his interest in the company but the grocery chain continued to grow and it carried his name until its dissolution.

"McBride's stores now under new management" read the headline in the January 3, 1946 *Leader-Post*.

J. M. Sinclair Ltd. of Regina purchased the company's capital stock and merged the McBride's wholesale depots at Regina and Moose Jaw with the Sinclair depots at those two points. The former McBride's retail stores in Saskatchewan were purchased by the employees and most continued to operate under the trade name McBride's.

The paper reported: "This sale to J. M. Sinclair Ltd. brings to an end a colourful saga in Saskatchewan business which began with the opening of the first McBride's store in Weyburn. . . . The first McBride merchandising venture in Regina was a self-service store opened in 1918. This store was closed after a short time.

"In 1921, another store was opened in the basement of the Trading Company building but was later moved to another location.

"At its peak, McBride's Limited operated 36 stores in Saskatchewan, with 14 in Regina, nine in Moose Jaw and 13 at Swift Current, Weyburn and country points and had a total of more than 200 employees."

This Saskatchewan enterprise dissolved after WW II.

Hamilton Street and 12th Avenue

ROYAL BILLIARDS

2228 11th Avenue

*R*oyal Billiards was originally located at 1820 Hamilton Street, next door to the Royal Bank. Established by Sam Swain and his partner Andy Rusconi in 1918, the "Royal" moved to 2228 11th Avenue opposite the Canada Life Building in 1936. With 14 billiard tables and a barber shop, it was a popular gathering place and provided recreational activities for men of all ages who enjoyed the game of pool. In the early days billiard halls were restricted to men over the age of eighteen. In 1942 a sporting goods department was added to the business.

The proprietor, Sam Swain, was a popular host who got to know everyone who frequented the Royal. He died in 1961, and his son Jack took over the business. Royal Billiards remained at its 11th Avenue location for 40 years, until 1976, when it was demolished to make way for the Cornwall Centre.

Royal Billiards was relocated to 1815 7th Avenue and the name was changed to Royal Sporting Goods. The family-owned company continues to be operated by Jack Swain and his son David.

CAPITAL FLOUR AND FEED

1777 Wallace Street

*C*apital Flour and Feed was a typical corner grocery store. It opened in 1919 and operated at 1777 Wallace Street until 1924.

Prior to the establishment of large grocery chain stores in Regina, there was a grocery store on every street corner. In fact, old-timers recall it was not uncommon for seven corner stores to operate in a two-block radius.

Capital Flour and Feed moved to 912 11th Avenue in 1924. Alex Zaharik and his son Vas were the proprietors until the store closed in 1947.

WILLIAM ARGAN '84

PRINTWEST/PW GROUP

1150 8th Avenue

PrintWest, Regina and Saskatchewan's largest commercial printing company, with branches in Saskatoon, Calgary, Winnipeg, Ottawa and Toronto, is also Regina's oldest continuously operating print company.

Originating as Central Press in 1919, the print shop was first located at 1530 Albert Street, moving in 1921 to 1843 Albert Street, the former Saskatchewan Co-op Creamery building. James F. Hudson joined the firm in 1930, and in 1953 he and Lionel Allen bought out the previous owners to form Central Press(1953) Ltd. They moved the business to 1440 Scarth Street in 1957. Upon the death of his father in 1962, John Hudson purchased his father's shares. In 1967 Don Hudson joined his brother John as a shareholder. A corporate partnership was formed in 1972, uniting Central Press and Caxton Printing, owned by Alfred and Alex Graf. The new company was called Centax of Canada. In 1976 the Hudsons purchased all of the company shares. They also developed a new print niche in consumer books which captured national attention. *The Best of Bridge* cookbook developed into a new corporate division, Centax Books & Distribution, that has resulted in over 300 titles being published and over 7,000,000 books being sold across North America. In 1986, Centax of Canada was the only Saskatchewan company featured in the book *The Financial Post Selects the 100 Best Companies to Work For in Canada*.

M.C.Graphics was formed in 1988 when Centax of Canada merged with Modern Press of Saskatoon, printer of the Western Producer, then owned by the Saskatchewan Wheat Pool.

Meanwhile, Brigdens, specializing in prepress, photography and commercial art, began operations in Regina in 1966, as a branch office of the parent company in Winnipeg. They were located in the 1300 block of Hamilton Street. In 1969, led by Keith Critchley and Ron Driscoll, the Saskatchewan employees bought out the Winnipeg company and formed Brigden's of Saskatchewan. They set up Regina Fast Print at 1300 Hamilton Street in 1974. In 1976 Brigdens purchased a printing press and expanded into the print business. They moved to 1150 8th Avenue in 1978.

In 1989 DirectWest Publishers was created as a partnership with Keith Critchley and partners and Tim Young, representing SaskTel Yellow Page employees. Their first contract was the publishing of the SaskTel telephone directories. In 1990 DirectWest purchased Brigdens and Regina Fast Print.

In 1992, with the printing industry undergoing massive changes the major printing companies in Saskatchewan negotiated a merger: Sask Wheat Pool/M.C.Graphics, under the guidance of John Hudson; Midwest Litho, Saskatoon, under Merv Wilson; Brigdens under Keith Critchley. The new company was called PrintWest Communications Ltd. with the head office in Regina and Keith Critchley as president and CEO. By 1997 the employees had purchased Saskatchewan Wheat Pool and Midwest Litho shares. In 1998 Critchley moved to chairman of the board and Wayne UnRuh became president and CEO.

In addition to traditional "ink on paper", PrintWest/PW Group has diversified its services to include publishing, electronic communications and fulfillment. In 1998 PW Group was formed as a trade name to serve Canadian Associations. Today, PW Group consists of PrintWest (locations in Regina [head office], Saskatoon and Calgary), Centax Books/Publishing Solutions (Regina), Mister Print Productions (Saskatoon), August Communications (Winnipeg) and PW Group offices in Ottawa and Toronto.

PrintWest has played an active role in a wide range of community and charitable events throughout its history. PrintWest is a long-standing partner of Regina's sporting community and the arts, including the Roughriders, Rams, Pats, Leader-Post Carrier Foundation, MacKenzie Art Gallery and Regina Symphony Orchestra. The company is particularly proud of its association with Parkinson's disease research. An annual golf tournament, the PW Classic, as of 2002 has raised over $300,000 for Parkinson's research.

COCA-COLA BOTTLING COMPANY

1748 Cornwall Street/355 Henderson Drive

*R*egina's first Coca-Cola bottling plant and distribution fleet opened for business on July 28, 1919.

By 1920 it was one of 75 companies across Canada that was under contract to bottle and distribute Coca-Cola.

1748 Cornwall Street

Coca-Cola has occupied two other buildings since its early years in Regina, including one at Victoria Avenue and Park Street and its present site in the Ross Industrial area.

355 Henderson Drive

SASKATCHEWAN CO-OP CREAMERY

Southwest corner of 11th Avenue and Albert Street

he Saskatchewan Co-op Creamery building was built in 1920, sold to the provincial government in 1943, and then sold back to the Creamery in 1950.

From the time the Creamery was built, until the mid-fifties, a livery stable was located off Angus Street behind the main building. It housed the horses that pulled the delivery wagons. The horses were so dependable and knew their routes so well that they were able to find their way back to the barn in the severest of winter snow storms, even when there was absolutely no visibility and their routemen were unable to guide them.

Not shown in this drawing was another huge illuminated sign, mounted to the roof of the building, which featured three flashing stars advertising "Esso Three Star Gasoline". At night the sign could be seen as far east as Balgonie. It was from this advertising slogan that Hockey Night in Canada, sponsored by Imperial Oil, originated the "three stars" selected at the end of every game, a tradition which is still carried on today.

Dairy Producers took over the Co-op Creamery building in 1971. For several years, prior to being demolished in 1995, the building served as the location of the Regina Food Bank.

SCHWANN TRADING COMPANY

12th Avenue and Halifax Street

S chwann Trading Company celebrated its success by building a
new home in 1931. Joe Schwann, an
independent grocer, attributed his
growth to "the close personal attention given every order" and his rigid
cutting of overhead expense.

"That policy has brought me a lot of
high class trade," he told the
Leader-Post. "I firmly believe that
satisfied customers tell their friends."

Schwann started his business at 12th
Avenue and Halifax Street in 1920. A few
years later he opened a meat department,
with W. J. Barr in charge. That arrangement lasted until his
lease expired three years later and he was forced to sell out. At that time, he and his family went east on a trip.

On his return to Regina, the business was for sale, so Schwann bought it back. From that time the business continued to
grow. When the Maple Leaf Stores burned down in 1931, Schwann again secured the services of Mr. Barr, who was put in
charge of the meat department in the new store.

Work began on the Schwann Trading Company in February 1931 and it opened in April of that year. The plans called for
the building to be placed 45 feet on 12th Avenue and 50 feet on Halifax Street, the front portion being a modern grocery
store and meat market and the rear portion laid out as apartments. The total cost of the building was about $10,000.

KENDRICK'S NEWS STAND

Southeast corner of Scarth Street and 11th Avenue

F or years, Henry Kendrick sold newspapers and magazines to customers who passed his hut on Scarth Street, next to the post
office. The blind news vendor set up his business in December 1923.
For 18 years he sold his wares from an old hut, until June 1941 when
the Lions Club of Regina supplied him with funds to build a new business office.

The June 7, 1941 *Leader-Post* described his new business: "All the
modern conveniences of a small hut are Mr. Kendrick's here. In winter or summer, snow and rain can't bother him, nor can cold and heat.
It's part of the Lions' activities, helping the blind, and this effort is just
one in many they have managed in recent years. Mr. Kendrick will
likely sell a few thousand papers more than usual toward the end of
this month, when Lions from all over Saskatchewan, North Dakota
and South Dakota gather for the great district convention. This
blind newsie is one man who will extend a warm welcome."

In 1951 it came to the attention of city officials that Fred Kendrick, Henry's son, was operating the stand. In January 1953
the Lions Club informed the city it was disassociating itself from the stand.

In 1953 the Scarth Street landmark was closed down by the city engineer's department. The department removed the stand,
saying that the stand was no longer being operated by the blind person originally in charge and "the practice of laying
papers out on the street by the operator detracts from the general appearance of the area."

ARMY AND NAVY DEPARTMENT STORE

Northwest corner of Broad Street and 11th Avenue

*E*stablished by Sam Cohen in 1924, as the British Army surplus store, this was "Canada's Original Discount Store". Sam came to Regina from Seattle via Vancouver. He was a good marketer who fully understood the difficult business conditions of the depression, with the result that the store soon developed into a distress merchandise clearance outlet renamed the Army and Navy.

The store became the gathering place for the many farmers living in rural communities surrounding Regina.

Army and Navy Department Store gained a reputation, which continued through 1980s, of offering top-line name merchandise which had been obtained from other stores in distress or bankruptcy, at bargain prices.

The store acquired the nickname "Antoine's" as prominent Reginans shopped there on a regular basis to pick up name-brand bargains.

Army and Navy also became famous for daily radio programs aired on CKCK Regina, and later CHAB Moose Jaw, entitled "Pleasant Memories" and "Golden Memories", hosted by W. M. Schultz. The format was aimed at a rural audience, acknowledging birthdays, weddings and anniversaries. "Golden Memories" was the oldest continuous radio program in Canada.

Sam Cohen moved to Vancouver in 1942 and opened stores throughout the west. The head office, however, remained in Regina until the chain closed its Regina store in 2000.

ARMY AND NAVY SUPER MARKET

Northeast corner of Broad Street and 11th Avenue

*I*n 1941, the Army and Navy Super Market, a diversification of the department store, moved into what was previously one of the McBride's store locations.

"One of the finest stocks of groceries and food in Saskatchewan is available to the housewives of Regina and district in the food department of the Army and Navy stores. . . . Thousands of dollars of stock is ever on hand for the choice of discriminating buyers. Shelf after shelf is well laden with high quality goods. Tables bear other stocks. The whole store is well laid out, with a view to making the buying of food supplies for the home a pleasant and easy duty. . . . Huge quantities of groceries are handled weekly in this popular grocery centre of Regina. For instance, in one week, the store disposes of two carloads of fresh vegetables and fruits of high quality. An average of five tons of canned goods move into consumers' hands every week." – July 26, 1941

Leader-Post

A staff of 24 people catered to the needs of thousands of customers who shopped weekly at the Army and Navy's popular Super Market.

In charge of the food department was J. Silzer, a well-known Regina grocery man who had more than 20 years of experience in merchandising in Saskatchewan.

BIRD FILMS CAMERA SHOP

Scarth Street

Bird Films was owned by Dick Bird who was seldom around. While he was away family members operated the store.

Bird, born in Leamington Spa, Warwickshire, England, in 1892, came to Regina in 1921 with his wife Pansy Myrtle Fern Nix and their daughter, Yvonne; their other daughter Jeanne was born in Regina a year later. They opened the camera and film shop just at the beginning of the depression. Established in 1928 as a local business, long before national chains existed, Bird Films was a popular outlet for shutterbugs. The store moved several times from its original downtown location, settling at last at the Golden Mile Shopping Centre. Bird Films Co. Ltd. is still owned and operated by members of the Bird family.

The depression years were difficult times for any business, but Bird was creative and enterprising. He was a professional photographer and loved his work. During the thirties he produced a weekly radio program on CKCK entitled "Camera Trails", which he narrated in story form, about his exciting adventures around the world with his camera.

Reliving his travelling experiences, Bird's radio show was about nature and conservation. He formed a club called Camera Trailers, of thousands of prairie children and adults, some as old as ninety. Unfortunately, times were tough and when Bird could no longer afford the ten-dollar-a-week cost for air time the program was abandoned.

As a freelance film photographer Bird travelled the world, visiting 68 countries, often under dangerous circumstances. He covered Mexican uprisings, the Spanish Civil War, Hitler Youth rallies, WW II, famine in China, the torture of Koreans in Japan, and countless other events of world interest. However, as time passed he became more interested in nature photography and for several years he worked for Walt Disney.

Although not a portrait photographer like Yousef Karsh, he and Karsh were the only two Canadians to become Fellows of the Royal Zoological Society of London and the Photographic Society of America. Dick's first wife died in 1937. He later married his assistant, Ada Bovee, from Avonlea, and they spent many years photographing nature and promoting conservation. Dick received an Honorary Doctorate from the University of Regina in 1976.

GENERAL MOTORS PLANT

Northwest Corner of 8th Avenue and Winnipeg Street

*T*o meet the heavy demand for new cars in Saskatchewan, General Motors made the decision to build a new plant in Regina in 1927.

Located on 38 acres of land between Toronto and Winnipeg Streets, on 8th Avenue, the assembly plant was designed by Hamilton architects Hutton and Souter and constructed by Smith Brothers and Wilson. The plant and office space of 370,000 square feet took six months to build.

The first cars rolled off the assembly line in December 1928. This plant produced the first all-Canadian-made Chevrolet with a six-cylinder motor. The modern assembly line was capable of producing a car every four minutes, with a capacity output of 150 cars a day. At its height of production the plant had 850 employees. It was designed to produce 30,000 units per year, but closed down in 1930 because of the market crash and the Great Depression.

The plant reopened in 1931, adding Oldsmobiles to its line of Chevrolets and Pontiacs. In 1941, shortly after WW II began, the Canadian Government took over the plant and renamed it Regina Industries Ltd. It produced war materials and over 1,000 people worked there in 1943, at the peak of wartime production (see page 21). Automobile production was not resumed after the war, and portions of the complex were used for national defence purposes until the mid-1960s.

In 1967 the complex was sold to the province, and the buildings have been subdivided into warehouse space, business and office rental units.

Ventilator Stacks

REGINA MOTOR PRODUCTS

1850 Albert Street

*F*rom 1929 to 1944, Regina Chevrolet Sales Limited was located at 1753 Cornwall Street. K. C. Leith was president, and E. Moynan was manager and director. In 1944 the company moved to 1850 Albert Street, and in 1947 the building was enlarged to provide 22,000 square feet of floor space. At this location there were 40 repair stalls, a shop control tower and new equipment.

A new building was erected at 1827 Albert Street in 1950 to house the body and paint shop. This provided additional stalls to keep pace with Regina's increasing car population.

After 22 years of service, the company changed hands in 1952 and Regina Motor Products was incorporated with W. B. Ledingham as president and general manager.

In 1979 Regina Motor Products moved to a new site on Albert Street just south of the Trans-Canada Highway.

Regina Motor Products is a third-generation family company. Blaine Ledingham succeeded his father as president and general manager in 1970, and Blaine's son Jason became president in 2000.

CROWN BAKERY LIMITED

1375 Hamilton Street

*G*uided tours of Crown Bakery were available at its open house held December 2 to 20, 1929. The new bakery was capable of producing 75,000 loaves of bread per week.

Describing itself as the finest bakery in western Canada, the bakery's open-house ad stated: "The new oil-burning oven is the first of its kind in Western Canada. . . . every loaf is baked perfectly and evenly for the same length of time. The first loaf placed IN the oven is the first loaf OUT and the last loaf in is the last loaf out.

"Then we have installed a marvelous new Rotary Cake Oven (also of the traveller type) the first of its kind in Western Canada. A new water-cooled, high speed dough mixer, the most modern dough-dividers, dough rounders and dough proofers are further examples of the modern type of scientific equipment you will see in operation when you visit this great new bakery."

When the bakery opened it was equipped with stables to accommodate horse-drawn-carriage home delivery. Weston Bakeries has occupied the building since 1938.

BROADWAY POPCORN STAND

Corner of Broad Street and 11th Avenue/Corner of Victoria Park and 12th Avenue

*I*n 1908 John Alecxe came to Canada from Romania and began farming in the Kayville area. He moved his family to Regina in 1919 and, in 1929, after a variety of jobs, including interpreter (he spoke nine languages), John set up a popcorn business in Regina.

"I met a Greek who had married a Romanian woman, and from him I bought an old popcorn stand and had my boys sell popcorn from it." (*National Museum of Man Mercury Series*, national Museum of Canada, Ottawa, 1977)

Alecxe built a second popcorn and peanuts wagon and his two teenaged sons, Tom and Harry, went to work selling popcorn and freshly roasted peanuts at the southwest corner of Victoria Park, across from Knox-Metropolitan Church, and at the corner of Broad Street and 11th Avenue. Every day they pushed their wagons downtown from the Alecxe home on Edgar Street.

In 1933 the World's Grain Fair in Regina also witnessed the beginning of Broadway Popcorn at the Regina Summer Fair. In 1938 John and his sons built a stationary popcorn stand at the Metropolitan Theatre on Broad street. In the 1960s the stand was across from the Regina Ballroom on Victoria Avenue, beside Greenberg's Drugs. It went back downtown on Broad Street near 11th Avenue when Harry Alecxe began operating it full time in 1970.

"It's a Regina business landmark, even though it isn't as grand as the Hotel Saskatchewan, as historical as the city's train station, or even as well known as the Leader-Post. The landmark is the Broadway Popcorn Stand, a small wooden shack that has stood on Broad Street since the late 1930s." – February 4, 1984 *Leader-Post*

The stand finally came to rest in 1990 near one of the wagons' original locations on 12th Avenue, across from the Capitol Theatre, the northeast corner of Victoria Park. Harry retired the old Broadway Popcorn Stand in 1992 when the city medical officer insisted on having a washroom built into the small stand. Broadway Popcorn was known for a quality product, good relations with the community and friendly conversation. Everybody who came to the stand went away with a bag of popcorn, whether or not they could pay for it.

The participation of Broadway Popcorn at the Regina Summer Fair continues. John's grandson, Ken Alecxe, operated the Broadway Popcorn Stand with his family, as part of the 2002 Summer Fair, in its original location in front of Centennial Park. The Alecxe family donated the oldest of the original antique popcorn wagons to the Regina Plains Museum in 1997.

CUDMORE'S POPCORN STAND

North side of 12th Avenue, near Rose Street

*J*ohn Guy Cudmore was known to generations as "The Popcorn Man". A native of Prince Edward Island, Cudmore came to Regina in 1915. He purchased his coach-shaped stand from Chicago and it was located in the downtown area in 1939.

Originally on the east side of the 1900 block Hamilton Street, in 1966 Cudmore had to move it to the north side of 12th Avenue, near Rose Street, to make way for the new Hudson's Bay Company.

Cudmore attracted wide public attention when the city's building inspector and medical health officer would not issue permits for the stand at the new location. Finally, city council gave special permission for the popcorn vendor to carry on his business.

"From then on, the red, white and blue stand became a popular source of not only popcorn, but Mr. Cudmore's own brand of philosophy, and both won the favour of people in all walks of life, from children to professors." – May 10, 1971 *Leader-Post*

Although Cudmore maintained ownership of the stand until his death in 1971, he retired from being a full-time vendor after he suffered a heart attack earlier that year.

TRIANON BALLROOM

1800 block Smith Street

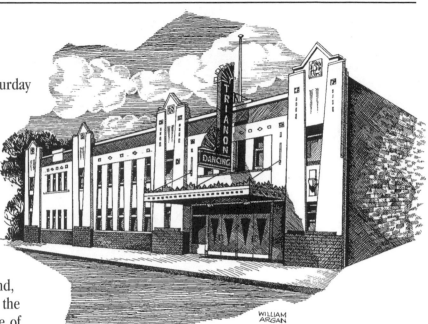

WILLIAM ARGAN

*T*he Trianon was the place to be on Saturday night. On December 17, 1929, Dave Mills and his Orchestra provided music for the first dance in the Trianon Ballroom. Forty-eight years later, the Cottonpickers played the last waltz. In the intervening decades most of the famous bands of the "Big Band" era, and dozens of house bands, entertained as thousands of couples danced and romance budded and bloomed.

Designed by architects Storey and Van Egmond, and built by Poole Construction Co. Ltd., the Trianon was named after the official residence of Louis XIV of France. The 100-by-80-foot ballroom was surrounded on three sides by a mezzanine floor furnished with comfortable chesterfields and chairs; in many respects it resembled a palace.

The word most often used to describe the Trianon in its heyday was futuristic. The Trianon quickly became everything its founders had hoped. The club's reputation for quality entertainment and luxurious surroundings made it a popular gathering place for people of all ages. The young came to socialize and indulge in the latest dance crazes, while their more sedate elders came to watch.

"Big Bands" on tour, including Guy Lombardo, Stan Kenton, Charlie Barnet, Ted Fio Rito, "Spike" Jones, The Six Fat Dutchmen and Frankie Yankovic, all played the Trianon. Famous Canadian groups included Don Messer, Bobby Gimby, and Mart Kenny and the Western Gentlemen. Gene Dlouhy and his orchestra, Walter Budd and his Blossoms were popular local favourites.When Frankie Yankovic performed over two thousand people would crowd the dance floor, all doing the polka. Often, owner Ross Sneath would sit in for a drum set.

During the 1930s through the 1970s, the Trianon hosted many events other than dances: $100 dinners, bonspiel banquets, conventions, bazaars, fashion shows and wrestling, but the dances are what made the place famous. In the late 1950s and early 1960s, the Trianon even had Saturday afternoon teen "Sockhops" which were broadcast on radio.

Owner Ross Sneath said that the liveliest dances he remembered were right after WW II, when the soldiers came home. There were many single people around who didn't know anyone, and they came to the Trianon to make friends.

One of the most popular social events was the annual "Tea Dance" graciously hosted by Ross Sneath and his wife, Marguerite. When the Trianon closed in 1977 it brought to an end a wonderful and memorable period in Regina's history. The building was demolished in 1981 and was replaced by Trianon Towers, a senior's high-rise complex.

SAFEWAY STORES

*T*his Safeway store, located at Winnipeg Street and Victoria Avenue, was one of three Safeway stores that opened in Regina on December 21, 1929.

The other locations were Albert Street and 15th Avenue, and Elphinstone Street and 13th Avenue.

Opening day prices at the stores included bread for five cents a loaf, a pound of butter for 38 cents, two pounds of cranberries for 43 cents, a box of Japanese oranges for 99 cents, and two pounds of Emperor variety grapes for 25 cents.

A tin of pure strawberry, raspberry or black currant jam sold for 43 cents and galvanized pails were 15 cents – one per customer.

Just in time for Christmas, fresh-killed turkeys sold at 23 cents a pound. "Turkeys drawn and cleaned with the sinews pulled – free of charge" – announced the ad.

Another store ad read: "The location of a Safeway store in your community or neighbourhood eliminates all necessity for making long, tiresome trips downtown to buy your foodstuffs to best advantage. Your local Safeway store is one of 3,000 of the most modern food shops on the American continent."

Winnipeg Street
and
Victoria Avenue

Eventually, the many small neighbourhood Safeway stores gave way to fewer and larger stores located in strip malls and major shopping centres.

Victoria Square Safeway

S. S. KRESGE CO. LTD.

1911 to 1913 11th Avenue

S. S. Kresge opened in 1930 at 11th Avenue and occupied the building until the late 1980s. The three-storey building had been erected in 1910 to house the business operations of George S. Wood, the local harness and hardware merchant. Prior to Kresge's opening, $40,000 of alterations were done to the store.

S. S. Kresge had features new to the city. The chute where freight was dropped from the ground level to the basement storage rooms had a slide that handled fragile articles without breakage, and in the basement there was a paper baler that baled waste paper from the wrappings of new merchandise.

A few days before the store opened, the restroom was used as an instruction room, with a cash register and other equipment with which the girls were given lessons in speed and accuracy.

Also in the rest room was a large square piano. The room was fitted with wicker easy chairs, a long wicker settee and chairs with a wide side arm for use during lunch hours.

The *Leader-Post* reported: "The building, which is immediately west of the Champlain Hotel on 11th Avenue, has a new type of front, being entirely of bronze and glass, with two entrances on 11th Avenue.

"The soda fountain, which is of the most modern type, has electrical refrigerator and power. All metal in the fountain accessories is mono-metal, stainless and non-corroding."

BROWN'S AUCTION ROOMS LTD.

1766 Osler Street

*B*rown's Auction Rooms was started by B. F. Brown in 1932. Born in Summerset, Iowa in 1897, Brown came to Canada in 1913 with his family and settled in Creelman. Along with nine others from Creelman, he enlisted in the army in WW I. He served in France and then in northern Russia from 1916 to 1919. After the war he returned to Creelman to farm.

Brown worked at various auctions and then took an auctioneering course by correspondence. With the drought and depression he decided to give up farming. In 1932 he held his own auction and moved to Regina. After getting his family settled in Regina, he had the grand total of $52.00 with which to start his own business. There was no credit in those days; everything had to be paid for in advance. He rented a building in downtown Regina and bought a Model A truck for $12.00. After placing ads in the *Leader* and the *Daily Star,* and obtaining his auctioneer and business licenses, along with necessary miscellaneous items, he was left with $5.00.

Brown made house calls to people advertising in the miscellaneous columns, and convinced a number of them to consign their goods to him. He assured them they would get more money if the goods were sold by auction. He soon had several auctions weekly and Brown's Auction Rooms became a reality. The business was an immediate success, and it was evident a much larger building was necessary. At this time the property at 1766 Osler Street was acquired, the current Brown's location.

In the early years, farmers would leave their horses and wagons at nearby Market Square, arranging to meet at Brown's or the Army and Navy, both popular places for rural people to shop.

In the late 1930s and early 1940s, Brown's was a household name in Regina and throughout Saskatchewan. Most homes had at least one, if not several, appliances or pieces of furniture from Brown's.

Brown became a Canadian citizen in 1944, and served in the 40th Field Artillery Regiment (Reserve) with the rank of Captain.

B. F. Brown sold the company to his son Clarence in 1951. Clarence Brown later sold the company to George Leichert and Blake MacKay.

In 2002, in its 70th year in business, Brown's is still thriving.

CONSUMERS' CO-OPERATIVE REFINERIES LIMITED

*T*he story of Consumers' Co-operative Refineries Limited began in 1933. Horses, which had been the dominant source of farm power for centuries, were giving way to petroleum-fuelled tractors. This was especially true in the Regina area, where the broad level prairie was well suited to the first tractors and combine harvesters.

As petroleum use increased, farmers looked for ways to reduce the cost of this important crop input. Many farmers had experience in the benefits of co-operation through joint purchases of other farm inputs. These efforts often resulted in the formation of local co-ops. With this strong and successful co-operative tradition, farmers formed oil co-ops to reduce the price of fuel.

Oil co-ops soon found that petroleum profits were shifting from the retail sector to the refinery, where the co-ops were not represented. In the midst of a world depression, serious drought and poor market prices for farm products, the bold response by the oil co-ops, in the winter of 1933/1934, was to launch a drive to build a refinery. In the middle of an economic catastrophe, this handful of visionaries, some of whom risked their own farms as security, believed they could build their own refinery.

Incorporated in 1934, the World's First Co-operative Refinery, a 500-barrel-per-day Skimming Plant, went "on stream" in 1935. In the first year of operation the plant achieved savings almost equal to the initial investment.

In 1939 CCRL built a long-awaited Cracking Plant which was essential to increase the yield of gasoline. It also increased production to 1,500 barrels of crude oil a day. In 1944 CCRL merged with Saskatchewan Co-operative Wholesale Society under the name Saskatchewan Federated Co-operatives Limited. Further expansion, to 5,000 barrels a day, opened in 1951.

A series of expansions over the next 20 years increased expansion to 50,000 barrels of crude per day in 1974. The early eighties brought a new chapter to the CCRL story. Canada and the rest of the world faced an energy crisis, and domestic supplies of light sweet crude dwindled. Saskatchewan and Canada were determined to secure the nation's energy future by

developing the vast reserves of heavy-oil. To do so, Canada needed a heavy oil upgrader to change heavy crude into a product suitable for further processing by conventional refineries.

After three years of construction of the mega project, which integrated an upgrader with CCRL existing refinery units, the Co-op Refinery/Upgrader Complex went on stream in 1988. It continues to be an important source of the energy needed to drive the agricultural industry as well as serve the needs of other petroleum users.

The Co-op Refinery/Upgrader Complex is one of Regina's most important industries and largest employers. The story of Consumers' Co-operative Refineries is a story of leadership, a story of success against almost impossible odds. CCRL celebrated its 67th Anniversary in 2002.

NEIL MOTORS

Northeast corner of Smith Street and 11th Avenue

A. E. Neil moved from Ontario to Saskatoon in 1912. There he was in the grocery business until 1927. "But this age is the motor era and Mr. Neil dropped groceries to go into the motor car field."

Neil Motors opened for business in Regina March 1, 1934 and sold 76 cars that year. Two years later the dealership had record sales of well over 300 Dodge and DeSoto cars.

Described in the *Leader-Post* as one of Regina's busiest and best-known families, the Neil family – father, son and daughter – ran the business. A. E. Neil was president, his son B. L. Neil, an "able assistant to a busy father", and Maxine Neil, "also an able assistant in the business of the firm."

The company opened for business at the southeast corner of 11th Avenue and Smith Street. Steady growth necessitated opening a new garage and service station across the street, on the northeast corner of 11th Avenue and Smith Street. The firm kept the southeast property for displaying used cars in the winter months and offices were located in the new garage, across 11th Avenue.

An ad in the December 17, 1936 *Leader-Post* read in part: "Fully equipped garage and storage – a pillarless storage and service floor – the garage man's fondest dream is now a reality with the innovation of a suspension roof. All the ease and convenience of outside parking now brought under cover." The service station had four "self computing pumps" and there was "no waiting for a complete and speedy Bumper to Bumper Service – economical and time-saving – that's what John Motorist wants."

Neil later built a second outlet at the corner of Albert Street and 12th Avenue. A low-rise office building, the Neil Professional Building, has since replace the Neil Motors building at this location.

Neil obviously knew what his customers wanted. The firm's constant expansion meant jobs for 34 Reginans in 1936. Business expanded to a Swift Current branch that same year to serve the needs of the western end of the province.

Bert Neil succeeded his father, Albert, as president and he ran Neil Motors until his sudden death in 1965 at the age of 54. A group headed by Paul Rousseau, who had been Neil Motors sales manager, purchased the company and the name was changed to Crestview Chrysler. Rousseau later sold the business to Ted Knight and entered politics.

FOODLAND

Northeast corner of Broad Street and 11th Avenue

*T*he doors of one of western Canada's largest groceterias swung open in Regina on March 28, 1935.

"The new groceteria boasts twice the extent of the original Foodland store which will incidentally continue in operation at 1794 Hamilton Street. Groceries, fruits and meats will be principal commodities – which brings the customer round to inspecting the longest single meat counter in the west. . . . All refrigeration is by means of air, doing away with the older-type chemicals." – March 27, 1935 *Leader-Post* Two tall tins of Carnation milk "from contented cows" sold for 19 cents. Red Rose tea was 45 cents a pound and Red Rose coffee was 39 cents a pound, while Nabob tea was 47 cents a pound and Nabob coffee was 39 cents a pound. A pint of Johnson's paste polishing wax sold for 53 cents and two boxes of Canada cornstarch were 19 cents.

Louis Krivel, manager of the new store, opened the first Foodland store in 1933. Upon the second store's opening, his brother I. Krivel managed the older store. This store became the Army and Navy Super Market.

Krivel sold the store at 11th Avenue and Lorne to Sam and Vivian Rootman in 1944. They later opened a second store at the corner of Hill Avenue and Montague Street and a third at 76 Stapleford Crescent.

At its peak, Foodland, when owned by the Rootmans, was the largest independent grocery store in Western Canada, with 1,000 charge accounts, free delivery (11 trucks), 75 employees and the first SaskTel answering machine in Saskatchewan. In 1966 the Rootmans sold the stores to the store manager, Cecil Jones. The Hill Avenue store still operates under the name Lakeview Fine Foods and is owned by Ken and Don Nasheim.

UNITED CIGAR STORES

11th Avenue and Broad Street/Hamilton Street/Cornwall Street/12th Avenue and Scarth Street

*E*stablished in the 1930s as retail outlets for Imperial Tobacco Co., United Cigar Stores were familiar landmarks in downtown Regina.

Changing streetscapes, with the building of new high-rise office buildings and shopping centres, saw the closing of the United Cigar Stores for redevelopment in the late 1970s. The stores, which sold tobacco, newspapers, confections and souvenirs, were relocated in the Regina Inn, the Cornwall Centre and the Northgate Mall. New stores were later opened in the Regina Airport and the Delta Hotel on Saskatchewan Drive.

THE BALMORAL CAFE

Hamilton Street between 11th and 12th Avenues

"*C*offee Row" – Where Sportsmen Gathered – In the late 1930s through the 1970s, the Balmoral Cafe, owned by Nick Pappas and his brother Sam, was a popular place for sports personalities to meet for coffee and discuss former and current sporting events. Usually, the self-appointed host for these gatherings was Al Ritchie, who would discuss at length his past experiences in both hockey and football for anyone who wanted to listen. These sessions usually included diagrams of plays, and strategies for future football games, drawn on table napkins.

Nick Pappas

Al Ritchie

Ritchie's audience usually included Greg Grassick, Angie Mitchell, Archie Biggart, Dave Dryburgh, Scotty Melville and Ken Preston. These impromptu gatherings grew so popular in the late 1940s that CKCK radio sports broadcaster Lloyd Saunders hosted a daily radio program called "Coffee Row".

Lloyd Saunders

There were other downtown locations where sportsmen met during the same period, including the Ritz Cafe operated by Chris Protopappas on Scarth Street, and National Billiards owned by hockey player Murray Armstrong and Jack Farquahar, just down the street from the Ritz.

Later, in the 1970s and 1980s, there was the LaSalle Hotel owned by Jim and Harry Kangles (see page 175) just a few doors down from the Balmoral. The LaSalle became a favourite meeting spot for football players such as Jack Gotta, George Reed and wrestling promoter Nick Zubray. However, none of the others equalled the fame of "Coffee Row" at the "Bal".

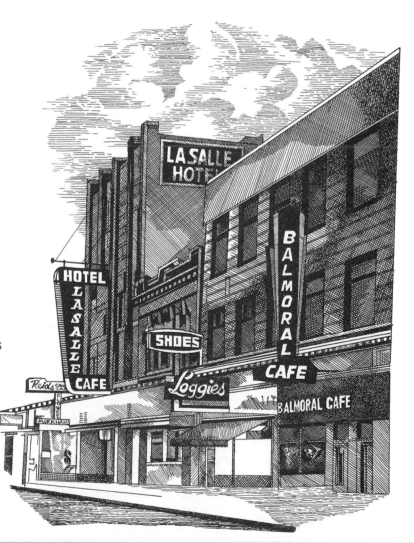

SHERWOOD

The Credit Union concept was born out of economic need. Like the hard times faced throughout the prairies in the 1930s, drought in Germany during the mid-1800s spawned the Credit Union concept. Poverty was the common link and community co-operation and the Christian belief, "Do as you would be done by", were the cures.

Credit Unions came to Saskatchewan in the spring of 1937 – after years of hardship – with the passing of the Credit Union Act. The purpose of the Act was "the promotion of thrift among its members at legitimate rates of interest exclusively for provident and productive purposes. In other words a membership devoted to pooling resources and then borrowing from that pool, where every member is an owner and every owner has an equal vote in the operation of the co-operative."

The predecessor of today's Sherwood Credit Union was the Regina Co-operative Savings and Credit Union. It was the fourth Credit Union incorporated under the Act, on September 27, 1937. It started with 30 members and total assets of $200. In 65 years it has grown into an organization of more than 63,000 members and assets in excess of $816 million, servicing Regina and surrounding southern communities.

"Being a community-owned company," says Susan Zwarych, Marketing Manager for Sherwood Credit Union, "it's important to be involved with the community."

She's right. Even the name elicits a community response, Sherwood being the name of the rural municipality surrounding the city. But it's not all in the name. Sherwood Credit Union donates between $150,000 and $250,000 per year throughout the community.

That money goes toward four areas the Credit Union envisions as vital to community development – Health, Sports and Recreation, Education and Social Development. Sherwood has put hundreds of thousands of dollars into capital campaigns for hospitals across southern Saskatchewan and has donated for the purchase of equipment such as the CT Scanner at the Pasqua Hospital, named in honour of the Credit Unions of Saskatchewan.

Sherwood Credit Union supports the Saskatchewan Roughriders and the community with the Fat Cat Family Fun Zone at

Sherwood Place
1960 Albert Street

5th Avenue and Elphinstone Street

Wallace Street and
Victoria Avenue

CREDIT UNION

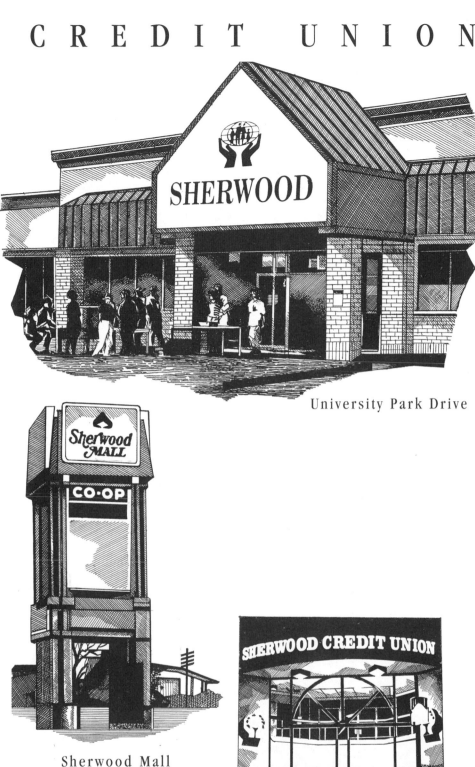

University Park Drive

Sherwood Mall
Rochdale and McCarthy
Boulevards

Sherwood Place

all Rider home games, providing family-priced tickets. Sherwood also supports many community amateur sports, in an effort to keep kids active and healthy, having fun, and promoting teamwork.

Sherwood staff work with community schools to help children understand banking, learn about saving money and, through various partnerships, allow high-school students to learn the business side of banking. The Credit Union provides money to neighbourhood libraries and volunteers to read stories to children, to allow them to work with adults other than parents and teachers.

Charitable and non-profit organizations in Regina benefit from the Credit Union's philosophy of community. The Credit Union provides support to organizations like Habitat for Humanity, with staff volunteering to pound nails as well as serve as board members. Sherwood encourages its staff to participate in these types of community projects and events. Corporate challenges in events like the Terry Fox campaign and MS Walk allow staff to interact with the community, take their families and raise the corporate profile. The United Way of Regina is an annual beneficiary.

Credit unions are unique in the banking world in that the members choose a board of directors. This gives Sherwood a stronger connection to the community as decisions are made locally, with community interests at heart. For instance, many banks have been closing branches in the past several years, but Sherwood continues to open branches in areas like East Regina. "Our branches cover the city well," Zwarych says. "It's important to have location accessibility, receptive to the needs of the community."

Sherwood's innovation doesn't end with community. It is at the leading edge of customer service and technology, being the first bank in Canada to introduce automated banking in the 1970s, the first with telebanking and at the forefront of Internet banking.

On January 1, 2003, Assiniboia Credit Union, once known as the largest agricultural-based credit union in the world, along with Moose Jaw Credit Union, the oldest existing credit union in the province, and Sherwood, the largest credit union in the province, will unite. The combined unions will operate under the new name CONEXUS, a latin term meaning "to join or unite".

CONEXUS, with headquarters in Regina, will be the ninth largest credit union in Canada.

CREDIT UNION CENTRAL

2055 Albert Street

*T*he story of Credit Union Central begins with the start of the credit union movement in Saskatchewan in 1937. Inexperience by early leaders, mostly unpaid volunteers, and the rapid growth of credit unions in every part of the province resulted in the organization in 1938 of the Credit Union Federation of Saskatchewan.

In 1941, under the visionary leadership of Tom Molloy, Saskatchewan credit unions recognized the growing need for additional financial services for credit unions and their members, and responded with the creation of the Saskatchewan Co-operative Credit Society. The Credit Union Federation and the Credit Union League operated separately until 1975 when they merged and adopted the trade name Credit Union Central.

Thomas M. Molloy

Credit Union Central is an umbrella association for the Saskatchewan credit unions. It is a central service agency and acts as a financial intermediary, providing a wide array of services for individual credit unions.

The head office building at the corner of Albert Street and 13th Avenue was completed in 1976.

KRAMER TRACTOR

Pasqua Street North and Highway 11

Robert A. Kramer

R. A. Kramer was born in California and became a naturalized Canadian in 1922. His family farmed near Lethbridge and he taught school in rural Alberta before entering the construction industry. Kramer came to Regina from Calgary in 1944 to take over the Caterpillar tractor dealership from Albert Olson. He purchased a building located at 6th Avenue and Halifax Street from the Beer Barrel Company, and it became the headquarters of Kramer Tractor Company Ltd.

Unfortunately, when Bob assumed the Caterpillar dealership, he had nothing to sell as Canada was at war, in addition, the building he had purchased had been leased to the Australian Government to store bales of wool. The wool was being stored there as a safeguard against possible invasion of Australia by the Japanese.

The war ended shortly thereafter and Kramer soon became a strong community leader. An astute businessman with a strong entrepreneurial spirit, Kramer Tractor expanded and flourished under his leadership. An avid sportsman, he was president of the Saskatchewan Roughriders on two occasions. He took the team to the Grey Cup in 1951. He was also president of the Western Interprovincial Football League, chairman of the United Way, director of the Regina Airport Board, director of Ducks Unlimited and St. Michael's Retreat House, and received the papal order of Knight Commander of St. Gregory.

Kramer Tractor moved to a new facility at Pasqua Street North and Highway 11 in 1977. The company name was changed to Kramer Ltd. in 1991.

Kramer Ltd. has been a family-held operation since 1944. Following the retirement of Robert A. Kramer in 1965, his son Donald E. Kramer was named president. In 1995 Timothy R. Kramer became president and Donald became chairman of the board.

Kramer Ltd. has grown with Saskatchewan's resource-based economy, serving the industries of mining, road building, oil, natural gas, forestry, electrical and agriculture. The company has service centres throughout the province as well as a parts facility at the Kumtor Mine (Cameco) in Kyrgyzstan. In 1998 Kramer Ltd. was inducted into the Saskatchewan Business Hall of Fame. Accepting the honour on behalf of the firm, Tim Kramer said, "Three factors have resulted in the success of Kramer, first is an honest customer base which can only be found in Saskatchewan where a handshake is held in as high regard as a legal document. Second is a supplier, Caterpillar. . . . third . . . Kramer's employees . . . "

Donald and Claire Kramer have been strong supporters of the MacKenzie Art Gallery. The Kramer IMAX Theatre in the Science Centre is named after them. The family has also supported many other cultural and charitable community activities.

A partnership between Kramer Ltd. and Winston Knoll Collegiate, signed May 25, 1999, provides for enrichment of curricular and extracurricular activities, to encourage students to stay in school and provide teachers and students with a first-hand look at the skills and abilities required after students leave school.

WESTERN TRACTOR LTD.

10th Avenue and Halifax Street

George Solomon

estern Tractor Ltd. was founded by Regina-born George Solomon in 1945. The company was a distributor of heavy industrial equipment throughout Saskatchewan.

The company was an outgrowth of the original company, Solomon and Sons, started by George Solomon's father, Fred. In the beginning it was an excavation company and Regina's first gravel contractor. They owned the only steam shovel in the city at the time.

Fred came to New York from Romania in 1900 and arrived in Regina in 1905. He was a construction laborer who had little difficulty finding work digging ditches. He was hired as construction foreman of Regina's new legislative building, where he coordinated the rigging and supervised the hoisting of the top crown. He also oversaw the stonework of the Hotel Saskatchewan. In his early days, before marriage, he spent his leisure hours in conversation with other workers in local bars and hotels. Fred realized his future success lay in the need for more hotels and rooming houses. The St. Regis Hotel at the corner of 11th Avenue and Osler Street was one of his first investments.

George learned well from his father's tutelage, and the original small family business was instrumental in the development of many successful Regina-based businesses, including Western Tractor, Canadian Hydrocarbons, Interprovincial Steel and Pipe Corporation (Ipsco), Sterling Cranes Ltd., Central Canadian Distillers and Western Transport. At one time George Solomon was one of Saskatchewan's largest employers. As the company diversified and became involved in extensive real estate development, the name of the company changed to Western Ltd.

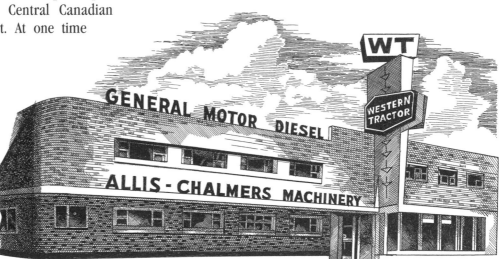

George Solomon received the Duke of Edinburgh Award, the Saskatchewan Order of Merit, the Order of Canada and received an Honourary Doctorate of Law from the University of Regina. "Western Spirit" a modern sculpture depicting geese in flight, located at the corner of 11th Avenue and Hamilton Street, was dedicated to Solomon's industrialism and philanthropy. A director of the Bank of Montreal, the Potash Corporation of Saskatchewan, Ocelot Industries, Carling O'Keefe Breweries, International Paints (Canada) Limited and many others, he was also a director of the YMCA and the Salvation Army, and served on advisory boards for the Canadian Council for Christians and Jews, the Boy Scouts of Canada, the Vanier Institute and the Canadian Association for Retarded Children.

Following in their father's footsteps, Western Ltd. actively continues property development and management in western Canada under the leadership of George's daughters: President Vaughn Solomon-Schofield and company Directors Sharon Dyksman and Adrian Burns.

THE CO-OPERATORS

1822 Albert Street/1920 College Avenue

*T*he Co-operative Life Insurance Company was incorporated in 1945. In 1947 a syndicate of co-operatives, including Co-operative Life Insurance Company, purchased the Veteran Block at 1822 Albert Street. Co-op Life moved its home office from a house in downtown Regina to the Veteran Block, which was renamed the Co-op Block.

In 1952 Co-op Fire and Casualty Company was incorporated and the two companies occupied the second and third floors and most of the basement. Other occupants of the Old Co-op Block included Sherwood Credit Union and Credit Union Central. They also relocated to new space and the Co-op Block on Albert Street was demolished.

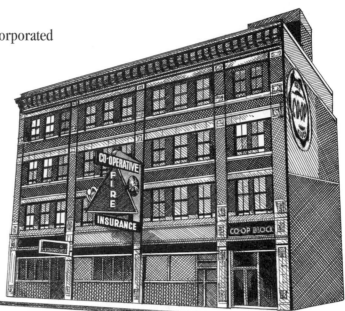

1822 Albert Street

In 1961 the two companies had outgrown the old location and a new building was designed by Stock, Keith and Associates. Constructed by Hilsden and Co. at 1920 College Avenue, the new building became the home of Co-op Life and Co-op Fire and Casualty Company. In 1964 the companies merged under a new name, CIS Group of Companies.

Continued growth of CIS necessitated expansions in 1972 and 1978, which quadrupled their space in the building. CIS merged with the Co-operators Group of Companies of Ontario and the new name became "The Co-operators".

With head offices in Regina, The Co-operators is the largest Canadian-owned multi-line insurer, with 4,000 employees and 450 exclusive agents.

1920 College Avenue

REDHEAD EQUIPMENT LTD.

705 Henderson Drive in Ross Industrial Park

R edhead Equipment got its start in 1948 under the name of W. F. Fuller Machinery Limited. Gordon Redhead, born in Regina in 1923, worked for Fuller Machinery until 1968, at which time he purchased the business and changed the name to Redhead Equipment Ltd.

Gary Redhead, Gordon's son, joined the family business in 1969. He worked with his father until 1980, when he bought his father's interest in Redhead Equipment Ltd. and became the president and CEO.

Since 1948, the Redhead family has built a reputation as one of Saskatchewan's premiere suppliers of new and used motor graders and heavy construction equipment, agricultural equipment and heavy trucks.

Redhead Equipment was originally a Champion motor grader dealer, but expanded in 1971 to also become the John Deere construction equipment dealer. In 1990 they diversified operations further by adding Mack trucks. In 1991 Redhead Equipment resigned as the John Deere dealer and acquired the Case Equipment dealership, including both construction and agricultural equipment. In 1998 Champion was purchased by Volvo Construction Equipment. As a result, in 2001 Redhead Equipment added Volvo Construction Equipment to its product line.

In 1998 Redhead Equipment Ltd. purchased Southwest Pro-Ag, an agricultural implement dealership in Swift Current, Saskatchewan, further expanding the company into southwestern Saskatchewan.

Today, Redhead Equipment Ltd. is a diversified company serving the trucking, construction, oil and gas, and agricultural industries in Saskatchewan from six state-of-the-art facilities, employing over 200 people, with two locations in Regina, two in Saskatoon, one in Lloydminster and one in Swift Current. Redhead Equipment is currently ranked as one of the largest equipment dealers in Saskatchewan and is the second-largest truck dealer. To better serve its growing business, Redhead equipment constructed facilities in Swift current in 1993 and in Lloydminster and Regina in 1997, earning themselves a cover story in *Border Business Magazine*.

Redhead Equipment is pleased to support the community by contributing to numerous local and national charities. In recent years they have contributed to the Hospitals of Regina Foundation as their primary charitable recipient.

Redhead Equipment is also committed to supporting community events and supports many provincial sports teams such as the Saskatchewan Roughriders, Regina Pats and Moose Jaw Warriors, as well as numerous local sports teams and community organizations.

Redhead Equipment Ltd. has received many awards over the years for both customer service and sale achievements, including several from Mack Trucks, Champion, Case and, in 2001, the Volvo Outstanding Achievement Award for highest North American market share.

CAIRNS HOMES LIMITED

776 Broad Street

Jim Cairns

W hat started as a small house builder in 1952, with only two employees, grew to become Saskatchewan's largest employer, involved in land development, housing, prefab plants and the lumber-supply-business.

Cairns Homes Limited was founded by D. J. (Jim) Cairns, from Bengough, Saskatchewan. An ambitious young man, after serving with the Royal Canadian Air Force, Jim was eager to go into business for himself.

Cairns first major project was to set up the 50 Home Club, building the first homes in Saskatchewan under the Canada Housing and Mortgage Corporation. The idea was to provide a standard plan with design options that could be packaged and produced in volume at the lowest cost. The customers in the club had young families, like Cairns himself, who had come out of the service needing affordable accommodation. The project was so successful that the original target of 50 homes grew to 78 in the first year.

Under the leadership of Cairns, assisted by Rod Gerla, Roy Grozell and Tom Shepherd, the company had steady growth for the next 20 years, with branches throughout the province. By the late 1950s Cairns was producing more than 200 homes annually. The company expanded to Alberta in 1970 because of favourable marketing opportunities, building houses in Red Deer and Edmonton. In 1973, Nu-West Development Corporation, a Calgary-based public company, purchased Cairns Homes Limited and the two companies merged. Cairns Homes, with its head offices in Regina, continued to operate independently, under its own board of directors. Cairns Homes Limited moved into the Calgary housing market in 1973, and expanded into Winnipeg in 1979. Also in the 1970s, Cairns, a wholly owned subsidiary of the Nu-West Group Limited, moved into commercial and income property development.

In 1989 Carma Developers Ltd. bought the company and amalgamated it into their operation. They continued to use the Cairns name in Regina and Winnipeg until the assets were sold to Dundee Development Corporation in 1997. Although the Cairns name has disappeared, Dundee continues the Regina land development and residential housing operations started by Jim Cairns in 1952.

Areas in Regina developed by Cairns include Glencairn, Glencairn Village, Sherwood Estates, McCarthy Park, Lakewood, Lakeridge, Parkridge, Creekside, Woodland Grove, Garden Ridge, Varsity Park, Wascana View and Gardiner Park. Cairns was also involved in developments in Whitmore Park, Albert Park, University Park and Uplands.

From 1952 to 1997 over 23,000 homes and lots were crafted and developed in western Canada under the Cairns name, this would be equivalent to the number of houses in a city larger than Moose Jaw.

GENE'S LTD.

Going on 50!

In 2004 Gene's Ltd. will celebrate its 50th anniversary.

In 1954 Gene Ciuca, with partners Frank Sojonky and Sam Stewart, opened Canada's first drive-through, drive-in restaurant on Highway #6 south, a summer-only enterprise.

Gene had previously partnered with Oscar Abdoulah in The Last Chance drive-in, and with Frank in the Blue Band Cafe and The Savoy. That fall they bought Ernie's lunch at Lorne Street and 14th Avenue and renamed it Gene's on the Avenue. The thought was to provide the same great food to sit-down customers in the winter, but the real purpose was to hold the suppliers and creditors at bay. "The Avenue" became the favourite spot of the University of Regina crowd, especially the Fine Arts Department. It was closed on Tuesdays, but the side door was open for a bowl of tomato soup and a grilled cheese sandwich.

An empty space in the back of Gene's on the Avenue became L'Habitant Steak House. The small 28-seater gained national acclaim, and was a perennial pick of *Where to Eat in Canada* and one of MacLean's magazine's top 10. It was the special-occasion restaurant for Reginans for many years.

In 1958 Chicken On The Way home-delivery service opened in the basement of Gene's on the Avenue. It was a great idea – but a lousy product. In his travels, Gene had run across an old guy with a pressure cooker and a recipe for fried chicken, so he tracked down the Colonel and signed up for the Kentucky Fried Chicken franchise for Regina. Gene's was the fifth franchise in Canada, fifty-fourth in the world. By the time the KFC stores were sold to Pepsico in 1991, Gene's Ltd. operated eight outlets in Regina and Fort Qu'Appelle.

Last Chance Drive-In

LAST CHANCE CURB SERVICE

Coca-Cola

DRINKS DOGS SHAKES CHIPS

Col. Sanders Recipe
Kentucky Fried Chicken®
A CANADIAN COMPANY
Regina and Fort Qu'Appelle

L'HABITANT
1711 Victoria Avenue

WALDOS
3970 Albert Street

Geno's
1515 Albert Street

Old Gold
3970 Albert Street

SAMMY'S PIZZA
THE 4th DIMENSION

River Heights Shopping Centre

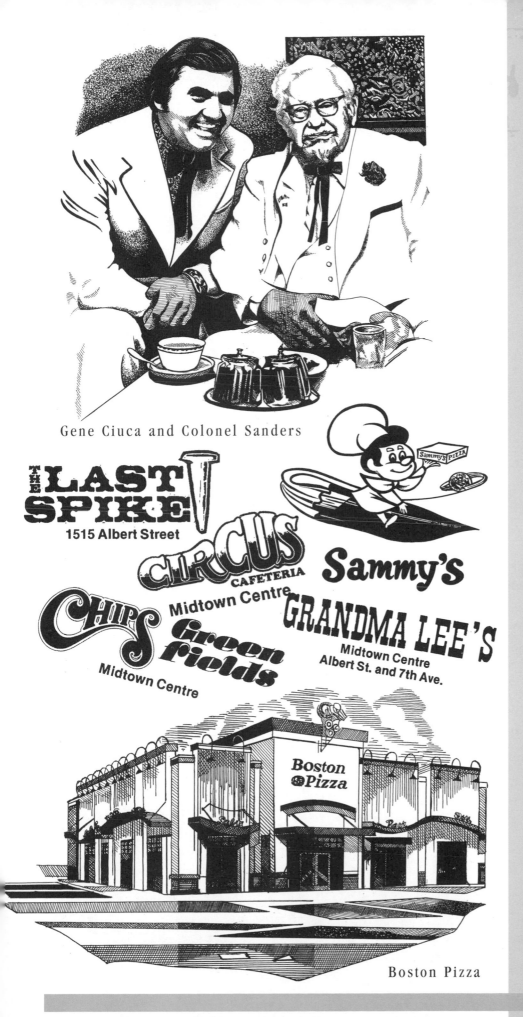

Gene Ciuca and Colonel Sanders

THE LAST SPIKE
1515 Albert Street

CIRCUS CAFETERIA
Midtown Centre

Sammy's

CHIPS
Midtown Centre

Green Fields
Midtown Centre

GRANDMA LEE'S
Midtown Centre
Albert St. and 7th Ave.

Boston Pizza

Boston Pizza

In addition to his many successful business interests, Gene was a major supporter of the arts in Regina. Over the years, Gene's Ltd. has maintained this generous support for the arts and other community projects.

Gene bought out Sojonky and Stewart, and in 1966 Wayne Steadman became Managing Partner. Gene passed away in Florida in 1984, and Steadman carried on his tradition with the help of partners, Gary Tremblay, Bill Rudichuk and Ed Katchur.

Over the years Gene's Ltd. opened several restaurants, many of them firsts for Regina – Sammy's Pizza and the Fourth Dimension Coffee House in the River Heights Shopping Centre. George Carlin, Joni Mitchell, The Guess Who, Don McLean and many more played the 4D over the years.

Other restaurants were: Geno's and The Last Spike at Albert Street and Dewdney Avenue, Circus Cafeteria in the Midtown Centre, Waldo's and The Old Gold at Albert Street and Parliament Avenue.

Geno's Pizza and Pasta Restaurants were converted to Boston Pizza in the mid-1990s as part of an arrangement to develop Boston Pizza restaurants in Saskatchewan. Gary Tremblay, longtime General Manager of Gene's Ltd. bought the company's interest in 2001 and is continuing to build Boston Pizzas in the province.

Today, Gene's Ltd. is primarily in the property development and management business. Aubrey Steadman, General Manager, joined the firm in 2001 after a career with KPMG and Deloitte and Touche Inc. as a management consultant.

To mark its 50th anniversary in 2004 the company plans a reunion weekend July 3rd and 4th. A committee is already working out plans and gathering lists of alumni. When you think of all the great people who worked toward the success of all those restaurants, over all those years – you know that's going to be some party!

genes.reunion@access.ca

MILKY WAY

910 Victoria Avenue

A familiar sight to Reginans has been the red and white Milky Way which has opened for the summer season every year since 1956. Frank and Margaret Anne Boldt and Lorne and Carole Boldt purchased the business in 1980.

Over the years, the Milky Way has gone through many renovations and operators, but it has remained as one of the favourite pit stops for ice-cream lovers in the city. When the stand opened only hard ice cream was served, but that changed in the mid-1960s when a soft-ice-cream machine was purchased.

The Milky Way opens just prior to Easter and offers 32 flavours of hard ice cream and six flavours of soft ice cream seven days a week from 11 a.m. to 11 p.m. It closes on the Thanksgiving weekend – a sure signal summer is over.

BRANDT INDUSTRIES LTD.

Pinkie Road

I n 1938 Brandt Electric was founded by Abram Peter Brandt. Located at 705 Toronto Street, Brandt designed and built innovative products, including one of the first grain augers available in Canada.

Gavin Semple of Craven, Saskatchewan joined Brandt Electric in 1972 and purchased the company in 1976. His son Shaun Semple has become president. Over the years Brandt Electric became Brandt Industries Ltd. The company celebrated its 60th Anniversary in 1998. It is now the 27th largest corporation in Saskatchewan.

Brandt invents, manufactures and distributes hundreds of industry-leading products across Canada and the world. It is a diverse company, with five independent divisions – agricultural equipment manufacturing, custom-engineered products, light industrial equipment dealerships, John Deere construction equipment dealerships and road rail equipment manufacturing.

Brandt Industries Ltd. employs over 1,000 people and services markets in North America, South America, Europe, Asia and Australia. It has sales of $450 million.

The Brandt Group of Companies was chosen as one of Canada's 50 Best Managed Private Companies in 1994 and again in 2001. In August 2002, Brandt purchased a British Columbia company, thereby making its Brandt Tractor Division the largest private company in the world selling John Deere's forestry and construction equipment.

IPSCO INC.

Armour Road

*I*n 1956 Prairie Pipe Manufacturing was incorporated at the urging of the government of the day. A number of diversification projects were undertaken in the province at that time, including cement making, shoe making and brick making, but one of the few to survive was IPSCO – the company that grew out of the original Prairie Pipe.

The idea behind Prairie Pipe was to supply the pipe needs for the natural gas network that SaskPower had under construction at the time. A pipe mill was constructed that began production in 1957. When Prairie Pipe first started operations it purchased the steel it required from outside the province. This dependence on outside steel sources led to the incorporation of a second company, Interprovincial Steel Corporation Ltd., that would gather scrap steel from western Canada and the northwestern United States and melt it into a new product, suitable not only for Prairie Pipe's needs but also for a variety of other customers. A short time later the companies became one entity under the name Interprovincial Steel and Pipe Corporation. The name changed some 30 years later to IPSCO Inc. – the name by which it had become generally known.

Those involved with IPSCO in the early days might be surprised at the amount of growth in the company since that time. IPSCO expanded in numerous ways. Its product lines have been expanded to include tubular products for oil and gas exploration, oil and gas transportation, pipe that can be found in farm implements and in sprinkler systems. In addition, its steel products go into these tubular products as well as into bridges, electrical transmission towers, wind turbines, ships, and products which have a myriad of other uses.

IPSCO has also grown geographically. From its roots in Regina have come two more steelmaking facilities, in Iowa and Alabama. Pipemaking and coil-processing facilities can be found in four Canadian provinces and five US states.

The company's sales have topped the billion-dollar mark, and its steelmaking production capacity exceeds 3-million tons of steel a year.

IPSCO's presence in Regina has been vital. Employing up to 1,000 people, the company also operates a wildlife park and pool, available free to the public. Cultural organizations, health providers and social-aid organizations have long looked to IPSCO for support of their work.

IPSCO is a dynamic company with deep roots in Regina. It produces materials accepted across the continent, from pipelines to tractors, wind turbines to ships – IPSCO supplies the materials.

SASKATCHEWAN POWER BUILDING

2025 Victoria Avenue

*D*esigned by local architect Joseph Pettick and opened in 1963, the Saskatchewan Power Building is distinguished by its curvilinear design in the Expressionist style. Other notable features of the "Y" shaped building include the arcade/drive-through area and its open floor plan. There is a small art gallery, the Gallery on the Roof, and an observation deck on the 13th floor of the building.

In 1964, the City of Regina arranged for the Saskatchewan Power Corporation to supply power for the city. Power had previously been generated at the Regina Power Plant (see page 49).

From 1909 to 1940 this was the site of St. Mary's Separate School. The school building was later occupied by the Reliance School of Commerce, from 1942 to 1947, and by Trans-Canada Airlines (now Air Canada), until 1950. The Regina bus depot moved into the building and remained there until 1959, when the depot was moved to 2041 Hamilton Street.

THE BAY DEPARTMENT STORES

12th Avenue between Rose and Hamilton Streets

*A*lthough the Hudson Bay Company is one of the oldest still active companies in the world, it did not take on a new approach to retailing until 1912, when it planned a chain of department stores in western Canada, which laid the foundation for its emergence as one of Canada's leading retailers. By 1970, downtown department stores had been built in each of the major cities of western Canada, including Regina. The Regina store was located on 12th Avenue between Rose and Hamilton Streets, on what were formerly the sites of the Regina Theatre, Regina Steam Laundry and Saskatchewan Motors.

The company then moved into eastern Canada through acquisitions and launched an ambitious expansion program into the suburbs of most major Canadian cities. This was followed by the acquisition of Zellers in 1978 and the Robert Simpson Co. in 1979.

In 1999 Sears Canada bought out Eaton's which had gone bankrupt, at which time the Eaton's store in the Cornwall Centre was closed as Sears already had a retail outlet in the Cornwall Centre. At that point, The Bay closed its original store on 12th Avenue and, in 2000, The Bay took over the former Eaton's store in the Cornwall Centre.

SGI SASKATCHEWAN HEADQUARTERS

2260 11th Avenue

*A*s part of the Provincial Government's commitment to preserve Regina's downtown core, the Saskatchewan Government Insurance Headquarters Building (the C. M. Fines Building) was built in 1979, adjoining the Cornwall Centre on 11th Avenue and Lorne Street.

The 20-storey building was designed by Pettick Phillips Partners Architects Ltd, and constructed by PCL Construction Management Inc. The building is of structural steel, metal deck and concrete floors with aluminum and glass curtainwall cladding. It contains three levels of below-grade parking.

The building was named in honour of C. M. Fines, to recognize his contribution in the establishment of government insurance in Saskatchewan.

Clarence Fines arrived in Regina as a 24-year-old vice-principal at Thomson School, and later became principal of Albert, Benson and Strathcona schools. He became active in politics and was a popular alderman on city council. He later became provincial treasurer in the government of Saskatchewan under Premier T. C. Douglas. He became known in New York, on Wall Street, as the "bankers' socialist" who took the province from near bankruptcy to a debt-free position before his retirement from government at age 55.

Fines was in charge of the Government Finance Office from 1947 to 1960 and was chairman of Saskatchewan Government Insurance from 1948 until 1960. He died in Florida in 1993 at the age of 88.

PHOENIX GROUP

335 Hoffer Drive

*T*he Phoenix Group started as a one-person advertising agency, founded in 1982 by Graham Barker.

Twenty years later, that one-person agency has become a 25-person, full-service communications agency which is one of the largest in the province. Continued growth forced the agency to move through several locations, including the 11th floor of the North Canadian Oils Building, and several historic buildings in downtown Regina, before locating at 335 Hoffer Drive in 1997.

In the past 20 years Phoenix has also gone through numerous other changes to keep up with the impact of new technology. Phoenix launched Digital and Eggplant Interactive (Web site, CD-Rom, animation and banner design and development) Divisions in 2000.

Phoenix is involved with more than innovative ideas within the advertising industry. Ideas that help and support the community are also paramount. Phoenix has become known for its passion for helping people.

The Phoenix Group was recognized as Regina's 2002 Business of the Year by the Regina Chamber Of Commerce Paragon Awards, which is a tribute to their community involvement.

The Phoenix Group, as a Community Partner, has sponsored pages 308 and 309 featuring the Saskatchewan Roughriders.

THE CANADA TRUST TOWER

1904 Hamilton Street

*T*he 12-storey Canada Trust Office Tower was built in 1985. Located on the site of the R. H. Williams/Robert Simpson Company Department Stores, at the corner of 11th Avenue and Hamilton Street, the tower was the Saskatchewan headquarters of Canada Trust until it merged with TD Bank in 2000.

The tower was designed by architect Bob Ellard and the IKOY partnership, and constructed by Dominion Construction Ltd. for the Bentall/Western Ltd./Canada Trust consortium.

GREYSTONE MANAGED INVESTMENTS

1230 Blackfoot Drive

*F*ounded in 1988, Greystone Managed Investments was initially entrusted with assets previously managed by the Saskatchewan Department of Finance. Greystone has grown from having 25 Saskatchewan-based clients, mainly public sector pension funds, to over 1,000 clients, ranging from some of the largest Canadian corporate and government pension plans to high-net-worth individuals from across Canada. Working from this solid base, Greystone has grown to become the 12th largest pension investment manager in Canada, with over $13 billion of assets under management. Outgrowing its original office space at 3303 Hillsdale within five years, the firm moved down the street to its current quarters at 1230 Blackfoot Drive in 1994.

Regina-based Greystone has over 60 employees, who form the majority ownership of the firm, with branches in Edmonton and Winnipeg. The technology of the 21st century affords Greystone, located in Regina, the possibility of maintaining a major profile in the pension investment industry in Canada, whereas in years gone by this was only deemed possible to companies centered in Toronto. The strength of the firm has been built on a solid team-based approach to investment management. Greystone's investment management team is led by President Rob Vanderhooft, who in 2002 was named one of Canada's Top 40 under 40 by The Globe and Mail's *Report on Business* Magazine. Superior client investment returns, generated by this team, have resulted in the growth of new client assets of over $1 billion a year since 1999.

Greystone is committed to giving back to the community by encouraging its employees to donate their time and resources to local charities. Deputy chairman and CEO Don Black leads by example. Don has represented Greystone with major sponsorships and in an advisory capacity for a number of local initiatives, including Habitat for Humanity Regina, the Saskatchewan Indian Federated College and the Regina United Way.

Greystone, as a Community Partner, has sponsored pages 112 and 113 featuring the Regina Public and Catholic Schools.

SASKENERGY PLACE

1777 Victoria Avenue

*U*ntil the late 1980s, Saskatchewan's power and natural gas services were both provided by one Crown Corporation – SaskPower. In 1988, however, SaskEnergy was created as a separate Crown Corporation whose purpose was to distribute natural gas throughout the province. SaskEnergy, and its wholly owned subsidiary TransGas, continue to provide natural gas transmission and distribution management and administrative services from the head office at 1777 Victoria Avenue, but the company did not always operate out of its current location.

For the first few years after its creation, SaskEnergy was based out of a series of temporary head offices: The Financial Building at 2101 Scarth Street; The Terrace Building at 2221 Cornwall Street; the Chateau Tower at 1920 Broad Street. Through a two-phase relocation in August 1991 and August 1994, SaskEnergy corporate office functions were consolidated into the SaskEnergy Tower (Grenfell Towers) at 1945 Hamilton Street. Upon expiry of the SaskEnergy lease, the head office was moved in October 2001 to its current location, SaskEnergy Place at 1777 Victoria Avenue.

More than 370 SaskEnergy and TransGas employees work in the head-office building, with approximately 1,000 employees in total working throughout the province. Through SaskEnergy's 64,000 kilometre distribution system, the company provides natural gas service to more than 317,000 homes, farms, and commercial and industrial customers in nearly 600 communities across Saskatchewan.

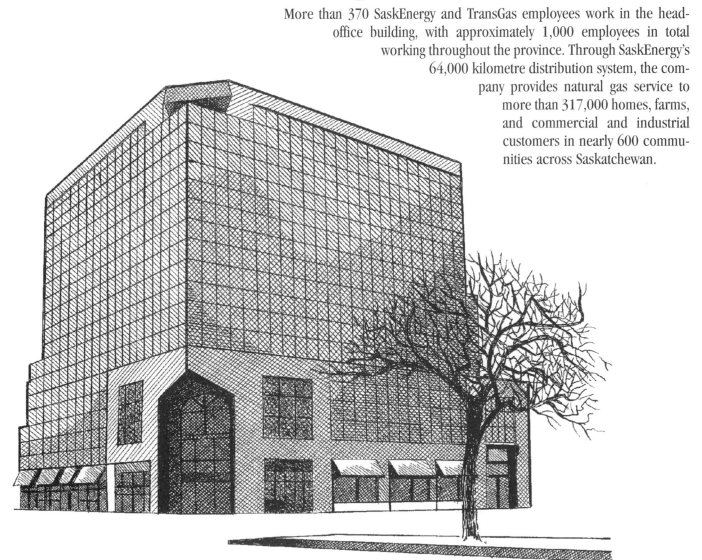

SaskEnergy, as a Community Partner, has sponsored pages 288 and 289 featuring Regina's YMCA and YWCA.

SHOPPING CENTRES IN REGINA

*A*fter WW II, in the late 1940s, strip malls began to appear in the new residential neighbourhoods of most cities, outside the downtown core. Strip malls were followed by major shopping centres located in rapidly expanding suburbs throughout North America.

In 1955 the Golden Mile Plaza, located on south Albert Street at 25th Avenue, became the first major shopping centre in Regina. The Golden Mile was followed by the Northgate Mall on Albert Street North, the Normanview Mall on McCarthy Boulevard North, the Sherwood Mall on Rochdale Boulevard in Northwest Regina, Southland Mall in south Regina on Gordon Road and Albert Street, and Victoria Square on Victoria Avenue East.

Concern about preserving the downtown core resulted in commitment from the provincial government to support a major redevelopment on the north side of 11th Avenue between Hamilton and Cornwall Streets, which resulted in the construction of the Cornwall Centre, SGI Tower, SaskTel Tower and an adjoining high-rise apartment in 1981.

In 1988, as part of the downtown redevelopment commitment, the province, in cooperation with the City of Regina, assisted in the building of the Saskatchewan Trade and Convention Centre and a 12-storey office tower connected to the Ramada Renaissance Hotel, which later became the Delta Hotel, on Saskatchewan Drive opposite Casino Regina.

The Cornwall Centre contains 85 stores, including Sears and The Bay. It is 100 per cent owned by Cadillac Fairview, and is connected to office towers. It is the largest shopping centre in southern Saskatchewan.

WILLIAM SELBY RESIDENCE

Lorne Street and 11th Avenue

William Selby

"*O*n May 25, 1883, the first boy to be born on the townsite turned up at the home of Lieutenant-Colonel and Mrs. John W. Selby, then situated on the corner of Lorne Street and 11th Avenue, where the Donahue Block now stands.

"This child was baptized in St. Paul's Anglican Church and was the first birth to be entered on the parish register. He was christened William John Percival and is today an exceedingly well-known Regina citizen, where he directs the activities of the Boy Scout organization. When this the first male to be born in Regina was about seven years old, the family moved back to Ontario, but as William Percival Selby grew up to young manhood he felt an irresistible urge to again visit the scene of his birth, and early in the present century, he returned to Regina where he has been engaged in a number of useful activities." – September 29, 1936 *Leader-Post*

The paper also noted, "The first child born in the new capital of Regina was Mary Rowell who arrived in this somewhat melancholy vale of tears just five days before Christmas, 1882." After Rowell's birth there was no increase in Regina's population until Selby's birth.

Built in 1882, the Selby house was one of the very first buildings in Regina. Handmade iron nails were used entirely in its construction. In 1910 the house was moved to 2614 Albert Street. Within the house's walls, plans were laid for Regina's first Anglican congregation, a vestry selected and a building committee put to work. On its threshold on December 13, 1882, Reverend A. Osborne was welcomed as the first rector of St. Paul's Anglican Church.

Selby was regarded as "The Father of Scouting in Saskatchewan." He organized the Coronation contingent of Boy Scouts in 1911 and 36 Scouts were sent overseas from Saskatchewan. He formed the first Boy Scout band in 1912. In 1917 he devoted his full time to Boy Scouts' work, completing more than 35 years without a break. Selby took 25 Saskatchewan Scouts to the world jamboree in Britain in 1929. He wore the Silver Wolf Award, Scouting's highest decoration, presented to him by Lord Baden-Powell during a Regina visit in 1929.

Selby rejoined the provincial government when he relinquished his full-time scouting duties in 1938, and worked in the Department of Agriculture and the Bureau of Publications. He had served for more than 36 years in St. Paul's Church, which his father had helped to build. Selby died in 1945 at the age of 62.

DEMETRIUS WOODWARD RESIDENCE

560 Albert Street

"City's oldest house torn down" was the *Leader-Post* headline in the August 29, 1960 issue. "A remnant of Regina's earliest history will be torn down and replaced by a Coronation Park shopping centre." reported the *Leader-Post*.

Built in 1883 by Demetrius Woodward, Regina's first settler, the house was a landmark in the city.

In 1882 Woodward left Norfolk, Ontario to look for rich farming land on the prairies. He took a CPR train as far as Brandon, the western terminus of the railway, and travelled as far as Fort Qu'Appelle by a Red River cart drawn by oxen. The soil was too light at Fort Qu'Appelle for his liking, so Woodward continued on to Pile of Bones, where he camped north of the little settlement of tents on May 18, 1882.

Soon after, Woodward returned to his eastern home to bring his wife and five children west. He arranged for a load of lumber to be sent out, and when his family arrived preparations were underway to build a sturdy frame house, spacious enough for a large family.

During the early days of his homesteading, Woodward almost lost his valuable property because the city attempted to take it over. He and other nearby homesteaders "engaged the services of a brilliant lawyer, Dalton McCarthy, who was able to uphold the rights of the homesteaders."

LIEUTENANT-GOVERNOR AMÉDÉE FORGET RESIDENCE

*T*his is the 1883 home of Amédée Emmanuel Forget, the man who twice held the position of lieutenant-governor. From 1898 to 1905, Forget was lieutenant-governor of the North-West Territories, then lieutenant-governor of the new province of Saskatchewan from 1905 to 1910.

Forget's first visit to Regina from Quebec was in 1878 when he reported on the trial of Louis Riel's assistant, Ambrose Lepine, for a French language newspaper. As he covered the story, Forget became interested in the life of the Indians.

He returned to Saskatchewan from Quebec years later and, after serving in several positions in the Territorial administration, he became Indian Commissioner in 1895.

The appointment of Forget as lieutenant-governor was popular. Within a short period of time, he and his wife, Henriette, established their positions as leading Regina citizens, hosting many gatherings.

The couple entertained at a state ball in conjunction with the opening of the legislature the year that Regina became a city.

"On that occasion of the first New Year's levee following this auspicious civic milestone 81 gentlemen, most correctly attired in high silk hats, morning coats and striped trousers, called on the vice regal representative to pay their respects." – *Leader*

In 1911 Forget was appointed to the Senate, where he sat until his death on June 8, 1923. Upon her husband's death, Mrs. Forget entered a convent where she stayed until her death in 1928.

Forget Street is named after the popular couple.

PETER McARA RESIDENCE

2013 Victoria Avenue

*F*orty-four years' residence in the same Regina house is something of a record. It was established by Peter McAra — ex-mayor, ex-alderman, pioneer and respected businessman (see page 37).

The house held a record, too. It was the oldest residence still on its original property, on the original townsite.

Colonel Hugh Richardson, the judge who tried Riel, had this house built in 1884, when Regina was just graduating from the tent and shanty stage. The property comprised five, 27-foot lots.

McAra bought the house from Judge Richardson in 1904 for $5,500. He had the partial basement fully dug out and the house placed on a cement foundation. The fireplace was converted to a fixture of utility and beauty with tiles and oak paneling, carved simply and beautifully in a Greek acanthus design.

On June 30, 1912, from his circular staircase, McAra saw the Metropolitan Church in ruins following the devastating cyclone.

R. H. WILLIAMS RESIDENCE

2152 Rose Street

*N*ot only did Regina's major department store, Glasgow House (see page 190), prosper for years, so did its owner, R. H. Williams. He built this house on Rose Street in what was then considered the better area of Regina.

R. H. Williams and his family were active in the community's church and social life and he played a prominent role in municipal politics, serving two terms as mayor, in 1891 and 1909 (see page 34).

In 1936 the Salvation Army purchased Williams' 14-room residence and converted it into the Eventide Home for elderly men.

G. T. MARSH RESIDENCE

1925 Victoria Avenue

*T*his frame, two-storey house, with extensive verandahs and a south-facing sunroom, belonged to one of Regina's first citizens. George Terry Marsh arrived in Regina in 1883 and was mayor of Regina during the 1895 Territorial Exhibition (see page 35). After this exhibition, the town purchased the exhibition site and it has become the permanent site of Regina Exhibition Park.

A member of the congregation of St. Paul's Anglican Church, Marsh donated the land, on the northeast corner of 12th Avenue and McIntyre Street, where St. Paul's Church was built. When he left Regina he donated the land on Victoria Avenue where his house was located for a new Assiniboia Club building (now Danbrys and the Assiniboia Club). Marsh was president of the Assiniboia Club in 1888 and again in 1904 to 1906.

His son George Marsh Jr. married Annie Whitmore and lived next door at 1945 Victoria Avenue, the current location of Golf's Steak House.

George Marsh's daughter Florence married A. E. Whitmore, who was also a major contributor to the community and, in particular, the exhibition. Whitmore was "instrumental in having the World Grain Show brought to Regina in 1933, and set aside one of his large farms as a demonstration plot for growing tests of grain entered in the world-wide show that year." – *Leader-Post*

A photograph in *The Tattler*, of September 29, 1906 shows Mr. and Mrs. Marsh in their new 10 H. P. Cadillac, one of the first cars in Regina. Marsh later moved from Regina to Toronto.

JACOB W. SMITH RESIDENCE – 1ST MAYOR OF REGINA

Victoria Avenue

A majestic verandah, graced with white pillars, topped with Ionic capitals, welcomed visitors to the Neoclassical-style home of Regina's first mayor. This three-storey brick house was further distinguished by a turret and a substantial third-floor balcony with a pediment supported again by pillars with Ionic capitals. A widow's walk with a graceful wrought iron balcony crowned the roof of the house.

A town councillor in 1884 and 1887, Smith was also town mayor in 1902. He became the City of Regina's first mayor in 1903 and was re-elected in 1907 (see page 34). A merchant, he had the Smith Block constructed at 1755 Rose Street in 1907. He was also a renowned curler.

Mrs. J. W. Smith is mentioned in Drake's *Regina* as one of the "untrained volunteer nurses" who helped care for the sick in the early 1890s, when the closest public hospital was in Medicine Hat.

F. N. DARKE – FIRST RESIDENCE

Southwest corner of Victoria Avenue and Scarth Street

*T*his was the first home of Francis N. Darke. "Frank Darke came to Regina in 1892, when it was little more than a village of mud streets. And since then he had taken part in practically every phase of civic life of any importance starting off in the wholesale and retail meat business, Mr. Darke was the leader in his business for 15 years." – July 18, 1940 *Leader-Post*

Mayor in 1898, at the age of 35, he was also a member of the Board of Trade for many years, a director of the Saskatchewan Exhibition Association, of the Saskatchewan Tuberculosis Sanatorium, and a governor of Regina College for 24 years. An avid amateur gardener, in 1909, with Canon George Hill, Darke reorganized the Horticultural Society to give leadership to a civic beautification campaign.

Darke's house pictured here, with mature landscaping, was prominent in a 1907 photograph of Regina. The elegant three-storey brick residence had a distinctive widow's walk on the roof and a deep verandah that wrapped around the Scarth Street frontage to the side yard on Victoria Avenue.

This photograph also showed Victoria Avenue and Scarth streets as unpaved dirt roads. However, a sturdy wooden sidewalk bordered the houses on both roadways.

Darke later sold this property in the mid-1920s to the CPR for the construction of the Hotel Saskatchewan (see page 172).

CHIEF JUSTICE W. M. MARTIN RESIDENCE

2042 Cornwall Street

"*H*on. William Melville Martin, who often has been called 'Saskatchewan's grand old man,' first hung out his shingle as a lawyer in Regina in 1903, just two years before provincial autonomy." – July 8, 1965 *Leader-Post* Martin joined his cousin James Balfour, KC in the practice of law. In 1908 he was elected to the House of Commons where he served until 1916 when he became premier of Saskatchewan. He also served as Education Minister, drawing on his earlier background as a teacher.

In April 1922, Premier Martin resigned and in May he was appointed a judge of the Saskatchewan Court of Appeal. He was appointed Chief Justice of Saskatchewan in 1941, a position he occupied until he retired, at age 84, in 1961. After WW II, he chaired the federal commission charged with revising the Criminal Code of Canada. He had turned down an opportunity to become a member of the Supreme Court of Canada; he preferred to stay in Saskatchewan.

The son of an Ontario Presbyterian minister, Judge Martin led the formation of First Presbyterian Church in 1925, after the Knox Presbyterian Congregation voted to join the United Church.

Following is a tribute to Chief Justice Martin by Premier T. C. Douglas: "As a Member of the House of Commons of Canada, as Premier, and as Chief Justice of Saskatchewan, Hon. W. M. Martin has for fifty-three years given devoted and unselfish service to our Province. He has earned the gratitude and affection of the people of Saskatchewan who will remember him as one of the architects of this great Province. His sincerity and resolute integrity, his natural dignity and modesty, will ever remain a model of conduct for men in public life. On the occasion of his retirement the Government of Saskatchewan, on its behalf and on behalf of the people of Saskatchewan, acknowledge a lasting debt to him and express the hope that Providence will grant him many more happy rewarding years." April 7, 1961 *Leader-Post*

Martin watched as the house at 2042 Cornwall Street was built in 1903. After he married in 1906, he and Mrs. Martin moved into the house on May 1, 1907. He lived in this house until his death in 1970.

The spacious three-storey house had three large sunrooms, two facing west and once facing south. The large verandah with striped awnings was on the east side of the house. The barn, opening onto the back lane behind the house, shows that horses and carriages were the standard mode of transportation when the house was built.

In the above illustration, showing Cornwall Street paved with crosscut wooden blocks, the Martin family, including the three sons Walter, Douglas and Kenneth, are shown in a new 1920 Packard in front of their house.

After Chief Justice Martin died, his residence was demolished, but the legal nature of the property was retained. An office building was constructed at 2042 Cornwall Street. Called Martin Place, it was home to the law office of Rendek, Kaufman, Embury, and in 2002 it holds the offices of MacKay and McLean, barristers and solicitors. In addition to his political and

judicial pursuits Judge Martin was also president of the Saskatchewan Red Cross, the King George V Jubilee Cancer Fund, the CNIB, and he served as Grand Master of the Masonic Lodge of Saskatchewan. In 1959 Martin Collegiate was named in his honour.

Mrs. W. M. (Violette) Martin, in whose memory a beautiful stained-glass window was dedicated in First Presbyterian Church, was a soprano gold medal soloist, a graduate of the Toronto Conservatory of Music, and a soloist at the first concert of the Regina Orchestral Society in 1908. She was the first president of the provincial IODE and the Violette Martin Children's Hospital at Fort San was named in recognition of her work with the IODE.

W. F. A. TURGEON RESIDENCE/
TURGEON INTERNATIONAL HOSTEL

2310 McIntyre Street

*T*urgeon House is a historic home that's been on the move.

When it was built in 1907, the 6,000-square-foot house was originally located at 2320 Angus Street and belonged to W. M. Logan, the first manager of the Northern Bank (later the Northern Crown Bank).

In 1910 the Honourable William F. A. Turgeon, Saskatchewan's second Attorney-General, moved in. Turgeon was one of Canada's most prominent public figures whose career over 54 years included lawyer, judge, politician and diplomat.

Appointed Attorney General in 1908, the youngest attorney general in Canada, Justice Turgeon left politics to sit on the Supreme Court of Canada. For the next 25 years he headed many royal commissions studying Canada's economic life, grain transportation and textile trades. After three years as Chief Justice of Saskatchewan, he served Canada for 15 years as ambassador to Argentina, Chile, Mexico, Belgium, Ireland and Portugal. He died in 1969 at the age of 92.

In 1920 Justice Turgeon was named to the Order of the Knights of St. Gregory for his service to country and church, both in Canada and abroad. He was one of the first Canadians to receive the Order of Canada Medal. A "remarkable man with a tremendous mind . . . A man with a quiet and retiring disposition, Justice W. F. A. Turgeon served his community, province and nation with unhurried competency and a brilliant lucidity that characterized his life as a jurist." – *Archdiocese of Regina*

Turgeon owned the house for ten years before he sold it to Claude H. Palmer. Since the Palmer's departure in 1932, the house had a succession of owners, and was divided into a 10-suite rooming house in 1944.

In 1981 the house was owned by the Saskatchewan Housing Corporation, which was going to demolish it and three other houses on the block to make room for a co-operative apartment building. Heritage Regina fought to save it because of its historical and architectural significance. The city continued to refuse to designate it a heritage property so, in November 1981, Heritage Regina bought the house for $1 and turned it over to Hostelling International – Saskatchewan. However, the house could not remain where it was. In November 1981, it was moved temporarily to an empty lot on 2300 block Albert Street. In July 1982, the house moved to its permanent location at 2310 McIntyre Street, and the city granted the Turgeon House heritage status in September 1982.

Opened as the Turgeon International Hostel in May 1983, the facility won the first Ivy Devereux Award for the most outstanding hostel in Canada in 1986. In May 1987, the Historic Sites and Monuments Board of Canada placed a plaque at the site commemorating Turgeon and his association with the building.

J. K. McINNIS RESIDENCE

1503 Victoria Avenue

*B*uilt in 1907, the John McInnis house, a large Classical-style, house "features prominent Gothic-influenced gables, accentuated by half-timbering, hipped dormers and broad eaves with dentils. A plain frieze separates the second floor from the first, which is built of rusticated concrete blocks. Originally, the house was surrounded on three sides by a verandah."

McInnis and his wife, Hannah, arrived in Regina in 1891 from Manitoba where McInnis had been a teacher. Upon arrival he took a position as editor of the Regina *Journal*, a rival to Nicholas Flood Davin's Regina *Leader*. His assistant was Walter Scott who became Saskatchewan's first premier in 1905.

Also in 1891, Regina's first ethnic organization was formed, the St. Andrew's Society. At a memorable haggis feast J. K. McInnis and N. F. Davin, inveterate newspaper rivals, both performed: McInnis a sword dance; Davin brought greetings from the Irish.

McInnis, with Scott, bought the *Journal* in 1891 and renamed it the *Weekly Standard*. Fourteen years later he pioneered the first daily newspaper in Saskatchewan, the *Daily Standard*. It was only one of McInnis' many business interests. Worth millions, he owned a publishing company and had substantial real estate investments. He sold land to Imperial Oil and subdivided and developed much of Eastview.

"Mr. McInnis relished politics . . . He fought his most vigorous political battle in the Dominion election of 1896, when he stood as an independent candidate against Nicholas Flood Davin, a Conservative and by then former owner of the *Regina Leader*. Pressed for money, Davin had sold the *Leader* to McInnis' former associate Mr. Scott in 1895 . . . The campaign culminated dramatically on election day, June 23 1896. When the count was in McInnis and Davin were tied with 1502 votes. It fell to the returning officer to cast the deciding vote. He did. For Mr. Davin."– Hryniuk and Perry, *Regina: A City of Beautiful Homes*

Davin won the election with 1503 votes. McInnis later immortalized the count when he inscribed the number "1503" on his home. Denied a role as a Member of Parliament he turned his attention to city politics. He sold his newspaper in 1913 to the *Daily Province* in order to devote himself to politics.

After McInnis' death, his family continued to live at 1503 Victoria Avenue until 1927. In 1928 Bruce McInnis added an apartment building, the Bruce Apartments, to the south side of the house. The site was designated a Municipal Heritage Property in 1984.

BARR RESIDENCE/HALDANE HOUSE

2102 Scarth Street

*T*his building was erected in 1907 as a residence for George H. Barr, QC, of the law firm Barr and Sampson. The house was designed by the Toronto firm of Darling and Pearson. The design is distinguished by the truncated corner tower, the M-shaped gable and a beautiful stained-glass window on the north side of the building.

Barr was the first lawyer to be called to the bar in the new province of Saskatchewan in 1905. He was the first lawyer in Regina to be an expert on constitutional law. Barr was a city alderman in 1916 and 1917 and a co-founder of Fidelity Life Assurance. He was also on the first board of directors for the Regina Public Library and he lobbied for the establishment of Regina College.

Barr sold his home to Dr. Morris Shumiatcher in May 1956. Extensive renovations were done by Smith Brothers & Wilson. Since this was the first Regina "home" turned into an office, the process of rezoning was lengthy. The renovations were completed and the Shumiatcher law firm moved in April 1957, at which time "Haldane House" was incorporated into the name and address of the firm. Dr. Shumiatcher called it Haldane House after British lawyer, statesman and philosopher, Viscount Richard Burdon Haldane, who was also twice Lord Chancellor of England. Dr. Shumiatcher, as a philosopher with a passion for the law, felt a kinship with Haldane.

Dr. Shumiatcher and his firm practiced at Haldane House from 1957 to 1997, although his private practice had commenced in 1949.

Dr. Shumiatcher, because of his interest in social matters, had been asked by Premier T. C. Douglas to write the Saskatchewan Bill of Rights which was adopted in April 1947. This was the very first Bill of Rights, even before the United Nations. He had four cases before the Privy Council in England at a time when lawyers on this side of the Atlantic had to go by ship. Once or twice they had to come back before their cases were heard, and reschedule, because the Privy Council had had a long sitting and needed a holiday!

Dr. Morris C. Shumiatcher, OC, SOM, QC, authored *Welfare: Hidden Backlash* and *Man of Law: A Model* (also see page 268).

Haldane House was sold in 2000 to Mervyn Phillips, also a lawyer, to be used for his law practice.

GODWIN/HARDING RESIDENCE/BISHOP'S COURT

2128 McIntyre Street

*F*redrick A. Godwin, a Saskatchewan Building Construction Limited superintendent, owned this house when it was built in 1908. The "house is distinguished by its verandah posts. . . . The posts are of limestone, cut from quarries in Tyndal, Manitoba, but roughened to look as if they are native fieldstone. They are among the few examples in Regina of a decorative device known as 'Richardsonian rustification'. Named after American architect H. H. Richardson who introduced this Italian Renaissance device, originally used in villas in Italy, to domestic architecture.

"The posts complement the yellow Lumsden brick, exposed beams and brown board trim of this Shingle-style Arts and Craft house. They are also the finishing touch that give 2128 McIntyre its cottage-like warmth and charm. . . .

"The house is best known as Bishop's Court. Residence of Malcolm Taylor McAdam Harding, fourth bishop of the Anglican Diocese of Qu'Appelle. He had come to Canada from England in 1887, when he was 24, to do missionary work in Manitoba for the Anglican Church. He moved to Qu'Appelle in 1903. In 1908 Dr. Harding married Emma Caswell. . . . Consecrated as the Coadjutor Bishop of the Diocese in St. Paul's Anglican Church in Regina in 1910, the first bishop to be consecrated in the Diocese, Dr. Harding moved the headquarters of the Diocese from Indian Head to Regina in 1911. The Diocese purchased 2128 McIntyre that year. The residence just three blocks south of Saint Paul's Church served as Bishop's Court and the Harding family home for 15 years. . . .

"It was through Bishop Harding's efforts that work on the great building scheme of the Diocese began in 1912. [The new headquarters was constructed on 15 acres of land on 16th Avenue (later College Avenue) and was to consist of four buildings – St. Chad's College, a school, a bishop's residence and a cathedral.] Three of these buildings were built and still stand on College Avenue just east of Broad Street: St. Chad's College, designed by Portnall and Clemesha; the school, known as St. Cuthbert's House; and the Synod House completed in 1926. [Plans for the cathedral were abandoned as the Diocese incurred heavy debts.]

"The Hardings lived at 2128 McIntyre Street until 1927, when they moved to Winnipeg. In 1934, Dr. Harding was elected Bishop of Rupert's Land and Archbishop of the Province of Rupert's Land, an office he held until his retirement in 1942. [Harding died in 1949.]" – Hryniuk and Perry, *Regina: A City of Beautiful Homes*

J. L. ROWLETT PARSONS/T. H. ROBERTSON/ VICTOR SIFTON RESIDENCE

2301 15th Avenue

J. L. Rowlett Parsons, president of Parsons Construction and Engineering Company, built this home in 1910. He lived here until leaving for active service in WW I and upon his return, until 1924.

The exterior design of this brick and shingle house exhibits Late Gothic Revival elements. It is dominated by a centred brick-clad projection which extends above the main eave line and features half-timbering in a front-facing gable, an oriel window on the second floor and an impressive entrance. The entrance includes a stained-glass window in the transom panel under the stone Tudor arch.

T. H. Robertson, president of Saskatchewan Building and Construction Company, and Victor Sifton, president of the Leader Publishing Company, also lived in this house.

The house was converted into apartment suites in 1956 and acquired by the Salvation Army in 1971. It became Grace Haven home for girls.

DR. MORRIS AND JACQUI SHUMIATCHER RESIDENCE

2520 – 2500 College Avenue

*B*uilt in the Cotswood Cottage style in 1910 for Maughan McCausland, a lawyer, this was one of the first houses on what was then 16th Avenue. The McCauslands lived in the house until 1934. Mrs. McCausland then rented the house until 1946, when she sold it to Cyril Blackall.

The Blackalls changed the appearance of 2520 College Avenue, adding what is now the main entrance reception area. They also reinstalled the original rolled roof. Grace Blackall was the manager of Mademoiselle's Ladies Wear.

The Shumiatchers purchased the house in 1956 from the Blackalls. The garage was built in 1957 and was styled to conform to the Tudor-style main house. The additional lawn property was purchased in 1969. Over the years the Shumiatchers have made small changes within the house. In 1983, a stained-glass feature window, designed by Ed Schaeffer, was installed in the dining room.

The one-storey house next door, at 2500 College Avenue, was built in 1920. Robert Hutchinson, President of the Saskatchewan Brewers Association lived here for many years. The Shumiatchers purchased the house in 1974. Previous to the Hutchinsons' ownership, there were stories regarding the house's use as a rum-running warehouse during Prohibition. Extensive renovations were made by the Shumiatchers from 1982 to 1986, including the amalgamation of the two houses through the construction of an interior walkway.

The Duke and Duchess of Kent stayed at the Shumiatcher home in 1989.

Morris Shumiatcher was born in Calgary. He took his ITS training in Regina at the RCAF compound. After the war, he was invited by Premier T. C. Douglas to work with the new CCF government on its legislative program, including the Saskatchewan Bill of Rights. Litigating on behalf of the government's innovative legislation programs took him to the Supreme Court of Canada and the Judicial Committee of the Privy Council in London, England. At this time he met Jacqueline Clay and they were married in Toronto in 1955. For many years they worked together at Haldane House, the location of Dr. Shumiatcher's law practice (see page 265).

Dr. Shumiatcher served as Honorary Consul General for Japan for Saskatchewan and was made a member of the Order of the Sacred Treasure by the Emperor of Japan in 1987. He was also president of the Regina Symphony Orchestra and the MacKenzie Art Gallery. He was appointed an Officer of the Order of Canada, received a Distinguished Service Award from the Canadian Bar Association and received the Saskatchewan Order of Merit.

Jacqui Shumiatcher established her own company in 1956, Managerial Services Ltd. She has been president of the Canadian Club, Regina Film Club, Regina Council of Women and has received the B'nai' Brith Society award, the Canadian Women's Mentor Award, the Saskatchewan Order of Merit and an Honorary Doctorate from the University of Regina.

The Shumiatchers are respected patrons of the arts in Regina, including Globe Theatre and the Regina Symphony. There are Shumiatcher Theatres at the University of Regina and the MacKenzie Art Gallery. Their outstanding collection of Inuit art was donated to the MacKenzie Art Gallery and is housed in the Shumiatcher Sculpture Court.

WALTER HILL RESIDENCE

2990 Albert Street

*B*uilt in 1911 for Mr. and Mrs. Walter Hill, for $18,000, this house was designed by the Regina architectural firm of Clemesha and Coltman. "The home was based on an English house admired by the Hills and copied, reduced by one quarter. . . . its references are Jacobean: elaborate chimneys, a steeply pitched roof and stone parapets, and strings of double-hung windows with stone mullions." The highest quality materials and craftsmanship were employed. The house had a central vacuum system and an in-house telephone system connecting all the rooms to the kitchen.

In 1912 the Regina cyclone knocked out the north wall of the house.

"Mr. Hill, born near Guelph, Ontario arrived in Saskatchewan in 1899. While attending Regina's Normal School, he met his future wife, Grace O'Connor, who was from Halifax. They married in 1905. Mr. Hill taught at Edenwold, where he spent his week-ends writing insurance policies for the local homesteaders, which led him to a full-time position as an insurance agent based in Regina. When organizing his territory he realized there was more money to be made in land development and, in 1903, he joined the McCallum brothers to form the McCallum Hill Company.

"A year later the company purchased 11,000 acres north of Swift Current and brought in a homesteader for each section. McCallum Hill soon became the foremost real-estate company in Regina as well, with the homes of two of the partners setting the tone for the development for what is now Old Lakeview. . . .

"The Hills were also the parents of James, Edward, Frederick, Robert and two daughters who died shortly after birth. It was a lively family: Frederick kept his homing pigeons in the stable loft, Robert played the piano in the library-cum music room and James conducted wireless experiments in the [large third floor] billiard room. Tragically, James was killed in 1930 while testing a mono-plane in Winnipeg." – Hryniuk and Perry, *Regina*

In addition to his business interests, Walter Hill was a city alderman from 1923 to 1926. Mrs. Hill lived in the house until she died in 1959, and Mr. Hill until he died at age 93. The Hill house at 2990 Albert Street was declared a Municipal Heritage Property in 1982.

Frederick W. Hill bought McCallum Hill from his father in 1953 and has developed the company into one of Saskatchewan's largest businesses (see page 180). In addition to his successful business ventures, Fred Hill has served as a Regina City alderman, from 1954 to 1955, on the Advisory Board of Campion College, Chancellor of Notre Dame College, as a director of the Canadian Imperial Bank of Commerce, Headway Corporation Limited, the CTV Network Limited and the Saskatchewan Roughriders.

For his services as a pilot in WW II, in the RCAF and then the US Army 15th Air Force, he was awarded the Air Medal with three oak clusters and the Distinguished Flying Cross. He is a recipient of Canada's highest distinction for outstanding merit and public service, the Order of Canada.

KERR RESIDENCE

2326 College Avenue

*I*n 1911 Lorence V. Kerr was only 26 when he married Edith Muriel Buck and commissioned architect Frank Portnall to design a residence for them at 2326 16th Avenue (later College Avenue). The design chosen was a Jacobean Revival-style house, "a carriage house, coachman's quarters and stables attached to the main house formed an "L" on the property. The design attracted considerable attention because of its large square tower, a feature unique in Regina at that time. . . .

"Kerr was a self-made man, able to take advantage of the opportunities in turn-of-the-century Western Canada for young men of ambition, courage and daring." Born in Stratford, Ontario, he came to Regina in 1903. A teacher by profession, he had a shrewd business sense and an entrepreneurial spirit. "Before long, he was heading the Kerr land Company, operating his enterprises out of the Northern Crown Building. His investments included large holdings of farm and city property in Saskatchewan, as well as development interests in Alberta. By 1910 he had built Regina's first sky-scraper, the five-storey Kerr Block on the 1700 block of Scarth Street and, with another Regina businessman, T. B. Patton, had formed the Kerr-Patton Coal Company.

"The house . . . suggests the wealth and prestige of British country baronial life, and the Kerrs did their part to uphold the impression. They were part of Regina's social set that included other real-estate men such as Edgar D. McCallum and R. L. Parsons. Their interests included riding and raising blue-ribbon horses. . . . Mr. Kerr's rise to fortune in Regina had been swift, and the family's stay in Regina was short. By 1921, their impressive house had become the residence of Harry Bronfman of Yorkton." – Hryniuk and Perry, *Regina*

WILLIAM ARGAN

Part of the well-known Seagram's distilling Bronfman family, by 1923 Harry Bronfman, too, had moved on to join his brother Sam in expanding the Seagram's empire.

"In 1929, the year of the stock market crash, two families, the Edgar D. McCallums and the William G. Yules, resided at 2326 College Avenue. Extensive changes occurred in 1942, when portions of the building were turned into apartments. When William Chadwick of Army and Navy Department Stores became owner renovations were undertaken to restore some of its original character. In 1972 the grand house ceased to be a private residence and was converted to commercial use." – *Ibid.*

For several years, Frances Olson Realty, Regina's only all-female realty company, was located here.

FARAWAY HOUSE

Douglas Park

*T*his big square brown brick home was built about 1912 by A. B. Cook, an astute businessman who served for many years as Regina's sheriff and later became the first superintendent of Fort San.

Faraway House is a name familiar to old-time Reginans. The home stood on five acres of land, far from any settlement, in Douglas Park southeast of the Power House (now the Science Centre) facing Wascana Lake. The property was a country retreat, isolated from the city. In Faraway House, in winter, the living-room fireplace would be ablaze and the scent of fresh cut flowers would waft from the adjoining conservatory. House dances, snowshoeing and sleighing parties were the order of the day.

In summer the Faraway House property was a prairie wonderland. There were well-kept tennis courts, croquet grounds on the lawn, a former RCMP riding horse, a small boat to cross the narrow strip of Wascana Creek, and a raft with a diving board for swimming in Wascana Lake. There was a barn that housed horses and, in earlier days, a milking cow. Because of its separation from the city there was always an aura of mystery surrounding the premises. There were many stories and rumours, none of which were true.

When Cook received the appointment to Fort San, Faraway House was sold to Dr. E. A. McCusker (see pages 199 and 285) who, with his mother and nieces, made his home there for many years. The Hamilton MacLeans lived there for a time and latterly it was owned by the *Leader-Post*.

During their Regina residence, Faraway House was the Victor Sifton family home. Mr. Sifton was a familiar figure in fine weather, walking the many miles from his downtown business office to Faraway House. The last occupants, shortly before its demolition in 1962 to permit expansion of Wascana Centre Authority, were Mr. And Mrs. Percy Keffer.

EDWARD McCALLUM RESIDENCE

2930 Albert Street

F. Chapman Clemesha designed this massive Tudor Revival house which features extensive stonework, half timbering, an impressive bay window with leaded glass and an elongated portico off the south side. It was built for Edward Donald McCallum at a cost of $30,000 in 1912. Edward, originally a teacher, and his brother Ernest teamed up with Walter Hill to form McCallum Hill and Company in 1903.

"The design draws on the grandeur of feudal days. The living room, for example, has been likened to a medieval hall with its 19-foot open-beamed ceiling, minstrels' gallery at the top of the grand staircase, and the oriel window, traditionally the high seat of the lord. Other medieval references include newel posts shaped like lanterns, and a built-in settle next to the broad limestone fireplace with its mantle carved in a pattern of acorns and bay leaves. . . . McCallum kept horses in the stable and coach house at the rear of the property, and played polo at the Wascana Country Club. Mrs. [Alice] McCallum, played the grand piano in the living room, tended their adopted daughter Muriel, and rode about town in her electric car." – Hryniuk and Perry, *Regina*

In the late twenties the McCallums moved to an apartment at 2326 College Avenue. In 1939 Mr. McCallum died from injuries suffered in a car accident while returning from a Winnipeg business trip.

"The house at 2930 Albert Street had been sold to Dr. Hugh MacLean, a prominent surgeon and active socialist. Dr. MacLean helped found the University of Saskatchewan Medical School and, long after his move to California in 1953, corresponded with Premier Tommy Douglas regarding establishment of a hospital insurance scheme."

Eye, ear and nose surgeon Dr. Harold Graham lived in the house until it was purchased in 1943 by Jack Rowand, president of Waterman-Waterbury, and strong supporter of the Saskatchewan Roughriders. Rowand was on the management committee for 22 years and was inducted into the Roughrider Plaza of Honor in 1990. He "installed a humidifying system to preserve the oak panelling that was featured throughout the home, and converted the spacious third-floor master suite into an apartment." His wife, Jessie, undertook an extensive refurbishment and decorating program to restore the home to its original splendor.

Architect Gordon Arnott took possession in 1972, and "retained the rented apartment, modernized the kitchen and enclosed the front screened sunroom with glass. The original design of the exterior and the main living areas has remained largely untouched." – *Ibid.*

In 1997 the residence was purchased by Mr. Mayo Schmidt, Saskatchewan Wheat Pool CEO.

RIGBY/POOLE/BAROOTES/ALPORT RESIDENCE

2805 McCallum Avenue

*B*uilt in 1912 for William Rigby, a clerk in the Regina Land Titles office, this elegant home was designed by architect Frank Portnall in a Tudor-influenced style. Ernest E. Poole bought the residence in 1923 and made major changes to the interior, to reflect more classical tastes.

Dr. Staff and Betty Barootes purchased the house in 1954. Dr. Barootes was born in Toronto and educated in Saskatoon. He attended the University of Saskatchewan where he obtained a degree in medicine in 1940. He was a prominent Regina urologist who led the Keep Our Doctors campaign against Medicare as proposed by Premier T. C. Douglas and the CCF government in 1961. Dr. Barootes remained politically active throughout his medical career and was appointed to the Senate in 1984. "Staff", as he was called, was considered to be one of the hardest working Senators to ever represent Regina and Saskatchewan. He died in 2000.

The Barootes home was purchased by Dr. Ted Alport and his wife, Karen, in 1986 and underwent further additions and renovations.

A distinguishing feature of this house was the flags flying from the front gable flagpole, a Union Jack flown by Rigby, a Canadian flag flown by Barootes.

WILLIAM MASON RESIDENCE

3118 Albert Street

*I*n 1913, this eclectic house was constructed for William and Helen Mason. It was designed by architect James Puntin, who also designed Darke Hall and the Albert Memorial Bridge.

"The high massing of the roof was of the East Coast Shingle style, the gambrel roof was borrowed from the Dutch Colonial style, the half-timbering and parapet were of the Tudor period, and the original wrap-around veranda with doric columns derived from the Neoclassical style. . . . during the 1950s conversion of the home into revenue property, the staircase and gallery were removed and the open ceiling of the hall was closed. The maid's back staircase now provides access to the second storey.

"The living room, dining room and upstairs den are essentially unchanged. All have open beam ceilings, battens below the high, broad plate rails, and brick fireplaces with interior warming shelves and maid's bells. While all floors and the woodwork in the dining room and den are of oak, the living room and remaining hall are finished in rosewood-stained birch. The latter is a rich contrast to the ornate brass door handles and the fine inlay of a lighter wood in the two sets of pocket doors off the hall.

"The original decor was rustic, with leather-like wallpaper, pictures of English hunting scenes, and paintings by family friend James Henderson. Hanging in the hall were the heads of a moose and wild sheep shot by Mr. Mason.

"An authentic rustic setting was achieved outside. A screened enclosure kept chickens and pigeons, and a large barn housed a cow and, for the pleasure of the daughter and three sons, a pony and horse. These were tended by a caretaker who lived with his wife, the maid, in a suite on the third floor.

"Such amenities were easily afforded by Mr. Mason, born in 1866 in Toronto and long-time employee of Canada Permanent Mortgage Corporation. He moved to Regina in 1905 to open a branch office, and eventually served as an alderman and mayor of the city as well [see page 39]. Although his wife, Helen, was an invalid – a dumb waiter carried her trays to the second floor – they entertained in a grand fashion, with musicians in the ministral's gallery playing for the frequent dances held in the three rooms below." – Hyrniuk and Perry, *Regina*

The Masons lived here until 1948 when Mrs. Mason died at age 80. Mr. Mason died three years later at age 85.

JAMES GRASSICK RESIDENCE

1604 College Avenue

Built in 1913, this was the home of James Grassick, his wife, Jessie, and their children until Grassick's death in 1956. It then became the residence of his daughter's family. Lillian Fairley and her husband, Fes, lived here until the late 1960s when it was demolished to make way for apartment construction.

Like so many grand homes constructed during this tremendous growth period for Regina, it was an impressive three-storey house. It included three fireplaces, a driveway and a covered carriage/carport on the west side that led to a four-stall barn, later used for a garage, at the rear of the property.

James (Jim) Grassick was one of Regina's most public-spirited men. He served ten years as a public school trustee, six years as councillor, four terms as mayor and five years as a MLA.

Born in Fergus, Ontario, Grassick moved with his family to Rapid City, Manitoba in 1878. Four years later they arrived in Regina, travelling by ox-cart, braving the mud, mosquitoes and sloughs (through which the oxen sometimes needed help in swimming).

Grassick's formal education was minimal. He received some schooling in Ontario and Winnipeg, but when he came to Regina he attended school for only four months before leaving to help on the farm. In his early years he worked at Mallory's Dairy, and during the 1885 Northwest Rebellion he transported military supplies from Fort Qu'Appelle to Battleford using his father's team. He then worked as a clerk in Mowat's general store and on the Mowat brothers' ranch at Avonlea. In 1889 he bought his own ranch and started the first of many businesses. He was a partner of Robert McKell, who had a cartage and livery business at 1821 Osler Street. Grassick bought out McKell and continued the business until 1906. At that time he started the business he kept for the next fifty years, the Capital Ice Company, located at 8th Avenue and Halifax Street. Grassick hauled ice from Boggy Creek, east of Regina, and Wascana Lake to sell (mostly to hotels and butcher shops). Later he built a reservoir at his farm and filled it with city water every fall in order to provide ice for his customers.

The Grassicks were dedicated parishioners of Knox Presbyterian Church (later Knox Metropolitan) where Grassick was on the Board of Managers for 35 years. He was a director of the Regina Exhibition Board for 25 years and of the Boxing/Wrestling Commission for 33 years.

Grassick was an agent for Imperial Oil, president of the Regina Foundry (previously Regina Machine and Iron Works) and a shrewd real estate investor. He also bought F. N. Darke's butcher business and ran it for a year.

In 1956, when Grassick was 88 years old, he was walking across Highway 1 just east of the city to look at a field of wheat. He apparently did not see a westbound car and despite the driver's best efforts he was hit and died shortly thereafter.

W. H. FLOOD RESIDENCE

1400 College Avenue

William Hamilton Flood, real estate developer, made his fortune from land sales. Born in Paisley, Ontario in 1881, he arrived in Regina in 1903.

Establishing the Flood Land Company, General Builders Company, the Queen City Development Company and the Regina Grain Company, Flood took advantage of the influx of immigration to open large tracts of unsettled lands for agriculture.

In 1912, the 30-year-old Flood began building this home at 1400 16th (College) Avenue. Unlike most Reginans, Flood used the designs of an American architect. The house was built for $10,000.

"The house is unique in Regina. It's an example of the Prairie School of Architecture made famous by Frank Lloyd Wright. Fourteen hundred College Avenue would be right at home in the Oak Park or River Forest areas of Chicago, which contain many of Wright's early buildings and are a visual record of his development of this indigenous American style.

"The low-pitched hipped roof of the two-and-one-half storey house features widely overhanging eaves which are double bracketed. The veranda, porte cochere and garage are attached asymmetrically and tied to the house by rusticated shingle and stucco finishing and broad base of brown brick. The whole is united by horizontal bands and mouldings. The veranda, with its whimsical butterfly cut-aways, encloses the main entrance and a second recessed entry that leads to the rear of the house.

"The front door opens onto a spacious hallway containing the main staircase. Through an archway is the oak-beamed living room, where gleaming oak floors reflect a fieldstone fireplace in front of which Mr. Flood's brown bear-skin rug once reclined. At one time, wine-coloured tapestry covered the living room walls. French doors lead to the sunporch, and a large square archway opens onto a dining room originally covered in tapestry of deep blue. The room is accented by wainscoting that reaches to the height of the plate rail." – Hryniuk and Perry, *Regina*

Besides his business interests, Flood was a member of the Assiniboia Club, the Regina Golf Club, the Wascana Country Club and played polo at grounds near the Wascana Country Club. In a stable at the back of his property, Flood kept ponies and employed a groom to care for them.

During WW I, the Floods moved to Ottawa where he served as a commissioned officer from 1916 to 1919. During this time the Flood house was used as a Canadian military residence. The Floods moved from the house in 1927.

From 1950 to 1971 the house was occupied by a succession of Saskatchewan-area commanders of the Canadian Army.

The house was designated a Municipal Heritage Property in 1983 and was the recipient of the 1988 Municipal Heritage Awards in the exterior and interior restoration categories.

T. B. PATTON RESIDENCE/NICOL COURT

2398 Scarth Street

*D*esigned by Clemesha and Portnall, this house was constructed in 1913 at a cost of $10,000 for Thomas B. Patton, a prominent sports promoter. Patton arrived in Regina from Hamilton, Ontario in 1901. He made speculative investments in real estate before entering into a partnership to form the Kerr-Patton Coal Company with Lorence V. Kerr in 1910. Kerr built an impressive home just down the street at 2326 College Avenue during the same period. Patton's wife, Elizabeth, said to be a tireless community and volunteer worker, was actively involved in the promotion of women's rights, the Regina Music Club and the Canadian Red Cross.

In 1918, the house was purchased by Dr. Charles F. Paradis, one of the founders of the Regina Patricia's (now the Pats) Hockey Club. The Paradis family lived here until 1929.

During the thirties this fine home was converted into apartments. The law firm of MacLean, Keith and Kelly acquired the house in 1976. Four years later they received a Heritage Canada Regional Award of Honour for its adaptive re-use. The name "Nicol Court" commemorates Alistair M. Nicol, a former principal of the firm.

The exterior design of the building is an unusual interpretation of the Georgian revival style, with strong classical influences. It is particularly distinguished by the broad sweep of the two-storey bow windows on either side of the front entrance. These windows are composed of individually curved glass lights, and their overall curvature is reflected in the cut of the eaves. A curved hood supported by wooden columns appears above a fanlight transom at the entrance. Also of interest is the second-story window, above the entrance, which is decorated with a scroll moulding motif.

B. F. MARSHALL RESIDENCE

3022 Victoria Avenue

B. F. Marshall built this large three-storey Tudor Revival-style residence at 3022 Victoria Avenue in 1914. Constructed after the Regina earthquake of 1909 and the cyclone of 1912, it was the only house in Regina at that time that was engineered and constructed to withstand gale-force winds and be safe in earthquakes and other natural disasters.

"Mr. Marshall could certainly afford the $24,000 it cost to build this lavish home, which was described as one of the most beautiful brick buildings in the city. Born in Fitzroy, Ontario, in 1844, and trained as a blacksmith and carpenter, Marshall arrived in Saskatchewan in 1903 after trying his hand at farming in Nebraska. He soon had large land holdings north and west of Regina, and owned 11 farms, including a dairy large enough to supply milk to the city. He also subdivided one of his farms into lots, and sold land to the Grand Trunk Pacific Railway for its rail yards in north Regina." – Hryniuk and Perry, *Regina*

Mr. Marshall died in 1925. His widow, Mrs Mary Marshall, sold this magnificent mansion two years later and in 1939 it was subdivided into apartments.

Mark Silver, who restored the Canada Life Assurance Building (see page 207), purchased this house in the mid-1980s and worked at restoring it.

HARRY READ RESIDENCE

3100 Albert Street

*T*his landmark home was constructed for Mr. And Mrs. Harry Read. They had moved from Hagersville, Ontario to Regina in 1906. He founded Regina Plumbing and Heating in 1908 and built this south Albert Street residence in 1914.

"Designed by F. Chapman Clemesha, and constructed for about $13,000, it originally was a house of Georgian proportions, classic detailing, and the wide flaring eaves of Prairie School influence. The eclecticism of its style was furthered by side wings with bracketed doric columns framing the Georgian Windows. The south wing, which was a conservatory, was connected to the north wing, which was a screened veranda, by a terrace. . . .

"A row of outbuildings, including a stable, garage and a suite for the caretaker, were joined to the house by a pergola with doric columns. That also outlined the two wings. Atop the out buildings was a cupola and weathervane, and above the square arch to the rear courtyard was a medallion proclaiming the year of construction. . . .

"But 1914 was also the beginning of WW I and Mr. Read signed up, leaving his wife and two children to move into the home without him." The family was reunited in 1918 upon his return and they lived in the house until 1943. The home was sold to Regina automobile dealer E. Moynan. "Several successive families lived there until 1953, when it was purchased by the Sisters of Social Service. The veranda was enclosed to become a chapel for the celebration of daily mass by a Campion College priest, and the sunroom and the gardener's apartment served as classrooms for the teaching of three elementary grades.

"In 1973 the house returned to private ownership. Its deterioration ended 13 years later, when an architect [Robert Croft] and his wife bought it and carried out major renovations.

"The first floor was extended forward with a marbled vestibule, a music room off the dining room, and a sunroom off the living room. A new and imposing port-modern portico relocated the main entrance, originally on 21st Avenue, to Albert Street. Two wide dormers linked by a clerestory window were added to the roof to create a third-floor master suite.

"Inside, the living room retained its battens, plate rail and the plain brick fireplace with its flanking columns. The oak flooring was refinished and extended. The kitchen was enlarged, the veranda became a library, the conservatory became a family room, and the main hall, den and part of the pergola became a games room." – Hryniuk and Perry, *Regina*

The residence enjoyed a reincarnation and has returned to be the landmark it was in 1914.

JAMES BRYANT/ROGER PHILLIPS RESIDENCE

3220 Albert Street

"The son of an Ontario minister, Mr. Bryant had received his education at Upper Canada College, Queen's University and the University of Manitoba before moving to Regina to establish a law firm in 1906. Distinguishing himself in the field of criminal law, it was said "no Bryant clients were hanged."

An avid horticulturist, Bryant won "the top Regina Horticultural Society Prize for eight consecutive years" for the magnificent gardens behind his house. Mr. Bryant played a part in the beautification of Regina as well. Minister of Public Works during the Conservative government of 1929 to 1934, "he was responsible for the dredging of Wascana Lake, the creation of its islands and the building of the Albert Memorial Bridge. . . .

"A long-time president of the Saskatchewan School Trustees Association, chairman of the Regina School Board and an admired public speaker, he was remembered long after his death in 1945 as the originator of the provincial Bryant Oratorical Contest. He was also remembered for his bright red wig. After his political defeat in 1934, Mr. Bryant and his wife, Mabel, who was also active in community and political affairs, moved to Saskatoon where he was appointed a district judge.

"The Bryant Home built in 1914, was designed by Frank Portnall in the Queen Anne style. Like most early Regina homes, however, it incorporates elements of other styles as well. While the window proportions are pure Queen Anne, the half-timbering and quatrefoils are in the Tudor style, and the buttresses, the use of stucco and the arch of the porte cochere are reminiscent of the Arts and Craft style. The decorative bargeboards allegedly are copied from those of Penrith Abbey in England.

"The interior is one of simplicity and fine craftsmanship: the parquet oak floors of the living room, dining room and large hall off the side entrance are bordered with a geometric design of various woods; the broad spindles of the hall staircase feature cutouts of a stylized leaf; and the newel posts and fireplace surround are carved with a dogwood design. In the tiny brass and green-tiled fireplace of the master bedroom is a hinged plate that swings out to receive a kettle for making tea." – Hryniuk and Perry, *Regina*

The trees and bushes are mature now and provide graceful privacy for the well-maintained Japanese garden that Roger and Ann Phillips have created. They have restored this gracious house that had been used as a revenue property for many years.

HERBERT McCALLUM RESIDENCE

3238 Albert Street

*I*n 1915, Herbert McCallum and his wife, Florence, built this magnificent home. "Designed by architect William Van Egmond it was built for $25,000, and shows the influence of Prairie School architecture. Its low-pitched hip roof has wide eaves; the veranda forms a dark, horizontal line, and the symmetry illustrates a later Prairie School development. The half-timbering is a reference to the Tudor style often found in the earlier homes of Frank Lloyd Wright.

"Originally, the veranda had wide open arches, which characterize this home of generous proportions and sturdy, yet grace-ful lines. Inside, the two living room bay windows were recessed behind gentle arches, and the built-in china cabinet in the dining room was similarly arched. The opening of the 15-foot limestone fireplace in the living room was semi-elliptical, its keystone echoing those of the basement windows.

"The huge living room and dining room, which remain essentially unchanged, open through pocket doors off a large, cen-tral hall and staircase, all of which are panelled with oak to a height of eight feet. The ceilings of the living and dining rooms are coved with oak and cross-hatched with oak beams." – Hrnyiuk and Perry, *Regina*

Herbert McCallum came west with his two brothers, Edward and Ernest, and teamed up with Walter Hill to form McCallum Hill and Company. However Herbert, his wife and two sons returned to eastern Canada in 1923.

In 1928 the house was bought by Dr. Fredrick Corbett, a surgeon and pioneer in cancer research, who arrived in Regina in 1911. Frederick and Mabel Corbett and their children Frederick, Dorthea and Isabel lived in the house for 20 years. Isabel Corbett married Dr. Trevlyn Darke, son of F. N. Darke.

In 1949 the Sisters of the Precious Blood bought the house and "for the next 12 years members of this cloistered Roman Catholic Order used the dining room as a visiting parlor. The living room was the chapel, where Bibles were stored in the fireplace and mass was celebrated behind a screen. The eight sisters slept in the attic, ate at long tables in the billiard room, and sewed church linens and vestments in the butler's pantry." – *Ibid.*

The house is now divided into suites.

YOUNG/COHEN/PATTERSON RESIDENCE

2800 Albert Street

*B*uilt in 1921 for J. Ridgely Young, the manager of Sun Electric Products, this house was purchased by Samuel J. Cohen who lived in it from 1925 to 1942. Cohen founded the British Army Store (subsequently the Army and Navy chain) in 1924, and later used the house as a residence for his store managers.

In 1952 this house became the residence of a man of many political accomplishments in Saskatchewan – William J. Patterson. "As premier of Saskatchewan, he was not only the first native (born), but also a WW I veteran and the first bachelor to hold that office." – June 11, 1976 *Leader-Post*

In 1915, Patterson was commissioned a lieutenant in the 10th Canadian Mounted Rifles. He went overseas with that unit and served with the Canadian Light Horse in France. He was wounded in August 1918 and celebrated the armistice in a London hospital bed. When he returned to Saskatchewan in 1919, he studied law for about a year before establishing an insurance and real estate business in Windthorst. In 1921, at the age of 35, he was first elected to the legislature. He was provincial treasurer, minister of highways and minister in charge of telephones until 1935, when he became premier. Two years later, he married.

Patterson was honoured many times throughout his years as premier. "One of the most colourful was Dominion Day, 1937, when he was given the title of Ka-Nee-O-Teai (Leader of Men) by the Peepekisis tribe of the File Hills Reserve. The Indians danced to the beat of a tom-tom in a dried lake bed in honour of their new warrior chief." – June 11, 1976 *Leader-Post*

While premier, Patterson met King George VI and Queen Elizabeth when they came to Regina in 1939. Patterson relinquished his office to T. C. Douglas and the CCF in 1944. As Lieutenant-Governor from 1951 to 1958, Patterson covered the province's 1955 Golden Jubilee. A decade later he was chairman of the committee that chose the Saskatchewan Jubilee Flag.

In 1968, Rene Rottiers, manager of Association of Culturelle Franco Canadienne Association, resided in this house. In 1970, the association purchased it as an office facility. Three years later it was sold and restored as a private home. This California-style bungalow, with extensive fieldstone used on the foundation walls and two fireplace chimneys, was designed by Storey and Van Egmond.

F. N. DARKE – SECOND RESIDENCE

2210 College Avenue

*F*rancis N. Darke commissioned the prominent local architect Francis Portnall to design his home in the Jacobean variant of the Late Gothic Revival Style in 1926. Built by Poole Construction, the most notable feature of the building is its Tyndall stone facing.

This Darke residence on College Avenue and Cornwall Street is directly across from two examples of Mr. Darke's great generosity to the City of Regina. In 1910 he contributed $85,000 and helped raise another $40,000 toward establishing Regina College, which he served as a governor for 24 years.

Both Mr. and Mrs. Darke took great interest in education and the arts. Strong Methodists, the Darkes became part of the Knox-Metropolitan United Church congregation. Mrs. Darke was founder and president of their Marionettes organization. She belonged to the Regina Federation of Artists, the Regina Sketch Club and the Arts and Crafts Society, and was on the original executive of the YWCA. The Darkes had four sons Clifford, Vernon, Clarence and Trevlyn.

Mr. Darke donated property and securities valued at $124,185 to Regina College for the purpose of erecting a music and art building. Darke Hall was "a temple of the arts" (see pages 36, 134, 142 and 261).

Frank Darke died at age 77 in 1940; Mrs. Darke died at age 93 in 1964.

The Darke residence was converted into a funeral home.

*T*he original owner was R. H. Cook, founder of Cook's Insurance and a director of the Regina Brewing Company, which became Sick's, then Molson – hence the beer bottle bottoms imbedded in a diamond shape on the west gable.

Built in 1929, this house was designed by architects Storey and Van Egmond. The design embodies a free interpretation of Tudor-Revival style, featuring a crenellated stair tower, Fort William red brick and stone trim, leaded windows and extensive half-timbering. Interest in the exterior is created by hood mouldings over the tower windows, decorative handmade rainspout heads, the drop finials from the apex of the gable and the twin chimneys. Quatrefoils are above the leaded den windows which contain small heraldic designs. This same design is on the windows of the tower and some interior doors.

The staircase curving up to the tower is of oak with wrought iron shaped like an elongated "S", as on the exterior of the north chimney. Architect Stan Storey liked to leave his initial "S" on all his structures.

The leaded pane windows and oak were imported from England. Pegging, a technique used in interior construction is an uncommon and expensive sign of craftsmanship. Wood pegs are used instead of nails.

The house was sold to Cyril Malone when Cook moved to Toronto. Malone was a lawyer and also a director of Sick's Brewery. He was aide-de-camp to Lieutenant-Governor McNab at the time of the 1939 royal visit. He bought the house the day his son Edward was born and sold it to Robert A. Kramer the day Edward left home for university. Edward Malone, also a lawyer, was a MLA and Leader of the Opposition, and was appointed to the Court of Queen's Bench.

Kramer, a local Caterpillar tractor dealer, commissioned architect Clifford Wiens to design extensive renovations to update the kitchen, bathrooms and second-floor bedrooms. The basement was lowered to accommodate a billiard room. The table was mounted on a hoist so it could be lowered for extra seating when a movie screen dropped from the ceiling. A sound system was installed throughout the house.

Kramer was an avid outdoorsman and sportsman. He was an honourary life member of Ducks Unlimited, a past president of the United Way and the only director of the the Saskatchewan Roughriders to become president of the team on two separate occasions, in 1951 and 1960. He was inducted into the Saskatchewan Roughrider Plaza of Honor in 1990.

The house was sold to Ward B. Johnston, president of Ward Johnston Electric, and the son of Victor E. Johnston, founder of the company. Patricia and Ward Johnston were strong supporters of the arts, locally, at the provincial level and nationally. The residence was sold in 1995 to R. W. Shirkie, a geological consultant.

ALBERT COURT

Northeast corner of Albert Street and 13th Avenue

*1*909 was an extremely busy year for commercial and residential construction in Regina. One such project was the completion of Regina's first apartment block, Albert Court apartments, on the northeast corner of Albert Street and 13th Avenue

Designed by Storey and Van Egmond and built by T. H. Robertson, President of The Saskatchewan Building Construction Co., the building is described in the *Regina Leader* dated June 12, 1909 "an apartment block as complete as any in the west." The three-storey structure featured suites of six and seven rooms, finished throughout in hardwood. The exterior was of stucco finish. The article goes on report that there were two laundries in the basement supplied with soft water from large storage tanks.

Albert Court apartments were replaced by the Credit Union Central building in 1976.

MADRID APARTMENTS

1726 College Avenue

*T*his 14-suite apartment block was erected in 1927 for Dr. Charles H. Dixon, a prominent dentist who arrived in Regina in 1918. He served as an alderman from 1929 to 1932 and again in 1934 and 1935.

Designed in a Mediterranean-influenced style by architects Storey and Van Egmond, it is faced primarily with brick and highlighted with door surrounds, pedimented parapets, panels, mouldings and medallions, all executed in stucco. Other notable features include the elaborate rounded-arch entrances, similarly arched windows appearing in triplets at the main floor level, and four bull's-eye windows at the southern end of the west face.

Attached to the east end of the apartment building, on College Avenue, was a separate residence which was the home of Dr. Emmett McCusker, another prominent doctor, sportsman and politician who lived there for many years (see pages 199 and 271). In 1954 Madrid Apartments was purchased by Ross Sneath who retained possession until 1986.

This apartment building was the location for some of the scenes for the movie *Sins of the Father* in 2000, starring Andy Garcia. The home of the late Joanne Wilson, at the corner of 20th Avenue and Albert Street, was also used in the movie.

THE BALFOUR APARTMENTS

2305 Victoria Avenue

James Balfour was a prominent early citizen of Regina. He was mayor of Regina in 1915 and 1931. He was also Regina's town clerk for several years and the first city clerk.

In the late 1920s, Balfour commissioned the architectural firm of Stan E. Storey and Van Egmond to design an apartment building on the site of his then current residence. The architects designed a seven-storey, "H" shaped building in Baronial style, with Mediterranean-influenced detail. The building was constructed in 1929 by Smith Brothers and Wilson, using many locally manufactured materials, including brick from Dominion Brick and Clay Products of Claybank, Saskatchewan and cut stone from Alex Young Limited of Regina.

Erected in the hot dry summer of 1929, "there wasn't a drop of rain to slow construction," according to C. Morley Willoughby, whose father and associates built the Balfour Apartments. At the time, the Balfour was Western Canada's most prestigious high-rise and the hub of Regina society. The most luxurious suites rented for $180 a month, a great deal of money during the Depression, and for a time the American ambassador to Canada rented a suite in the Balfour. Six-foot-wide hallways, oak hardwood floors, high ceilings, walnut baseboards and tile bathrooms all lent a touch of elegance to the Balfour. A tea room in the basement was a meeting place for some of Regina's most prominent citizens.

The Balfour was the largest and tallest apartment building in the province until 1955, when Tower Gardens was constructed on Broadway Avenue at Winnipeg Street. It was also the first to be equipped with self-operated elevators. When the building was sold by the Balfour family in 1984, City Council approved the plan to change the Balfour from rental accommodation to owner-occupied suites in 1985. Phase one of the $3-million-plus redevelopment was completed in 1987. The building's 92 suites were renovated into 60 luxury condominiums which sold for between $50,000 to $150,000 per unit.

The building received Municipal Heritage designation in 1993 and was declared a Provincial Heritage Property later the same year.

FRONTENAC APARTMENTS

2022 – 2024 Lorne Street

"One of the most modern in design" is how the Frontenac Apartments were described when the 56-suite apartment block opened in 1929.

The apartments were erected by Provincial Apartments Ltd. at a cost of $200,000. Provincial Apartments Ltd. was a Regina company formed in the fall of 1928 by a group of Regina businessmen, following the city's promise to General Motors of Canada Ltd. to meet the housing demand caused by the influx of a large number of employees from Oshawa and other Canadian points to work in the motor and other manufacturing plants.

Facing eastward on Lorne Street, just south of Victoria Avenue, the Frontenac apartments were within easy walking distance of any business place in the centre of the city.

Smith Brothers and Wilson were the general contractors and Stan E. Storey and W. G. Van Egmond were the architects.

The Mayfair Apartments, containing 29 suites, on 14th Avenue and Retallack Street, were also erected in the summer of 1929 by Provincial Apartments Limited.

TOWER GARDENS

1100 Broadway Avenue

First suburban high-rise apartment building – when built in 1955, Tower Gardens was the tallest apartment building in Regina at that time. It was to be the first of five 10-storey apartments, each containing 137 suites, on a site bounded by College and Broadway Avenues and Winnipeg and Montreal Streets.

Tower Gardens section "A" was designed by architects McCudden and Robbins of Regina and constructed by Bird Construction Co. Ltd. The project was developed by Graybar Holdings (Sask) Ltd. of Winnipeg.

The site was purchased from the provincial government with options on the other four parcels for the other buildings. After several delays and option extensions Graybar allowed the options to lapse and construction of the remaining buildings did not proceed.

Owned by RDL Management of Saskatoon, Tower Gardens is under lease to Regina Lutheran Home to be used as a senior citizens' apartment complex. In 2002, almost fifty years after the first tower was built, plans have been completed by the Regina Lutheran Care Society for construction of a second high-rise apartment to the immediate west of Tower Gardens. The 11-floor, 123-unit facility is called Broadway Terrace. The $20-million development will include a 15-bed personal care home.

YMCA

For more than a century, the "Y" has provided programs and services that promote healthy spirit, mind and body.

In 1890 far-sighted pioneers formed a provisional YMCA in Regina. Meetings were conducted in various churches, halls and homes in the downtown area. In 1907 the YMCA was incorporated in Regina with a mission to "develop the Christian character and usefulness of its members and to improve the mental, spiritual, social and physical condition of young men." By 1911 the official membership of the Regina YMCA was 325, with 80 junior members.

In 1947, with the assistance of the Regina Y's Men's club, a parcel of land was purchased at Echo Lake for a residential camp. The YMCA has provided a summer camping experience at Camp Ta-Wa-Si ever since. A Ta-Wa-Si experience helps campers build their self-esteem as they live and work with others and face new challenges in an outdoor environment.

Most people know the YMCA through the health, fitness and recreation programs. But there's always been a lot more to the Y than swimming and working out. The Y promotes the health and well-being of individuals and communities in everything they do – child care, employment, international development, education or community outreach. The Y is a place where everyone is welcome. By bringing people from all walks of life together, and encouraging a contribution from all, the Y helps people become the best they can be, as leaders, participants, athletes, instructors, volunteers and staff.

After more than a century of service, the Y remains as committed to building strong kids, strong families and strong communities as in 1890.

First YMCA – 1890 to 1908

W. F. Eddy building, 1751 Scarth Street, the "Y" occupied the floor above the barber shop. The opening of its reading room was memorable because on November 15, 1890 electric lights were turned on for the first time. The YMCA was the only place in Regina lighted by electricity that evening.

Northwest corner of
12th Avenue and
Cornwall Street
1908

Y W C A

First YWCA – 1909 to 1912

1950 Lorne Street

The first YWCA was temporarily housed in the second *Leader* newspaper building.

WILLIAM ARGAN '84

1912 to 1970

1950 Lorne Street

1970 –

1940 McIntyre Street

Sponsored by SaskEnergy

arch 14, 1910 saw the creation of the YWCA of Regina. In 1911 the cornerstone for the first YWCA was laid at 1950 Lorne Street.

In 1910, 800 girls worked in Regina. As women were beginning to find their place in business and industry they found that the YWCA provided housing, social interaction and recreational programs. On June 30, 1912, the cyclone struck Regina, demolishing the new building. It was repaired and in 1925 a swimming pool was added.

During WW I the YWCA was criticized for employing foreign girls. Post-war problems included inflation. The YWCA attracted the lonely, the unemployed and the destitute. Programs such as gymnastics, CGIT and summer camp began. In the 1930s girls arrived at the YWCA penniless, without jobs. An employment service placed girls in household jobs.

Traveler's Aid and Housing Registry was established during WW II. At times not a single bed or chesterfield was available in the house; women slept in easy chairs or on gymnasium mats.

In 1944 the YWCA coordinated a conference asking for increasing school-leaving age, opportunities for vocational training, equal pay for equal work, subsidies for heads of families, increased grants to widows, old-age pensioners and disabled persons.

The new YWCA opened on February 6, 1970 at 1940 McIntyre Street. For a few years the YWCA thrived with its new building. However, when city leisure centres opened there was a serious decline in swimming registration and both pools were forced to close by 1995.

In the new millennium the "Y" returned to its roots, offering social, housing and recreational programs to women and their families, developing solid plans to ensure its existence for years to come.

REGINA CURLING CLUB

20 block Halifax Street

*T*he Regina Curling Club, founded in 1889, was situated on the southwest corner of Rose Street and 12th Avenue. In 1907, when four sheets of ice became too few, the club purchased six lots on the 20 block Halifax Street and built a new nine-sheet curling club for a total cost of $8,250. Early patrons of the club included Mr. White, then General Superintendent of the CPR; Indian Commissioner, A. E. Forget who later became the province's first lieutenant-governor; Lieutenant-Governor McIntosh; Commissioner L. A. Herchmer of the NWMP and F. W. G. Haultain, MLA, who later became Chief Justice of Saskatchewan.

In 1895 the club entertained the Governor General of Canada, the Earl of Aberdeen, who was elected an honourary member. The first bonspiel held in the new rink was named the Citizen's Bonspiel and opened December 14, 1909 with 85 rinks competing. The club also opened its doors to lady curlers that year. By 1914 the ladies' club was well established.

In 1912 the club suffered damage during the June cyclone, forcing officials to raise fees to pay for repairs. Sunday curling was allowed in 1936. In 1951, the first artificial ice plant was installed at a cost of $30,000. In 1952, the first of the annual shirtsleeve bonspiels was established.

In 1952 a group of curlers from the Regina Curling Club decided to build their own curling rink, Regina's fifth. The Wheat City Curling Club opened in January 1953 at 10th Avenue and Alexandra Street with five sheets of ice and two lounges. Lieutenant-Governor W. J. Patterson delivered the first rock. Chairman Percy Shore, President Barney Krivel and board members, Dr. Stan Abrams, Al Linds, Dr. Alex Mintz and Pete Minovitch officiated. Rabbi Hartstein gave the dedication prayer. While the founding members were Jewish, the club was open to all nationalities and faiths.

Avonlea's Garnet Campbell won the Macdonald Brier Tankard at the Regina Club in 1955. In 1958 the Curlodrome opened, marking Canada's first pay-as-you-play curling facility.

Disaster struck on April 16, 1961 when a fire started in the upstairs lounge of the Regina Curling Club. High winds hampered firefighters and the 52-year-old building was gutted, causing $52,000 in damages. However, the ice plant was saved. In 1961/1962 the Regina club reopened with six sheets of ice on the same Halifax Street site. In 1962 and 1963, Ernie Richardson's team won two of its four world curling titles while playing out of the Regina Club. In 1973 the Regina Club's Harvey Mazinke team also won the Brier.

In 1981, after functioning in the red for several years, the club building was put up for sale. The following year, the Regina Curling Club reached an agreement with the Regina Exhibition Association to function out of the Curlodrome.

In 1989 the Regina Curling Club celebrated its 100th anniversary. Regina Exhibition Park shut down the Curlodrome and the Regina Curling Club in 1994 because the City of Regina insisted that Regina Exhibition Park assume the $135,000 the club owed in back taxes.

THE CURLING RICHARDSONS

*F*rom hobby sport to dreams fulfilled – the Richardson family wasn't planning on becoming four-time world curling champions when they first started to play the game. They took up curling as something to do in the winter time, when the construction business wasn't busy.

They became fans of the game as they followed the success of the Curling Campbells – when the Campbells won the Brier in 1955. Soon curling became more than a

Ernie   Sam   Arnold   Wes
Four-Time Canadian Curling Champions
World Curling Champions – 1963

pastime and the team steadily improved. Early on Ernie, as skip, struggled with his confidence. At one point he was so shaken that he wanted his cousin Arnold to take over as skip. Things turned around in 1959 and Ernie skipped his all-Richardson rink of Sam, Wes and Arnold to the Canadian Men's Curling Championship and their first World Curling title.

The all-Richardson rink successfully retained both the Canadian and World Championships again the following year, and they did it again in 1962. An unprecedented fourth Canadian Championship and World Championship were won in 1963 by the Ernie Richardson rink, which now had Mel Perry in place of Wes, who had withdrawn from the team for health reasons. The Ernie Richardson team won a fifth Saskatchewan Brier in 1964.

The Richardson rink is the only team in Canadian curling history to have won four Canadian Championships. Ernie was installed in the Saskatchewan Sports Hall of Fame in 1971 as an individual and the team, including his brother Sam, cousins Arnold and Wes, and Mel Perry, who had replaced Wes for the 1963 season, were named to the Saskatchewan Sports Hall of Fame in 1973. The team was also inducted into the Canadian Sports Hall of Fame and the Canadian Curling Hall of Fame.

In 1978, Ernie was named an Order Of Canada recipient, but it was an honour he wanted to turn down. He did not want to accept the award as an individual but would rather have it presented to the team. He finally accepted the award at the urging of his teammates. He did so because he was told the pin would be presented in a way that would include all of the members of the team.

The Richardsons have long been admired, not only for their curling ability, but, equally, for their friendliness and their desire and efforts to develop the sport of curling.

THE HARVEY MAZINKE CURLING TEAM

*I*n 1973, the Regina Curling Club's own Harvey Mazinke and his team, consisting of Bill Martin, George Achtymichuk and lead Dan Klippenstein, had dominated their opposition all year. They won every cashspiel they played, every game in their club, and in the southern and provincial playdowns. Mazinke also skipped his team to a 9 and 1 record in the 1973 Edmonton Brier.

The World Championship, "The Silver Broom", was played in 1973 before the Mazinke team's hometown crowd, at Regina's Exhibition Stadium. Local and pre-tournament favourites, the Mazinke team went through the entire week undefeated, until the final rock in the extra end of the final game of the World Championship. They suffered a bitter blow when the ice turned against the curlers in the biggest game of the year – it melted. Mazinke's final rock could not navigate through the watery surface of Exhibition Stadium. They lost their final game and the World Championship.

Going into this game the team had a competitive record of 68 wins and one loss . . . a truly remarkable feat!

George
Achtymichuk

Dan
Klippenstein

Harvey
Mazinke

Bill
Martin

Canadian Curling Champions – 1973

Harvey Mazinke played in three Briers and one Silver Broom, putting his name on the curling record book as a Canadian Champion.

He was one of the key people responsible for getting Labatt's involved in sponsorship of the Brier. He was a member of the Advisory Board for Labatt's Saskatchewan, and host President during the period of the Olympic Games in Canada when curling was included in the program as a demonstration sport. He was also involved with the International Curling Federation, acting as liaison with the Calgary Olympics.

Mazinke was President of the Saskatchewan Sports Administration Centre and served as Chairman of the Board of Governors for the University of Regina.

ARENA RINK

Robinson Street at 14th Avenue

*T*he Arena rink was built in 1910 by the Pearce brothers of Pense and was used for ice and roller skating and for hockey.

"The size of the rink may be gathered from the fact that its measurements will be 190 feet x 110 feet and the proprietors claim that the sheet of ice provided will be the largest in the city." – October 21, 1910 *Leader*

The December 28, 1910 edition of the *Leader* reported: "Regina's new skating rink, which is now under construction will be the second largest rink in Canada and the largest this side of Winnipeg, the Amphitheatre rink of Winnipeg being the largest. On the ground floor of the two-storey building were two waiting rooms and a front rotunda, enclosed with glass, that faced the ice. The second storey was divided into hockey rooms and had a bandstand that was directly over the rotunda. There are two rows of windows around the entire building, which will give ample light. The building will be lighted by electricity. There will be 48 electric globes over the sheet of ice, each having 200 candle power and a 24-foot reflector. They will be run up the centre and around the sides of the ice.

"The seating capacity is approximately 2,000. Four rows of seats will be run around the entire ice with the exception of the south end, at which end the ice will run to the outside wall.

"The approximate cost of the building is between $13,000 and $14,000. . . . It is hoped to have the building completed by New Year's day and to open on that day. The formation of ice has already been started and it will not be long before there will be a good sheet of ice. There will be skating every afternoon and evening with the exception of every other Monday evening when the rink will be thrown open for hockey only." – December 28, 1910 *Leader*

After the collapse of the Wascana Winter Club's roof in 1974, all Regina rinks were inspected. Within months the Arena Rink was condemned. It was later torn down to make way for an apartment development.

CALEDONIAN CURLING CLUB

2225 Empress Road

*A*t pioneer-day curling events, visiting town and country teams congregated in local hotels and some of the friskier curlers set the traditional bonspiel mood of conviviality by replaying the last end in the hotel corridor at midnight – with chamber pots.

The first Caledonian Rink was a Skating and Hockey Rink built in 1895 at Cornwall Street and 11th Avenue. On March 9, 1904, despite furious opposition, the Regina building inspector refused to allow a championship game between Regina and Moose Jaw to be played. The game was forfeited. Later that evening, after midnight, the roof collapsed.

The Caledonian Curling Club had its beginnings at a meeting on October 7, 1915 in the Slater & Finlayson store on Dewdney Avenue where 18 men discussed forming a second curling club in the city. A week later, at another meeting, a motion was passed to organize the Caledonian Curling Club. A. R. Tingley approached city council, requesting the use of an implement building on the exhibition grounds. His request was granted and eight sheets of ice were installed.

In 1919, the club moved to a brick stable, and in 1926 to the "cow barn" rink with nine sheets of ice. The club had 14 sheets of ice when it moved to the Grain Show Building in 1933, but during WW II the Callie returned to the cow barn. When the war ended, the club moved back to the Grain Show Building.

As early as 1928, the Callie boasted the largest membership of any curling club in the world. In the 1930s, with 14 sheets of ice under one roof, it was the biggest club. That distinction lasted until the early 1960s when a 24-sheeter was built in Calgary. Another first for the club was the introduction of high school curling in 1932. Club members are certain that their high school club was the first in Canada.

In the fall of 1968, the club explored the feasibility of obtaining a new building. After years of hard work, the dream became a reality when the first draw in their new building took place on November 13, 1978. Another dream came true during the 1979/1980 season when club curlers, Marj Mitchell, Nancy Kerr, Shirley McKendry and Wendy Leach won the Ladies' Canadian and World Championships.

In more recent years, the Callie Club is remembered as the home of the Sandra Schmirler team, including Jan Betker, Joan McCusker and Marcia Gudereit. Schmirler, a three-time Canadian and World Champion and Olympic Gold Medalist, died from cancer at the age of 36. On March 6, 2000, the 12 sheets at the Caledonian Curling Club were quiet as the rink's lounge and upstairs viewing areas were packed with about 150 people watching the nationally televised memorial service for Schmirler. The crowd at the Callie included the 2000 provincial champion June Campbell and her Callie teammates.

THE MARJ MITCHELL CURLING TEAM

wo dates will forever be associated with Marj Mitchell's World Champion women's curling team – March 22, 1980, when Mitchell, Nancy Kerr, Shirley McKendry and Wendy Leach became Canada's first Women's World Curling Champions, and October 18, 1983, the day Mitchell lost her battle with cancer.

Playing out of the Caledonian Curling Club in Regina, the Mitchell team was together only a short time because of the untimely death of their skip. They will best be remembered for winning Canada's first Women's World Curling title.

Marj
Mitchell

Nancy
Kerr

Shirley
McKendry

Wendy
Leach

Women's World Curling Champions – 1980

All of the members of the team were talented, but it was Mitchell who elevated the rink to the world championship level. Her teammates considered her a skip ahead of her time. Strategy was a big thing with Marj. She skipped a chess game on ice. Her teammates believed that they won as many games on strategy as on playing skill. Mitchell, as skip, simply outsmarted the other teams.

The team, made up of Marj Mitchell, skip; Nancy Kerr, third; Shirley McKendry, second; Wendy Leach, third, was named to the Saskatchewan Sports Hall of Fame in 1981.

THE SANDRA SCHMIRLER CURLING TEAM

*T*he Sandra Schmirler curling team was formed in 1990. The following year the team won its first Saskatchewan Women's Curling Championship.

Two seasons later the Schmirler team, curling out of the Callie Club, captured their second Saskatchewan championship. At the Scott Tournament of Hearts in Brandon, in 1993, the Schmirler team outclassed the opposition and claimed their first Canadian Championship.

Later, at the World Curling Championships in Geneva, the team continued their strong play to win the 1993 Women's World Curling Championship for Canada; the first Saskatchewan team to claim victory since the Marj Mitchell team won in 1980.

The following season, as Team Canada, the team captured its second straight Canadian Championship and travelled to Germany to defend its World title. The Schmirler team emerged victorious. This was the first time in history a Canadian women's curling team had won back-to-back world championships.

The team did not curl together in 1996, but reunited for the 1997 playdowns, with Sandra Schmirler as skip; Jan Betker, third; Joan McCusker, second; Marcia Gudereit, lead. In 1997 Anita Ford played fifth and later became the team's coach. Without missing a beat, they won the provincial championship in January, the Scott Tournament of Hearts in Vancouver – the Canadian Women's Curling Championship, and they represented Canada in Switzerland, becoming the only women's curling team in history to win three world championships.

The Schmirler team was named Saskatchewan Sports Team of the Year for 1993 and 1994, and was inducted into the Saskatchewan Sports Hall of Fame in 1997. Later, on a spectacular eighth-end shot by skip Sandra Schmirler, the team qualified to represent Canada at the 1998 Olympic Winter Games in Nagano, Japan. Atina Ford, Anita's daughter, was added as a spare.

During the 1990s the Schmirler team had done much to improve the quality of women's curling. Public interest was at its peak following their Olympic Gold Medal win in Nagano, the first time that curling was included as an Olympic sport.

A little over a year later, two months after the birth of her second daughter, Jessica, doctors diagnosed Sandra with cancer. She died at age 36 in March 2000, almost two years to the day after the Schmirler Team Canada Gold Medal win.

Sandra Schmirler

Jan Betker

Joan McCusker

Marcia Gudereit

Women's World Curling Champions – 1993, 1994, 1997
Women's Curling first Olympic Gold Medalists – 1998

ROYAL REGINA GOLF CLUB

*E*stablished as the first golf club in the province, the Regina Golf Club survived mosquitoes, fire and several changes of location. It began in 1899 when a group of Regina businessmen, lawyers and members of the North-West Territorial government got together to start a golf club. F. W. G. Haultain, Attorney-General for the North-West Territories, was elected club president and Lieutenant-Governor A. E. Forget was named honorary president.

Originally located south of 16th (College) Avenue, clouds of mosquitoes, following a herd of cows that wandered daily across the course, forced a change of location two years after the opening of the club.

On the invitation of the North-West Mounted Police, the club moved to a course commonly known as the Barracks. The club continued to use the Barracks course until 1905. In 1906 the club reorganized and resumed its possession of the quarter section of land in what is now the Crescents area of Regina. A clubhouse was built in 1907. In 1910 Commissioner Perry invited the club to return to the Barracks course. "A dressing room was provided in the south end of the old recreation hall at the Barracks, the course was prepared and the greens made ready for the opening, but rains delayed it for two weeks, and by that time the grounds outside of the fairways were covered with grass of such length that the players in many instances were unable to conclude their games because of having lost their balls in the rough." – June 3, 1924 *Leader* Later that year the course improved and became quite playable.

The Regina Golf Club clubhouse was moved to the medical residence of the RCMP in 1911.

In 1924 the club opened their own clubhouse. Three years later, in 1927, it was completely destroyed by fire. Members rallied together and the clubhouse was rebuilt in 1928. With some additions and changes, that clubhouse served the membership until 1999 when it was demolished to make way for a new clubhouse.

Over the years, there have been many improvements to the course. Stanley Thompson, Canada's leading golf architect, redesigned the course in 1925. In 1956 an irrigation system was installed and it was upgraded in 1985. Present-day improvements include the construction of another new green.

The new clubhouse, designed by Ellard Croft Design Group and built by Dura Structures, was constructed over the 1999/2000 winter season, in six months, and was opened to the membership soon after the start of the 2000 season.

Throughout its long history the Royal Regina has produced many great golfers. The most consistent winner is Joanne Goulet, who has won 33 City Championships and 21 Provincial Championships over a span of 51 years. She was also a member of the Saskatchewan team that won the Canadian Senior Ladies Championships in 1985 and 1990.

Joanne was inducted into the Saskatchewan Sports Hall of Fame in 1980. The City of Regina named the Joanne Goulet golf course in Westhill Park in her honour in 1993.

There are only five Canadian golf clubs which have been given Royal designation. In recognition of the Regina Club's long history, its ties with the RCMP and the high standard it has maintained over the years, Lieutenant-Governor Jack Wiebe bestowed the rare honour on the province's oldest golf club on January 20, 1999. The club is now known as the Royal Regina Golf Club. The last previous club to receive the "Royal" designation was the Royal Colwood in Victoria in 1931.

WASCANA COUNTRY CLUB

S ituated on 100 acres of land south of Wascana Creek, the Wascana Country Club opened on May 25, 1912 with 300 members in attendance. The property was purchased for $11,215 in 1910 from the estate of William C. McIntyre of Montreal who had acquired it from the CPR in 1884 for three dollars per acre. On June 16, 1911, the Wascana Country Club was incorporated by an Act of Parliament.

The *Leader* stated the 100-acre site would provide for many kinds of sports. It continued, "A large stable has been provided for the horses of the members. Nine holes of the golf links are ready for use and were declared to be as good as the time used in their construction would permit. Another nine are being prepared and as soon as these are complete they will be used and the rest will be put in first-class shape. This is the only branch of sport provided so far. A portion of the ground has been set aside for polo." The polo field, on the present 16th fairway, did not survive beyond WW I.

The clubhouse, erected from plans prepared by Storey and Van Egmond, was a one-storey building with a large "lounging" room, 33-feet square, in the centre. A unique feature of this room was a four-way fireplace built in the centre of the room. "The ladies' and gentlemen's dressing rooms are also on the first floor while the dining room has been arranged at the end of the broad verandah. The servants' rooms are in the attic."

The greens were seeded with hardy fescue and clover in the early years and hand-watered from a tank. Any mowing on the primitive fairways was done with a horse-drawn scythe mower. At each teeing ground were waist-height boxes with sand and water. "Tees" were made by wetting the sand and shaping it into a cone to hold the ball. Painted on the tee boxes were the names of each hole, the number and the length. Eventually sand was no longer used, but water remained until the advent of ball washers.

In the early days, all the golf clubs were handcrafted by the professional from wooden head blanks or forged iron heads and hickory shafts, all of which were imported, first from Scotland and later from the United States.

Dressing for the occasion was important at Wascana Country Club. Before 1920, female golfers wore long dresses and large hats and men wore jackets and knickers, although on very hot days the jackets could be removed. This formal dress continued in the 1940s, when a shirt and tie were required wear on Sundays and, in the clubhouse, a jacket was mandatory. Old boots with logger's hobnails driven into the soles were the foot attire worn while golfing.

Disaster hit the clubhouse in September 1929 when it was razed by fire. Property loss totalled $10,000 and the loss of golf clubs in the locker room was $7,000. All of the club records for the first 18 years were lost in the fire.

Club competitions continued in 1930, so it is assumed that the clubhouse was rebuilt and in use a year after the fire. The new clubhouse was built on the site of the old. The verandah, which had extended on three sides, was now only on the eastern end of the building.

Irrigation mains were installed in 1944 and a complete watering system was installed in 1987. This watering system was computerized in the late 1990s.

In 1946 the club bought three sections of dormitory buildings which were surplus to the Royal Canadian Air Force. Two of the buildings became an addition to the west end of the clubhouse for locker-room space.

Located east of the present pro shop, the third building was renovated into living quarters for staff. In 1962 the building became a workshop and office for the greens' superintendent.

In 1961, in an effort to provide its membership with a first-class golf course, 40 acres of land was acquired south of the club property to provide a driving range facility. At the same time the road allowance extending north from the southwest corner of the club's property was ceded to the club.

A new clubhouse was opened on September 22, 1961. The honour of cutting the ribbon and declaring the club officially open was given to the member with the longest and most senior continuous membership, Lorne Johnson. He had been a club member since 1917 and was club champion three times.

The two-level clubhouse and improved greens were valued at nearly a quarter of a million dollars.

The club's second
pro shop was built in 1975 by
Dick Bell Construction at an approximate
cost of $53,000. The structure replaced the old shop
that had been on the bank of Wascana Creek, north of the existing
clubhouse. In the last seven years, renovations to the pro shop have included enlarging the storage area for power carts.

In its 91-year history there have been many changes to the golf course and clubhouse facilities. In 1993 major renovations and expansions were undertaken in the clubhouse, including the addition of locker rooms, a new dining room on the northwest side of the club, and a 19th-hole restaurant named the Spike Lounge.

The Wascana hosted the CPGA Trans America Championships, an open tournament run by the Canadian PGA for Canadian professionals, in 1993. Over the years, noted golfers Gary Player, Moe Norman, Bobby Locke and Stan Leonard have played at the Wascana Golf Club.

A new master plan was approved for redevelopment of the golf course and construction began in 1997. The layout of the golf course changed considerably. Twenty acres of land was acquired from Wascana Centre for the development of three new holes on the front nine, which is the west side of the golf course. Land owned by the club on the south perimeter of the front nine was used for the development of another three new holes on the east side. As part of the development of the master plan, relocation and reconstruction of new undulated greens was also undertaken.

Many members have volunteered their time and expertise to serve the Wascana Club over the past 91 years. One notable volunteer was Jim Kangles who was Club Captain for 22 years. Jim passed away in 1998 and the Jim Kangles Memorial Junior Scholarship is awarded annually in his honour.

WASCANA COUNTRY CLUB STREET CAR LINE

*I*n the early days of the Wascana Country Club few members owned cars and only a small number owned a horse and buggy. For the majority of the members, walking the three-and-a-half miles to the 18-hole golf course was a challenge, so their solution was a street car service to the club.

In 1911 the Regina Municipal Railway was completed, and operated with a terminus on Albert Street at McCallum Avenue. Members of the club approached city council with a proposal to extend the existing track to the club. The southern boundary of the city, at that time, was 10 blocks south of the terminus at 25th Avenue. The club would finance, build and operate the line from there. By the agreement, the club and securers would bear the cost of $59,767. Any loss in the line's operation was the club's responsibility and all materials were city property.

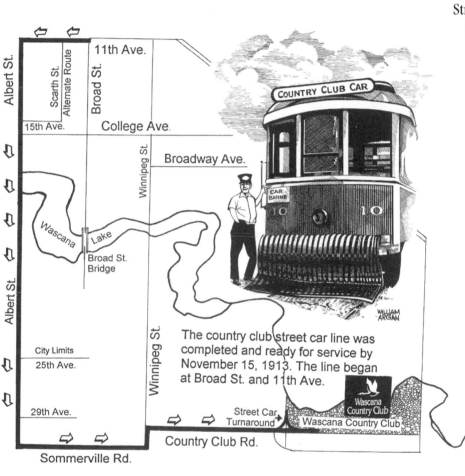

The country club street car line was completed and ready for service by November 15, 1913. The line began at Broad St. and 11th Ave.

When the line was completed in 1913, it went south of 25th Avenue on Albert Street for seven blocks to Sommerville Road (a name that disappeared in the Whitmore Park subdivision). It then proceeded east to the club to the end of the line, opposite the eighth green where a small roofed but open shelter with back-to-back benches was situated. The fare was five cents each way. For several years the line was a paying proposition, with golfers and sightseers utilizing it. The four-wheeled trolley went back and forth to the club four times on weekdays and six times on Sundays and holidays.

When the war ended in 1918, the car was the predominant means of transportation. By the early 1920s, drifted soil and weeds choked the street car line. Shortly after 1923, the overhead wires and supporting poles were removed by the Sherwood Municipality, but the steel track was left.

In the "dirty thirties" the track was torn up in nine days by homeowners who were afraid they'd lose their homes through tax arrears, so many worked out the obligation. The salvaged steel covered the cost and left a credit balance for the city.

GYRO CITIZEN'S GOLF CLUBHOUSE

College Avenue and Elphinstone

*T*he Regina Gyro Club, a service organization, lobbied city council for land to establish the Gyro Citizen's Golf Club in the summer of 1925. The club began to use the land the following year, but it wasn't until 1927 that city council gave permission to place the course where Les Sherman Park is now located.

There were two existing golf courses when the Gyro opened. The first public course opened in the spring of 1897 and was located in the area south of Wascana Creek and just west of Albert Street (present-day Lakeview). Two years later the Regina Club was formed and a clubhouse was constructed in the vicinity of what is now Leopold Crescent.

Golf was a favourite summer pastime for Reginans, so the Gyro quickly grew from a 9-hole to an 18-hole course.

Although the club showed a profit during the war years, it wasn't able to overcome financial difficulties in the mid-1950s and it closed in 1955.

LAKEVIEW PAR 3 GOLF CLUB

Kings Road north of Hill Avenue

"*S*outh Lakeview will have golf" was the headline in the August 17, 1963 edition of the *Leader-Post*.

The article continued: "An 18-hole 'pitch and putt' course will be developed in the South Lakeview district next year. Thursday night city council approved the development of the golf course on park site land previously sought by the Regina Rams. Initial cost of the 18-hole par-three course is estimated at $40,000. The 30 acres of land for the course is situated between Pasqua Street and Kings Road and north of Hill Avenue. Funds for development of the golf course will be taken from money in the South Storm Channel Park Development Account."

Discussions at city council about building a ball diamond or golf course in South Lakeview started in 1961. Once a golf course was decided upon, it was designed by Harry Brinkworth, director of the City Parks Department.

The course opened for play in May 1966 and in July of that year Mayor Henry Baker officially threw the switch to turn on the 12, 400-watt mercury vapour lamps at the opening ceremony.

Over the past 34 years the club has seen some changes. The building that is now the machine shed was used as a temporary clubhouse and a deck was added in 1991. J. P. Lord Construction was the contractor to build the clubhouse which opened officially on September 6, 1966.

Marion Lafoy Carr, manager of the course from 1966 to 1988, organized a men's club and a ladies' club. The men's club is no longer in existence but the ladies' club has flourished.

CENTRAL PARK

Hamilton Street and 14th Avenue

A sure sign of summer was the flocking of sports enthusiasts to Central Park, described as "Regina's most popular sports rendezvous when Old Sol is shining" in a 1948 edition of the *Leader-Post*. Men's and ladies' intercity softball was played at the park, which took its name from Central Collegiate – a block to the immediate south.

In the late 1930s through the 1950s, ladies softball reigned supreme, playing before crowds of 3,000 per game. Teams were the Army and Navy Bombers, coached by Kappy Kaplan; the British Consols, the Maefairs and the Diamonds. Other coaches and managers were Len Barker, Willie Francis, Sam Portigal and Gordon Balfour.

The calibre of softball was so good that several players, including Mary Baker, Daisy Junor and Millie Warwick, were invited to play in the All-American Girls Professional Baseball League, formed during WW II. Mary, Millie and Daisy were inducted into the Saskatchewan Sports Hall of Fame along with another player from Saskatchewan, Arleene Noga. A movie of the League was made in 1991. Entitled *A League Of Their Own*, it starred Geena Davis, Tom Hanks, Madonna and Janet Jones, who is married to Wayne Gretzky.

Mary Baker

Daisy Junor

In a December 8, 1987 *Leader-Post* interview, Junor and Baker reacted to their inclusion in the Baseball Hall of Fame in Cooperstown, New York: "I thought 'Golly, I'm going to be in the Hall of Fame with Ted Williams and Joe DiMaggio,' recalls Regina-born Daisy Junor, 67, who played for the South Bend Blue Sox from 1946 to 1949. 'It really is the thrill of a lifetime.'

"Baker, another Regina product, was one of 20 Saskatchewan players and 48 Canadians to play in the league. Nicknamed 'Bonnie', she was a four-time all-star catcher. . . . 'My first contract was for $150 a week and it was like $3 million to me. I left here making $17 a week.'

"Fans clamored for autographs. Junor and DiMaggio were interviewed – together – on a Chicago radio station, and Baker appeared in television's 'What's My Line'. In Havana, the girls outdrew the Dodgers during concurrent 1947 spring-training exhibitions. 'It was the most exciting time of my life,' says Baker. 'I didn't know how long it would last, but I didn't care. I was realizing a dream.'"

From 1901 to 1932 the park's northeast corner was the site of Victoria Hospital and, subsequently, Regina College. It was also a home for "incurables" and the city's first commercial high school. Central Park has been a key part of the downtown residential neighbourhood, now known as the Transitional Area, and the entire city since 1909.

In the late 1980s, the Transitional Area Community Society and the City of Regina discussed redeveloping the park. The redesigned open space was developed with a heritage theme. It was completed in 1990 when it received a $250,000 city grant to install walkways, shuffleboards, a ball diamond and a gazebo. At that time, softball found a new home at Kaplan Field in the Mount Pleasant Park area. The southern half of Central Park addresses the historic relationship between the park and the former Central Collegiate by arranging the formal design components along an axis extending from the original north entrance of the school. The project received a 1991 Municipal Heritage Award in the Heritage Open Space category.

RAILWAY/CPR PARK

7th Avenue and Broad Street

B y 1909 Regina had nearly 40 distinct sports organizations. Prominent local business-men gave strong financial support to the pro-fessional baseball and lacrosse teams. Fans packed CPR Park and, later, Dominion Park to watch them play. The CPR Park was laid out in the late 1890s. When the railway extended its freight sheds in 1909, CPR Park could no longer be used by local sports clubs.

DOMINION PARK

The block from 6th to 7th Avenues and Rose to Broad Streets

P ictured competing in Dominion Park are the Roughriders playing the Winnipeg Rowing Club in 1913. The Roughriders won the Western Championship 14 times between 1914 and 1936.

In 1917 the City sold Dominion Park, a public reserve, to the T. Eaton Company. The federal government intervened and confiscated the proceeds of the sale, approximately $100,000, claiming Regina had acted illegally in selling the property. In 1927, through arbi-tration proceedings, Regina recovered part of the purchase price on the con-dition that the money be used for park development.

The T. Eaton Company erected its mail-order facility on this site in 1917 and later added a retail outlet. It constructed an addi-tion to the east of the Eaton's store (the Eaton's Dominion Mall) in 1967. The company remained at this location until 1981 when it moved to the Cornwall Centre.

WILLIAM
ARGAN

he Saskatchewan Rough-
riders are a team rich in tradition. For over 90 years
football has been more than
just a game to Roughrider
fans, it has become a way of
life. "Rider Pride" is known
worldwide as the passion Roughrider fans
have for their football team. Not only have
the Saskatchewan Roughriders provided
their fans with many on-field stories and
memories, but the club also has a fascinating off-field history.

The legend of Saskatchewan Roughrider
football began on Tuesday, September 6,
1910. On that historic night the Regina
Rugby Club was formed which, by the way,
was first intended to be a rowing club.
History was made again later that year as
the Regina Rugby Club played its first
game. The lives of football fans in
Saskatchewan were changed forever. Even
though the Regina team, dressed in their
purple and gold uniforms, lost a nail-biter,
7-6 to Moose Jaw, the love affair began.

In their second season, their colours were
changed to blue and white to match those
of the Regina Amateur Athletic Association.
1912 saw another uniform change to red
and black, colours that would be used for
the next 36 years.

The Regina team was very competitive in
the early years under player/coach Fred
Ritter. He led the squad to two Western
Championships in their first four years, the
first in 1912. During the Club's first 21
years, they won the Western Championship
15 times.

The 1924 season was significant in
Saskatchewan football history as the
Regina Rugby Club changed its name to
the Regina Roughriders. Earlier that year
the Ottawa Rugby Club dropped the Rough
Rider nickname they had used since the
1890s in favour of the name "Senators".
The Regina Club jumped at the chance to
adopt the Roughrider name.

Football historians in Saskatchewan claim
two versions as to where the team name
originated. The first states that
Saskatchewan "Roughrider" comes from
the North-West Mounted Police, who were
called Roughriders because they broke the
wild horses used by the force. The second
version comes from a Canadian group of
soldiers who joined Teddy Roosevelt to
fight in the Spanish-American war.
Roosevelt's troops became known as the
Roughriders.

Dean Griffing

Al Ritchie

Greg Grassick

Ken Preston

Eagle Keys

Glenn Dobbs

Ron Atchison

Bill Clarke

ROUGHRIDERS

Ed McQuarters

Ron Lancaster

George Reed

Alan Ford

Tom Shepherd

Kent Austin

Ray Elgaard

Roger Aldag

Sponsored by **Phoenix Group**

Some of Teddy's "Roughriders" settled around Ottawa while others moved out west. It is believed that Ottawa's Rough Riders got their name from the Ottawa Valley lumberjacks who rode log booms down the Ottawa River.

1948 proved to be another important year in the history of the football club. The Club changed its name from the Regina Roughriders to the Saskatchewan Roughriders. The main reason for the switch was the heavy financial burden of running a team; renaming them the Saskatchewan Roughriders was a call for province-wide support.

This move was critical to the longevity of the club. Only the undying support of fans, business, media and volunteers from every corner of the province has enabled the Roughriders to defy the odds and remain a viable part of Canadian professional football for over 90 years.

In 1948 Jack Fyffe made an indelible mark on Saskatchewan. While on a business trip to Chicago Fyffe, an executive committee member, purchased two sets of nylon green and white uniforms at a discounted price. It is ironic that an organization that battles annually for financial survival, would have the colour of its uniforms decided by a bargain price.

Even though The Green and White has taken Saskatchewan fans on an emotional roller coaster ride, from the ultimate highs – Grey Cup Championships in 1966 and 1989 – through the lows of losing seasons . . . the passion of Rider Pride lives on. The names have changed over the years as the torch has passed to many who have dedicated their time and efforts to keep football alive in Saskatchewan, people such as: Fred Ritter, Al Ritchie, Dean Griffing, Greg Grassick, Bob Kramer, Ken Preston, Eagle Keys, Ron Atchison, Bill Clarke, Ron Lancaster, George Reed, Ed McQuarters, Tom Shepherd, Roger Aldag, Ray Elgaard, Kent Austin and Alan Ford, to name but a few. Many unsung players, coaches and volunteers have also left their mark on this proud franchise. The Plaza of Honor Cairn in front of Taylor Field is a testimony to the building blocks of the organization, those who played an important part in making Rider Pride the envy of the CFL. It has often been said, "Once a Roughrider always a Roughrider", and everyone ever associated with the Club can take heart in knowing they helped create the legend of Saskatchewan Roughrider football.

REGINA RAMS FOOTBALL CLUB

Mount Pleasant Park

*T*here was a time, not long ago, when you could drive along Albert Street in south Regina, and come across the little shack that wasn't. It wasn't good for much, but its image has stood the test of time and to this very moment it stands as a symbol of just how far the University of Regina Rams have travelled in their often glorious and mostly unequalled history.

It was on a field where the T. C. Douglas Building now stands that the Regina Rams used to practice, and a shack, complete with mice and holes in the wooden walls and leaks in the roof, served as the dressing room. This was the worst practice facility you could imagine, but the Rams, in those days of Bert Ianone and Bill Ciz, didn't know any better.

They practiced on a field that might once have known grass, but had turned to cracked dirt and dust, and occasionally they would lose a player to an injury suffered when he failed to navigate the many gopher holes that pockmarked the place. The players in those days didn't mind long practices. It kept them from having to go into the dressing room, which looked as if it was but a good Saskatchewan wind gust from falling down.

It wasn't until the mid-1960s that everything about the Regina Rams turned around, and what a swift and dramatic turnaround it was. In the span of two lightning years, the Rams went from so-so members of junior football to a team laying the foundation to create a dynasty that may never be surpassed.

A new group of local businessmen got involved with the Rams in time for the 1965 season, well-known Reginans R. C. (Scotty) Livingstone, Rafe Chadwick, Peter McCafferty, Joe Kanuka, Erwin Strass, Ken Wheeler, George Hambly and Reg Forsyth, to name a few.

The first thing they did was find a new head coach. They went after the very best. Gordon Currie had established himself as the greatest high-school coach Saskatchewan had ever seen. He had coached the Balfour Tech Redmen to baseball championships, but where he excelled was in football. In a remarkable coaching career, Currie coached the Redmen to seven straight city and provincial high-school football championships.

So, in 1965, Currie signed on as head coach of the Regina Rams and he brought with him his capable assistant coaching staff of Al Relkey, Gil Wagner and Doug Killoh. That year, they coached both the Rams and the Redmen. In only his first year as coach of the Rams, Currie performed what would become the "usual" magic. The Rams made it to the playoffs, won the league championship, and got as far as the Western final, where they lost to the Edmonton Huskies. When the Western final was over, Currie and the Rams returned to Regina, arriving just in time for Currie to head over to Taylor Field where his Balfour Redmen were playing the city championship. Arriving just in time for the start of the game, Currie coached the Redmen to victory and finished off his last season in high school football by winning yet another provincial championship.

The 1966 season was Currie's first year as fulltime head coach of the Rams. His days as Balfour's coach were over, although he continued to teach and eventually became a principal in the Regina Public School system.

When that 1966 season began, the Rams had a definite Balfour look to them. The Class of '66 at Balfour had followed their coach to Mount Pleasant. Why Mount Pleasant? Because in 1966, the Rams executive, guided by Erwin Strass, who owned his own construction company, erected a brand new clubhouse at Mount Pleasant. They now had their own clubhouse and their own practice field, complete with lights.

Gordon Currie

Not only had the Rams become the envy of junior football, their facility was also the envy of some Canadian Football League teams, including the Saskatchewan Roughriders, who continued to practice on the infield of a racetrack and had a cramped dressing room under the grandstand at the old Exhibition Park. Later, the Rams' practice facility was named after Scotty Livingstone, whose son Dick and grandson Jarrod became Ram fans with a devotion that continued well into the new century.

Currie armed his new Ram team with familiar faces. He brought along his entire offensive backfield of quarterback Richard Seitz, fullback Ken Newman and running backs Mel Fiissel and Stan Mustatia. Eventually, those four would become as unstoppable in junior football as they had been in high-school football.

In 1966 the Rams did what only a couple of years earlier would have seemed impossible. They won their first Canadian junior championship, taking the Leader-Post Trophy back to Regina for the first time in their history.

By the time Currie retired as coach of the Rams, in 1976, the Rams had won six Canadian junior championships and the dynasty had been established. It would continue. During the 33 years from 1966 to 1998, the Rams played in 17 Canadian championships and won 15 of them (1966, 1970, 1971, 1973, 1975, 1976, 1980, 1981, 1986, 1987, 1993, 1994, 1995, 1997 and 1998), and they did that with only four head coaches. Mel Fiissell succeeded Currie as head coach and then gave way to Jerry Zybtnyiuk. One of Jerry's assistant coaches was a former Ram linebacker by the name of Frank McCrystal, who would become the Rams' head coach in 1984. In 2002 he is still their head coach. For many of those who were part of the Rams' program it became impossible to leave. Frank McCrystal was one. Another was Frank's teammate Bernie Schmidt who developed into one of the most dependable receivers and kick returners in Ram history. Bernie took his exceptional knowledge of the game into the coaching ranks alongside McCrystal.

Over the the years, a number of outstanding players passed through the Rams' system. Bob Poley and Roger Aldag became Canadian Football League all-stars after having found their "football feet" with the Rams – Poley coming to the Rams from Hudson Bay, Aldag from Gull Lake. More recently, Regina native Jason Clermont ended a spectacular career with the Rams by being drafted in the first round of the 2002 CFL College Draft by the B.C. Lions. In his rookie year he made their starting line-up as a slotback. Another local player who dominated at the linebacker position in both the junior and college levels was Jeff Zimmer.

There were outstanding junior quarterbacks such as Lenny Knoll, Dean Picton and Darryl Leason. Running backs from the early days such as Barry Radcliffe and Garry Andrews excelled. Linemen such as Bill Deal, Bill Salloum, Larry VanMoorlehem, Brian Illerbrun and Ron Nicholson all learned much from Ram line coaches Wagner and Killoh.

The Rams got their actual beginning in 1954 when the two Regina junior teams of the day – the Bombers and the Dales – amalgamated and took the name Rams. In 1998, the Rams chose to complete a 45-year history in junior football. In what was at the time a daring move, one with many unknowns, the Rams pulled out of junior football and put together a unique arrangement that saw them become the University of Regina Rams. Many thought the move dangerous for the Rams, that they would be out of their league, too small and too inexperienced.

Those who knew the Rams knew better. On the day in 1998 that the Rams played their final junior game, by winning their 15th Canadian championship, at home in Taylor Field, the Rams celebrated in their dressing-room. Frank McCrystal stood off at the side and as he looked at the trophy as it sat in the middle of the dressing room floor, he said aloud, to himself, "I wonder what the Vanier Cup looks like."

It wouldn't take him long to find out. In only their second season of university football, the Rams ended the century by winning their way all the way to the Canadian championship. They didn't win the Vanier Cup that year, but they had served notice that come the new century, the name Regina Rams would continue as a beacon for success.

Del Wilson

Murray Armstrong

Al Ritchie

Bob Strumm

Bob Turner

Bill Hicke

Bill Hay

Murray Balfour

T he Regina Pats are to junior hockey what the RCMP training depot is to Regina, what the Saskatchewan Roughriders are to Canadian Football, the Montreal Canadiens are to hockey, and the New York Yankees are to baseball. They are irreplaceable in the historical landscape of sport in Regina.

Since the Regina Pats were formed in 1917, they have survived wars, droughts, a cyclone, recessions and a depression. The Pats represent more than the city of Regina, they represent the strength of hockey in Canada.

The Pats are the flagship franchise for every junior team in the country. They are a blueprint for longevity and, on occasion, for brilliance. The Pats have been around longer than most institutions in the province.

The Pats were named after the Princess Patricia's Light Infantry, one of Canada's most esteemed army corps. Named after Princess Patricia, the daughter of the Governor General, the Duke of Connaught, the regiment began with 1,098 officers and men, most of whom were born in England, many of whom now live in Regina.

The Regina Patricia's name was shortened in 1923 to the Regina Pats. Other than the years of WW II, the Pats have not missed a beat since 1917. During the war period, two junior teams were organized to fill the void. It took urging from sportsmen like Beattie Ramsay, Clarence Mahon and Dave Dryburgh, *Leader-Post* sportswriter, to convince the hierarchy of the Commandos and the Abbotts to merge so that the Pats could be reactivated in 1946.

Great Abbott and Commando junior players, all from Regina, such as Jack Wilkie, Bill Giokas, Jim Owen, Bill Folk, Mo Young, Del Wilson, Red Staley, Dunc Fisher, Jim Fairburn and Gordon Knutson, were given the honour of wearing the blue and white, and once again the Pat tradition was alive.

P A T S

Fran Huck

Doug Wickenheiser

Dennis Sobchuk

Clarke Gillies

Ed Staniowski

Dale Derkatch

Brent Parker

Brad Stuart

Derek Morris

The Pats are a lot of things. They are Al Ritchie, perhaps the most legendary hockey coach this province has ever seen. They are Reginans Murray Armstrong and Bud Ramsay, Len Rae, Art Kirkpatrick, Bill Hicke, Bob Turner, Terry Harper and Murray Balfour, some of whom won Stanley Cups. The Pats are Fran Huck, Stan Gilbertson, Mike Fischer and Ernie Hicke.

The Pats are also Dennis Sobchuk, Greg Joly, Clarke Gillies, Gord "Red" Berenson, Ed Staniowski, Glen Burdon, Dale Derkatch and Robbie Laird. They are Del Wilson, Doug Wickenheiser, Mike Blaisdell, Bart Hunter and Darren Veitch. They are Sandy Archer and Normie Fong. Some of the most successful coaches in Canadian junior hockey history are guys like Al Ritchie (the Silver Fox), Murray Armstrong, Bob Turner and Bryan Murray.

The Pats have won four Memorial Cup Championships, in 1925, in 1928 and 1930, twice under Ritchie and once under Howie Milne. In 1974 Bob Turner ended the 44-year drought with perhaps the greatest Pat team of all time.

There was a time when the Pats' roster was made up mostly of Regina kids who came up through the ranks of the Regina Parks League and the Pat minor hockey system. With the establishment of the draft system, players from other centres, like Jeff Shantz, Jason Smith, Jeff Friesen, Josh Holden, Brad Stuart and Derek Morris, have joined the team and worn the Pat colours.

The Regina Pats Hockey Club is 85 years old, but they're hardly showing their age. There is strength in their stride; dreams still dance in their eyes; there is hope in their hearts. Under ownership of the Parker family, they are always preparing for next year and another chance at the Memorial Cup.

AUDITORIUM RINK/SHERMAN THEATRE

Southeast corner of 12th Avenue and Rose Street

R. B. Ferguson built the Auditorium Rink on the southeast corner of Rose Street and 12th Avenue, across the street from the curling rink that had been built earlier on the southwest corner (later location of the Regina Theatre and The Bay department store). Curling began in February 1890.

In January 1905 the Auditorium Rink was used to provide extra sheets of ice for the first Saskatchewan Curling Association Bonspiel being hosted at the curling rink across the street.

In the summer months the rink was home to the Sherman Theatre (see page 180). It was also the site of Saskatchewan's inaugural ball in September 1905, celebrating Saskatchewan's new status as a province.

In March 1914, in the Auditorium Rink, the Regina Vics defeated Grand Mere, Quebec, 6-4 and 4-1 to win the Allan Cup (senior hockey) final.

The rink went up in flames in April 1921.

AMPHITHEATRE AND WINTER FAIR BUILDING

Regina Exhibition Grounds

*T*he Amphitheatre and Winter Fair Building was built in 1913 and opened in February 1914. The building was turned over to the 77th Battery when war was declared in 1914. The structure was used as a military barracks and drill hall until fire destroyed it on December 19, 1917.

During the war, hockey games were played in the Arena Rink on Robinson Street and the Auditorium Rink at Rose Street and 12th Avenue.

EXHIBITION STADIUM

Regina Exhibition Grounds

At the end of WW I public works projects were begun by the city the province and the federal government. In 1919, the erection of Exhibition Stadium, the largest in the West, was the most prominent public project. The stadium was built on the Exhibition Grounds on Pasqua Street and used as a horse show arena and hockey stadium. When an artificial ice plant was installed in 1939, the Stadium name was changed to Queen City Gardens. It was renamed Exhibition Stadium in 1949.

Prior to the opening of the Centre of the Arts, many entertainment and other events were held in either the Armouries or the Stadium.

The Stadium was home to many junior and senior hockey teams; the Pats, the Rangers, the Capitals, the Victorias and the Aces. In the early days the ice hockey rink extended from the north walls to the south walls. The ice surface was about 230 feet long.

In the 1930s, with Lord and Lady Baden-Powell in attendance, the World Boy Scout Jamboree was held in the Stadium. Political rallies were also held in the Stadium. The strikers used the stadium as a place to camp when they stopped in Regina during the On-To-Ottawa March in 1935.

The Stadium was the site of several Memorial and Allan Cup playoff games, and Brier and Silver Broom curling championships. It was also home to the annual Light Horse Show and Winter Fair; the first Kinsmen Five-Car Bingo, with 6,000 players in attendance; the Kinsmen Sportsman and Boat Show, with an indoor "lake" to display boats; Wascana Winter Club Ice Shows, including Disneyland on Ice, Spacerama and TV on Ice. The RCMP Musical Ride, for their 100th Anniversary Pageant in 1973, took place at the Stadium.

Louis Armstrong, the Beach Boys and many other famous entertainment groups performed in Exhibition Stadium. Poor sound, primitive bench seating, but we all thought it was great.

The 6,000-seat Regina Agridome, completed in 1977, replaced the Exhibition Stadium as a hockey arena.

Today, for six months of the year the Exhibition Stadium offers rental ice for hockey, ringette and broomball. In the summer season the building is used for cattle and horse shows.

REGINA RANGERS WIN ALLAN CUP

WE DUNNIT GANG! – METCALFE

☆   ☆   ☆   ☆   ☆

Drama in Dressing Room after Victory
THE KIDS GO WILD!

The Cinderella Kids of hockey who laughed at defeat when it stared them in the eye, Regina Rangers reached the end of the rainbow and wrote a happy ending to the MOST ASTOUNDING CHAPTER IN ALL ALLAN CUP HISTORY.

Coach Fred Metcalfe

REGINA RANGERS – CINDERELLA TEAM WINS ALLAN CUP

*I*n 1941 Canadian senior hockey teams played for the Allan Cup, the top award in Canadian senior hockey, second only to the Stanley Cup in the National Hockey League.

The Regina Rangers, with several youngsters in their first year and a few veterans, under coach Freddie Metcalfe, a former Regina Pat coach, assisted in the background by Coach Al Ritchie, surprised every team they met throughout the season. Strong goalkeeping by "Sugar" Jim Henry, defensive work by Al "Bud" Sandelack and Garth Boesch, and the brilliant play of the "kid" line of Grant Warwick, Frank Mario and Scotty Cameron took the team to the Allan Cup finals against the heavily favoured Sydney Millionaires, a team stacked with seasoned talent.

Not expected to win, and on the brink of elimination, the Rangers kept their Allan Cup hopes alive with a 1-1 tie in Saskatoon, setting the stage for the final game in Regina May 2, 1941. The game was played in the Exhibition Stadium (Queen City Gardens) before 6,700 fans on a hot sweltery night which created a waist-high fog three feet above the ice. The Rangers won 3-0 in dramatic fashion. No one in the crowd saw Alf Kunkel's second-period goal because of the ice-level fog.

In 1949, when the Allan Cup was still the top award in Canadian Hockey, another great Regina senior team, the Regina Caps, lost to Ottawa in the famous "egg-shaped" rink final. However, the talented, underrated "cinderella" Rangers, who played with such dogged determination, have to be considered the greatest senior hockey team to represent Regina in Allan Cup history.

JACK HAMILTON ARENA

1010 McCarthy Boulevard

Jack W. Hamilton

*J*ack Hamilton was a sports builder. He was active as a coach, manager and official in three different sports. He was coach and manager of the Regina Vics Hockey Club from 1925 to 1927. Under his leadership the team was a potent force in Saskatchewan league play and in the Western Canada playoffs.

Hamilton, as an executive member, was associated with baseball and hockey teams in southern Saskatchewan. He also served on the Western Canadian Rugby Football Rules Committee for six years. He was a member of the Canadian Olympic Committee for seventeen years and was a Governor of the Saskatchewan Junior Hockey League.

Hamilton was the president of six different sports organizations during a period extending from 1947 through 1960. He was president of Queen City Gardens in 1938 when artificial ice was first installed in a sports facility in Regina. He remained active until 1949, when Queen City Gardens was renamed Exhibition Stadium.

Hamilton had the distinction of being one of only two people to hold the presidency of both the Canadian Amateur Hockey Association and the Amateur Athletic Union of Canada.

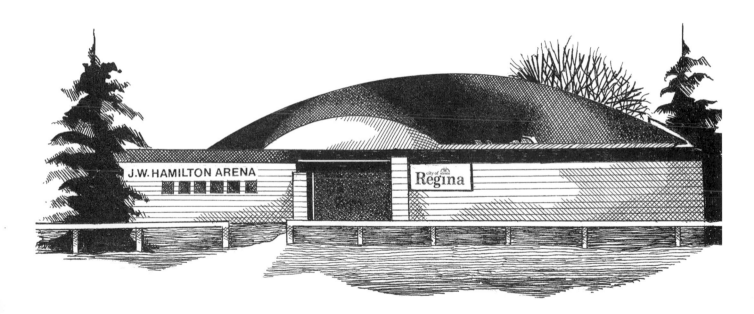

For his achievements Jack Hamilton received a Life Membership in the Saskatchewan Hockey Association. He received the Coronation Medal awarded by King George VI and was recognized by the Province of Saskatchewan during the 1955 Jubilee Celebrations. He was selected Optimist Club Senior Sportsman in 1967.

In his honour, the City of Regina renamed the community rink on McCarthy Boulevard the Jack Hamilton Arena. The rink was built in 1974.

JACK W. STAPLES ARENA

444 Broad Street North

*J*ack Staples was appointed director of the Regina Parks Department in 1946, a position he held for 35 years. Prior to joining the Parks Department, he had worked with the YMCA since his early teens. He had held several positions with YMCA auxiliary services in Scotland, England and Italy during WW II.

As parks director, Staples was instrumental in the organization of many major programs, some of which are still in operation. His favourite programs included the Children's Parade, the operation of summer playgrounds and the Parks League Hockey program. He was an avid sportsman and served on the Regina Pats Minor League Hockey Committee from 1947 to 1961.

A native Reginan, Staples received several Canadian Parks and Recreation Awards and, in 1967, a Centennial Medal, for his outstanding contributions to Canada. In 1968, he was named Senior Sportsman of the Year by the Regina Optimist Club. He was a former secretary of the Canadian Parks and Recreation Association of Canada, and an Honorary Director of the Regina Pats. He died in 1978, and the hockey arena on north Broad Street was named after him by the City of Regina. The arena was built in 1971.

Jack W. Staples

CLARENCE MAHON ARENA

130 Brotherton Avenue

Clarence Mahon

*C*larence Mahon was born in Ottawa and came to Regina in 1915. He worked as an accountant until he established his own real estate firm in 1931.

Mahon was an outstanding hockey player. He was known to all Regina fans in the 1930s, when senior hockey was in its heyday and there was intense rivalry between teams. He was a defenceman for the Regina Victorias and, later, founder, coach and manager of the rival Regina Aces.

He continued to be a strong hockey supporter and became a member of the rink committee of the Regina Exhibition Association. Mahon was involved when the two junior Regina teams, the Abbotts and the Commandos merged after WW II, in 1946, to reactivate the Pats.

He served as the Pats' manager that first year. He was an active director of the Regina Exhibition Association for many years and was president in 1962.

Mahon also contributed to the business community. He was co-founder of the Regina and Saskatchewan Real Estate Boards and a past vice-president of the Canadian Real Estate Association. He was on the city planning council, the Regina Executive Association and served on the vestry of St. Mary's Anglican Church.

In recognition of his many contributions, the city named Clarence Mahon Arena in his honour. It was built in 1975 on Brotherton Avenue in Glencairn.

MURRAY BALFOUR ARENA

70 Massey Road

*M*urray Balfour was a home-grown boy who played hockey on the outdoor rinks and in the Parks League Hockey program. He graduated from Parks League Hockey and played for the Regina Pats for 2 years before finishing his junior eligibility for the Ottawa-Hull junior Champions.

From the Junior Pats he went to the NHL Chicago Blackhawks where he played on the famous "Million-Dollar Line". His teammates were Bill Hay, also a former Pat, and the "Golden Jet" Bobby Hull.

Murray died unexpectedly of cancer early in his career.

In his honour, the City of Regina named the hockey rink on Massey Road in Hillsdale/Whitmore Park the Murray Balfour Arena. The rink was built in 1975.

Murray Balfour

DOUG WICKENHEISER ARENA

1127 Arnason Street North

*B*orn in Regina, Doug Wickenheiser was a star hockey player for the Regina Pats for three years, 1977 through 1980. Doug had outstanding seasons and was the first overall NHL draft pick by the Montreal Canadiens in 1981. He was traded to the St. Louis Blues in 1983 and enjoyed three successful seasons, until he was sidelined by a serious knee injury.

Wickenheiser later played for the Hartford Whalers, Vancouver Canucks, New York Rangers, Washington Capitals, the Canadian National Team and in Europe. Diagnosed with cancer, Wickenheiser died in 1999.

The Regina Pats retired his sweater number, 12, in his honour, and the rink portion of the Northwest Leisure Centre was named after him.

Doug Wickenheiser

AL RITCHIE MEMORIAL CENTRE

2230 Lindsay Street

Al Ritchie

*A*l Ritchie came to Regina with his family before WW I. During the war he was an artilleryman, and was a prisoner of war for a year.

Ritchie was a coach of the Regina Roughriders in the days of senior football, when they ruled the west year after year. He coached both junior football and the Regina Pats hockey teams, and is the only man in history to have won National Championships in both.

Ritchie's football team won 56 consecutive games and nine western championships, but never a Grey Cup. He coached four straight Grey Cup losers, 1929 to 1932, but it was his persistent and fighting spirit that laid the groundwork for the east-west rivalry that is now the Canadian Football League.

He played a major role in organizing the Regina Pats junior football and hockey clubs. He coached the Pats hockey club when they won the Memorial Cup in 1925, and under his leadership they won again in 1928 and in 1930. As great a coach as he was, he never wore skates!

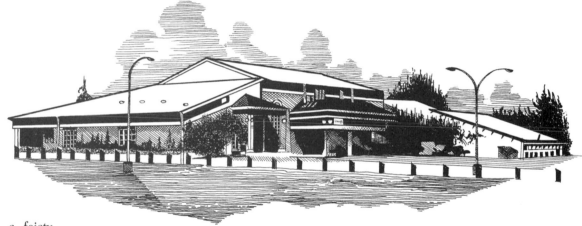

Ritchie was a feisty coach who inspired his players to perform at their best. Everybody knew the "Silver Fox". He was not only a coach, but a teacher, an ambassador and a friend to all who knew him. In later years, as Western Canada scout for the New York Rangers, he was identifiable by his ever-present cigar and coonskin coat, and was a familiar figure at rinks throughout the province. Hundreds of young hockey players owe their start to Al Ritchie.

Players such as Dick Irvin, Johnny Gottselig, Gordon Pettinger, Freddie Metcalfe, Murray Armstrong, the Warwick brothers, Scotty Cameron, Huddy Bell, Jim Henry, Bill Giokas, Dunc Fisher and Gus Kyle were able to pursue professional hockey careers because of his recommendations.

Al Ritchie was named to Canada's Sports Hall of Fame in 1965, The Saskatchewan Sports Hall of Fame in 1966, and inducted into the Saskatchewan Roughrider Plaza of Honor in 1987. When the City of Regina Community Centre was constructed in 1967 on Lindsay Street in east Regina, it was named in his honour.

THE SUNDOWN OPTIMIST BUFFALO GALS

1991 Baton Twirling Team

Stacy Singer

*T*he Buffalo Gals Baton Twirling Club was founded by Maureen Johnson in 1967, Canada's Centennial Year, and 24 years later the club reached the pinnacle of success – a World Championship.

The Buffalo Gals began to experience success within two years of forming. In 1959 they travelled to the CNE in Toronto and won gold in the Corps Championships. During the 1970s, the newly named Sundown Optimist Buffalo Gals performed and competed at international venues. In 1974 and 1976 they captured the coveted "Little Brown Jug" at the prestigious America's Youth on Parade. The Buffalo Gals were the first Canadian group to win these Corps Championships, which were at the time the highest level of international competition in baton twirling. In 1978 they swept the Canadian Championships in all events and age divisions.

During the 1980s the Buffalo Gals moved onto the international scene. At their first World Championship in Paris, France, in 1987, they placed fifth and were on the the international medal podium for the next three years; World Silver in 1988 in Nagoya, Japan; World Bronze in Lausanne, Switzerland in 1989; World Silver in 1990 in San Antonio, Texas.

In 1991, the Buffalo Gals travelled to Podova, Italy to represent Canada at the World Championships for the fifth straight year. Canada had never won a world championship in team competition and expectations were high for this Regina team.

Formed in 1987, the team used a formula of outstanding coaching, led by Maureen Johnson, and strong individual competitors, which included Stacy Singer. A previous individual gold medal winner, Singer was eight years old when she won the gold medal in the junior (under 13) division at the World Baton Twirling Championship in Germany in 1985. She won the gold again at age eleven in the freestyle event in Japan, She went on to win six consecutive gold medals. Working as a team, the Buffalo Gals became Canada's first World Championship gold medal team in 1991.

The team was inducted into the Saskatchewan Sports Hall of Fame in 1996, and Maureen Johnson was inducted into the Saskatchewan Sports Hall of Fame in 2000.

THE REGINA SPORTPLEX

1717 Elphinstone Street.

*T*he Regina Sportplex is a multi-purpose recreation facility that is owned and operated by the City of Regina under the Community Services, Parks and Recreation Department. Together, the Fieldhouse and Lawson Aquatic Centre create the largest recreation facility in Saskatchewan.

In 1975, the Lawson Aquatic Centre was built to provide an indoor facility to accommodate the Western Canada Summer Games competitive swimming events. In 1987, through a joint venture with the provincial government, municipal government and the Western Canada Summer Games Committee, the facility was expanded to include a $6.4-million fieldhouse.

The Sportplex accommodates special events (sporting and non-sporting) and is widely used by the general public and sport groups. The Sportplex provides Regina residents the opportunity to enhance their leisure lifestyle, provides facilities for athletes to train and compete and provides a first-class facility for major community events. The combined attendance for both the aquatic centre and the fieldhouse is over 600,000 visitors annually.

The Lawson Aquatic Centre was designed by Recreation Development Association and Western Consultants and named in honour of Bevan K. J. (Bev) Lawson. People who worked in aquatics knew Bevan Lawson as Mr. Water Safety. He was the first Director of Water Safety for Saskatchewan's Red Cross. He has been called a legend in his own time as he did so much to promote aquatics. Bev did his phenomenal swan dive at the age of 72 at the official opening of the Lawson Aquatic Centre. He was born in 1903 in Leyton, Essex, England, and died in 1977.

The Fieldhouse was designed by IKOY Partnership and the prime consultant was Reid Crowther. The facility was first used for basketball and volleyball events during the Western Canada Summer Games in August 1987.

SANDRA SCHMIRLER LEISURE CENTRE

3130 East Woodhams Drive

Sandra Schmirler

S andra Schmirler was born in 1963. She began to curl in her hometown of Biggar and continued to compete while attending the University of Saskatchewan. She graduated with a Bachelor of Science in Physical Education in the spring of 1985 and moved to Regina, looking for employment and to extend her curling career.

She found employment at the North West Leisure Centre as a lifeguard and swimming instructor, a position she was overqualified for but enjoyed. Her fellow staff members at the centre nicknamed her "Schmirler the Curler".

Arriving in Regina, Schmirler first joined the Kathy Falhman rink, which included Jan Betker. The team won the provincial championship and a trip to the Scott Tournament of Hearts in Lethbridge. The team stayed together for two years, at which time Sandra and Jan formed the Schmirler Rink. Joan Inglis (who became McCusker) and Marcia Gudereit were added. The team became legendary over the next decade.

When Schmirler married, she played under the name Sandra Peterson. Later, when she remarried, she changed her name back to Schmirler. Sandra was a keen competitor with a positive attitude and strong personality. She was a leader and an inspiration to her team members. She was a clutch shotmaker who could make what the team called the big "circus" shot when it counted.

Sandra was admired and loved by all who knew her. When she wasn't curling she was employed as manager of the South East Leisure Centre in Windsor Park. The centre, built in 1990, was renamed "The Sandra Schmirler Leisure Centre" in 2000 by the City of Regina, after Sandra's premature death from cancer (see page 296).

The centre has a pool, whirlpool and weight room. The building also houses the Sunrise Branch of the Regina Public Library.

WASCANA LAKE

ascana Centre, covering 931 hectares, is one of the largest in-city parks in North America. The beautifully landscaped park surrounds a 120-hectare lake located in the heart of Regina.

The Centre is the home for a large permanent flock of Canada geese, and each fall Regina and Wascana Centre are a stopover for flocks of Canada geese and other waterfowl migrating south for the winter.

In the summer the park is filled with joggers, canoeists, sailors and kayakers. The Wascana Centre Authority's ferries that take picnickers to Willow Island are the only power craft allowed on the lake.

Pile O' Bones Sunday, held at the end of July, marks the beginning of the Buffalo Days Exhibition. The event, billed as Canada's largest outdoor picnic, attracts thousands of people to the park as do the Lanterns on the Lake Festival and the Dragon Boat Festival.

The park is also used for winter activities such as the Waskimo Winterfest, held in February. Skating on the lake and cross-country ski trails also provide fun for thousands of people.

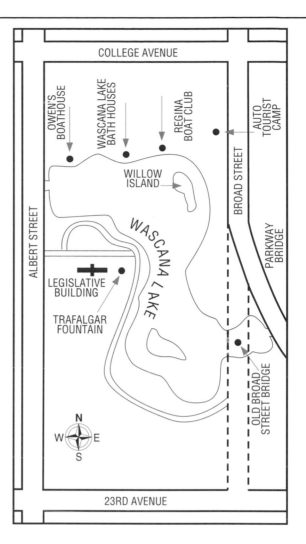

WILLIAM ARGAN '82

OLD BROAD STREET BRIDGE

he old Broad Street Bridge, built in 1909, showed signs of structural defects in 1953 and was demolished in 1960. Fearing collapse the city asked the provincial government to repair it, but the government rejected the proposition.

The old bridge was located about 1,000 yards west of the new bridge. Owners of the old bridge, the provincial government, didn't agree with the city that the bridge should be closed. However the old bridge was removed and Lakeshore Drive was extended after traffic problems were created by motorists attempting to drive onto Broad Street from the old bridge.

The concrete abutment of the old bridge can be seen on the west side of the current Wascana Parkway Bridge.

REGINA BOAT CLUB

*T*his Regina Boat Club, located on Wascana Lake, was built in 1909 and was destroyed in the 1912 cyclone.

REGINA BOAT CLUB

*T*he second Regina Boat Club was built in 1912 and demolished in 1964.

SUNDAY IN THE PARK

 Sunday concert at the bandshell in Wascana Park in the 1930s was popular family entertainment.

WASCANA LAKE BATHHOUSES

*U*ntil it was destroyed in the 1912 cyclone, the Wascana Lake Bathhouse accommodated swimmers taking a dip in the lake.

This building, constructed in 1912, replaced the original bathhouse. There was also a third bathhouse; all three were built and owned by the City of Regina.

OWEN'S BOATHOUSE

North side of Wascana Lake

*O*riginally O'Brien's Boathouse, the Owen family owned the boathouse from 1928 to 1952 and lived in apartments in the upper level of the building. The boathouse was set on telephone pole pilings in Wascana Lake. The pilings had to be re-levelled every spring.

Winter activities included skating from the Broad Street to Albert Street Bridges, ice boating, ice tennis and toboggan sliding on specially constructed above-ground slides. In summer there were boat rentals, a confections' room and Saturday night dances.

front view

Owen's Boathouse was damaged by fire in 1940 but it was restored and provided a venue for entertainment, plus mooring for two Navy lifeboats during the war years. Up to 36 people at a time would tour the lake on the large motorized paddle-wheel boat, the "Queen Mary".

After illness and death in the Owen family, the boathouse was leased out for two years, from 1953 to 1954, but it was no longer a money-making venture so an equipment auction was held and the building was torn down.

back view

REGINA ROWING CLUB TEAM

Canadian Fours champions 1938

*T*he Regina Boat Club had an active competitive membership in the 1930s. Using man-made Wascana Lake as a training facility, club members won a number of national awards.

Regina's first entry in the Canadian Henley Regatta, held on the Welland Canal during 1938, was not taken seriously; few supposed that a riverless prairie centre could produce oarsmen, let alone champions. Nautical opinions were quickly revised, however, as the unheralded "landlubbers" from Regina triumphed in both the junior, 150-pound fours and the senior fours.

The members of the Regina Rowing Club team that won the Canadian Fours championship in 1938 were Harry Duckett (bow), Newt Hughes (second), Dick Priest (third) and Jack Peart (stroke).

VIEW OF LEGISLATIVE BUILDING FROM OWEN'S BOATHOUSE DOCKS

*T*aken circa 1940, Bill Argan drew this view from his own photograph collection.

REGINA AUTO COURT

*T*he Regina Auto Court opened in 1926 and served as a tourist campground. It was designated part of Wascana Park in 1957.

WASCANA BADMINTON/WASCANA WINTER CLUB

Albert Street and 19th Avenue

*T*he Wascana Badminton Club was built in 1930 and supported by nearly 250 members. In 1934, plans were prepared by Storey and Van Egmond and construction began on an extension to the badminton club to provide figure-skating facilities. Figure skating had its beginnings in Regina about 1930 with the formation of the Regina Skating Club. Upon completion of the skating rink extension, the club became associated with the Wascana Winter Club and moved into its clubhouse on Albert Street.

Only shareholder members were allowed full privileges of the club, however, non-members were admitted to skate.

In 1941 the Wascana Winter Club membership agreed to turn over the club facilities to the Department of National Defence. The HMCS Queen, the training ship in Regina, was located in the club. About 4,000 men were trained there for the Royal Canadian Naval Volunteer Reserve.

The *Leader-Post* reported in August 1941: "The armouries has every appearance of figuratively bursting at the seams with both the military forces and the naval division expanding almost daily. Regina division has expanded almost fourfold since the war's outbreak. . . . The Wascana Winter Club was chosen as a suitable building for the division and the department, as a preliminary step, asked city council in a letter whether the council would be prepared to grant exemption from taxation of the property for the duration of the war." Council agreed to the tax exemption for the balance of 1941. The building had an assessed value of $43,730.

The officer commanding Regina Division said the building would prove very satisfactory because, "there was ample drill space and its proximity to Wascana Lake would be welcomed."

When WW II ended the Navy returned the facility and the Wascana Winter Club resumed operations, adding a curling extension in 1950.

Wascana Winter Club/
HMCS Queen

From 1945 on, the complex provided recreational figure skating, badminton and curling facilities and was an active social centre for its members and their families. There was a strong figure-skating section under the leadership of people like Dr. DeWitt, Willa Haughton, Amy Kaltenbruner, Bert Penfold, Dr. Urban Gareau and Bill England. Many great skaters were produced, some of whom later skated professionally. Dick Salter toured with American ice shows for years. Barry Green was Donna Atwood's skating partner with Ice Capades, Joan and Margie Penfold pursued skating careers and Margie (Sandison) became an International skating judge. The DeWitt twins, Joan and Jean (Owen), skated professionally with Barbara Ann Scott and later with Sonja Henie's Hollywood Ice Revue.

The badminton section, led by Harry Robbins and Barry Ursel, produced champions Clara Ehman Lovett, Don Hodges, Sid Lowthian, Ted and Pat Child, Tom Drope, Art Booth and Jim Cuthbert. The curling section was headed by Ted Culliton, Neil Scheuerwater and Ed Petersmeyer.

In the days before large touring ice shows, the Wascana Winter Club staged a number of professionally produced ice shows that played before capacity audiences at Exhibition Stadium. Top guest stars were Otto and Maria Jelinek, Barbara Paul and Robert Wagner and Wendy Greiner. The casts included all members of the skating section, young and old. Costumes were designed by Pat Haug and made by the many volunteers, headed by Mildred Babey, Joyce Weicker and Yvonne Ellis. Some of the shows they produced were Disneyland On Ice, Spacerama and TV on Ice.

The roof of the curling and skating section of the club collapsed under heavy snow in March 1974. After that the remaining portion of the facility was used by the Wascana Badminton Club.

"Fire razes badminton club" read a May 5, 1977 headline in the *Leader-Post*. "Two brick chimneys rising out of charred, smouldering ruins were all that remained Thursday morning after a two-alarm fire Wednesday night destroyed the Wascana Badminton Club, formerly the Wascana Winter Club, at Albert Street and 19th Avenue."

The Wascana Winter Club was a vibrant family recreational centre and sports facility for many Reginans. Its closure was a great loss for the community.

CIVIL SERVICE/LAKESHORE TENNIS CLUB

Legislative Grounds, Wascana Centre

*T*he game of tennis has been part of Regina's sporting and social life since the end of the nineteenth century. The Regina Tennis Club began operations in 1883, when the town was barely a year old. The courts were located on Dewdney Avenue, near the Indian Office. Sometime during the first decade of the Twentieth century, the club moved to a site in Victoria Park.

By 1915, the Regina Tennis Club was in a new location, near the north end of Albert Street Bridge on 19th Avenue near Wascana Creek. It remained there until 1930, when it was relocated to provincial property east of Albert Street at Hill Avenue, in Wascana Park.

The new facilities included a large new clubhouse, 12 courts, a high fence, and hot and cold showers. At that time, the new Regina Tennis Club was described as "among the finest in the west".

There were 19 tennis clubs in the city in 1915, all members of the Regina Tennis League. One of the clubs was the Civil Service Club, the other clubs were Carmichael Club, Catholic Club, Knox Club, Methodist Club, Metropolitan Club, St. Mary's Anglican Club, St. Paul's Anglican Club, Wesley Club, Westminster Club, CNR Club, City Club, Collegiate Club, General Hospital Club, North Side Club, Montague Club, Regina College Club, Saskatchewan Co-op Elevator Club and the Saskatchewan Wheat Pool Club.

The Civil Service Tennis Club, located just south of the Legislative Building, was founded in 1915. Eighty-seven years later it is the only club of the original Regina Tennis League that remains. In 1973 the club changed its name to the Lakeshore Tennis Club. Nestled amongst Wascana Park's lofty firs and poplars, off Lakeshore Drive, the complex consists of a clubhouse and five floodlit hard-surface courts. In 1915 the Civil Service Club had fewer than 35 members; in 2002 the Lakeshore Club has a membership of 278.

The Regina Tennis Club was forced to move from the legislative grounds in 1958 to make way for building expansion within Wascana Centre. They moved for a short time to the Lakeview Par Three Golf Course site but ceased operation in 1964.

Over the years the Regina and the Civil Service (Lakeshore) Tennis Clubs provided recreational and competitive tennis for thousands of Regina citizens, and produced several provincial and national champions. Bill Ebbels won the Saskatchewan Singles crown a record eight times between 1948 and 1967, and was runner up on seven other occasions. He was also the first chairman of the Leader-Post Carrier Foundation.

Don Hodges won the Singles Western Canadian Championship in 1948. On numerous occasions between 1941 and 1951, Don held the Provincial Mixed Doubles, Singles and Doubles championships for Saskatchewan, Manitoba and Alberta. Others Reginans who have won Saskatchewan Championships over the years are Art Sihvon, Sid Lowthian, Garth Kennedy, Len Turner and Bob Fuller, to name a few.

ALBERT MEMORIAL BRIDGE

*T*he bridge was built at a cost of almost $250,000 and was undertaken in conjunction with improvements to Wascana Lake. It replaced the first bridge built in 1908 by Parsons Construction Company. The 1908 bridge had replaced the timber and dirt dam that had created Wascana Lake.

After the discovery of King Tut's tomb in 1923, the Egyptian craze came to Regina and two symbols – the lotus flower and the papyrus plant – became part of the bridge's balustrades and lamp posts.

The project was described as Bryant's Folly, after the provincial Minister of Public Works. At the bridge's opening, the Honourable J. F. Bryant said to the throng of people: "The bridge was designed by Messrs. Puntin, O'Leary and Coxall, and was erected and brought to completion under the skilled and loving care of Lieut.-Col. O'Leary M.C. and two bars – the bars being given for gallant conduct under fire in reconnoitering, designing and constructing two bridges on Flanders Fields. It was fitting that the memorial bridge should be erected by one who served with distinction in the Great War.

"The work on the bridge is honest work, the material in the bridge is honest material, and the price paid for that work and material is an honest price. The government and the city have spared neither pains nor expense in an endeavor to make the bridge worthy of the object for which it is intended."

Dedicated to fallen soldiers, the Albert Street Bridge was the government's first war memorial erected on behalf of the Saskatchewan people. "This beautiful structure is but additional evidence of the honour, we, of this province, are prepared to do (for) the memory of the men who have died for us in the Great War," said Premier J. T. M. Anderson as he addressed the 10,000 people gathered for the bridge's opening on November 10, 1930.

According to the November 11, 1930 edition of the *Leader-Post*: "The bridge itself was decorated with flags, 68 in number, equally divided between the Union Jack and the Red Ensign, along the balustrades and on the pylons at the ends of the structure. The uniforms and accoutrements of the Royal Canadian Mounted Police, the infantry units, the sea cadets and Royal Canadian Naval Volunteer Reserves, drawn up in formation over the central arch of the bridge, added colour to the scene."

The Albert Memorial Bridge was constructed using hand tools and horse-drawn wagons as a make-work project at the beginning of the Depression. Wages of 45 cents an hour were paid to unskilled labourers while elsewhere 35 cents was being paid for similar work. A total of 1,302 men were given work on the bridge and nearly 2,000 contributed to the job.

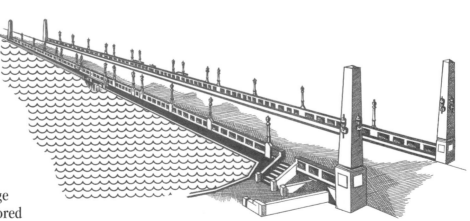

Designated a Municipal Heritage Property in 1984, the bridge was restored in the late 1980s at a cost of $1.4 million.

TRAFALGAR FOUNTAIN

Legislative Grounds, Wascana Centre

*O*ne of a pair designed by Sir Charles Barry, architect of the Houses of Parliament, London, England, this fountain stood in London's Trafalgar Square from 1845 to 1939. The fountain was officially dedicated in August 1963 by Viscount Amory, British High Commissioner to Canada, to the founding of the North-West Mounted Police headquarters in Regina in 1882. The other fountain is in Ottawa.

The fountain is constructed of red granite from Scotland. It is centred on an octagonal base of coloured terrazzo in the garden east of the Legislative Building.

SPEAKERS' CORNER

Southwest corner of Wascana Park, Wascana Centre

*S*peakers' Corner in Regina's Wascana Centre is a Canadian version of the original in England. The large gas lamps at the entrance once stood near Speakers' Corner in London's Hyde Park. They were removed when London traffic routes were modernized. The birch trees were brought from Runnymede Meadow, where King John signed the Magna Carta in 1215. Symbolizing free speech at the municipal level, the columns surrounding the central podium are from Regina's old City Hall, which was built in 1908 and demolished in 1964.

The official opening and dedication ceremonies for Speakers' Corner were performed by Lord Mountbatten of Burma on April 12, 1966. The April 13, 1966 edition of the *Leader-Post* read: "Despite the cold, overcast day, Lord Mountbatten said there was only one way to open a speakers' corner – with a speech – and for 10 minutes he reminisced about his association with Canada, his career and his friendship with Dr. A. C. Taylor of Regina, formerly his physician in Burma."

Mountbatten said the 1,600-acre Wascana Centre project, being developed jointly by the provincial government, the University of Saskatchewan and the city was "imaginative and stimulating" and one of which Reginans may be proud.

To celebrate Canada's 99th birthday in 1966, civic, provincial and federal government speakers were invited to expound their views on matters of public concern.

In August 1966, hundreds gathered to hear speakers promoting the end of the Vietnam conflict. T. C. Douglas, leader of the New Democratic Party, drew a crowd of 250 people when he was guest speaker at a Regina Vietnam Action Committee meeting held at Speakers' Corner. He said it was time for the Canadian government to speak out about the conflict in Vietnam in an effort to bring peace to the people of "that unhappy country." Douglas concluded: "As Canadians we should be shouting: 'For God's sake stop' for in this critical hour of human history, silence is criminal."

KWAKIUTL TOTEM POLE

Wascana Centre, east end of Hill Avenue

*T*his totem pole was a gift to the people of Saskatchewan by the Native Indian Peoples of British Columbia to commemorate the centenary of the union of the province of British Columbia with Canada on July 20, 1871.

The Kwakiutl are a people who live on Vancouver Island, Queen Charlotte Island and northwestern British Columbia.

The pole was carved in Vancouver, British Columbia by Mr. Lloyd Wadhams of the Nimpkish Indian Band. It is located in the picnic area in the southwest part of Wascana Centre, directly east of Hill Avenue boulevard.

GLOCKENSPIEL

Victoria Park

*L*ocated in the northeast corner of Victoria Park, near the intersection of Scarth Street and 12th Avenue, is a glockenspiel or bell tower.

Erected in the fall of 1985, this set of 23 bells hangs in several tiers on a 30-foot bell tower. The bells are cast from brass, manufactured in Germany, and weigh from 24 pounds to 117 pounds, each contributing to a musical scale with a range of two octaves. They are sounded electronically and controlled by a mechanism housed in the polished red granite base.

The bells can be made to chime at specified times of the day and are played either by programmed tapes or by an electronic keyboard.

A Heritage Regina 1985 project, the glockenspiel project began with a $10,000 donation from the heritage committee and Regina's Market Square.

The estimated cost of the project totalled $60,000, which was raised through private and public donations.

At the site of the glockenspiel a plaque states: "The harmonious chiming of the bells is a symbol of the way in which groups of different heritages come together to enrich the life of this city."

DIEFENBAKER HOMESTEAD

Lakeshore Drive, Wascana Park

A s an eleven-year-old, John Diefenbaker helped his father build the three-room family home that now stands in Wascana Centre. The home where "The Chief" lived between 1906 and 1910 was moved from Borden to Regina in 1967. It was dedicated an historic site on August 31 of that year.

Restored with the former prime minister's input, the homestead's contents included some original pieces that were donated by the family, such as the kitchen table, sewing machine and the kitchen stove, as well as a T. Eaton Co. fall and winter catalogue from 1901/1902, and a jar of saskatoons canned in 1923.

The smaller home of an uncle, Ed Diefenbaker, was originally located near the Diefenbaker home and was included at the site.

Diefenbaker was born September 18, 1895 in Ontario. His family moved to Saskatchewan in 1903 and lived on the homestead near Borden from 1905 to 1910. In 1910 the family moved to Saskatoon where Diefenbaker studied law. Following overseas service in WW I, Diefenbaker set up his law practice in Wakaw, and it was there that he entered politics as a village councillor.

In 1956 John Diefenbaker became leader of the federal Progressive Conservative Party and was elected Prime Minister of Canada in 1957. He held office until 1963. Following his term as Prime Minister he continued to be an active Member of Parliament.

On August 16, 1979, at the age of 83, John Diefenbaker died at his Ottawa home. He is buried on the campus of the University of Saskatchewan in Saskatoon next to his second wife, Olive.

The Diefenbaker Homestead was closed in 2001 as operating costs became too high for the level of tourist interest.

ASSINIBOIA CLUB/DANBRY'S

1925 Victoria Avenue

*T*he Assiniboia Club, a male bastion for years, began as a musical club in 1882. In May 1883 the Musical Club changed its name to the Assiniboia Club, after the District of Assiniboia, a subdivision of the old North-West Territories. A. J. L. Anson was elected as its first president. Thus began one of Western Canada's oldest and best-known private clubs. From the start it was a rendezvous for the elite as nearly every prominent man in Regina and district belonged.

Corner of 12th Avenue and Hamilton Street

This building, located at the corner of 12th Avenue and Hamilton Street from 1886 to 1893, represented the third change of address for the club.

Membership in the Assiniboia club over the years is a lesson in the province's history. Through its doors passed Saskatchewan's leaders in business and community life, and those who helped shaped the province's destiny.

Even before Saskatchewan was named a province, and while it was still part of the North-West Territories, all of its premiers enjoyed honourary membership in the Assiniboia Club, as did the lieutenant-governors. The same honour went to all the mayors of Regina before and after Regina achieved city status.

Following three temporary homes, this building was erected in 1893 and demolished in 1912. Regina's first skyscraper, the McCallum Hill Building, was erected in its place.

Northwest corner of 12th Avenue and Scarth Street

This is the Assiniboia Club as it was built in 1912 (see page 260). The club closed its doors in 1994.

In 1996, Garry and Margaret Huntington purchased the Assiniboia Club building from the Bank of Montreal. Over the next year the Huntingtons renovated the building and converted the main floor into Danbry's, a contemporary restaurant. In July 1997, the building reopened with the Assiniboia Club returning to the top two floors as a private business club. The restoration has been very successful and the building has been awarded municipal and provincial heritage restoration awards.

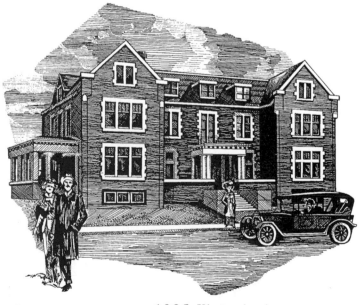

1925 Victoria Avenue

ODD FELLOWS HALL

2080 Rae Street

*T*he Odd Fellows and Rebekahs of Regina are part of a worldwide fraternal organization that has been on the North American continent for 183 years.

The Three Links – the symbol of the organization – denotes the ideals which the members strive to portray: friendship, love and truth.

In the formative years of the fraternity, it was unusual for people to lend a helping hand to those in need, to be concerned about the welfare of others or to establish programs that would benefit all people. That is one of the reasons that this group of men became known as Odd Fellows. The name and the ideals continue today.

Members of the Regina Odd Fellows and Rebekahs provide funds and manpower to support many projects which benefit our community. Their main project is the preservation of eyesight. They have donated over $100,000 during the last 15 years to purchase equipment for the Pasqua Hospital's eye department, and prisms are provided free of charge to patients through their funding.

Other projects include bursaries and scholarships to local students, low-interest educational loans, citizenship awards for schools, sponsorship of Little League and Minor Hockey, a United Nations annual educational tour to New York, fundraising for the Arthritis Society of Saskatchewan, and donations to Souls Harbour Mission, the MS Society, the Heart and Stroke Foundation and Transition House.

An Odd Fellow Lodge, Regina Lodge No. 6, was first established in Regina on August 23, 1893 and a Rebekah Lodge, Naomi No. 3, was established on June 2, 1908. Today, there are two Odd Fellow Lodges, three Rebekah Lodges, an Encampment, a Canton and a Ladies Auxiliary to the Canton.

Sometime prior to 1914, the Lodges began to meet at a hall located at 2229 15th Avenue. Shortly thereafter the organization purchased a cottage at 2305 Lorne Street. In 1952 the 15th Avenue hall was sold to the Archiepiscopal Corporation of Regina and the Lorne Street cottage was sold to a private individual. The Odd Fellows and Rebekahs moved into their new hall at 2080 Rae Street in July 1952. Today, 248 Rebekahs and 100 Odd Fellows still call this location home.

MASONIC TEMPLE

1930 Lorne Street

*O*riginally this site was occupied by the YMCA, until the 1912 cyclone levelled that structure.

In 1906 the Masons built their temple on 11th Avenue, but by the 1920s this fraternal organization, along with its affiliated youth and women's groups, had outgrown those quarters. A new and larger temple at 1930 Lorne Street was designed by the architects Portnall and Reilly and was dedicated in 1926. Interior millwork was done by the local Western Manufacturing Company.

The central main entrance is framed with Doric columns and reached by a flight of stone steps with curved balustrade walls.

The fraternity of Freemasonry is the oldest, largest and most widely known in the world. It dates back hundreds of years, to when stonemasons and other craftsmen working on building projects gathered in shelter houses or lodges.

WA WA SHRINE TEMPLE

2065 Hamilton Street

*U*ntil the completion of the Wa Wa Temple in 1955, Shriners had never had their own building. In earlier years, Shrine activities centered around the Masonic Temple on Lorne Street. Any shows staged, such as the Shrine's annual ceremonial, were held at City Hall, in the ballroom of the Hotel Saskatchewan or in Exhibition Stadium.

The cornerstone for Regina's Shrine Temple was laid May 18, 1955.

Shriners belong to an international fraternity with members throughout Canada, the United States and Mexico. The Shrine is best known for its colourful parades, its distinctive fez and its official philanthropy – Shriners Hospitals for Children.

At a cost of $17 US per second, Shriners operate 22 hospitals in Canada, the US and Mexico for children up to age 18. Patients are never charged for any care or service received at the hospitals and transportation costs to the hospital and home are covered, for the child and one parent, by Shriners.

The hospitals are largely funded by endowments, wills and gifts. In Saskatchewan, 17 Shrine Clubs raise money through a travelling circus, a calendar and local events.

Every Shriner is first a Mason. A man is a fully accepted "Blue Lodge" Mason after he has received the required degrees. After that he may join other organizations such as York or Scottish Rites, and he can become a Noble of the mystic Shrine.

ELKS OF CANADA

2629 29th Avenue

T he National Head Office of the Elks of Canada is located in south Regina. Founded in 1912, the head office was moved to Regina from Winnipeg in 1976.

The Elks Club is the largest all-Canadian, fraternal organization in Canada with 300 lodges and 20,000 members. They are committed to their vision of being the most progressive family-focused organization in Canada, meeting community and member needs and expectations.

Membership is open to any person, male or female, of good reputation, a believer in a Supreme Being, an adherent of lawful government and having reached the age of majority as established by the province or authority in which the Lodge is located.

Their main charity, The Elks & Royal Purple Fund for Children, has an impact on thousands of Canadians annually.

THE HUNT CLUB

Southeast corner of Victoria Avenue and Rose Street

B uilt in 1909 as Edward McCarthy's home, this gracious residence was destined to house a series of Regina service clubs and organizations.

McCarthy had established a general store on Broad Street in 1883 (see page 188). As an alderman in 1899, and from 1903 to 1904, he advocated municipal ownership of electric lights, street railways and water works.

Edward McCarthy

The site of the Waldorf Lodge in 1920 and from 1937 to 1948, this building was also the home of the Canadian Legion. It later housed the Royal Order of Moose. The Hunt Club took it over from 1953 to 1961. The building was demolished in 1964.

WILLIAM ARGAN

VICTORIA CLUB

1300 Victoria Avenue

*T*he Victoria Club dates back to 1923, when a group of Danube Schwabian Reginans, predominantly from the villages of Zichydorf and Gyorgyhaza, Banat, Austria, Hungary saw the need for a community organization in the heart of Germantown. A benevolent society was established, and a small group of 23 held their first meetings in the Nestman Block on 11th Avenue and Ottawa Street. Membership grew quickly and the group moved to Kleisinger Hall on Ottawa Street.

Wanting their own clubhouse, the Victoria Club was built in 1925. The club installed two bowling alleys in 1930. Leagues were formed and continue to flourish, making it unique among other private clubs in the city.

First known as the German Canadian Club the name was changed to Victoria Hall between 1940/1941 because of anti-German sentiment. It was later renamed the Victoria Club.

The club has undergone many changes over the years. As a result of a disastrous fire in 1975, the downstairs portion was completely rebuilt. More recently, the entire building has had extensive renovations.

The 750 members of the Victoria Club celebrated its 77th anniversary in 2002 with further renovations and building expansion, including automating the 70-year-old bowling alleys.

HUNGARIAN CULTURAL CLUB

1925 McAra Street

*I*n 1922, the Hungarian Club's first building was located on the south side of Victoria Avenue near McAra Street. At that time the club was open to those of Hungarian descent and offered social and cultural opportunities for the club's 60 members.

As membership increased the quarters became too small. The first building was sold and construction began on the second building at 1925 McAra Street in 1962. The club opened in 1963.

The club was built from members' donations and it was mainly the members who volunteered to construct the building. This building provided roomier accommodations, including a club bar, a dining room, a room to play cards and a hall, with a dance floor, that can seat 250 people.

Cultural activities at the club include three levels of dance groups plus a Hungarian language class held on Sundays for children and adults.

In the 1950s many Hungarians fled their native country after the Hungarian revolution. In Regina they found a place where they could celebrate their culture and customs. The Hungarian Cultural Club is now open to everyone.

ROMANIAN CANADIAN CULTURAL CLUB

726 Victoria Avenue/639 Victoria Avenue

*T*he Romanian Canadian Cultural Club "Mihail Eminescu" of Regina celebrated its 70th anniversary in 1998. Mihail Eminescu was the greatest of all Romanian poets. Application to have the club incorporated was made on March 21, 1928 and the first hall at 726 Victoria Avenue was purchased in April of the same year. The first ladies' auxiliary of the club, the "Romanian Ladies Association M. Eminescu" was organized in 1931.

In 1951 the old hall was sold and a building at Victoria Avenue and Broder Street was purchased. The three levels were used for small gatherings and social events while other halls were rented for larger events.

The grand opening of a new hall – the Regina Ballroom – took place on August 15, 1955. Additions in 1966/1967 included the Banastir Room (for small gatherings), a beverage room, a restaurant and a larger members' club room and lounge. Additions and renovations were made in 1972/1973 to bring the complex to its present size.

Cultural activities over the years have included seasonal concerts, programs, theatrics, a music school, various dance groups and language classes. Other activities include banquets, dances, bazaars, picnics and many fundraising and social events.

The "Daughters of the Canadian Romanian Club", better known as the DCRCs, were organized in 1955. The remaining members of the "Romanian Ladies Association M. Eminescu" joined them a few years later. The Eminescu Romanian Dancers were organized in 1965 to participate in Saskatchewan's jubilee and Canada's centennial. The group has represented the club across Canada and the United States. In 1979 they did a performance tour in Romania. They were the first Romanian group from outside the borders of Romania to do such a tour.

The Romanian Canadian Cultural Club, Mihail Eminescu, was also known for its support of local charities, sport and other organizations. The club has participated in numerous festivals and other activities organized or promoted by the Regina Multicultural Council.

The club closed its doors in 2002 due to financial difficulties.

GERMAN-CANADIAN SOCIETY HARMONIE

1727 St. John Street

*T*he German-Canadian Society Harmonie provided a sense of home for the immigrants who came to Regina after WW II, said club member, Rose Engelhardt. "You wanted to be with people and share the same experiences. We were young and we liked to dance and to our own music. We had a few men who played accordion, saxophone and drum and a lot of singing went on."

The club began after an ad in 1955, in *Der Courier,* the German-language newspaper, invited all German immigrants to a meeting to organize a German Club. On May 12, 1955 the German-Canadian Society Harmonie was started in the Quebec Hall, with 80 members. The Soccer Club Concordia and the *Volksliederchor Harmonie* joined as subgroups, and a theatre and bowling group were also founded.

In 1956 shares to finance a clubhouse were sold and the club became a non-profit shareholder organization. A year later, property on 1727 St. John Street was bought and the building was remodelled by volunteers. The club received a club licence from the city in 1958 and the clubhouse opened that year.

In 1960 the Harmonie club opened a library in the clubhouse with German books and the German Language School became a subgroup. In 1963, the club was licensed to serve alcoholic beverages and the women's auxiliary became a sub-group. By 1964 the clubhouse was paid for. Four years later the old clubhouse was torn down and work began on the new building which was erected in 1969. The club held an exhibition of about 3,000 German books in 1973 and, for the first time, the German Club held a three-day Oktoberfest for the public at the Exhibition Grounds.

In 1978 Mosaic was celebrated in the clubhouse. The annual festival presents the cuisine, song and dance of Regina's various ethnic groups in pavilions scattered across the city. The Maypole was erected in front of the clubhouse to coincide with the festival. The club celebrated a red letter year in 1989. The Berlin Wall came down and Germany was united. It was also the year that members burned the club mortgage.

SERBIAN CANADIAN CULTURAL CLUB

1876 Wallace Street

*T*he Serbian Canadian Cultural Club first opened in 1967 at 928 11th Avenue. It operated at this location until 1989 when the Serbian Orthodox Church bought the property at 1876 Wallace Street, the site of the former Settlement House, and erected a new building for the club.

The club's 1,200 members participate in a number of fundraisers to benefit charities – the main one being The Hospitals of Regina Foundation.

The club promotes its culture through its church – the Serbian Orthodox Holy Trinity Church – the first Serbian church built in Canada (see page 85). In August 1991 the exiled prince of Yugoslavia, Prince Alexandar Karadjordjevic, visited Regina to celebrate the Church's 75th anniversary.

Members from all walks of life belong to the club's various subgroups, including the golf club, which began in the early 1990s and has 100 members. There are also hockey, baseball, volleyball, soccer and floor hockey teams. Members enjoy playing shuffleboard, pool and darts, and they are in the process of organizing a folk dance group.

Church Name Day, held six weeks after Easter, is open to the public. At that time Regina people can experience Serbian food and dancing.

A painting in the club by one of the members illustrates the expulsion of the Serbs from Kosovo, by the Turks, in 1389.

The colours red, blue and white are significant to the club. Red represents the blood given for freedom; blue represents freedom of the air; white represents freedom as a whole. Found throughout the club is a cross with four Cs representing the motto for all Serbs: "Only Unity Will Save Serbs".

G. MARCONI ITALIAN CLUB

2148 Connaught Street

*I*n 1953 the G. Marconi Italian Club became a non-profit organization. Before they owned their own club the Italians met in the basement of Holy Rosary Cathedral.

Construction began on the G. Marconi Italian Club in the spring of 1971. It was funded and constructed by a group of Italian immigrants who received no grants from anyone. They are now known as the founding members. The club's first president was Ernesto Bresciani. The official opening of the new Italian Club was in March 1972.

The original building was approximately 7,000 square feet and it included a banquet hall, kitchen and a members' bar. An additional 7,000 square feet was added in 1985/1986, housing an additional banquet hall and classrooms upstairs.

On the club's 25th anniversary, a commemorative plaque was made recognizing the founding members. There are approximately 200 Italian families that are members, and about 300 Canadian families that are honourary members.

A number of groups perform under the umbrella of the Italian Club: the 35-member dance group, *Le Campagnole* Italian dancers which traveled to Ottawa to dance on Parliament Hill on Canada Day in 2000; the Italian School, *Scuola Italiani*, which runs four different classes and is open to anyone; the Abruzzo Association, whose annual dance is always a sellout; the Fish and Game Association, *Cacciattore*, which has annual awards for the best catch.

The club books many functions such as weddings, dances, anniversaries and tournaments. As well, the family-focused club holds special family functions throughout the year, such as the annual Christmas party, barbecues, an annual golf tournament and curling bonspiel.

The club sponsors many sports groups, such as baseball, darts, soccer and shuffleboard, and every year it raises money for Telemiracle.

SENIOR CITIZENS' CENTRE OF REGINA INC.

2134 Winnipeg Street/2404 Elphinstone Street

*T*he Citizens' Centre on Winnipeg Street, which was officially opened with great fanfare on January 7, 1981, was the triumph of a large group of determined seniors.

It had begun with the opening of the Seniors' Activity Centre at 1511 11th Avenue in 1965. The seniors gained larger quarters and full-time social and recreational facilities in 1966 with assistance from the city. Increased demands for services and the need for more space necessitated three more moves in the next ten years, the last of which was to the old Peart's Hardware building at 1725 11th Avenue.

The Regina Senior Citizens' Centre on Elphinstone Street, offering a range of programs, had opened September 19, 1977.

2134 Winnipeg Street

However, the real victory was won when the Winnipeg Street Centre was opened in the fall of 1980, with ample space, including a 400-seat auditorium, full meal service and a wide range of programs, crafts and activities. The *Leader-Post* reported: "For the more than 2,400 members of the Regina senior citizens' centre, the road to the new $1.3 million-dollar building, which was officially opened Wednesday, was paved with picket signs and letters and phone calls to politicians."

The Regina City Council had agreed to pay $636,000; the province provided $518,000; Wheat City Kinsmen raised $100,000, and the Lakeside Lions and Regina Rotary Clubs provided funds for equipment and furnishings. New Horizons funded the kitchen equipment.

In 1982 the Lakeside Lions donated a 24-passenger bus, and the seniors then formed a tour group to organize trips for seniors. Since then the Wheat City Art Club was formed (1985) and a senior bicycling group (1989). Lists of activities at the Winnipeg Street and Elphinstone Senior Citizens' Centres, published weekly in the *Leader-Post*, include snooker, exercise classes, computer classes, cribbage, painting, whist, bridge, dance, bingo, quilting, home maintenance and housekeeping, cycling on the bike path, and more.

Senior Citizens' Service, a separate organization established in 1971 to upgrade the living conditions, physically and emotionally, of seniors living in their own homes, developed a wide range of programs, many volunteer. There were maintenance and housekeeping programs, snow shovelling, a grow program to share garden produce, visitor programs, Operation Identification to help with crime situations, Operation Alive to promote well-being, plus Surveillance and Support Programs. The services were shut down briefly due to lack of funding, but they reopened in 1993 and once more home maintenance and housekeeping services were provided to seniors living in the city. In 1996 the Services and the Centre merged to provide a wider range of services and programs.

2404 Elphinstone Street

At almost 120 years of age, the *Leader-Post* is one of the oldest businesses in Regina and the province. the *Leader* was established on March 1, 1883 as a weekly newspaper and covered some of the "firsts" in the province's history even before it was a province. Nicholas Flood Davin was the first owner/editor. He was a lawyer/journalist who was a friend of Sir John A. Macdonald. He covered events like the hanging of Louis Riel and is best known for getting an exclusive interview by posing as a priest and conducting the interview in French right under the nose of a watchful guard only hours before Riel was hanged.

The newspaper has had several owners over the last 12 decades, including the province's first premier, Walter Scott, and his successor W. F. Kerr. In 1920 T. Buford Hooke, who started out as a copy boy, held the paper but sold it in 1927 to the Sifton family, who owned the *Leader-Post* for nearly 70 years, the longest of any owner. In the mid-1990s Conrad Black took over ownership of the paper under a "black" cloud of controversy. The current owner, CanWest Global, is headed by the Asper family of Winnipeg. As major players on the Canadian television scene for several years, the Aspers have initiated a crossover between television and newspapers, taking the Leader-Post into a new realm.

The *Leader-Post* has played a significant role in the province by being there for every major story over the past century and providing a credible historical account of these momentous occasions. From the Northwest Rebellion to the establishment of the province in 1905, through two world wars and Medicare, not to mention football and politics – the lifeblood of the province.

The Leader
1883 to 1891
Victoria Avenue
between Hamilton
and Rose Streets

Nicholas Flood Davin,
founder of the
Regina *Leader*

The Leader
1891 to 1905
Hamilton Street between
South Railway and 11th
Avenue

The Leader
1905 to 1913
Southwest corner
of 11th Avenue and
Hamilton Street

P O S T

The Leader-Post
1913 to 1964
Hamilton Street
between
11th and 12th
Avenues

WILLIAM
ARGAN '84

Leader-Post
1964 –
1964 Park Street

The *Leader-Post* is also a leader in the community by supporting hundreds of groups and causes over the course of a year, from literacy to schools to a host of non-profit organizations and projects, such as the Christmas Cheer Fund. In 1986 the paper spearheaded the formation of the Leader-Post Carrier Foundation which honours Leader-Post carriers and provides scholarships for the youth of Regina and southern Saskatchewan as well as providing money to various community groups. Today, the paper still provides arm's-length support by providing financial and administrative help to the Foundation. Speaking of paper carriers, it is the young boys and girls and adults who are the front line between the public and the business."You can have millions of dollars of equipment, hundreds of people and hours of work," says Bob Hughes, the paper's executive editor, "and it is nothing if the delivery people can't get out the paper."

The *Leader-Post* employs about 1,600 carriers, children and adults, and they still deliver it in the traditional way. "It's the only way to get it there," says Hughes. "We switched to morning delivery in November 1996 to better serve readers. It had a great impact on the carrier force but they have done well.

"Hundreds of community leaders got their start as carriers," he adds. "Young carriers learn life experience, earn money and learn responsibility." The *Leader-Post* has been an integral part of Regina for its entire history and will continue to be over the next 120 years and beyond.

THE LEADER

Victoria Avenue between Hamilton and Rose Streets

*D*uring Territorial days, in 1883, Nicholas Flood Davin started Regina's first weekly newspaper, The *Leader*, in this building on Victoria Avenue.

1883 to 1891

THE LEADER

Hamilton Street between
South Railway and 11th Avenue

*I*n 1891 the *Leader* moved to this stone and brick structure in the 1700 block Hamilton Street. The *Leader* was in this building in 1895 when Walter Scott purchased it. He edited the paper until 1900. Scott was the first premier of the province of Saskatchewan.

1891 to 1905

THE LEADER

Southwest corner of 11th Avenue
and Hamilton Street

S oon after Saskatchewan became a
province, the *Leader* published a
daily newspaper called the *Morning
Leader*. The paper was located in this
three-storey building.

1905 to 1913

WILLIAM
ARGAN '84

WILLIAM
ARGAN '84

1913 to 1964

THE LEADER-POST

Hamilton Street between 11th and 12th Avenues

T he *Leader* moved into this building in 1913.
In 1928, Armadale Company Limited, owned
by the Sifton family, purchased and managed the
Leader as well as *Saskatoon's StarPhoenix*. On
April 7, 1930, the Regina paper's name changed to
the *Leader-Post* for morning and afternoon edi-
tions.

This building was also the original home of CKCK
Radio, the first radio station in Saskatchewan, established by the newspaper in 1922.

The *Leader-Post* expanded and circulation increased,
necessitating a move to its present location at 1964
Park Street

The *Leader* building was designated as a Municipal
Heritage Property in February of 1987.

CKCK RADIO

*T*he original CKCK studios were located on the top floor of the old Leader-Post Building on Hamilton Street. The transmitters were on the same floor as the studios and the transmitting towers (horizontal antenna) were on the roof. The towers were lined with lights. There were special platforms at the top of each tower on which were mounted very strong searchlights. Former staff member Lyman Potts recalled one night when the lights failed at the Regina airport, the CKCK tower searchlights were focused on the landing field and late-arriving aircraft landed safely.

The tower lights came into unusual use again in 1933 for the official opening of the World's Grain Exhibition in Regina. The lights were trained on the entrance to the Regina Exhibition grounds. To a traveller at night the lights were the first sight of Regina, until they were removed in the 1940s after the transmitter was relocated to Victoria Plains (Boggy Creek) in 1937.

The early days at CKCK featured a one-man show – the legendary Bert Hooper. He was the first engineer, announcer, producer and only staff member.

CKCK Radio 1922
Hamilton Street between
11th and 12th Avenues

Highway 6 South

From 1922 to 1928 there was no continuous broadcast service. Programming was interrupted by Hooper's meals, program preparation, holidays and janitorial duties.

In 1928 Williams Department Store (which sold radios) came up with an idea for continuous service. When CKCK went off the air, the R. H. Williams Department Store station would fill in. Thus radio station CHWC was born, with studios in the Kitchener Hotel, owned by the Williams family.

CKCK continued to operate its transmitter from the heart of the city while CHWC tried to reach the rural areas. CHWC installed their transmitter, consisting of two tall telephone poles with wires strung between them which provided the antenna, at Pilot Butte. They shared the same frequency. When CKCK went off the air, listeners in Regina had to turn up the volume control to hear CHWC, which became known as "The Glasgow House Station". The two stations formally signed "on" or "off". Transmitters had to be switched on and off and there were pauses of up to 60 seconds.

Radio was popular and expanded quickly as technology improved. Hooper was joined by other radio pioneers, Horace Stovin, Pete Parker and Knight Wilson, and new studios were built on the second floor of the Leader-Post Building.

Horace Stovin   Pete Parker   Knight Wilson   Bert Hooper

The studios were state of the art, specially constructed on springs which lined floors, walls and ceilings beneath the finishes, to prevent any vibrations from penetrating the studios. The studios remained there until 1964 when they moved to Park Street in the new Leader-Post Building.

The first decade of CKCK radio featured many firsts. In 1923 the first church broadcast in the British Empire, from Carmichael Church; the first play-by-play hockey broadcast by Pete Parker, between the Regina Caps and the Edmonton Eskimos, played at Exhibition Stadium; the longest remote-control broadcast to that time, of the Prince Albert Music Festival. Some 307 miles of telephone lines were involved.

W. N. Shultz
Longest record for
Sunday programs

In 1927, CKCK joined with 20 other stations to form the first coast-to-coast network in Canadian history, to carry a broadcast celebrating the Diamond Jubilee of Canada's Confederation.

Gee Johnson
News Butcher

Horace Stovin took over operation of the station in 1929 and introduced many innovations, one of which was the introduction of newscasting. He invented the "News Butcher", prepared and read by *Leader-Post* reporter Gee Johnson, four nights a week on a Western Canada network.

The 1930s and 1940s were the great days of radio in Regina and across Canada. Innovation abounded. Some 97,000 Regina and district people swarmed into the Regina Exhibition's Confederation Building in 1936 to watch live sports, news, weather broadcasts and musical entertainment. Bleachers were built to accommodate the crowds. This "Palace of Glass", the re-creation of a complete radio station behind glass, through the combined efforts of CKCK and CHWC radio stations, was the only such station on the continent and the first time most people could see the operation of a radio station. The sound travelled 20 miles before it reached the audience on the other side of the glass. Following the exhibition the two stations merged and CKCK continued the "Palace" for another four years, building a new and larger station in the Grain Show Building.

Ross McRae
Beaver Award Winner—
Radio's Oscar

Many successful Canadian broadcasters and station managers spent a good portion of their broadcasting careers at CKCK radio : W. A. Speers, Al Smith, A. J. Balfour, Lyman Potts, Don A. MacMillan, W. V. Chestnut, Ross McRae, Wilf Collier, Barry Wood and Don Dawson.

In 1942 Harold Crittenden became general manager of CKCK, he was the youngest station manager in Canada. In 1943 the station received the Billboard Award from New York's Billboard magazine. The inscription read in part: "In recognition of outstanding achievement in radio publicity based on exhibits from the United States and Canada." Crittenden said that CKCK donated 22,000 hours of radio time to worthy organizations during the year. The station's service to the community entered into the judges' decision.

CKCK was the strongest and most popular radio station in Saskatchewan for many years. It earned the nickname "Mighty Mike" because its radio signal was so strong it could be heard right across Saskatchewan and into the northern US. CKCK was heavily involved in almost every community event with its radio personalities, the "Guys and Gals". CKCK featured the "Open Line Show" with Lorne Harasen, the "Morning Mayor" with Johnny Sandison, and newsman Jim McLeod. Other personalities included Doug Alexander, John Wells, Fred Sear, Ken Singer, John Badham, Lloyd Saunders and "Porky" Charbonneau.

Continued on the next page.

Mighty Mike

CKCK was part of the Armadale Communications network owned by the Sifton family which included CKTV and *The Leader-Post*. Armadale was required by CRTC to divest its Regina interests and the station was sold. As competition increased, and formats changed, CKCK lost its popularity and its listening audience diminished. The station discontinued operations in 2001.

CKCK RADIO

1922 Park Street

Michael C. Sifton

Clifford Sifton

RADIO STATION CHWC/KITCHENER HOTEL

1763 Rose Street

*T*he Kitchener Hotel was originally built by R. H. Williams in 1907 as a three-storey department store. In 1918 the store was converted into the Kitchener Hotel (see page 176).

Radio station CHWC became the second radio station in Regina in 1926. Also owned by R. H. Williams Department Store, they began operating from a room on the top floor of the store where the transmitter was located.

CHWC's studio was eventually relocated to the Kitchener Hotel, in sample rooms previously used by travellers to display their wares. The walls were so thin that listeners could hear a flushing toilet from next door. As a result CHWC's call letters, in some circles, came to stand for "Can Hear Water Closet".

CHWC, the R. H. Williams Glasgow House station shared broadcast frequency with CKCK, which was owned by George Bell of the *Leader*. However, CKCK had a distinct advantage as its transmitter, located on the roof of the Leader building, was much stronger than CHWC's transmitter, which was outside the city at Pilot Butte. Listeners constantly had to adjust their sets as the stations took turns on the air each day (see page 352).

The station was part of the Western Broadcasting Bureau, the "Prairie Loop", that included 15 stations in Manitoba, Alberta and Saskatchewan. CHWC's daily program lineup featured Child and Gower Piano Co. Hour of Fine Music, National Music Supply Programme, Metropolitan Theatre Organ and weekly Amateur Hours. CHWC ceased operation in the mid-1930s.

A.D. 1907

THE KITCHENER

CJRM/CKRM RADIO

2060 Halifax Street

James Richardson

Fred W. Hill   Paul J. Hill

*F*ounded in 1926 by James Richardson of James Richardson and Sons of Winnipeg, CJRM broadcast studios were located in Moose Jaw. Richardson established the outlet to provide farmers with daily stock quotations, a service still provided by its successor, CKRM.

CJRM relocated to the Fidelity Life building in Regina in 1936. The call letters were changed to CKRM in 1943. The station format was directed to a broad rural audience with a strong emphasis on sports. In the 1930s and early 1940s sports events were covered by Grant Carson, who was followed by Johnny Esaw. Esaw created the "Roughrider Quarterback Club", broadcast live from the Grand Theatre, and later the Rex Theatre, every Sunday night.

"On Air" personalities included Bill Walker, Bob and Tom Hill, Al Smith, Johnny Sandison, Frank Flegel, Roy Brown, Fred King and Lorne Harasen. CKRM continues to be the voice of the Roughriders and the Regina Pats.

Johnny Esaw

In 1954 CKRM moved to their present location in the former Hebrew School at 2060 Halifax Street. The station was sold by James Richardson in 1941 to Trans-Canada Communications Ltd. CKRM, along with FM stations 104.9 the Wolf and Lite 92 are now owned by Harvard Broadcasting, a subsidiary of the Hill Group of Companies. When CKCK discontinued broadcasting in 2001, CKRM assumed their location on the radio dial and became 620CKRM.

Jim McLeod
CKCK-TV News Anchor

Lloyd Westmoreland
CKCK-TV Manager

On the afternoon of July 27, 1954, a television signal originated from a small, unassuming building on the open prairie east of Regina. In scores of urban and rural homes, a test pattern flickered and sharpened on newly purchased television sets. CKCK Television was on the air.

Owned and operated by Armadale Communications Ltd. of Toronto, which also owned CKCK Radio, CKCK-TV was Saskatchewan's first television station and Western Canada's first privately owned television station. Although it is now recognized as CTV Regina, a proud member of the CTV Network, CKCK Television began its broadcast history as a CBC affiliate.

Many people were responsible for the initial organization and building of CKCK Television, but two veteran broadcasters, Harold Crittenden and Lloyd Westmoreland stand out as the driving force behind the evolution of television in Saskatchewan. Crittenden, formerly General Manager of CKCK Radio, came to Channel 2 in 1954 as the station's first General Manager. Westmoreland was CKCK Television's first Sales Manager and became Assistant General Manager in charge of programming.

Programming in the mid-to-late 1950s was dominated by comedy variety shows, such as The Jackie Gleason Show and Texaco Star Theatre starring Milton Berle, as well as western serials like The Rifleman and Roy Rogers.

Channel 2 usually started its broadcast day at 4 p.m., but viewers had their television sets turned on hours before, listening to the music and watching the test pattern. Local musical and variety programs were popular and they were all produced live in the CKCK studio.

In the 1960s colour was the most noticeable innovation and broadcast video tape recorders were introduced. CKCK-TV also became a CTV affiliate. Viewers saw the introduction of a wider variety of shows – sports, dramas, musicals and documentaries. From "Laugh In" to "Kids Bids", television was becoming very popular.

CKCK Television's mobile unit was first used at the Regina Exhibition in 1964. It enabled CKCK-TV to broadcast live on-the-scene reports for "Telepulse", the daily news service.

In 1977 Armadale sold CKCK Television to Frederick W. Hill of Regina. It became part of Harvard Communications Ltd. and ended the legal affiliation with its longstanding partner, CKCK Radio.

During the 1970s and 1980s, CKCK-TV, managed by Bruce Cowie, dominated the television airwaves in southern Saskatchewan as its

CKCK

Harold Crittenden

Audy & Vidy

Bruce Cowie

locally produced news programs and commercials garnered soaring viewer ratings and national accolades. Much of the station's success was due to it focus on the community. CKCK-TV was enthusiastically involved in countless events and charity functions throughout Regina and southern Saskatchewan.

Station personalities hosted and participated in all manner of community initiatives, while CKCK-TV donated hours of airtime, a station philosophy that began the day CKCK-TV opened its doors and continues to this day.

In 1986 Harvard Communications Ltd. sold the station to Baton Broadcasting Incorporated of Toronto (now known as CTV Inc.), which also acquired CFQC-TV in Saskatoon, CIPA/CKBI-TV in Prince Albert and CICC/CKOS-TV in Yorkton. Common ownership and common purpose now linked the four major television markets in Saskatchewan, providing viewers throughout the province with expanded news coverage and locally produced programming.

As CTV Regina continued to serve, inform and entertain the community of Southern Saskatchewan throughout the late 1980s and into the 1990s, the television industry continued to evolve, both at the ownership level and in the areas of cable and satellite television expansion. The CTV family grew to include new services and channels such as TSN (The Sports Network), CTV Newsnet and The Discovery Channel. The revolutionary aspect of computer Internet communications converged with broadcast services and southern Saskatchewan viewers were faced with an almost overwhelming number of potential viewing choices. Yet, as in 1954, the loyalty of the viewing audience is still in the local focus and community commitment of CTV Regina.

As we take our first steps into the new millennium, CTV Regina is a member of CTV; a subsidiary of Bell Globemedia, Canada's premier multi-media company, which also owns The Globe and Mail and Bell Globemedia Interactive, the largest Canadian-owned family of Internet properties. Through all those changes, there has remained one constant — the mutual respect and loyalty between the people who work at CTV Regina and the viewing audience of southern Saskatchewan.

Starting from those five-hour broadcast days in 1954, two generations of viewers have embraced the little station located on the prairie east of Regina as their first choice for news, entertainment and community support, making CTV Regina, Saskatchewan's most-watched television station.

This viewer trust and loyalty inspires the staff of CTV Regina to uphold the traditions of broadcast excellence and community involvement that began with that first test pattern almost 50 years ago.

CBC/CANADIAN BROADCASTING CORPORATION

*C*BC radio, originally broadcast from Watrous, CBK540 on the radio dial, moved to Winnipeg for a short period in 1939. It then moved to new Saskatchewan headquarters in the Exner Building, 1840 McIntyre Street, Regina. The CBKT television studios that had been located in Moose Jaw, at CHABTV, also moved to a Regina location on the 1700 block Lorne Street.

In 1969 CBC made the first tentative plans to establish a consolidated broadcast facility in the City of Regina. Designs for the new building were prepared by the architectural firm of Wiens, Johnstone, Architects Limited, and were approved by Wascana Centre Authority in 1977. Construction by PCL Construction Ltd. got underway in 1981.

CBK540 – Watrous

1840 McIntyre Street

The design of the CBC building at 2440 Broad Street conforms with the Wascana Authority's master plan for Wascana Park and provides a perfect blend of beauty and functionality. Extensive landscaping and the choice of Tyndall stone for the exterior of the building designate the Broadcast Centre as a special anchor in a triangular concept with the Legislative Building and the Royal Saskatchewan Museum.

The interior of the building allows for easy access to the public in the dominating galleria space and public areas, but maintains functionality for studios, technical spaces and support services.

The building represents the culmination of years of intricate planning to accommodate the needs of CBC present and future. Layout, equipment space and design features all work together to make Regina's CBC Broadcast Centre one of the most modern and effective facilities of its kind in Canada.

The CBK transmitter located in Watrous is still in use. Its 50,000-watt signal beams over a listening area larger than any other in the world.

A state-of-the-art sound stage, linked to the adjacent CBC Regina Broadcast Centre, is located in the redeveloped Regina Normal School Building (see page 135). The $11.5-million centre is a partnership between the city, provincial and federal governments, and the Saskatchewan film and video industry.

Saskatchewan Property Management Corporation (SPMC) owns the building; SaskFilm operates and administers the program. SaskFilm, a non-profit agency that works to promote growth in the provincial film industry, is located in the centre. The University of Regina and Saskatchewan Institute of Applied Science and Technology (SIAST) lease classroom space.

The Canada/Saskatchewan Film, Video, Production and Education Centre is one of the largest film and video production centres in Western Canada.

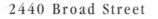

2440 Broad Street

CJME/Z99 RADIO/RAWLCO

2224 11th Avenue

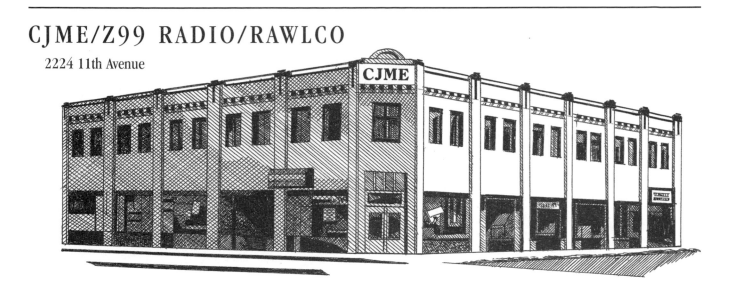

Radio station CJME was first granted a radio license to broadcast in 1959. Founded by Regina businessman J. M. (Marsh) Ellis, studios were originally located at 2224 11th Avenue

Ellis was a salesman in the radio department of the Robert Simpson Ltd. downtown store. He had spent the major part of his life in either the programming or engineering ends of radio. Before returning to Regina to establish CJME he had worked in radio stations in Regina, Trail, Medicine Hat and Minneapolis.

Midwest Broadcasting, owned by Ed Rawlinson of Prince Albert, purchased CJME in 1966. He sold the station to his sons Gordon and Doug in 1976 and the company name was changed to Rawlco Communications Ltd. CJME was located at 1771 Rose Street throughout the 1960s and 1970s, and moved to the Lloyd Building at the corner of Albert Street and 11th Avenue in 1977. The company name changed again to Rawlco Radio Ltd. and a new FM station, Z99, was added in 1982.

Rawlco, with head offices in Regina, grew dramatically during the 1980s, acquiring radio stations in Saskatoon, Calgary, Ottawa and Toronto. In 1988 the studios moved to a new building at 2401 Saskatchewan Drive. In 2001 CJME moved from 1300 to 980 on the radio dial.

STV/GLOBAL TELEVISION

370 Hoffer Drive

In 1987 STV Global went on air and became the third TV station in Regina to serve the Regina-Moose Jaw market area.

Located in Ross Industrial Park in northeast Regina, the station is part of the Global Television network owned by the Can-West Capital Corporation, started by I. H. Asper of Winnipeg in 1970.

Global has grown to become a strong national television network and Can-West, with its print, broadcast and Internet holdings, has created the most comprehensive, multiplatform international media company in Canada.

ACCESS

Early in the 1970s, the Regina Cablevision Co-operative was created to provide the citizens of Regina with the benefits of cable TV: a greater choice and variety of television programming . . . better technical TV quality . . . more channels at better prices . . . available and accessible communication between local groups and their neighbours through television.

The community-owned, non-profit service co-operative filed its application for a cable license with the Canadian Radio-Television and Telecommunications Commission (CRTC) in November 1975, and received approval on July 15, 1976, the beginning of a success story unique in communications history.

In the years since then, many changes have taken place, in the world, in the communications industry – and in the company that started out as Cable Regina.

The original co-operative has evolved into Access Communications Co-operative Limited, an organization which greatly exceeds anything its founders might have imagined. Today, Access is much more than "cable", and a great deal more widespread than "Regina", providing an ever-expanding selection of the newest communication technologies to an ever-growing base of subscribers.

In the mid-90s, the co-operative began to extend its services beyond Regina, first to Regina Beach, Buena Vista and Kinookimaw, White City, Emerald Park and Copper Sands, and then to Weyburn and Estevan, followed by Yorkton, Melville, Norquay, Canora, Kamsack, Theodore, Springside, Saltcoats, Bredenbury, Churchbridge and Esterhazy.

Early in 2002, a merger was approved between Access Communications Co-operative Limited and Battlefords Community Cablevision Co-operative, which added the communities of North Battleford, Battleford, Meadow Lake, Lashburn, Maidstone, Unity, Wilkie, Biggar, Kindersley and Rosetown to the Access service picture.

1976 to 1978
2419 11th Avenue

1978 to 1979
2500-2502 11th Avenue

1979 to 1989
102-1911 Park Street

COMMUNICATIONS

from 1989
2250 Park Street

ACCELERATE
WITH
US

from April 17, 2000
2250 Park Street

With 84,000 cable TV customers and 30,000 Internet customers in 30 communities, 200 employees and $60 million in assets, Access Communications Co-operative Limited became the seventh largest cable operation in Canada.

The steadily-increasing list of services provided by Access Communications includes specialty programming such as pay-per-view movies and events without the need for a "black box", dial-up and high speed Internet access, advanced paging systems, a community channel available to residents in each location within Access' service areas, Rogers AT&T Wireless cellular phone service and accessories, and more than 200 channels of high-quality digital television.

From its very beginnings, Access Communications has been a vital part of the communities it serves, supporting thousands of community events and activities. Access has played an integral role in fundraising initiatives for hundreds of community groups, as well as the Access Communications Children's Fund, which receives support from individual donations, employee fundraising, and the annual Rotary Carol Festival.

Many groups have taken advantage of Access7 community channel facilities and air time to hold telethons or live auctions to raise funds, and develop programming which broadens community awareness about their objectives and activities.

To assist in these endeavours, Access relies extensively on community programming volunteers. Volunteering provides an opportunity for people of all ages and all walks of life to learn new skills, meet new people, enjoy new experiences, and give something back to their communities. Access expresses its recognition and appreciation for the contribution of these community participants in many ways, including the unique provision of insurance coverage for its volunteers.

The members, Board, management, staff and volunteers of Access Communications Co-operative Limited are proud of their past and committed to the future with a dedication that grows stronger each year. As they say at Access – "We're not just part of the community – we're the heart of the community!"

REGINA EXHIBITION

The Regina Exhibition Association Ltd., originally the Assiniboia Agricultural Association, has served Regina and the province since 1884. In that year, soon after the railway had reached Regina, the first event brought together 150 individuals to exchange goods, information and experiences at the Scarth Building, near existing Victoria Park. Annual events continued and became fairs, which remained local in character until the Canadian government sponsored the Territorial Fair in 1895 in an effort to stimulate interest in the North-West Territories.

The Canadian government and Territorial Legislature provided financial assistance, and the Canadian Pacific Railway offered to transport exhibits to and from the exhibition free of charge. Following much controversy, a new site was chosen on the west side of town, where a 1,000-seat grandstand, a two-storey main structure and three frame buildings were constructed. This was to become the Regina Exhibition's permanent home. Regina was left so exhausted by the fair of 1895 that another was not held until 1899. Since then, there never has been a summer without a Regina Exhibition, despite the fact that the grounds were twice expropriated by the Canadian government for training and accommodating troops during World Wars I and II.

In 1907, the legislature of the newly formed province of Saskatchewan passed "An Act to incorporate the Regina Agricultural and Industrial Exhibition Association Limited". The act set out the objectives of the Association to exhibit products, goods, merchandise, machinery, paintings; and to exhibit several breeds of horses and other animals as well as to provide entertainment and amusement. Most importantly, it empowered the Association to erect

Amphitheatre and Winter Fair Building
1913 to 1917

Exhibition Stadium/Queen City Gardens
1919 –

World's Grain
Exhibition and
Conference
1933

ASSOCIATION LTD.

The Midway

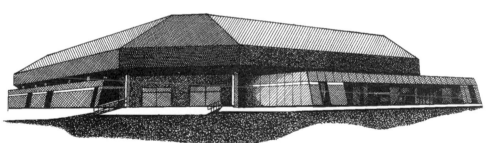

BUFFALO DAYS

Agridome
1978 –

Queensbury Centre
1987 –

any structures needed to carry out the objectives. The Act paved the way for the great Dominion Exhibition of 1911. In preparation for the event the Federal government provided finances to rebuild the grandstand to accommodate 4,000 people and construct stabling for 100 race horses.

Dan Elderkin was appointed Exhibition Manager in 1913, a position he held for 29 years. The Amphitheatre and Winter Fair Building was built the same year and opened in 1914. It was turned over to the 77th Battery when WW II was declared.

During WW I, hockey games were played at the Auditorium Rink at 12th and Rose Street and at the Arena Rink on Robinson Street. The Exhibition Stadium was built in 1919. The largest stadium in the west, Exhibition Stadium was part of a federal and provincial public works project.

Hockey games have been played at Exhibition Stadium since 1919. It was upgraded with an artificial ice plant in 1939 and renamed Queen City Gardens. It was the home of such Regina teams as the Vics, Aces, Vic-Aces, Allan Cup Rangers, Western League Capitals, Junior Abbotts and Commandos, Monarchs and the Pats. Curling competitions such as the Silver Broom and the Brier were played in the Gardens. In 1949 the name was restored to Exhibition Stadium. The Stadium roof was blown off in a cyclone in the 1960s and the grandstand roof suffered a similar fate in the 1970s.

During the 1920s, racing, professional baseball, cockfighting, pitbull dogfights and giant horsepulling competitions provided entertainment at the Stadium. The Regina Roughriders played their games in front of the grandstand.

Continued on the next page.

*T*he Amphitheatre was used as a military barracks and drill hall until destroyed by fire in 1917. Fire was a constant danger for exhibition buildings in those early days. Shortly after Elderkin took office a disastrous fire destroyed the grandstand and spread to the Industrial and Agricultural Building. Rebuilding began at once and was ready for the annual summer fair. The grandstand burned again in 1917 during fair week. Although it was crowded there were no serious injuries.

WORLD'S GRAIN EXHIBITION AND CONFERENCE

*B*y far the biggest event in the history of the Regina Exhibition was the two-week World's Grain Exhibition and Conference in 1933. It which attracted thousands of visitors. A huge U-shaped Grain Show building was built to house exhibits from 40 countries. Beautiful gardens were created in the centre of the U. Confederation Park was later developed to the west of the Grain Show Building, north of the bandshell. The east wing of the building became the Caledonian Curling rink (see page 294). With 14 sheets of curling ice under one roof, it was the largest curling rink in the world. The south and west wings of the building were destroyed by fire in 1955.

Grain Show Building

One of the main attractions during early summer fairs was machinery row, where dealers exhibited millions of dollars worth of farm machinery. However, marketing methods were changing and soon exhibitors wanted more specialized shows.

In 1978 the first Farm Progress was held. It became extremely popular, complementing the Canadian Western Agribition Livestock Show usually held in November. The same year the Buffalo Days Exhibition was named "Major Fair of the Year".

For many years the Exhibition Grounds provided the Saskatchewan Roughriders with administrative offices in the Exhibition Auditorium, dressing rooms in the grandstand and a practice field within the interior of the racetrack.

To accommodate demand for curling ice because of increased interest in the sport, the Saskatchewan Building was built in 1958 with 12 sheets of ice. The building was used for exhibits during the summer fair and in the winter provided a home for the Regina Curling Club, until 1994 when it became a Regina Soccer Association facility.

During this same period the Winter Fair, which featured the annual Light Horse Show and Spring Bull Sale, was also a popular attraction. As Regina was the home of the RCMP and horsemanship was part of their training program, including the famous "Musical Ride", their support greatly assisted the annual horse show. Under the guidance of RCMP member Cec Walker, and with the leadership of Chairmen Lyle Doan and Cliff Elder, the Regina Light Horse Show gained a reputation as one of the top ten indoor horse shows in North America.

With the opening of the Buffalo Buck Casino in 1969, and other specialized events like home and auto shows, activities at the Exhibition Grounds were no longer limited to seasonal summer activities, so the grounds were renamed Exhibition Park. The Regina Exhibition provided the leadership, in partnership with other Saskatchewan fairs, to operate the Saskatchewan Derby Sweepstakes, a lottery with prizes awarded on the results of a horse race, similar to the Irish Sweepstakes. The lottery continued until 1978 when it was taken over by Sask Sport Inc. and the Western Canada Lottery Foundation.

The 1960s are remembered for the Diamond Jubilee Exhibition, the construction of the Winter Fair Building, the first Saskatchewan Derby, and the adoption of the Buffalo Days theme featuring Pemmican Pete and Pemmican Pearl.

For years the midway arrived and set up on the grounds on a Sunday. Concessions were open and admission was free. It was named "Scotchman's Day" and the grounds were jam-packed with people. As the crowds increased, so did the dangers, and the decision was made to close the gates. To satisfy the tremendous interest in the summer fair, "Pile of Bones Sunday", with free entertainment, was organized by the Buffalo Days' committee. It is held in Wascana Park on the legislative grounds.

Other than a brief period during the war years in the early forties, the 1930s through the 1970s were the years of spectacular outdoor grandstand shows, glittering midways with thrilling rides and thoroughbred racing at what now had become the Provincial Exhibition.

Under the direction of Chairmen Bob Gillies and Jack Swain, the grandstand performances always played to capacity. Regina was on the Western Circuit, along with Brandon, Calgary, Edmonton and Saskatoon, and featured the top North American midways, including Johnny J. Jones, Rubin and Cherry, Castle, Erhlich and Hirsch, and Morris and Castle. Royal American Shows provided the midway from 1934 to 1942 but was replaced during the war years. Their show train wasn't available because the railway was pressed into military service. Royal American returned in 1946 and provided the midway until 1975 when they were replaced by Conklin Shows.

The commencement of the Market Cattle Livestock Show in 1971, by Canadian Western Agribition, placed heavy demands on the Regina Exhibition to provide the barn and exhibit space required for the rapidly expanding show. The Agribition Building was constructed in 1973 and the Exhibit Hall in 1978.

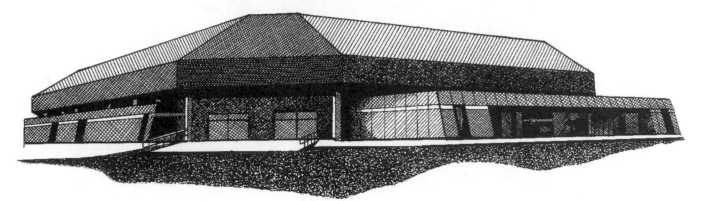

Agridome 1978 –

With profits realized from Saskatchewan Derby Sweepstakes, and financial support from the City of Regina, the Agridome was constructed in 1978. The Building chairman was Gord Staseson who was also chairman and project coordinator responsible for building the Canada Centre in 1981, and Queensbury Centre in 1987, at which time the antiquated outdoor grandstand was demolished.

When the Agridome opened it featured the Agridome Star Theatre as part of the summer fair, with such performers as Paul Anka, Dolly Parton, Bob Hope, Pat and Debbi Boone, Rich Little and Kenny Rogers. The Agridome has been the site of two Memorial Cups, two Briers, three Scott Tournaments of Hearts, the Canadian Figure Skating Championships, Skate Canada, and is the home of the Canadian National Arabian Horse Show Championships (Royal Red).

Racing was also a
part of the summer
fair, with the thorough-
breds provided by Speers
Raceway of Assiniboia Downs
of Winnipeg. The racing circuit
was similar to that of the midway.
Racing attracted large crowds during fair week, with handles of $300,000 daily.

The Regina Exhibition Association Limited manages Exhibition Park on a 102-acre site. The Park continues to provide a venue for entertainment and education for the community. Exhibition Park produces two annual major events, the Regina Summer Fair and the Canadian Western Farm Progress Show, and it facilitates the production of the Canadian Western Agribition and the Royal Red (the Canadian National Arabian Horse Show Championships). It also plays host to a myriad of events, attractions and other activities that have a direct financial impact on the City of Regina and the province.

INDEX

Graham, Harold M., 97, 272
grain prices, 17, 19
Grain Show Building, 294, 353, 365
Grand Hotel, 167
Grandma Lee's, 245
Grandstand, 17, 35, 363, 364, 368, 370
Grand Theatre, 184, 355
Grand Trunk Pacific Hotel, 171
Grand Trunk Pacific Railway (GTP), 37, 143, 154, 155, 278
Grant, George, 176
Grant, Gordon B., 42
grasshopper plagues, 19
Grassick, Greg, 235, 308, 309
Grassick, James, 36, 39, 40, 125, 275
Grassick, James, residence, 275
Grassick, Jessie, 275
Gratton Catholic School, 113, 116
Gratton, Father Damien, 113, 116
Gratton Roman Catholic Separate School District, 113
Graybar Holdings (Sask) Ltd., 287
Great Northern Railway, 154
Green and White, The, 308, 309
Green, Barry, 120, 331
Green, John, 110
Greer, Willie, 54
Grenfell Towers, 253
Grey, A. H. G., Earl (Governor General), 16, 60, 108
Grey Cup, 23, 26, 27, 28, 64, 309
Grey Nuns Hospital, 40, 89, 105, 106, 107
Grey Nuns, Order of, 105, 106
Greystone Managed Investments, 252
Griffing, Dean, 308, 309
Grisdale, Bishop, 76
Grisenthwaite, Jim, 127
Grolle and Portnall, 387
Groome, Roland J., 18, 158, 160
Grotsky, Isadore, 118
Grozell, Roy, 243
Guardo, J., 98
Gudereit, Marcia, 27, 294, 296, 324
Guess Who, The, 245
Gunn, Ellen, 126
Gyro Citizen's Golf Clubhouse, 304
Hacienda night club/The Pump, 177
Haldane House, 265, 268
Hambly, George, 310
Hamilton, Doreen E., 44
Hamilton Hotel, 169
Hamilton, Jack W., 317
Hamilton, William Cayley, 33
Hammond, Leslie, 42
Hanbidge Hall, 147
Harasen, Lorne, 353, 355
Harding House, 76, 78
Harding, Malcolm Taylor McAdam, 266
Harding residence, 266
Harmonie club, 344
Haro Financial, 195
Harper, Terry, 127, 313
Hartstein, Rabbi, 290
Harvard Broadcasting, a Hill Company Division, 195, 355
Harvard Communications Ltd., 83, 356, 357,
Harvard Developments Inc., 186, 194, 195
Harvard International Resources, 194
Harwood, R. J., 52

Haseltine, Lena, 130
Haslam, J. H., 170
Hastings, Earl, 124
Haug, Pat, 331
Haughton, Willa, 331
Haultain, F. W. G., 37, 135, 141, 290, 297
Hawks, Frank, 161
Hay, Bill, 120, 312, 320
Haynes, Arden, 120
Headquarters for the Armed Services, 64
Headquarters, North-West Mounted Police, 58
Hebrew School (Talmud Torah), 83, 355
Heintzman building, 196
Helmsing Funeral Chapel, 36
Henderson, James, 274
Henry, Jim "Sugar", 21, 316, 321
Herchmer, Commissioner, 114
Herchmer, L. A., 56, 114, 290
Herchmer, Mrs., 56
Herchmer Public School, 114
Heritage Regina, 335
Heritage Properties (Municipal, Provincial and Federal), 49, 51, 57, 61, 65, 67, 73, 75, 76, 138, 146, 152, 165, 166, 173, 207, 210, 263, 264, 269, 276, 277, 286, 306, 333, 335, 351
HMCS Queen, 40, 64, 330
Heughan, R. W. G., 63
Hewitt, Reverend W. J., 12
Hicke, Bill, 127, 312, 313
Hicke, Ernie, 313
Hicks, Mary, 120
Hill, Bob, 355
Hill, Edward, 269
Hill, Frederick W., 194, 269, 355, 356
Hill, Reverend Canon G. C., 138, 261
Hill, Grace (O'Connor), 269
Hill Group of Companies, 162, 166, 195, 355
Hill, James, 269
Hill, Mel, 22
Hill, Paul J., 126, 195, 355
Hill, Robert, 269
Hill, Tom, 355
Hillsdale subdivision, 98, 194, 320
Hill, Walter H. A., 194, 269, 272, 281
Hill, Walter, residence, 269
Hilsden and Company, 94, 241
Hilton, William W., 75
Hindu Temple, 103
Hinkson, E. W., 175
Hinkson, Frank, 175
Hinkson, Ted, 120
Hipperson Construction of Regina, 210
Hipperson, Donald, 118
Hird, C. E., 97
Historical gallery, Government House, 59
Historical Public Records Office, 139
Hitchcock, Tom, 52
Hockey, ladies club, 13
Hockey, Regina Professional Club, 174
Hodges, Don, 22, 120, 331, 332
Holden, Josh, 313
Holy Rosary Cathedral, 81, 89, 98, 123, 126, 346
Holy Rosary School, 123
Holy Trinity Serbian Orthodox Church, 85
Honan, Florence, 119
Honeyman, J. R. C., 138

Snyder Brothers, 208
Sobchuk, Dennis, 24, 313
Sobor (Pro-Cathedral), 88
Soccer Club Concordia, 344
Sojonky, Frank, 244
Solomon, Adrian (Burns), 240
Solomon and Sons, 240
Solomon, Fred, 240
Solomon, George, 124, 240
Solomon-Schofield, Vaughn, 240
Solomon, Sharon (Dyksman), 240
Sommerville Road, 303
Soofi, Fred, 165
Sotirios, Bishop, 103
Sound Stage Production Centre – Canada/Saskatchewan Production
    Studios, 135, 358
South East Leisure Centre, 324
Southland Mall, 22, 195, 254
Southland Mall Multiplex Theatre, 186
South Railway (Saskatchewan Drive), 200
South Saskatchewan Hospital Board, 107
South Saskatchewan Youth Orchestra, 141
Southwest Pro-Ag, 242
Spanier, Herb, 120
Sparrow, Spunk, 174
Speakers' Corner, 334
Speers Funeral Home, 198
Speers, George, 198
Speers, Marshall and Boyd Funeral and Furniture Store, 198
Speers, W. A., 353
Sport, Culture and Recreation Administration Centre, 61
Sportplex, 323
Sports Governing Associations, 61
Spring Bull Sale, 366
Sprowl, Ray, 198
S. S. Kresge Co. Ltd., 230
Stage West Dinner Theatre, 177
Staley, Red, 312
Standard, 16
Staniowski, Ed, 24, 313
Stankov, Don, 127
Stanley Park, 152
Staples, Jack W., 318
Staseson, Gordon W., 5, 118, 120, 370
Steadman, Aubrey, 245
Steadman, Wayne, 127, 245
Steelcon Construction Co., 93
Steele, S. B., 54
Steiger, Barbara (Kleisinger), 140
Sterling Cranes Ltd, 240
Stevenson, Theresa, 28
Stewart, Sam, 244
Stimpson, Doreen (Fisher), 120
Stock, Keith and Associates, 241
Stock market crash, 19
Stock Ramsay and Associates, 209
Storey, Edgar M., and Van Egmond, William, 77, 135
Storey, Stan, 64
Storey, Stan E., and Van Egmond, W. G., 34, 49, 65, 77, 83, 120, 131,
    138, 164, 174, 208, 212, 228, 282, 284, 285, 286, 287, 300, 330
Stovin, Horace, 352, 353
Strass, Erwin, 310, 311
Strathcona School, 118, 250
streetcar barns, 156
streetcars, 16, 34, 37, 49, 156, 157, 184

street paving, 37
Strumm, Bob, 312
Stuart, Brad, 313
STV/Global Television, 359
Styles, A. C., 64
Sud, Johannah, 130
Suffa, Father Augustine, 68, 94, 119, 122
Sullivan, Frank "Sully", 126
Summers, Bert, 176
Sunday School, 67
Sundown Optimist Buffalo Gals, 322
Sun Electric Products, 282
Sunrise Branch (Regina Public Library), 324
Super Market, Army and Navy, 223
Supreme Court of the North-West Territories, 33
Surjik, Myrtle Bainbridge, 120
Sutherland, Shirley (Douglas), 120
Swain, David, 218
Swain, Jack, 218, 369
Swain, Sam, 218
Synod House, 266
Synod of the Ecclesiastical Province of Rupert's Land, 77
Taché, Archbishop, 68
Taggart, J. G., 39
Talmud Torah, 83
Tattler, The, 260
Taylor, A. C., 334
Taylor Field, 27, 174, 309, 310, 311
Taylor, N. J. "Piffles", 174
Taylor, Sam, 63, 174
T. C. Douglas building, 24, 26, 144, 310
TD Bank, 252
TD Canada Trust office tower, 191
Teachers' College (Normal School), 43, 114, 115, 135
Team Canada, 296
T. Eaton Company, 215
telephones, 13, 16, 79, 202, 208, 209
temperance movement, 33
10 Field Regiment RCA, 64
tennis clubs, 332
Terrace Building, 253
Territorial Exhibition, 35, 36, 70, 362
Territorial Government, 13
Territorial Government buildings, 11, 57
Thatcher, Ross, 64, 109, 170
38 Brigade Group, 64
Thompson, Andrew, 130
Thompson, Stanley, 298
Thomson School, 112, 129, 250
Thomson, William Alexander, 129
Thorn, Tony, 163
thoroughbred racing, 371
Tiki Night Club, 177
Tilson, Abe, 127
Tilson, Red (Bill), 127
Tingley, A. R., 294
Todd, Frederick G., 23
Toth, Jim, 131
Toth, Joe, 216
Tow-cars, 49
Tower Gardens, 286, 287
Town bell, 52
Town Bylaws, 52
Town Hall, 30, 33, 50, 165
Town Trustees, 32

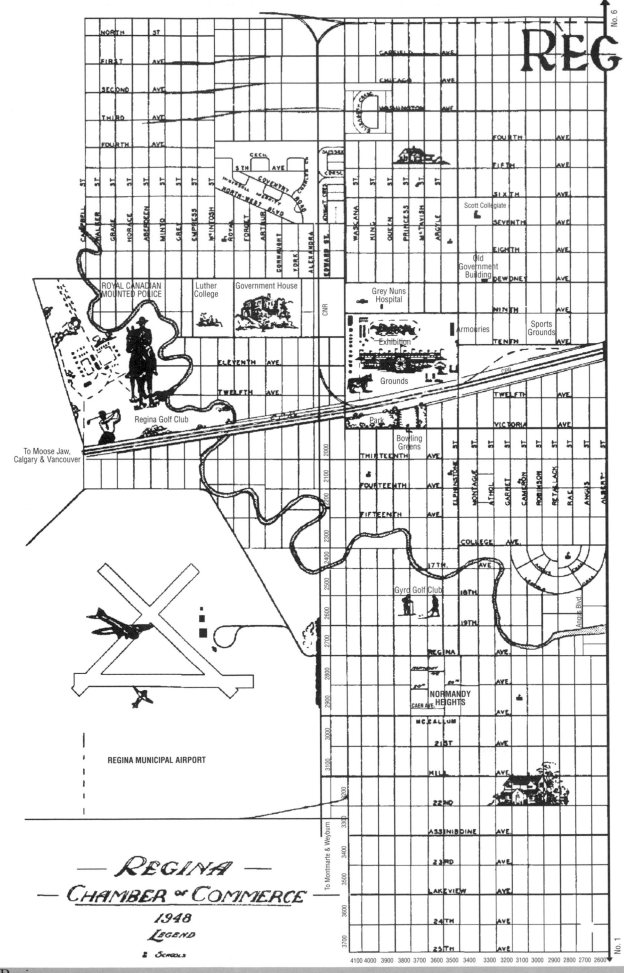

REGINA

CHAMBER of COMMERCE

1948

LEGEND

Schools